ADRIENNE
AND

POEMS
PROSE
REVIEWS AND CRITICISM

A NORTON CRITICAL EDITION

ADRIENNE RICH'S POETRY AND PROSE

POEMS

PROSE

REVIEWS AND CRITICISM

Selected and Edited by

BARBARA CHARLESWORTH GELPI

ALBERT GELPI

STANFORD UNIVERSITY

W · W · NORTON & COMPANY · *New York* · *London*

Copyright © 1993, 1975 by W. W. Norton & Company, Inc.
Printed in the United States of America
The text of this book is composed in Electra
with the display set in Bernhard Modern
Manufacturing by Maple-Vail
Book design by Antonina Krass
Library of Congress Cataloging in Publication Data
Rich, Adrienne Cecile.
    Adrienne Rich's poetry and prose: poems, prose, reviews, and
criticism / selected and edited by Barbara Charlesworth Gelpi,
Albert Gelpi.
        p.   cm.—(A Norton critical edition)
    Rev. ed. of: Adrienne Rich's poetry. 1st ed. 1975.
    Includes bibliographical references and index.
    ISBN 0-393-96147-8
    1. Rich, Adrienne Cecile—Criticism and interpretation.
I. Gelpi, Barbara Charlesworth.   II. Gelpi, Albert.   III. Rich,
Adrienne Cecile. Adrienne Rich's poetry.   IV. Title.
PS3535.I233A6   1993b   92-28640
811′ .54—dc20

W. W. Norton & Company, Inc., 500 Fifth Avenue, New York, N.Y. 10110
www.wwnorton.com

W. W. Norton & Company Ltd., Castle House, 75/76 Wells Street,
London W1T 3QT

0

Contents

Poems

Prose

Reviews and Criticism

Contents

Preface

The contents of *Adrienne Rich's Poetry and Prose* differ so widely from those of its predecessor, *Adrienne Rich's Poetry* (1975), that words like *revised* and *enlarged* became inadequate, and we needed to change the title as well. These changes are signs not of any repudiation of that earlier work but of Adrienne Rich's extraordinary, in fact phenomenal, achievements during the eighteen years that separate the two editions. In 1975 Rich's was already a poetic voice that had earned universal attention, a voice that both affected and effected her readers' process of self-creation through articulation, through speech. The long process of her own self-birthing that Rich described in "Necessities of Life" (1962), and in many other poems as well, was herald, companion, and coach to others around the world, women and men, struggling toward a new consciousness.

As we knew even then, Rich's was not a consciousness that rested in its own achievement. Then, as now, its characteristic self-injunction was "To pull yourself up by your own roots; to eat the last meal in / your old neighborhood" ("Shooting Script" [11/69–7/70]). But even someone deeply aware of Rich's intelligence, courage, and passion and of the flexibility and power of her poetic gift could scarcely have foreseen future works such as *Twenty-One Love Poems* (1974–76), *Sources* (1981–82), and *An Atlas of the Difficult World* (1990–91). This new edition, then, gives a long overdue compilation of Rich's work and a chart to her poetic journey. A selection like this one necessarily has to omit many important poems. We chose these to demonstrate the full range of Rich's achievement and to provide a balanced overview of her poetry.

Much more space was needed in this edition than in the last to represent, again only with works that seemed to us to mark certain high points, Rich's achievements in prose. In 1975 Rich had already written "When We Dead Awaken: Writing as Re-Vision" (1971)—an essay that continues to mark the point at which the second wave of feminism resoundingly reached shore. Our earlier edition contained that and "The Anti-Feminist Woman" (1972). The latter was, as it turned out, a glimpse toward what Rich was to accomplish in *Of Woman Born: Motherhood as Experience and Institution* (1976). But in 1975 we had no adequate foreknowledge of the contributions Rich was shortly to make to feminist theory. As *Of Woman Born*'s subtitle suggests, Rich was one of the first to investigate in depth the meaning of the slogan at the heart of the feminist movement, "The personal is political." She had very early and very clearly the radical insight that women's most supposedly "personal" experiences—their motherhood, their very sexuality—are shaped in large part by the male-dominated institutions in which they occur.

That structuring process is now so familiar that the signifiers for it have become jargon; *constructed* and *inscribed* are taken as the appropriate adjectives for the very word *consciousness*. But in both the past and the present Rich's thinking avoids and transcends the oversimplifications that create jargon. For her the fact that consciousness bears the marks and scars of oppressive institutions does not invalidate, much less destroy, the actuality of personal experience as a source and resource. Seeing the scars rather than denying them and using memory to grasp their causes and consequences together constitute the awesome "re-vision" undertaken in everything she writes. The most difficult but at the same time the most liberating aspect of this re-vision is that it involves the constant reassessment of the ways in which one has participated, whatever one's race, gender, or class, in one's own oppression. This focused and healing self-scrutiny so characteristic of Rich, so much the ground of her poetry's fused insights and of her prose analysis, has also been her central, though by no means her single, contribution to the methodology at the core of all feminist theorizing.[1]

"Three Conversations," our dialogue with Rich in *Adrienne Rich's Poetry*, was made redundant by the wealth and significance of the prose Rich has published since 1975, and that body of materials eliminated the need for new "conversations" in this edition. The numerous essays on Rich's work that have appeared in the intervening years and Rich's own self-analytical prose also transformed the critical section of this book. In the place of the criticism with a strong biographical cast that for good reason characterized early studies of her work, we have looked to essays that emphasize the qualities of her writing and of her situation as a twentieth-century American woman poet. As a link between the three different sections of the book, our index not only includes references for the first lines and titles of the poems but indicates those places in both Rich's own prose and the critical essays where particular poems are discussed.

Adrienne Rich's Poetry and Prose is, then, virtually a different book from *Adrienne Rich's Poetry*, and that is appropriate, given the changes it registers in Rich's thought, life, poetic production, and critical reception. But through these changes there remains continuity. To an interior interlocutor, the poet in *An Atlas of the Difficult World* says, "If you had known me / once, you'd still know me now though in a different /

---

1. We are grateful to Diane Middlebrook for pointing out this parallel between Rich's stance toward experience and the central concerns of feminist theory.

light and life." Her words apply more generally as well to her ongoing dialogue with all her readers. Through dramatic changes in the inner and outer places from which Rich writes and through changes in profoundly lived commitments, whether as a wife and mother or as a lesbian lover, Rich's abiding dedication to "living memory" means that earlier selves are not lost, much less repudiated, but transformed. The voice of a woman focusing her intelligence and her passion and shaping her language to the articulation of a constantly evolving, freshly realized identity and situation is the voice we know through all these differences.

Acknowledgments

We are grateful to the Stanford English Department for underwriting expenses we incurred while doing this revision of *Adrienne Rich's Poetry*. The reference librarians at Stanford's Green Library were an invaluable resource to us as we worked on the footnotes to the poems. Indeed, their zest transformed the potentially lonely task of source hunting into the communal pleasure of an intellectual scavenger hunt. Our thanks go to Karen Fiser and to Joellen Hiltbrand, whom we consulted as we were making editorial selections for this volume, and to Joellen for her help with other editorial labors such as photocopying and the pasting up of pages. George Hart assisted in the final stages with wonderful awareness, gusto, and sense of detail.

Above all, our thanks go to Adrienne Rich herself. While remaining rigorously separate from the process of selecting both her own work and the essays on it, she generously responded to questions, saving us hours in the library. While any errors or omissions are our own, her contribution was invaluable. We are grateful for this particular aid and rejoice in a friendship that has deepened over thirty years.

BARBARA CHARLESWORTH GELPI
ALBERT GELPI

POEMS

A single dot at the bottom of the text on a page indicates a break between stanzas.

From *A Change of World*
(1951)

Storm Warnings

The glass has been falling all the afternoon,
And knowing better than the instrument
What winds are walking overhead, what zone
Of gray unrest is moving across the land,
I leave the book upon a pillowed chair   5
And walk from window to closed window, watching
Boughs strain against the sky

And think again, as often when the air
Moves inward toward a silent core of waiting,
How with a single purpose time has traveled   10
By secret currents of the undiscerned
Into this polar realm. Weather abroad
And weather in the heart alike come on
Regardless of prediction.

Between foreseeing and averting change   15
Lies all the mastery of elements
Which clocks and weatherglasses cannot alter.
Time in the hand is not control of time,
Nor shattered fragments of an instrument
A proof against the wind; the wind will rise,   20
We can only close the shutters.

I draw the curtains as the sky goes black
And set a match to candles sheathed in glass
Against the keyhole draught, the insistent whine
Of weather through the unsealed aperture.   25
This is our sole defense against the season;
These are the things that we have learned to do
Who live in troubled regions.

Aunt Jennifer's Tigers

Aunt Jennifer's tigers prance across a screen,
Bright topaz denizens of a world of green.
They do not fear the men beneath the tree;
They pace in sleek chivalric certainty.

Aunt Jennifer's fingers fluttering through her wool   5
Find even the ivory needle hard to pull.
The massive weight of Uncle's wedding band
Sits heavily upon Aunt Jennifer's hand.

When Aunt is dead, her terrified hands will lie
Still ringed with ordeals she was mastered by.   10
The tigers in the panel that she made
Will go on prancing, proud and unafraid.

Afterward

Now that your hopes are shamed, you stand
At last believing and resigned,
And none of us who touch your hand
Know how to give you back in kind
The words you flung when hopes were proud: 5
Being born to happiness
Above the asking of the crowd,
You would not take a finger less.
We who know limits now give room
To one who grows to fit her[1] doom.   10

The Uncle Speaks in the Drawing Room

I have seen the mob of late
Standing sullen in the square,
Gazing with a sullen stare
At window, balcony, and gate.
Some have talked in bitter tones,   5
Some have held and fingered stones.

These are follies that subside.
Let us consider, none the less,

1. When the poem appeared in A *Change of World*, the phrase read "his doom." Amending the phrase in *Poems: Selected and New* the poet noted: "I have altered the [pronoun] not simply as a matter of fact but because [it alters], for me, the dimensions of the poem."

Certain frailties of glass
Which, it cannot be denied,   10
Lead in times like these to fear
For crystal vase and chandelier.

Not that missiles will be cast;
None as yet dare lift an arm.
But the scene recalls a storm   15
When our grandsire stood aghast
To see his antique ruby bowl
Shivered in a thunder-roll.

Let us only bear in mind
How these treasures handed down   20
From a calmer age passed on
Are in the keeping of our kind.
We stand between the dead glass-blowers
And murmurings of missile-throwers.

An Unsaid Word

She who has power to call her man
From that estranged intensity
Where his mind forages alone,
Yet keeps her peace and leaves him free,
And when his thoughts to her return   5
Stands where he left her, still his own,
Knows this the hardest thing to learn.

From *The Diamond Cutters and Other Poems* (1955)

Living in Sin

She had thought the studio would keep itself;
no dust upon the furniture of love.
Half heresy, to wish the taps less vocal,
the panes relieved of grime. A plate of pears,
a piano with a Persian shawl, a cat   5
stalking the picturesque amusing mouse
had risen at his urging.
Not that at five each separate stair would writhe
under the milkman's tramp; that morning light
so coldly would delineate the scraps   10
of last night's cheese and three sepulchral bottles;
that on the kitchen shelf among the saucers
a pair of beetle-eyes would fix her own—
envoy from some village in the moldings . . .
Meanwhile, he, with a yawn,   15
sounded a dozen notes upon the keyboard,
declared it out of tune, shrugged at the mirror,
rubbed at his beard, went out for cigarettes;
while she, jeered by the minor demons,
pulled back the sheets and made the bed and found   20
a towel to dust the table-top,
and let the coffee-pot boil over on the stove.
By evening she was back in love again,
though not so wholly but throughout the night
she woke sometimes to feel the daylight coming   25
like a relentless milkman up the stairs.

The Diamond Cutters

However legendary,
The stone is still a stone,

Though it had once resisted
The weight of Africa,
The hammer-blows of time   5
That wear to bits of rubble
The mountain and the pebble—
But not this coldest one.

Now, you intelligence
So late dredged up from dark   10
Upon whose smoky walls
Bison took fumbling form
Or flint was edged on flint—
Now, careful arriviste,[1]
Delineate at will   15
Incisions in the ice.

Be serious, because
The stone may have contempt
For too-familiar hands,
And because all you do   20
Loses or gains by this:
Respect the adversary,
Meet it with tools refined,
And thereby set your price.

Be hard of heart, because   25
The stone must leave your hand.
Although you liberate
Pure and expensive fires
Fit to enamor Shebas,[2]
Keep your desire apart.   30
Love only what you do,
And not what you have done.

Be proud, when you have set
The final spoke of flame
In that prismatic wheel,   35
And nothing's left this day
Except to see the sun
Shine on the false and the true,
And know that Africa
Will yield you more to do.[3]   40

1. Literally, one who has arrived; a social climber or upstart.
2. The queen of Sheba, famed for her attractiveness and intelligence, from a land located in the southwest corner of the Arabian peninsula. In the Old Testament, 1 Kings 10 describes her visit to the Israelite king Solomon.
3. For Rich's comment on this metaphor, see below, p. 259.

From *Snapshots of a Daughter-in-Law: Poems 1954–1962* (1963)

The Knight

A knight rides into the noon,
and his helmet points to the sun,
and a thousand splintered suns
are the gaiety of his mail.
The soles of his feet glitter   5
and his palms flash in reply,
and under his crackling banner
he rides like a ship in sail.

A knight rides into the noon,
and only his eye is living,   10
a lump of bitter jelly
set in a metal mask,
betraying rags and tatters
that cling to the flesh beneath
and wear his nerves to ribbons   15
under the radiant casque.

Who will unhorse this rider
and free him from between
the walls of iron, the emblems
crushing his chest with their weight?   20
Will they defeat him gently,
or leave him hurled on the green,
his rags and wounds still hidden
under the great breastplate?

1957

Snapshots of a Daughter-in-Law

1.

You, once a belle in Shreveport,
with henna-colored hair, skin like a peachbud,
still have your dresses copied from that time,
and play a Chopin [1] prelude
called by Cortot:[2] *"Delicious recollections*   5
float like perfume through the memory." [3]

Your mind now, moldering like wedding-cake,
heavy with useless experience, rich
with suspicion, rumor, fantasy,
crumbling to pieces under the knife-edge   10
of mere fact. In the prime of your life.

Nervy, glowering, your daughter
wipes the teaspoons, grows another way.

2.

Banging the coffee-pot into the sink
she hears the angels chiding, and looks out   15
past the raked gardens to the sloppy sky.
Only a week since They said: *Have no patience.*

The next time it was: *Be insatiable.*
Then: *Save yourself; others you cannot save.*
Sometimes she's let the tapstream scald her arm,   20
a match burn to her thumbnail,

or held her hand above the kettle's snout
right in the woolly steam. They are probably angels,
since nothing hurts her anymore, except
each morning's grit blowing into her eyes.   25

3.

A thinking woman sleeps with monsters.
The beak that grips her, she becomes. And Nature,
that sprung-lidded, still commodious

1. Frederic François Chopin (1810–49), Polish composer and pianist who settled in Paris in 1831.
2. Alfred Cortot (1877–1962), famous French pianist.
3. Cortot's notation for Prelude no. 7, Andantino, A Major, in the prefatory remarks of his *Chopin: 24 Preludes* (Paris, 1930).

steamer-trunk of *tempora* and *mores*[4]
gets stuffed with it all: the mildewed orange-flowers,   30
the female pills,[5] the terrible breasts
of Boadicea[6] beneath flat foxes' heads and orchids.

Two handsome women, gripped in argument,
each proud, acute, subtle, I hear scream
across the cut glass and majolica   35
like Furies[7] cornered from their prey:
The argument *ad feminam*,[8] all the old knives
that have rusted in my back, I drive in yours,
ma semblable, ma soeur![9]

4.

Knowing themselves too well in one another: 40
their gifts no pure fruition, but a thorn,
the prick filed sharp against a hint of scorn . . .
Reading while waiting
for the iron to heat,
writing, *My Life had stood—a Loaded Gun—*[1]   45
in that Amherst[2] pantry while the jellies boil and scum,
or, more often,
iron-eyed and beaked and purposed as a bird,
dusting everything on the whatnot every day of life.

5.

Dulce ridens, dulce loquens,[3]   50
she shaves her legs until they gleam
like petrified mammoth-tusk.

4. Literally, "times and customs," alluding perhaps to Cicero's phrase "O Tempora! O Mores!"
   in *Pro Rege Deiotaro* 2.31 ("Alas! for the degeneracy of our times and the low standard of our
   morals!").
5. Remedies for menstrual pain.
6. British queen in the time of the Emperor Nero who led her people in a large though finally
   unsuccessful revolt against Roman rule.
7. Greek goddesses of vengeance.
8. Feminine version of the phrase "ad hominem," referring to an argument that appeals to per-
   sonal interests, prejudices, or emotions rather than to reason or justice.
9. The last line of the poem "Au Lecteur" by Charles Baudelaire addresses "Hypocrite lecteur!—
   mon semblable,—mon frère!": "Hypocrite reader, like me, my brother"—not as here, "my
   sister."
1. Poem 754 in *The Poems of Emily Dickinson*, ed. Thomas H. Johnson (Cambridge, MA, 1955)
   2.574.
2. The Massachusetts town in which Emily Dickinson lived (1830–86).
3. Latin for "sweetly laughing, sweetly speaking." Horace (Quintus Horatius Flaccus), Ode 22,
   "Integer vitae," ll. 23–24.

6.

When to her lute Corinna sings[4]
neither words nor music are her own;
only the long hair dipping   55
over her cheek, only the song
of silk against her knees
and these
adjusted in reflections of an eye.

Poised, trembling and unsatisfied, before   60
an unlocked door, that cage of cages,
tell us, you bird, you tragical machine—
is this *fertilisante douleur?*[5] Pinned down
by love, for you the only natural action,
are you edged more keen   65
to prise the secrets of the vault? has Nature shown
her household books to you, daughter-in-law,
that her sons never saw?

7.

"To have in this uncertain world some stay
which cannot be undermined, is   70
of the utmost consequence."[6]
               Thus wrote
a woman, partly brave and partly good,
who fought with what she partly understood.
Few men about her would or could do more,   75
hence she was labeled harpy, shrew and whore.

8.

"You all die at fifteen," said Diderot,[7]
and turn part legend, part convention.
Still, eyes inaccurately dream
behind closed windows blankening with steam.   80
Deliciously, all that we might have been,
all that we were—fire, tears,
wit, taste, martyred ambition—

4. First line of a poem by Thomas Campion (1567–1620).
5. French for "fertilizing or life-giving sorrow."
6. From Mary Wollstonecraft, *Thoughts on the Education of Daughters*, London, 1787 [*Rich's note*].
7. Denis Diderot (1713–84), French philosopher, encyclopedist, playwright, and critic. "You all die at fifteen": "Vous mourez toutes a quinze ans," from the *Lettres à Sophie Volland*, quoted by Simone de Beauvoir in *Le Deuxième Sexe*, Vol. II, pp. 123–24 [*Rich's note*].

stirs like the memory of refused adultery
the drained and flagging bosom of our middle years.   85

9.

Not that it is done well, but
that it is done at all?[8] Yes, think
of the odds! or shrug them off forever.
This luxury of the precocious child,
Time's precious chronic invalid,—   90
would we, darlings, resign it if we could?
Our blight has been our sinecure:
mere talent was enough for us—
glitter in fragments and rough drafts.

Sigh no more, ladies.   95
             Time is male
and in his cups drinks to the fair.
Bemused by gallantry, we hear
our mediocrities over-praised,
indolence read as abnegation,   100
slattern thought styled intuition,
every lapse forgiven, our crime
only to cast too bold a shadow
or smash the mold straight off.

For that, solitary confinement,   105
tear gas, attrition shelling.
Few applicants for that honor.

10.

Well,
she's long about her coming, who must be
more merciless to herself than history.   110
Her mind full to the wind, I see her plunge
breasted and glancing through the currents,
taking the light upon her
at least as beautiful as any boy
or helicopter,[9]   115

8. An allusion to Samuel Johnson's remark to Boswell: "Sir, a woman's preaching is like a dog's walking on his hinder legs. It is not done well; but you are surprised to find it done at all" (July 31, 1763, *Boswell's Life of Johnson*, ed. George Birkbeck Hill [Oxford, 1934] 1.463).
9. "She comes from the remoteness of ages, from Thebes, from Crete, from Chichén-Itzá; and she is also the totem set deep in the African jungle; she is a helicopter and she is a bird; and there is this, the greatest wonder of all: under her tinted hair the forest murmur becomes a thought, and words issue from her breasts" (Simone de Beauvoir, *The Second Sex*, trans. H. M. Parshley [New York, 1953] 729). (A translation of the passage from *Le Deuxième Sexe* 2.574, cited in French by Rich.)

       poised, still coming,
her fine blades making the air wince

but her cargo
no promise then:
delivered   120
palpable
ours.

1958–1960

Antinoüs:[1] The Diaries

Autumn torture. The old signs
smeared on the pavement, sopping leaves
rubbed into the landscape as unguent on a bruise,
brought indoors, even, as they bring flowers, enormous,
with the colors of the body's secret parts.   5
All this. And then, evenings, needing to be out,
walking fast, fighting the fire
that must die, light that sets my teeth on edge with joy,
till on the black embankment
I'm a cart stopped in the ruts of time.   10

Then at some house the rumor of truth and beauty
saturates a room like lilac-water
in the steam of a bath, fires snap, heads are high,
gold hair at napes of necks, gold in glasses,
gold in the throat, poetry of furs and manners.   15
Why do I shiver then? Haven't I seen,
over and over, before the end of an evening,
the three opened coffins carried in and left in a corner?
Haven't I watched as somebody cracked his shin
on one of them, winced and hopped and limped   20
laughing to lay his hands on a beautiful arm
striated with hairs of gold, like an almond-shell?

The old, needless story. For if I'm here
it is by choice and when at last
I smell my own rising nausea, feel the air   25
tighten around my stomach like a surgical bandage,
I can't pretend surprise. What is it I so miscarry?
If what I spew on the tiles at last,
helpless, disgraced, alone,

1. A beautiful youth, favorite boy of the Emperor Hadrian, who drowned in the Nile, perhaps a
suicide, in A.D. 130. [I let the young man speak for me—*Rich's note.*]

is in part what I've swallowed from glasses, eyes,   30
motions of hands, opening and closing mouths,
isn't it also dead gobbets of myself,
abortive, murdered, or never willed?

1959

A Marriage in the 'Sixties

As solid-seeming as antiquity,
you frown above
the *New York Sunday Times*
where Castro,[2] like a walk-on out of *Carmen*,[3]
mutters into a bearded henchman's ear.   5

They say the second's getting shorter—
I knew it in my bones—
and pieces of the universe are missing.
I feel the gears of this late afternoon
slip, cog by cog, even as I read.   10
"I'm old," we both complain,
half-laughing, oftener now.

Time serves you well. That face—
part Roman emperor, part Raimu—[4]
nothing this side of Absence can undo.   15
Bliss, revulsion, your rare angers can
only carry through what's well begun.

When
I read your letters long ago
in that half-defunct   20
hotel in Magdalen Street
every word primed my nerves.
A geographical misery
composed of oceans, fogbound planes
and misdelivered cablegrams   25
lay round me, a Nova Zembla[5]
only your live breath could unfreeze.
Today we stalk

2. Fidel Castro (1927–), Cuban leader who on January 1, 1959, overthrew the regime of General Fulgencio Batista in a Marxist revolution.
3. Opera (1875) by George Bizet (1838–75) about a romance between a Spanish soldier and a gypsy woman.
4. Pseudonym of Jules Muraire (1883–1946), French character actor and comedian with a music-hall background.
5. A pair of islands off the Arctic coast of Russia and Siberia.

in the raging desert of our thought
whose single drop of mercy is   30
each knows the other there.
Two strangers, thrust for life upon a rock,
may have at last the perfect hour of talk
that language aches for; still—
two minds, two messages.   35

Your brows knit into flourishes. Some piece
of mere time has you tangled there.
Some mote of history has flown into your eye.
Will nothing ever be the same,
even our quarrels take a different key,   40
our dreams exhume new metaphors?
The world breathes underneath our bed.
Don't look. We're at each other's mercy too.

Dear fellow-particle, electric dust
I'm blown with—ancestor   45
to what euphoric cluster—
see how particularity dissolves
in all that hints of chaos. Let one finger
hover toward you from There
and see this furious grain   50
suspend its dance to hang
beside you like your twin.

1961

The Roofwalker

For Denise Levertov

Over the half-finished houses
night comes. The builders
stand on the roof. It is
quiet after the hammers,
the pulleys hang slack.   5
Giants, the roofwalkers,
on a listing deck, the wave
of darkness about to break
on their heads. The sky
is a torn sail where figures   10
pass magnified, shadows
on a burning deck.

I feel like them up there:
exposed, larger than life,
and due to break my neck.   15

Was it worth while to lay—
with infinite exertion—
a roof I can't live under?
—All those blueprints,
closings of gaps,   20
measurings, calculations?
A life I didn't choose
chose me: even
my tools are the wrong ones
for what I have to do.   25
I'm naked, ignorant,
a naked man fleeing
across the roofs
who could with a shade of difference
be sitting in the lamplight   30
against the cream wallpaper
reading—not with indifference—
about a naked man
fleeing across the roofs.

1961

Ghost of a Chance

You see a man
trying to think.

You want to say
to everything:
Keep off! Give him room!   5
But you only watch,
terrified
the old consolations
will get him at last   10
like a fish
half-dead from flopping
and almost crawling
across the shingle,
almost breathing
the raw, agonizing   15
air
till a wave

pulls it back blind into the triumphant
sea.

1962

Prospective Immigrants
Please Note

sexuality!

Either you will
go through this door
or you will not go through.

If you go through
there is always the risk   5
of remembering your name.

Things look at you doubly
and you must look back
and let them happen.

If you do not go through   10
it is possible
to live worthily

to maintain your attitudes
to hold your position
to die bravely   15

but much will blind you,
much will evade you,
at what cost who knows?

The door itself
makes no promises.   20
It is only a door.

1962

From *Necessities of Life: Poems 1962–1965* (1966)

Necessities of Life[1]

Piece by piece I seem
to re-enter the world: I first began

a small, fixed dot, still see
that old myself, a dark-blue thumbtack

pushed into the scene,   5
a hard little head protruding

from the pointillist's buzz and bloom.[2]
After a time the dot

begins to ooze. Certain heats
melt it.
        Now I was hurriedly   10

blurring into ranges
of burnt red, burning green,

whole biographies swam up and
swallowed me like Jonah.[3]

Jonah! I was Wittgenstein,[4]   15
Mary Wollstonecraft,[5] the soul

●

1. Entitled "Thirty-Three" when the poem first appeared in *The Paris Review* (Winter–Spring 1964).
2. The visual effect of a painting in the pointillist style. Pointillism is a postimpressionist school of painting exemplified by Georges Seurat and his followers. They reduced color to its constituent shades and painted in dots of those shades, to be blended by the viewer's eye into the appropriate colors.
3. Old Testament prophet who was swallowed by a great fish and released after three days (Jonah 1.17).
4. Ludwig Wittgenstein (1889–1957), a philosopher especially important for his work in linguistic analysis and semantics.
5. English feminist (1759–97), author of *A Vindication of the Rights of Woman*.

of Louis Jouvet,[6] dead
in a blown-up photograph.

Till, wolfed almost to shreds,
I learned to make myself   20

unappetizing. Scaly as a dry bulb
thrown into a cellar

I used myself, let nothing use me.
Like being on a private dole,

sometimes more like kneading bricks in Egypt.[7]   25
What life was there, was mine,

now and again to lay
one hand on a warm brick

and touch the sun's ghost
with economical joy,   30

now and again to name
over the bare necessities.

So much for those days. Soon
practice may make me middling-perfect, I'll

dare inhabit the world   35
trenchant in motion as an eel, solid

as a cabbage-head. I have invitations:
a curl of mist steams upward

from a field, visible as my breath,
houses along a road stand waiting   40

like old women knitting, breathless
to tell their tales.

1962

---

6. French director (1887–1957); also worked as an actor, designer, and technician.
7. The Israelites, when captive in Egypt, were set by the Pharaoh to making bricks for building his cities (Exodus 1.14).

In the Woods

"Difficult ordinary happiness,"[8]
no one nowadays believes in you.
I shift, full-length on the blanket,
to fix the sun precisely

behind the pine-tree's crest   5
so light spreads through the needles
alive as water just
where a snake has surfaced,

unreal as water in green crystal.
Bad news is always arriving.   10
"We're hiders, hiding from something bad,"[9]
sings the little boy.

Writing these words in the woods,
I feel like a traitor to my friends,
even to my enemies.   15
The common lot's to die

a stranger's death and lie
rouged in the coffin, in a dress
chosen by the funeral director.
Perhaps that's why we never   20

see clocks on public buildings any more.
A fact no architect will mention.
We're hiders, hiding from something bad
most of the time.

Yet, and outrageously, something good   25
finds us, found me this morning
lying on a dusty blanket,
among the burnt-out Indian pipes

and bursting-open lady's-slippers.
My soul, my helicopter, whirred   30
distantly, by habit, over
the old pond with the half-drowned boat

●

8. The line is borrowed, translated from the Dutch poet J. C. Bloem [Rich's note].
9. Sung by the poet's son David at play.

toward which it always veers
for consolation: ego's Arcady:[1]
leaving the body stuck   35
like a leaf against a screen.—

Happiness! how many times
I've stranded on that word,
at the edge of that pond; seen
as if through tears, the dragon-fly—   40

only to find it all
going differently for once
this time: my soul wheeled back
and burst into my body.

Found! Ready or not.   45
If I move now, the sun
naked between the trees
will melt me as I lie.

1963

The Trees

The trees inside are moving out into the forest,
the forest that was empty all these days
where no bird could sit
no insect hide
no sun bury its feet in shadow   5
the forest that was empty all these nights
will be full of trees by morning.

All night the roots work
to disengage themselves from the cracks
in the veranda floor.   10
The leaves strain toward the glass
small twigs stiff with exertion
long-cramped boughs shuffling under the roof
like newly discharged patients
half-dazed, moving   15
to the clinic doors.

●

1. An allusion to the phrase "Et in Arcadia ego" ("and I in Arcadia"). Bartolomeo Schidoni
   (1560–1616) wrote on a painting, "Et in Arcadia vixi" ("And I lived in Arcadia"). The painters
   Guercino, Poussin, and Reynolds later put the phrase "Et in Arcadia ego" on paintings.

I sit inside, doors open to the veranda
writing long letters
in which I scarcely mention the departure
of the forest from the house.   20
The night is fresh, the whole moon shines
in a sky still open
the smell of leaves and lichen
still reaches like a voice into the rooms.
My head is full of whispers   25
which tomorrow will be silent.

Listen. The glass is breaking.
The trees are stumbling forward
into the night. Winds rush to meet them.
The moon is broken like a mirror,   30
its pieces flash now in the crown
of the tallest oak.

1963

Like This Together

For A.H.C.

1.

Wind rocks the car.
We sit parked by the river,
silence between our teeth.
Birds scatter across islands
of broken ice. Another time   5
I'd have said: "Canada geese,"
knowing you love them.
A year, ten years from now
I'll remember this—
this sitting like drugged birds   10
in a glass case—
not why, only that we
were here like this together.

2.

They're tearing down, tearing up
this city, block by block.   15
Rooms cut in half
hang like flayed carcasses,

their old roses in rags,
famous streets have forgotten
where they were going. Only   20
a fact could be so dreamlike.
They're tearing down the houses
we met and lived in,
soon our two bodies will be all
left standing from that era.   25

3.

We have, as they say,
certain things in common.
I mean: a view
from a bathroom window
over slate to stiff pigeons   30
huddled every morning; the way
water tastes from our tap,
which you marvel at, letting
it splash into the glass.
Because of you I notice   35
the taste of water,
a luxury I might
otherwise have missed.

4.

Our words misunderstand us.
Sometimes at night   40
you are my mother:
old detailed griefs
twitch at my dreams, and I
crawl against you, fighting
for shelter, making you   45
my cave. Sometimes
you're the wave of birth
that drowns me in my first
nightmare. I suck the air.
Miscarried knowledge twists us   50
like hot sheets thrown askew.

5.

Dead winter doesn't die,
it wears away, a piece of carrion
picked clean at last,
rained away or burnt dry.   55

Our desiring does this,
make no mistake, I'm speaking
of fact: through mere indifference
we could prevent it.
Only our fierce attention   60
gets hyacinths out of those
hard cerebral lumps,
unwraps the wet buds down
the whole length of a stem.[2]

1963

After Dark

1.

You[3] are falling asleep and I sit looking at you
old tree of life
old man whose death I wanted
I can't stir you up now.

Faintly a phonograph needle   5
whirs round in the last groove
eating my heart to dust.
That terrible record! how it played

down years, wherever I was
in foreign languages even   10
over and over, *I know you better*
than you know yourself   I know
●

2. When this poem first appeared in *Poetry* (April–May 1965) it had the following sixth and
concluding stanza:

> A severed hand
> keeps tingling, air still suffers
> beyond the stump. But new
> life? How do we bear it
> (or you, huge tree)
> when fresh flames start spurting
> out through our old sealed skins,
> nerve-endings ours and not yet ours?
> Susceptibilities we still
> can't use, sucking
> blind power from our roots—
> what else to do but
> hold fast to the
> one thing we know,
> grip earth and let burn.

3. The poet's father, Dr. Arnold Rich.

you better than you know
yourself   I know
you   until, self-maimed,   15
I limped off, torn at the roots,

stopped singing a whole year,
got a new body, new breath,
got children, croaked for words,
forgot to listen   20

or read your *mene tekel*[4] fading on the wall,
woke up one morning
and knew myself your daughter.
Blood is a sacred poison.

Now, unasked, you give ground.   25
We only want to stifle
what's stifling us already.
Alive now, root to crown, I'd give

—oh,—something—not to know
our struggles now are ended.   30
I seem to hold you, cupped
in my hands, and disappearing.

When your memory fails—
no more to scourge my inconsistencies—
the sashcords of the world fly loose.   35
A window crashes

suddenly down. I go to the woodbox
and take a stick of kindling
to prop the sash again.
I grow protective toward the world.   40

2.

Now let's away from prison[5]—
Underground seizures!
I used to huddle in the grave
I'd dug for you and bite

my tongue for fear it would babble   45
—*Darling*—

4. The words that appeared on the walls of Belshazzar's feasting room and which the prophet Daniel interpreted correctly as signifying the king's downfall (Daniel 5).
5. Lear says to his faithful daughter Cordelia, captured and near death: "Come, let's away to prison" (Shakespeare, *King Lear* 5.3.8).

I thought they'd find me there
someday, sitting upright, shrunken,

my hair like roots and in my lap
a mess of broken pottery—   50
wasted libation—
and you embalmed beside me.

No, let's away. Even now
there's a walk between doomed elms
(whose like we shall not see much longer)   55
and something—grass and water—

an old dream-photograph.
I'll sit with you there and tease you
for wisdom, if you like,
waiting till the blunt barge   60

bumps along the shore.
Poppies burn in the twilight
like smudge pots.
I think you hardly see me

but—this is the dream now—   65
your fears blow out,
off, over the water.
At the last, your hand feels steady.

1964

"I Am in Danger—Sir—" [6]

"Half-cracked" [7] to Higginson, living,
afterward famous in garbled versions,
your hoard of dazzling scraps a battlefield,
now your old snood

●

---

6. Sentence in a letter from Emily Dickinson to Thomas Wentworth Higginson (1823–1911), a
   literary critic with whom she opened correspondence in 1862 and to whom she sent some of
   her poems (The Letters of Emily Dickinson, ed. Thomas H. Johnson and Theodora Ward, 3
   vols. [Cambridge, MA, 1958] 2.409). She writes: "You think my gait 'spasmodic'—I am in
   danger—Sir—You think me 'uncontrolled'—I have no Tribunal."
7. Higginson in a letter described Emily Dickinson as "my partially cracked poetess at Amherst"
   (The Years and Hours of Emily Dickinson, ed. Jay Leyda [New Haven, 1960] 2.263).

mothballed at Harvard[8]   5
and you in your variorum monument[9]
equivocal to the end—
who are you?

Gardening the day-lily,
wiping the wine-glass stems,   10
your thought pulsed on behind
a forehead battered paper-thin,

you, woman, masculine
in single-mindedness,
for whom the word was more   15
than a symptom—

a condition of being.
Till the air buzzing with spoiled language
sang in your ears
of Perjury   20

and in your half-cracked way you chose
silence for entertainment,
chose to have it out at last
on your own premises.

1964

Focus

For Bert Dreyfus

Obscurity has its tale to tell.
Like the figure on the studio-bed in the corner,

out of range, smoking, watching and waiting.
Sun pours through the skylight onto the worktable

making a jar of pencils, a typewriter keyboard   5
more than they were. Veridical[1] light . . .

Earth budges. Now an empty coffee-cup,
a whetstone, a handkerchief, take on

●

8. The Houghton Rare Books Library at Harvard University has a collection of Emily Dickinson
   manuscripts and memorabilia.
9. *The Poems of Emily Dickinson*, ed. Thomas H. Johnson, 3 vols. (Cambridge, MA, 1955).
1. Truthful; from *verus* true + *dicere* to say.

their sacramental clarity, fixed by the wand
of light as the thinker thinks to fix them in the mind.   10

O secret in the core of the whetstone, in the five
pencils splayed out like fingers of a hand!

The mind's passion is all for singling out.
Obscurity has another tale to tell.

1965

Face to Face

Never to be lonely like that—
the Early American figure on the beach
in black coat and knee-breeches
scanning the didactic storm in privacy,

never to hear the prairie wolves   5
in their lunar hilarity
circling one's little all, one's claim
to be Law and Prophets

for all that lawlessness,
never to whet the appetite   10
weeks early, for a face, a hand
longed-for and dreaded—

How people used to meet!
starved, intense, the old
Christmas gifts saved up till spring,   15
and the old plain words,

and each with his God-given secret,
spelled out through months of snow and silence,
burning under the bleached scalp; behind dry lips
a loaded gun.[2]   20

1965

---

2. See poem 754, "My Life—had stood a Loaded Gun–," in *The Poems of Emily Dickinson*, ed.
Thomas H. Johnson (Cambridge, MA, 1955) 2.574. See also above, p. 10, line 45.

From *Leaflets: Poems 1965– 1968* (1969)

Orion[1]

Far back when I went zig-zagging
through tamarack pastures
you were my genius, you
my cast-iron Viking, my helmed
lion-heart king in prison.[2]   5
Years later now you're young

my fierce half-brother, staring
down from that simplified west
your breast open, your belt dragged down
by an oldfashioned thing, a sword   10
the last bravado you won't give over
though it weighs you down as you stride

and the stars in it are dim
and maybe have stopped burning.
But you burn, and I know it;   15
as I throw back my head to take you in
an old transfusion happens again:
divine astronomy is nothing to it.

Indoors I bruise and blunder,
break faith, leave ill enough   20
alone, a dead child born in the dark.
Night cracks up over the chimney,
pieces of time, frozen geodes[3]
come showering down in the grate.

●

1. Constellation that dominates the winter in the Northern Hemisphere, named for a mythical hunter of gigantic size and great beauty. The belt and sword are stars in the constellation.
2. Richard the Lion Heart of England (1157–99) was captured by Leopold of Austria and imprisoned. According to legend, his faithful minstrel Blondel discovered his whereabouts.
3. Small, hollow, usually spheroidal rocks with crystals lining the inside walls.

A man reaches behind my eyes   25
and finds them empty
a woman's head turns away
from my head in the mirror
children are dying my death
and eating crumbs of my life.   30

Pity is not your forte.
Calmly you ache up there
pinned aloft in your crow's nest,
my speechless pirate!
You take it all for granted   35
and when I look you back

it's with a starlike eye
shooting its cold and egotistical spear
where it can do least damage.
Breathe deep! No hurt, no pardon   40
out here in the cold with you
you with your back to the wall. [4]

1965

The Demon Lover [5]

Fatigue, regrets. The lights
go out in the parking lot
two by two. Snow blindness
settles over the suburb.
Desire. Desire. The nebula   5
opens in space, unseen,
your heart utters its great beats
in solitude. A new
era is coming in.
Gauche as we are, it seems   10
we have to play our part.

A plaid dress, silk scarf,
and eyes that go on stinging.
Woman, stand off. The air
glistens like silk.   15

4. One or two phrases suggested by Gottfried Benn's essay "Artists and Old Age" in *Primal Vision*, edited by E. B. Ashton, New Directions [*Rich's note*]. Benn writes this advice to the modern artist: "Don't lose sight of the cold and egotistical element in your mission . . . With your back to the wall, care-worn and weary, in the gray light of the void, read Job and Jeremiah and keep going" (pp. 206–7).
5. A phrase that Samuel Taylor Coleridge uses in the poem "Kubla Khan."

She's gone. In her place stands
a schoolgirl, morning light,
the half-grown bones
of innocence. Is she
your daughter or your muse,   20
this tree of blondness
grown up in a field of thorns?

Something piercing and marred.
Take note. Look back. When quick
the whole northeast went black[6]   25
and prisoners howled and children
ran through the night with candles,
who stood off motionless
side by side while the moon swam up
over the drowned houses?   30
Who neither touched nor spoke?
whose nape, whose finger-ends
nervelessly lied the hours away?

A voice presses at me.
If I give in it won't   35
be like the girl the bull rode,
all Rubens flesh and happy moans.[7]
But to be wrestled like a boy
with tongue, hips, knees, nerves, brain . . .
with language?   40
He doesn't know. He's watching
breasts under a striped blouse,
his bull's head down. The old
wine pours again through my veins.

Goodnight, then. 'Night. Again   45
we turn our backs and weary
weary we let down.
Things take us hard, no question.
How do you make it, all the way
from here to morning? I touch   50
you, made of such nerve
and flare and pride and swallowed tears.
Go home. Come to bed. The skies
look in at us, stern.
And this is an old story.   55

6. On November 9, 1965, eight northeastern states and the Canadian province of Ontario were
   entirely without electricity because of a massive power failure, for periods ranging from thirty
   minutes in some areas to thirteen hours in others.
7. Europa, whom Zeus, taking the form of a bull, seduced and carried over to Crete. Peter Paul
   Rubens (1577–1640) painted the *The Rape of Europa.*

I dreamed about the war.
We were all sitting at table
in a kitchen in Chicago.
The radio had just screamed
that Illinois was the target.   60
No one felt like leaving,
we sat by the open window
and talked in the sunset.
I'll tell you that joke tomorrow,
you said with your saddest smile,   65
if I can remember.

The end is just a straw,
a feather furling slowly down,
floating to light by chance, a breath
on the long-loaded scales.   70
Posterity trembles like a leaf
and we go on making heirs and heirlooms.
The world, we have to make it,
my coexistent friend[8] said, leaning
back in his cell.   75
Siberia vastly hulks
behind him, which he did not make.

Oh futile tenderness
of touch in a world like this!
how much longer, dear child,   80
do you think sex will matter?
There might have been a wedding
that never was:
two creatures sprung free
from castiron covenants.   85
Instead our hands and minds
erotically waver . . .
Lightness is unavailing.

Catalpas[9] wave and spill
their dull strings across this murk of spring.   90
I ache, brilliantly.
Only where there is language is there world.
In the harp of my hair, compose me

---

8. "Peaceful co-existence" is a phrase used to describe the notion of détente between the United States and the USSR, the main adversaries in the Cold War between communist and noncommunist countries after World War II.
9. Trees with large leaves, showy clusters of whitish flowers, and long, slender pods.

a song. Death's in the air,
we all know that. Still, for an hour,   95
I'd like to be gay. How could a gay song go?
Why that's your secret, and it shall be mine.
We are our words, and black and bruised and blue.
Under our skins, we're laughing.

In triste veritas? [1]   100
Take hold, sweet hands, come on . . .
Broken!
When you falter, all eludes.
This is a seasick way,
this almost/never touching, this   105
drawing-off, this to-and-fro.
Subtlety stalks in your eyes,
your tongue knows what it knows.
I want your secrets—I *will* have them out.
Seasick, I drop into the sea.   110

1966

5:30 A.M.

Birds and periodic blood.
Old recapitulations.
The fox, panting, fire-eyed,
gone to earth in my chest.
How beautiful we are,   5
she [2] and I, with our auburn
pelts, our trails of blood,
our miracle escapes,
our whiplash panic flogging us on
to new miracles!   10
They've supplied us with pills
for bleeding, pills for panic.
Wash them down the sink.
This is truth, then:
dull needle groping in the spinal fluid,   15
weak acid in the bottom of the cup,
foreboding, foreboding.
No one tells the truth about truth,
that it's what the fox

---

1. Literally, "In sorrow, truth," playing upon the phrase "in vino veritas": "in wine (drunkenness), truth."
2. In the original version of the poem, this pronoun is "he." Rich explains in her preface to *Poems: Selected and New, 1950–1974* (New York: Norton, 1975) xv: "Very rarely, I've altered a verb or a pronoun because I felt it had served as an evasion in the original version."

sees from her scuffled burrow: 20
dull-jawed, onrushing
killer, being that
inanely single-minded
will have our skins at last.

1967

Implosions [3]

The world's
not wanton
only wild and wavering [4]

I wanted to choose words that even you
would have to be changed by   5

Take the word
of my pulse, loving and ordinary
Send out your signals, hoist
your dark scribbled flags
but take   10
my hand

All wars are useless to the dead

My hands are knotted in the rope
and I cannot sound the bell

My hands are frozen to the switch   15
and I cannot throw it

The foot is in the wheel

When it's finished and we're lying
in a stubble of blistered flowers
eyes gaping, mouths staring   20
dusted with crushed arterial blues

I'll have done nothing
even for you?

1968

---

3. An implosion is a violent collapse inward.
4. The first three lines are stolen, by permission, from Abbot Small [*Rich's note*]. Small was a
   student in one of the poet's classes.

On Edges

When the ice starts to shiver
all across the reflecting basin
or water-lily leaves
dissect a simple surface
the word *drowning* flows through me.   5
You built a glassy floor
that held me
as I leaned to fish for old
hooks and toothed tin cans,
stems lashing out like ties of   10
silk dressing-gowns
archangels of lake-light
gripped in mud.

Now you hand me a torn letter.
On my knees, in the ashes, I could never   15
fit these ripped-up flakes together.
In the taxi I am still piecing
what syllables I can
translating at top speed like a thinking machine
that types out *useless* as *monster*   20
and *history* as *lampshade*.
Crossing the bridge I need all my nerve
to trust to the man-made cables.

The blades on that machine
could cut you to ribbons   25
but its function is humane.
Is this all I can say of these
delicate hooks, scythe-curved intentions
you and I handle? I'd rather
taste blood, yours or mine, flowing   30
from a sudden slash, than cut all day
with blunt scissors on dotted lines
like the teacher told.

1968

Nightbreak

Something broken   Something
I need   By someone
I love   Next year

will I remember what
This anger   unreal
                                              yet   5
has to be gone through
The sun to set
on this anger [5]
                        I go on
head down   into it
The mountain pulsing   10
Into the oildrum   drops
the ball of fire.

Time is quiet   doesn't break things
or even wound   Things are in danger
from people   The frail clay lamps   15
of Mesopotamia [6]
row on row under glass
in the ethnological section
little hollows for dried-
up oil   The refugees   20
with their identical
tales of escape   I don't
collect what I can't use   I need
what can be broken.

In the bed the pieces fly together   25
and the rifts fill   or else
my body is a list   of wounds
symmetrically placed
a village
blown open   by planes   30
that did not   finish the job [7]
The enemy has   withdrawn
between raids   become invisible
there are
                no agencies
                                of relief
the darkness becomes utter   35
Sleep   cracked and flaking
sifts over the shaken   target

What breaks   is night
not day   The white

---

5. St. Paul's Epistle to the Ephesians, 4.26–27: "Never let the sun set on your anger or else you will give the devil a foothold."
6. Ancient country between the Tigris and the Euphrates rivers.
7. The poem's context is the Vietnam War.

scar   splitting   40
over the east
The crack weeping
Time for the pieces
                    to move
dumbly back
        toward each other.

1968

From *The Will to Change: Poems 1968–1970* (1971)

Planetarium

Thinking of Caroline Herschel (1750–1848)
astronomer, sister of William; [1] *and others.*

A woman in the shape of a monster
a monster in the shape of a woman
the skies are full of them

a woman   'in the snow
among the Clocks and instruments   5
or measuring the ground with poles'

in her 98 years to discover
8 comets

she whom the moon ruled
like us   10
levitating into the night sky
riding the polished lenses

Galaxies of women, there
doing penance for impetuousness
ribs chilled   15
in those spaces   of the mind

An eye,

       'virile, precise and absolutely certain' [2]
       from the mad webs of Uranusborg

●

1. In helping her brother, William (1738–1822), the discoverer of Uranus, Caroline Herschel
became a superb astronomer in her own right.
2. Phrase used by the Danish astronomer Tycho Brahe (1546–1601) to describe his own obser-
vations, but also applicable to the work of Caroline Herschel.

encountering the NOVA[3]

every impulse of light exploding
from the core
as life flies out of us

      Tycho whispering at last
      'Let me not seem to have lived in vain'[4]   25

What we see, we see
and seeing is changing

the light that shrivels a mountain
and leaves a man alive[5]

Heartbeat of the pulsar[6]   30
heart sweating through my body

The radio impulse
pouring in from Taurus[7]

      I am bombarded yet   I stand

I have been standing all my life in the   35
direct path of a battery of signals
the most accurately transmitted most
untranslatable language in the universe
I am a galactic[8] cloud so deep   so invo-
luted that a light wave could take 15   40
years to travel through me   And has
taken   I am an instrument in the shape
of a woman trying to translate pulsations
into images   for the relief of the body
and the reconstruction of the mind.   45

1968

3. Uranienborg, "castle in the sky," was the name of the observatory built in 1576 by Brahe. On
November 11, 1573, Brahe discovered the famous "New Star" in Cassiopeia.
4. Brahe's last words.
5. Alludes to 7.144 of the Qur'an: "And when his Lord manifested Himself on the mountain, He
broke it into pieces and Moses fell down unconscious."
6. Celestial object emitting pulses of radio waves; generally thought to be a remnant of a super-
nova, or exploding star.
7. The constellation in the Northern Hemisphere near Orion and Aries; also Rich's astrological
sign.
8. Of, pertaining to, occurring in, or originating in the Milky Way.

The Burning of Paper Instead of Children

*I was in danger of
verbalizing my moral
impulses out of existence.
—Daniel Berrigan,[9]
on trial in Baltimore.*

1. My neighbor, a scientist and art-collector, telephones me in a state
of violent emotion. He tells me that my son and his, aged eleven and
twelve, have on the last day of school burned a mathematics textbook in
the backyard. He has forbidden my son to come to his house for a week,
and has forbidden his own son to leave the house during that time. "The
burning of a book," he says, "arouses terrible sensations in me, memo-
ries of Hitler; there are few things that upset me so much as the idea of
burning a book."

Back there: the library, walled
with green Britannicas   10
Looking again
in Dürer's *Complete Works*
for MELANCOLIA,[1] the baffled woman

the crocodiles in Herodotus[2]
the Book of the Dead[3]   15
the *Trial of Jeanne d'Arc*[4] so blue
I think, It is her color

and they take the book away
because I dream of her too often

love and fear in a house   20
knowledge of the oppressor
I know it hurts to burn

2. To imagine a time of silence
or few words

9. Jesuit priest, pacifist, and writer (1921–). Active in protests against the Vietnam War, Berrigan
  and his brother, Philip, and seven others burned several hundred draft records at a Selective
  Service office in Catonsville, Maryland, for which they were tried and imprisoned.
1. Engraving personifying melancholy as a woman, by Albrecht Dürer (1471–1528), German
  artist.
2. Famous Greek historian of the fifth century B.C. In book 2, sections 68–70, of his *Histories* he
  describes crocodiles.
3. Translation of an Egyptian papyrus (the Papyrus of Ani) in the British Museum.
4. Translation by W. P. Barrett of the original documents relating to Joan of Arc's trial (London,
  1931). Joan of Arc (1411–31) was a French peasant girl who became a mystic and was led by
  voices to rally the French and lead their army against the English. Tried and burned at the
  stake as a witch, she was later canonized.

a time of chemistry and music   25

the hollows above your buttocks
traced by my hand
or, *hair is like flesh*, you said

an age of long silence

relief   30

from this tongue   this slab of limestone
or reinforced concrete
fanatics and traders
dumped on this coast wildgreen clayred
that breathed once   35
in signals of smoke
sweep of the wind

knowledge of the oppressor
this is the oppressor's language

yet I need it to talk to you   40

3. *People suffer highly in poverty and it takes dignity and intelligence to
overcome this suffering. Some of the suffering are: a child did not had
dinner last night: a child steal because he did not have money to buy it:
to hear a mother say she do not have money to buy food for her children
and to see a child without cloth it will make tears in your eyes.*[5]

(the fracture of order
the repair of speech
to overcome this suffering)

4. We lie under the sheet
after making love, speaking   50
of loneliness
relieved in a book
relived in a book
so on that page
the clot and fissure   55
of it appears
words of a man
in pain
a naked word
entering the clot   60

5. The prose was written by one of Rich's students in the Open Admissions Program at City
College of New York.

a hand grasping
through bars:

deliverance

What happens between us
has happened for centuries   65
we know it from literature

still it happens

sexual jealousy
outflung hand
beating bed   70

dryness of mouth
after panting

there are books that describe all this
and they are useless

You walk into the woods behind a house   75
there in that country
you find a temple
built eighteen hundred years ago
you enter without knowing
what it is you enter   80

so it is with us

no one knows what may happen
though the books tell everything

burn the texts   said Artaud[6]

5. I am composing on the typewriter late at night, thinking of today.
How well we all spoke. A language is a map of our failures. Frederick
Douglass wrote an English purer than Milton's.[7] People suffer highly in
poverty. There are methods but we do not use them. Joan, who could
not read, spoke some peasant form of French. Some of the suffering are:
it is hard to tell the truth; this is America; I cannot touch you now. In
America we have only the present tense. I am in danger. You are in
danger. The burning of a book arouses no sensation in me. I know it

6. Antonin Artaud (1896–1948), French surrealist poet who called for the destruction of the
   values and structures that inform Western culture.
7. Douglass (1817?–95), American black abolitionist. Son of a slave woman, he escaped to the
   North and became a strong voice against slavery; he wrote *Narrative of The Life of Frederick
   Douglass* (1845; rev. 1855). John Milton (1608–74), English poet and essayist.

hurts to burn. There are flames of napalm in Catonsville, Maryland. I know it hurts to burn. The typewriter is overheated, my mouth is burning, I cannot touch you and this is the oppressor's language.

1968

I Dream I'm the Death of Orpheus[8]

I am walking rapidly through striations of light and dark thrown
     under an arcade.

I am a woman in the prime of life, with certain powers
and those powers severely limited
by authorities whose faces I rarely see.
I am a woman in the prime of life   5
driving her dead poet in a black Rolls-Royce
through a landscape of twilight and thorns.
A woman with a certain mission
which if obeyed to the letter will leave her intact.
A woman with the nerves of a panther   10
a woman with contacts among Hell's Angels[9]
a woman feeling the fullness of her powers
at the precise moment when she must not use them
a woman sworn to lucidity
who sees through the mayhem, the smoky fires   15
of these underground streets
her dead poet learning to walk backward against the wind
on the wrong side of the mirror

1968

Our Whole Life

Our whole life a translation
the permissible fibs

and now a knot of lies
eating at itself to get undone

Words bitten thru words   5
●

8. Legendary Thracian poet who descended to the underworld to recover his dead wife, Eurydice. Jean Cocteau (1889–1963) wrote and directed a motion picture, *Orphée* (1950), modernizing the story. Scenes and images from the movie are used in the poem. Death, a woman riding in a Rolls-Royce guarded by motorcyclists with black leather jackets, comes for Orpheus and carries him through a mirror into the underworld on the other side.
9. Motorcycle club that originated in Oakland, California, and was widely viewed as something of an outlaw gang.

meanings burnt-off like paint
under the blowtorch

All those dead letters
rendered into the oppressor's language

Trying to tell the doctor where it hurts   10
like the Algerian
who walked from his village, burning

his whole body a cloud of pain
and there are no words for this

except himself   15

1969

A Valediction Forbidding Mourning [1]

My swirling wants. Your frozen lips.
The grammar turned and attacked me.
Themes, written under duress.
Emptiness of the notations.

They gave me a drug that slowed the healing of wounds.   5

I want you to see this before I leave:
the experience of repetition as death
the failure of criticism to locate the pain
the poster in the bus that said:
my bleeding is under control.   10

A red plant in a cemetery of plastic wreaths.

A last attempt: the language is a dialect called metaphor.
These images go unglossed: hair, glacier, flashlight.
When I think of a landscape I am thinking of a time.
When I talk of taking a trip I mean forever.   15
I could say: those mountains have a meaning
but further than that I could not say.

To do something very common, in my own way.

1970

1. This is also the title of a poem by the English Metaphysical poet John Donne (1572–1631),
written to his wife on the occasion of a trip to the Continent, during which he would be
separated from her.

Shooting Script
(11/69–7/70)[2]

Part I. 11/69–2/70

1.

We were bound on the wheel of an endless conversation.

Inside this shell, a tide waiting for someone to enter.

A monologue waiting for you to interrupt it.

A man wading into the surf. The dialogue of the rock with the breaker.

The wave changed instantly by the rock; the rock changed by the wave returning over and over.   5

The dialogue that lasts all night or a whole lifetime.

A conversation of sounds melting constantly into rhythms.

A shell waiting for you to listen.

A tide that ebbs and flows against a deserted continent.

A cycle whose rhythm begins to change the meanings of words.   10

A wheel of blinding waves of light, the spokes pulsing out from where we hang together in the turning of an endless conversation.

The meaning that searches for its word like a hermit crab.

A monologue that waits for one listener.

An ear filled with one sound only.

A shell penetrated by meaning.   15

---

2. Of the fourteen sections that make up this poem, four (1, 8, 13, and 14) are reprinted here.

Part II. 3–7/70

8.

For Hugh Seidman

A woman waking behind grimed blinds slatted across a courtyard
she never looks into.

Thinking of the force of a waterfall, the slash of cold air from the
thickest water of the falls, slicing the green and ochre afternoon
in which he turns his head and walks away.

Thinking of that place as an existence.

A woman reaching for the glass of water left all night on the bureau,
the half-done poem, the immediate relief.

Entering the poem as a method of leaving the room.   5

Entering the paper airplane of the poem, which somewhere before
its destination starts curling into ash and comes apart.

The woman is too heavy for the poem, she is a swollenness, a foot,
an arm, gone asleep, grown absurd and out of bounds.

Rooted to memory like a wedge in a block of wood; she takes the
pressure of her thought but cannot resist it.

You call this a poetry of false problems, the shotgun wedding of the
mind, the subversion of choice by language.

Instead of the alternative: to pull the sooty strings to set the
window bare to purge the room with light to feel the sun breaking
in on the courtyard and the steamheat smothering in the shut-off
pipes.   10

To feel existence as this time, this place, the pathos and force
of the lumps of snow gritted and melting in the unloved corners of
the courtyard.

13.

We are driven to odd attempts; once it would not have occurred to
me to put out in a boat, not on a night like this.

●

ll, it was an instrument, and I had pledged myself to try any
instrument that came my way. Never to refuse one from conviction
of incompetence.

A long time I was simply learning to handle the skiff; I had no
special training and my own training was against me.

I had always heard that darkness and water were a threat.

In spite of this, darkness and water helped me to arrive here.   5

I watched the lights on the shore I had left for a long time; each
one, it seemed to me, was a light I might have lit, in the old days.

14.

Whatever it was: the grains of the glacier caked in the boot-cleats;
ashes spilled on white formica.

The death-col viewed through power-glasses; the cube of ice melting
on stainless steel.

Whatever it was, the image that stopped you, the one on which you
came to grief, projecting it over & over on empty walls.

Now to give up the temptations of the projector; to see instead the
web of cracks filtering across the plaster.

To read there the map of the future, the roads radiating from the
initial split, the filaments thrown out from that impasse.   5

To reread the instructions on your palm; to find there how the
lifeline, broken, keeps its direction.

To read the etched rays of the bullet-hole left years ago in the
glass; to know in every distortion of the light what fracture is.

To put the prism in your pocket, the thin glass lens, the map
of the inner city, the little book with gridded pages.

To pull yourself up by your own roots; to eat the last meal in
your old neighborhood.

From *Diving into the Wreck: Poems 1971–1972* (1973)

Trying to Talk with a Man

Out in this desert we are testing bombs,

that's why we came here.

Sometimes I feel an underground river
forcing its way between deformed cliffs
an acute angle of understanding   5
moving itself like a locus[1] of the sun
into this condemned scenery.

What we've had to give up to get here—
whole LP collections, films we starred in
playing in the neighborhoods, bakery windows   10
full of dry, chocolate-filled Jewish cookies,
the language of love-letters, of suicide notes,
afternoons on the riverbank
pretending to be children

Coming out to this desert   15
we meant to change the face of
driving among dull green succulents
walking at noon in the ghost town
surrounded by a silence

that sounds like the silence of the place   20
except that it came with us
and is familiar
and everything we were saying until now
was an effort to blot it out—
coming out here we are up against it   25

●

1. Place; but also, in geometry, the configuration made by all the points that satisfy certain specified conditions—so, a location defined by a constellation of elements.

Out here I feel more helpless
with you than without you
You mention the danger
and list the equipment
we talk of people caring for each other   '   30
in emergencies—laceration, thirst—
but you look at me like an emergency   '

Your dry heat feels like power
your eyes are stars of a different magnitude
they reflect lights that spell out: EXIT   35
when you get up and pace the floor

talking of the danger
as if it were not ourselves
as if we were testing anything else.

1971

Waking in the Dark

1.

The thing that arrests me is
   how we are composed of molecules

   (he showed me the figure in the paving stones)

   arranged without our knowledge and consent

      like the wirephoto composed   5
      of millions of dots

      in which the man from Bangladesh [2]
      walks starving
         on the front page
         knowing nothing about it   10

   which is his presence for the world

2.

We are standing in line outside of something
two by two, or alone in pairs, or simply alone,

2. Formerly East Pakistan, which proclaimed independence in March 1971 and achieved sovereignty in December 1971, after the war between India and Pakistan.

looking into windows full of scissors,
windows full of shoes. The street was closing,   15
the city was closing, would we be the lucky ones
to make it? They were showing
in a glass case, the Man Without A Country.[3]
We held up our passports in his face, we wept for him.

They are dumping animal blood into the sea   20
to bring up the sharks. Sometimes every
aperture of my body
leaks blood. I don't know whether
to pretend that this is natural.
Is there a law about this, a law of nature?   25
You worship the blood
you call it hysterical bleeding
you want to drink it like milk
you dip your finger into it and write
you faint at the smell of it   30
you dream of dumping me into the sea.

                              3.

The tragedy of sex
lies around us, a woodlot
the axes are sharpened for.
The old shelters and huts   35
stare through the clearing with a certain resolution
—the hermit's cabin, the hunters' shack—
scenes of masturbation
and dirty jokes.
A man's world. But finished.   40
They themselves have sold it to the machines.
I walk the unconscious forest,
a woman dressed in old army fatigues
that have shrunk to fit her, I am lost
at moments, I feel dazed   45
by the sun pawing between the trees,
cold in the bog and lichen of the thicket.
Nothing will save this. I am alone,
kicking the last rotting logs
with their strange smell of life, not death,   50
wondering what on earth it all might have become.

---

3. Short story (1863) by Edward Everett Hale (1822–1909) about a naval officer who makes a
hasty wish never to see America again. It was made into an opera by Walter Damrosch and
produced at the Metropolitan Opera in 1937.

4.

Clarity,

       spray

blinding and purging

spears of sun striking the water   55

the bodies riding the air

like gliders

the bodies in slow motion

falling
into the pool   60
at the Berlin Olympics [4]

control; loss of control

the bodies rising
arching back to the tower
time reeling backward   65

clarity of open air
before the dark chambers
with the shower-heads

the bodies falling again
freely   70

         faster than light
the water opening
like air
like realization

A woman made this film   75
against

the law
of gravity

---

4. Allusion to the diving sequence from *Olympiad*, a film of the 1936 Olympic Games, directed
by Leni Riefenstahl.

5.

All night dreaming of a body
space weighs on differently from mine   80
We are making love in the street
the traffic flows off from us
pouring back like a sheet
the asphalt stirs with tenderness
there is no dismay   85
we move together like underwater plants

Over and over, starting to wake
I dive back to discover you
still whispering, *touch me*, we go on
streaming through the slow   90
citylight forest ocean
stirring our body hair

But this is the saying of a dream
on waking
I wish there were somewhere   95
actual we could stand
handing the power-glasses back and forth
looking at the earth, the wildwood
where the split began

1971

The Stranger

Looking as I've looked before, straight down the heart
of the street to the river
walking the rivers of the avenues
feeling the shudder of the caves beneath the asphalt
watching the lights turn on in the towers   5
walking as I've walked before
like a man, like a woman, in the city
my visionary anger cleansing my sight
and the detailed perceptions of mercy
flowering from that anger   10

if I come into a room out of the sharp misty light
and hear them talking a dead language
if they ask me my identity
what can I say but

I am the androgyne [5]   15
I am the living mind you fail to describe
in your dead language
the lost noun, the verb surviving
only in the infinitive
the letters of my name are written under the lids   20
of the newborn child

1972

Diving into the Wreck

First having read the book of myths,
and loaded the camera,
and checked the edge of the knife-blade,
I put on
the body-armor of black rubber   5
the absurd flippers
the grave and awkward mask.
I am having to do this
not like Cousteau [6] with his
assiduous team   10
aboard the sun-flooded schooner
but here alone.

There is a ladder.
The ladder is always there
hanging innocently   15
close to the side of the schooner.
We know what it is for,
we who have used it.
Otherwise
it's a piece of maritime floss   20
some sundry equipment.

I go down.
Rung after rung and still
the oxygen immerses me
the blue light   25
the clear atoms
of our human air.
I go down.
My flippers cripple me,
I crawl like an insect down the ladder   30

5. One who has male and female characteristics physically or, as intended here, psychologically.
6. Jacques Cousteau (1910–), French underwater explorer and author.

and there is no one
to tell me when the ocean
will begin.

First the air is blue and then
it is bluer and then green and then   35
black I am blacking out and yet
my mask is powerful
it pumps my blood with power
the sea is another story
the sea is not a question of power   40
I have to learn alone
to turn my body without force
in the deep element.

And now: it is easy to forget
what I came for   45
among so many who have always
lived here
swaying their crenellated[7] fans
between the reefs
and besides   50
you breathe differently down here.

I came to explore the wreck.
The words are purposes.
The words are maps.
I came to see the damage that was done   55
and the treasures that prevail.
I stroke the beam of my lamp
slowly along the flank
of something more permanent
than fish or weed   60

the thing I came for:
the wreck and not the story of the wreck
the thing itself and not the myth
the drowned face always staring
toward the sun   65
the evidence of damage
worn by salt and sway into this threadbare beauty
the ribs of the disaster
curving their assertion
among the tentative haunters.   70

●

---

7. Notched with rounded or scalloped projections.

This is the place.
And I am here, the mermaid whose dark hair
streams black, the merman in his armored body
We circle silently
about the wreck   75
we dive into the hold.
I am she: I am he

whose drowned face sleeps with open eyes
whose breasts still bear the stress
whose silver, copper, vermeil[8] cargo lies   80
obscurely inside barrels
half-wedged and left to rot
we are the half-destroyed instruments
that once held to a course
the water-eaten log   85
the fouled compass

We are, I am, you are
by cowardice or courage
the one who find our way
back to this scene   90
carrying a knife, a camera
a book of myths
in which
our names do not appear.

1972

The Phenomenology of Anger

1. The freedom of the wholly mad
to smear & play with her madness
write with her fingers dipped in it
the length of a room

which is not, of course, the freedom   5
you have, walking on Broadway
to stop & turn back or go on
10 blocks; 20 blocks

but feels enviable maybe
to the compromised   10

●

8. Gilded metal, such as silver, bronze, or copper.

curled in the placenta of the real
which was to feed & which is strangling her.

2. Trying to light a log that's lain in the damp
as long as this house has stood:
even with dry sticks I can't get started   15
even with thorns.
I twist last year into a knot of old headlines
—this rose won't bloom.

How does a pile of rags the machinist wiped his hands on
feel in its cupboard, hour upon hour?   20
Each day during the heat-wave
they took the temperature of the haymow.
I huddled fugitive
in the warm sweet simmer of the hay

muttering: *Come.*   25

3. Flat heartland of winter.
The moonmen come back from the moon
the firemen come out of the fire.
Time without a taste: time without decisions.

Self-hatred, a monotone in the mind.   30
The shallowness of a life lived in exile
even in the hot countries.
Cleaver,[9] staring into a window full of knives.

4. White light splits the room.
Table.   Window.   Lampshade.   You.   35

My hands, sticky in a new way.
Menstrual blood
seeming to leak from your side.

Will the judges try to tell me
which was the blood of whom?   40

5. Madness.   Suicide.   Murder.
Is there no way out but these?
The enemy, always just out of sight
snowshoeing the next forest, shrouded

9. Eldridge Cleaver (1935–), one of the theorists of the Black Panther Party who split with the
   party line by continuing to advocate violence. Refusing to serve a prison sentence for a crime
   of which he said he was not guilty, he was for a time an exile in Algeria.

In a snowy blur, abominable snowman   45
—at once the most destructive
and the most elusive being
gunning down the babies at My Lai[1]
vanishing in the face of confrontation.

The prince of air and darkness   50
computing body counts, masturbating
in the factory
of facts.

6. Fantasies of murder: not enough:
to kill is to cut off from pain   55
but the killer goes on hurting

Not enough. When I dream of meeting
the enemy, this is my dream:

white acetylene
ripples from my body   60
effortlessly released
perfectly trained
on the true enemy

raking his body down to the thread
of existence   65
burning away his lie
leaving him in a new
world; a changed
man

7. I suddenly see the world   70
as no longer viable:
you are out there burning the crops
with some new sublimate
This morning you left the bed
we still share   75
and went out to spread impotence
upon the world

I hate you.
I hate the mask you wear, your eyes
assuming a depth   80
they do not possess, drawing me

1. Village in South Vietnam whose inhabitants were massacred in March 1968 by an American army platoon.

into the grotto of your skull
the landscape of bone
I hate your words
they make me think of fake   85
revolutionary bills
crisp imitation parchment
they sell at battlefields.

Last night, in this room, weeping
I asked you: *what are you feeling?*   90
do you feel anything?

Now in the torsion of your body
as you defoliate the fields we lived from
I have your answer.

8. Dogeared earth. Wormeaten moon.   95
A pale cross-hatching of silver
lies like a wire screen on the black
water. All these phenomena
are temporary.

I would have loved to live in a world   100
of women and men gaily
in collusion with green leaves, stalks,
building mineral cities, transparent domes,
little huts of woven grass
each with its own pattern—   105
a conspiracy to coexist
with the Crab Nebula,[2] the exploding
universe, the Mind—

9. *The only real love I have ever felt*
was for children and other women.   110
Everything else was lust, pity,
self-hatred, pity, lust.
This is a woman's confession.
Now, look again at the face
of Botticelli's Venus,[3] Kali,[4]   115
the Judith of Chartres[5]
with her so-called smile.

2. The Crab (also called Cancer) is a constellation in the Northern Hemisphere near Leo and
    Gemini. A nebula is any diffuse mass of interstellar dust, gas, or both.
3. The reference is to the *Birth of Venus* by Sandro Botticelli (1447?–1510); the painting is now
    in the Uffizi Gallery, Florence.
4. Hindu goddess, wife of Shiva, often depicted dancing triumphantly on his body.
5. On the north portal of Chartres cathedral is a series of scenes depicting Judith's decapitation of
    the Assyrian general Holofernes (*Book of Judith* 8–13).

FROM A SURVIVOR59

10. how we are burning up our lives
testimony:

                the subway
                hurtling to Brooklyn
                her head on her knees
                asleep or drugged

la vía del tren subterráneo
es peligrosa[6]

                many sleep
                the whole way
                others sit
                staring holes of fire into the air
                others plan rebellion:
                night after night
                awake in prison, my mind
                licked at the mattress like a flame
                till the cellblock went up roaring

        Thoreau[7] setting fire to the woods

Every act of becoming conscious
(it says here in this book)
is an unnatural act

1972

From a Survivor

The pact that we made was the ordinary pact
of men & women in those days

I don't know who we thought we were
that our personalities
could resist the failures of the race

Lucky or unlucky, we didn't know
the race had failures of that order
and that we were going to share them

●

6. Spanish for "the subway track is dangerous"—part of a sign printed in English and Spanish in
    New York City subways.
7. Henry David Thoreau (1817–62), American essayist and poet, author of *Walden*. Once Tho-
    reau's campfire spread to the woods and threatened the town; his *Journal* describes the mixture
    of horror and fascination with which he watched it burn (*The Writings of Henry David Tho-*
    reau: Journal II, ed. Bradford Torrey [Walden edition, Boston, 1906] 21–26).

Like everybody else, we thought of ourselves as special

Your body is as vivid to me   10
as it ever was: even more

since my feeling for it is clearer:
I know what it could and could not do

it is no longer
the body of a god   15
or anything with power over my life

Next year it would have been 20 years
and you are wastefully dead
who might have made the leap
we talked, too late, of making   20

which I live now
not as a leap
but a succession of brief, amazing movements

each one making possible the next

1972

For the Dead

I dreamed I called you on the telephone
to say: *Be kinder to yourself*
but you were sick and would not answer

The waste of my love goes on this way
trying to save you from yourself   5

I have always wondered about the leftover
energy, water rushing down a hill
long after the rains have stopped

or the fire you want to go to bed from
but cannot leave, burning-down but not burnt-down   10
the red coals more extreme, more curious
in their flashing and dying
than you wish they were
sitting there long after midnight

1972

From *Poems: Selected and New 1950–1974* (1975)

Re-forming the Crystal

I am trying to imagine
how it feels to you
to want a woman

trying to hallucinate
desire   5
centered in a cock
focused like a burning-glass

desire without discrimination:
to want a woman like a fix

Desire: yes: the sudden knowledge, like coming out of 'flu, that the body
is sexual. Walking in the streets with that knowledge. That evening in
the plane from Pittsburgh, fantasizing going to meet you. Walking through
the airport blazing with energy and joy. But knowing all along that you
were not the source of that energy and joy; you were a man, a stranger,
a name, a voice on the telephone, a friend; this desire was mine, this
energy my energy; it could be used a hundred ways, and going to meet
you could be one of them.

Tonight is a different kind of night.
I sit in the car, racing the engine,
calculating the thinness of the ice.   20
In my head I am already threading the beltways
that rim this city,
all the old roads that used to wander the country
having been lost.
Tonight I understand   25
my photo on the license is not me,
my
name on the marriage-contract was not mine.

If I remind you of my father's favorite daughter,
look again. The woman   30
I needed to call my mother
was silenced before I was born.

Tonight if the battery charges I want to take the car out on sheet-ice; I
want to understand my fear both of the machine and of the accidents of
nature. My desire for you is not trivial; I can compare it with the greatest
of those accidents. But the energy it draws on might lead to racing a cold
engine, cracking the frozen spiderweb, parachuting into the field of a
poem wired with danger, or to a trip through gorges and canyons, into
the cratered night of female memory, where delicately and with intense
care the chieftainess inscribes upon the ribs of the volcano the name of
the one she has chosen.

1973

The Fact of a Doorframe

means there is something to hold
onto with both hands
while slowly thrusting my forehead against the wood
and taking it away
one of the oldest motions of suffering   5
as Makeba[1] sings
a courage-song for warriors
music is suffering made powerful

I think of the story
of the goose-girl who passed through the high gate   10
where the head of her favorite mare
was nailed to the arch
and in a human voice
If she could see thee now, thy mother's heart would break
said the head   15
of Falada[2]

Now, again, poetry,
violent, arcane, common,
hewn of the commonest living substance
into archway, portal, frame   20
I grasp for you, your bloodstained splinters, your
ancient and stubborn poise

1. Miriam Makeba (1932–), black South African singer.
2. See "The Goose Girl," in *The Complete Fairy Tales of the Brothers Grimm*, trans. Jack Zipes
   (New York: Bantam, 1987) 324.

—as the earth trembles—
burning out from the grain

1974

From an Old House in America

1.

Deliberately, long ago
the carcasses

of old bugs crumbled
into the rut of the window

and we started sleeping here   5
Fresh June bugs batter this June's

screens, June-lightning batters
the spiderweb

I sweep the wood-dust
from the wood-box   10

the snout of the vacuum cleaner
sucks the past away

2.

Other lives were lived here:
mostly un-articulate

yet someone left her creamy signature   15
in the trail of rusticated

narcissus straggling up
through meadowgrass and vetch [3]

Families breathed close
boxed-in from the cold   20

hard times, short growing season
the old rainwater cistern

hulks in the cellar

3. Climbing plant of the genus *Vicia*.

3.

Like turning through the contents of a drawer:
these rusted screws, this empty vial   25

useless, this box of watercolor paints
dried to insolubility—

but this—
this pack of cards with no card missing

still playable   30
and three good fuses

and this toy: a little truck
scarred red, yet all its wheels still turn

The humble tenacity of things
waiting for people, waiting for months, for years   35

4.

Often rebuked, yet always back returning[4]
I place my hand on the hand

of the dead, invisible palm-print
on the doorframe

spiked with daylilies, green leaves   40
catching in the screen door

or I read the backs of old postcards
curling from thumbtacks, winter and summer

fading through cobweb-tinted panes—
white church in Norway   45

Dutch hyacinths bleeding azure
red beach on Corsica

set-pieces of the world
stuck to this house of plank

I flash on wife and husband   50
embattled, in the years

●

4. Borrowed from a poem, "Stanzas," by Emily Brontë [*Rich's note*].

that dried, dim ink was wet
those signatures

5.

If they call me man-hater, you
would have known it for a lie   55

but the *you* I want to speak to
has become your death

If I dream of you these days
I know my dreams are mine and not of you

yet something hangs between us   60
older and stranger than ourselves

like a translucent curtain, a sheet of water
a dusty window

the irreducible, incomplete connection
between the dead and living   65

or between man and woman in this
savagely fathered and unmothered world

6.

The other side of a translucent
curtain, a sheet of water

a dusty window, Non-being   70
utters its flat tones

the speech of an actor learning his lines
phonetically

the final autistic [5] statement
of the self-destroyer   75

All my energy reaches out tonight
to comprehend a miracle beyond

raising the dead: the undead to watch
back on the road of birth

5. Abnormally subjective and withdrawn.

7.

I am an American woman: 80
I turn that over

like a leaf pressed in a book
I stop and look up from

into the coals of the stove
or the black square of the window   85

Foot-slogging through the Bering Strait[6]
jumping from the *Arbella*[7] to my death

chained to the corpse beside me[8]
I feel my pains begin

I am washed up on this continent   90
shipped here to be fruitful

my body a hollow ship
bearing sons to the wilderness

sons who ride away
on horseback, daughters   95

whose juices drain like mine
into the *arroyo*[9] of stillbirths, massacres

Hanged as witches, sold as breeding-wenches
my sisters leave me

I am not the wheatfield   100
nor the virgin forest

I never chose this place
yet I am of it now
●

---

6. Body of water lying between Alaska and the Kamchatka Peninsula of Siberia. Anthropologists surmise that the ancestors of the American Indians came from the Asian continent by this route when the land masses of Asia and North America were still joined.
7. Ship in which the Puritans, under the leadership of William Bradford (1590?–1657), came to New England. Anne Bradstreet (1612?–72), the first woman poet in America, was on board. Her collection of verse, *The Tenth Muse* (1650), is the first book of poems written in the New World.
8. Many African women went into labor and gave birth on the slave-ships of the Middle Passage, chained for the duration of the voyage to the dying or the dead [*Rich's note*].
9. Deep gully cut by an intermittent stream; a dry gulch.

In my decent collar, in the daguerrotype [1]
I pierce its legend with my look   105

my hands wring the necks of prairie chickens
I am used to blood

When the men hit the hobo track
I stay on with the children

my power is brief and local   110
but I know my power

I have lived in isolation
from other women, so much

in the mining camps, the first cities
the Great Plains winters   115

Most of the time, in my sex, I was alone

8.

Tonight in this northeast kingdom
striated iris stand in a jar with daisies

the porcupine gnaws in the shed
fireflies beat and simmer   120

caterpillars begin again
their long, innocent climb

the length of leaves of burdock
or webbing of a garden chair

plain and ordinary things   125
speak softly

the light square on old wallpaper
where a poster has fallen down

Robert Indiana's LOVE [2]
leftover of a decade   130

---

1. Picture made by an early photographic process.
2. This pop painting, a brightly colored arrangement of the letters of the word *love* in capitals, is by the American artist Robert Indiana, pseudonym of Robert Clark (1928–), and was a popular icon of the 1960s.

9.

I do not want to simplify
Or: I would simplify

by naming the complexity
It was made over-simple all along

the separation of powers   135
the allotment of sufferings

her spine cracking in labor
his plow driving across the Indian graves

her hand unconscious on the cradle, her mind
with the wild geese   140

his mother-hatred driving him
into exile from the earth

the refugee couple with their cardboard luggage
standing on the ramshackle landing-stage

he with fingers frozen around his Law   145
she with her down quilt sewn through iron nights

—the weight of the old world, plucked
drags after them, a random feather-bed

10.

Her children dead of diphtheria, she
set herself on fire with kerosene   150

(O Lord I was unworthy
Thou didst find me out)

she left the kitchen scrubbed
down to the marrow of its boards [3]

"The penalty for barrenness   155
is emptiness

my punishment is my crime
what I have failed to do, is me . . ."

●

3. Based on incidents described by Michael Lesy in *Wisconsin Death Trip* (New York, 1973).

—Another month without a show
and this the seventh year[4]   160

O Father let this thing pass out of me
I swear to You

I will live for the others, asking nothing
I will ask nothing, ever, for myself

11.

Out back of this old house   165
datura[5] tangles with a gentler weed

its spiked pods smelling
of bad dreams and death

I reach through the dark, groping
past spines of nightmare   170

to brush the leaves of sensuality
A dream of tenderness

wrestles with all I know of history
I cannot now lie down

with a man who fears my power   175
or reaches for me as for death

or with a lover who imagines
we are not in danger

12.

If it was lust that had defined us—
their lust and fear of our deep places   180

we have done our time
as faceless torsos licked by fire

we are in the open, on our way—
our counterparts

●

4. The speaker in these lines suffers from her barrenness as the one in the next four does from
repeated pregnancies.
5. A poisonous hallucinogenic weed. It has a spiky green pod and a white flower, and is also
known as jimson-weed, or deadly nightshade [*Rich's note*].

the pinyon jay, the small   185
gilt-winged insect

the Cessna[6] throbbing level
the raven floating in the gorge

the rose and violet vulva of the earth
filling with darkness   190

yet deep within a single sparkle
of red, a human fire

and near and yet above the western planet
calmly biding her time

13.

They were the distractions, lust and fear   195
but are

themselves a key
Everything that can be used, will be:

the fathers in their ceremonies
the genital contests   200

the cleansing of blood from pubic hair
the placenta buried and guarded

their terror of blinding
by the look of her who bore them

If you do not believe   205
that fear and hatred

read the lesson again
in the old dialect

14.

But can't you see me as a human being
he said   210

What is a human being
she said

●

6. Light airplane.

I try to understand
he said

what will you undertake   215
she said

will you punish me for history
he said

what will you undertake
she said   220

do you believe in collective guilt
he said

let me look in your eyes
she said

15.

Who is here. The Erinyes.[7]   225
One to sit in judgment.

One to speak tenderness.
One to inscribe the verdict on the canyon wall.

If you have not confessed
the damage   230

if you have not recognized
the Mother of reparations

if you have not come to terms
with the women in the mirror

if you have not come to terms   235
with the inscription

the terms of the ordeal
the discipline   the verdict

if still you are on your way
still She awaits your coming   240

7. Greek goddesses of vengeance (the Furies).

16.

"Such women are dangerous
to the order of things"

and yes, we will be dangerous
to ourselves

groping through spines of nightmare   245
(*datura* tangling with a simpler herb)

because the line dividing
lucidity from darkness

is yet to be marked out

Isolation, the dream   250
of the frontier woman

leveling her rifle along
the homestead fence

still snares our pride
—a suicidal leaf   255

laid under the burning-glass
in the sun's eye

Any woman's death diminishes me

1974

From *The Dream of a Common Language: Poems 1974–1977* (1978)

Power

Living   in the earth-deposits   of our history

Today a backhoe divulged   out of a crumbling flank of earth
one bottle   amber   perfect   a hundred-year-old
cure for fever   or melancholy   a tonic
for living on this earth   in the winters of this climate   5

Today I was reading about Marie Curie:[1]
she must have known she suffered   from radiation sickness
her body bombarded for years   by the element
she had purified
It seems she denied to the end   10
the source of the cataracts on her eyes
the cracked and suppurating skin   of her finger-ends
till she could no longer hold   a test-tube or a pencil

She died   a famous woman   denying
her wounds   15
denying
her wounds   came   from the same source as her power

1974

---

1. Polish-born chemist and physicist (1864–1934) who, after coming to France and marrying Pierre Curie, did pioneering research on radioactivity. The Curies discovered radium and isolated it from pitchblende. Marie Curie was the first person to be awarded the Nobel Prize twice.

Phantasia for Elvira Shatayev

*Leader of a women's climbing team, all of whom died in a
storm on Lenin Peak, August 1974. Later, Shatayev's
husband found and buried the bodies.*

The cold felt cold until our blood
grew colder   then the wind
died down and we slept

If in this sleep I speak
it's with a voice no longer personal   5
(I want to say   *with voices*)
When the wind tore   our breath from us at last
we had no need of words
For months   for years   each one of us
had felt her own *yes*   growing in her   10
slowly forming   as she stood at windows   waited
for trains   mended her rucksack   combed her hair
What we were to learn   was simply   what we had
up here   as out of all words   that *yes*   gathered
its forces   fused itself   and only just in time   15
to meet a *No* of no degrees
the black hole   sucking the world in

I feel you climbing toward me
your cleated bootsoles leaving   their geometric bite
colossally embossed   on microscopic crystals   20
as when I trailed you in the Caucasus[2]
Now I am further
ahead   than either of us dreamed   anyone would be
I have become
the white snow packed like asphalt by the wind   25
the women I love   lightly flung   against the mountain
that blue sky
our frozen eyes unribboned   through the storm
we could have stitched that blueness   together   like a quilt

You come (I know this) with your love   your loss   30
strapped to your body   with your tape-recorder   camera
ice-pick   against advisement
to give us burial in the snow   and in your mind
While my body lies out here
flashing like a prism   into your eyes   35

---

2. Range of mountains between the Caspian and Black seas.

how could you sleep   You climbed here for yourself
we climbed for ourselves

When you have buried us   told your story
ours does not end   we stream
into the unfinished   the unbegun   40
the possible
Every cell's core of heat   pulsed out of us
into the thin air   of the universe
the armature of rock beneath these snows
this mountain   which has taken   the imprint of our minds   45
through changes elemental and minute
as those we underwent
to bring each other here
choosing ourselves   each other   and this life
whose every breath   and grasp   and further foothold   50
is somewhere   still enacted   and continuing

In the diary I wrote: *Now we are ready*
and each of us knows it   I have never loved
like this   I have never seen
my own forces so taken up and shared   55
and given back
After the long training   the early sieges
we are moving almost effortlessly in our love

In the diary as the wind   began to tear
at the tents over us   I wrote: 60
We know now we have always been in danger
down in our separateness
and now up here together   but till now
we had not touched our strength

In the diary torn from my fingers I had written: 65
What does love mean
what does it mean   "to survive"
A cable of blue fire ropes our bodies
burning together in the snow   We will not live
to settle for less   We have dreamed of this   70
all of our lives

1974

Splittings

1.

My body opens over San Francisco like the day-
light raining down   each pore crying the change of light
I am not with her   I have been waking off and on
all night to that pain   not simply absence but
the presence of the past   destructive   5
to living here and now   Yet if I could instruct
myself, if we could learn to learn from pain
even as it grasps us   if the mind, the mind that lives
in this body could refuse   to let itself be crushed
in that grasp   it would loosen   Pain would have to stand   10
off from me and listen   its dark breath still on me
but the mind could begin to speak to pain
and pain would have to answer:

                                        We are older now
we have met before   these are my hands before your eyes   15
my figure blotting out   all that is not mine
I am the pain of division   creator of divisions
it is I who blot your lover from you
and not the time-zones nor the miles
It is not separation calls me forth   but I   20
who am separation   And remember
I have no existence   apart from you

2.

I believe I am choosing something new
not to suffer uselessly   yet still to feel
Does the infant memorize the body of the mother   25
and create her in absence?   or simply cry
primordial loneliness?   does the bed of the stream
once diverted   mourning   remember wetness?
But we, we live so much in these
configurations of the past   I choose   30
to separate her   from my past we have not shared
I choose not to suffer uselessly
to detect primordial pain as it stalks toward me
flashing its bleak torch in my eyes   blotting out
her particular being   the details of her love   35
I will not be divided   from her or from myself
by myths of separation
while her mind and body in Manhattan are more with me
than the smell of eucalyptus coolly burning   on these hills

3.

The world tells me I am its creature   40
I am raked by eyes   brushed by hands
I want to crawl into her for refuge   lay my head
in the space   between her breast and shoulder
abnegating power for love
as women have done   or hiding   45
from power in her love   like a man
I refuse these givens   the splitting
between love and action   I am choosing
not to suffer uselessly   and not to use her
I choose to love   this time   for once   50
with all my intelligence

1974

Twenty-One Love Poems

I

Wherever in this city, screens flicker
with pornography, with science-fiction vampires,
victimized hirelings bending to the lash,
we also have to walk . . . if simply as we walk
through the rainsoaked garbage, the tabloid cruelties   5
of our own neighborhoods.
We need to grasp our lives inseparable
from those rancid dreams, that blurt of metal, those disgraces,
and the red begonia perilously flashing
from a tenement sill six stories high,   10
or the long-legged young girls playing ball
in the junior highschool playground.
No one has imagined us. We want to live like trees,
sycamores blazing through the sulfuric air,
dappled with scars, still exuberantly budding,   15
our animal passion rooted in the city.

II

I wake up in your bed. I know I have been dreaming.
Much earlier, the alarm broke us from each other,
you've been at your desk for hours. I know what I dreamed:
our friend the poet comes into my room
where I've been writing for days,   5
drafts, carbons, poems are scattered everywhere,

and I want to show her one poem
which is the poem of my life. But I hesitate,
and wake. You've kissed my hair
to wake me. *I dreamed you were a poem,*   10
I say, *a poem I wanted to show someone* . . .
and I laugh and fall dreaming again
of the desire to show you to everyone I love,
to move openly together
in the pull of gravity, which is not simple,   15
which carries the feathered grass a long way down the upbreathing air.

III

Since we're not young, weeks have to do time
for years of missing each other. Yet only this odd warp
in time tells me we're not young.
Did I ever walk the morning streets at twenty,
my limbs streaming with a purer joy?   5
did I lean from any window over the city
listening for the future
as I listen here with nerves tuned for your ring?
And you, you move toward me with the same tempo.
Your eyes are everlasting, the green spark   10
of the blue-eyed grass of early summer,
the green-blue wild cress washed by the spring.
At twenty, yes: we thought we'd live forever.
At forty-five, I want to know even our limits.
I touch you knowing we weren't born tomorrow,   15
and somehow, each of us will help the other live,
and somewhere, each of us must help the other die.

IV

I come home from you through the early light of spring
flashing off ordinary walls, the Pez Dorado,[3]
the Discount Wares, the shoe-store. . . . I'm lugging my sack
of groceries, I dash for the elevator
where a man, taut, elderly, carefully composed   5
lets the door almost close on me. —*For god's sake hold it!*
I croak at him. —*Hysterical,*—he breathes my way.
I let myself into the kitchen, unload my bundles,
make coffee, open the window, put on Nina Simone[4]
singing *Here comes the sun.* . . . I open the mail,   10

---

3. Store on Broadway in New York City.
4. African-American singer, pianist, and composer (1933–), best known for protest songs of the
   1960s such as "Four Women" and "Mississippi Goddam." "Here Comes the Sun" is a song
   from the Beatles' 1969 album, *Abbey Road.*

drinking delicious coffee, delicious music,
my body still both light and heavy with you. The mail
lets fall a Xerox of something written by a man
aged 27, a hostage, tortured in prison:
My genitals have been the object of such a sadistic display   15
they keep me constantly awake with the pain . . .
Do whatever you can to survive.
You know, I think that men love wars . . .
And my incurable anger, my unmendable wounds
break open further with tears, I am crying helplessly,   20
and they still control the world, and you are not in my arms.

V

This apartment full of books could crack open
to the thick jaws, the bulging eyes
of monsters, easily: Once open the books, you have to face
the underside of everything you've loved—
the rack and pincers held in readiness, the gag   5
even the best voices have had to mumble through,
the silence burying unwanted children—
women, deviants, witnesses—in desert sand.
Kenneth tells me he's been arranging his books
so he can look at Blake and Kafka[5] while he types;   10
yes; and we still have to reckon with Swift[6]
loathing the woman's flesh while praising her mind,
Goethe's dread of the Mothers,[7] Claudel vilifying Gide,[8]
and the ghosts—their hands clasped for centuries—
of artists dying in childbirth, wise-women charred at the stake,   15
centuries of books unwritten piled behind these shelves;
and we still have to stare into the absence
of men who would not, women who could not, speak
to our life—this still unexcavated hole
called civilization, this act of translation, this half-world.   20

VI

Your small hands, precisely equal to my own—
only the thumb is larger, longer—in these hands

5. William Blake (1757–1827), English Romantic poet-prophet of human perfectability. Franz Kafka (1883–1924), Czech-born fiction-writer of human oppression.
6. Jonathan Swift (1667–1745), Anglo-Irish satirist and poet. The allusion is to a poem such as "Cadenus and Vanessa," which describes Swift's rebuff of Esther Vanhomrigh's love.
7. See act 1, scene 5, of *Faust, Part II* by Johann Wolfgang von Goethe (1749–1832), German dramatist, novelist, and scientist.
8. French writers Paul Claudel (1868–1955) and Andre Gide (1869–1951). In a 1947 interview, Claudel said, "I had a lot to do with Gide when I thought he was profoundly Christian . . . and I knew nothing of his abominable failing. . . . Yes up to the day I learnt of that . . . abyss" (*The Correspondence Between Paul Claudel and Andre Gide,* trans. John Russell [New York: Pantheon, 1952] 234). Gide was homosexual as well as anti-Christian.

I could trust the world, or in many hands like these,
handling power-tools or steering-wheel
or touching a human face. . . . Such hands could turn   5
the unborn child rightways in the birth canal
or pilot the exploratory rescue-ship
through icebergs, or piece together
the fine, needle-like sherds of a great krater-cup
bearing on its sides   10
figures of ecstatic women striding
to the sibyl's den or the Eleusinian cave—
such hands might carry out an unavoidable violence
with such restraint, with such a grasp
of the range and limits of violence   15
that violence ever after would be obsolete.

VII

What kind of beast would turn its life into words?
What atonement is this all about?
—and yet, writing words like these, I'm also living.
Is all this close to the wolverines' howled signals,
that modulated cantata [9] of the wild?   5
or, when away from you I try to create you in words,
am I simply using you, like a river or a war?
And how have I used rivers, how have I used wars
to escape writing of the worst thing of all—
not the crimes of others, not even our own death,   10
but the failure to want our freedom passionately enough
so that blighted elms, sick rivers, massacres would seem
mere emblems of that desecration of ourselves?

VIII

I can see myself years back at Sunion, [1]
hurting with an infected foot, Philoctetes [2]
in woman's form, limping the long path,
lying on a headland over the dark sea,
looking down the red rocks to where a soundless curl   5
of white told me a wave had struck,
imagining the pull of that water from that height,
knowing deliberate suicide wasn't my métier,
yet all the time nursing, measuring that wound.

9. Vocal and instrumental composition comprised of choruses, solos, and recitatives.
1. One of the Greek islands.
2. Figure from Greek mythology. Crippled in the foot by a snakebite on his way to the Trojan
   War, he was abandoned by his comrades on a desert island.

Well, that's finished. The woman who cherished   10
her suffering is dead. I am her descendant.
I love the scar-tissue she handed on to me,
but I want to go on from here with you
fighting the temptation to make a career of pain.

IX

Your silence today is a pond where drowned things live
I want to see raised dripping and brought into the sun.
It's not my own face I see there, but other faces,
even your face at another age.
Whatever's lost there is needed by both of us—   5
a watch of old gold, a water-blurred fever chart,
a key. . . . Even the silt and pebbles of the bottom
deserve their glint of recognition. I fear this silence,
this inarticulate life. I'm waiting
for a wind that will gently open this sheeted water   10
for once, and show me what I can do
for you, who have often made the unnameable
nameable for others, even for me.

X

Your dog, tranquil and innocent, dozes through
our cries, our murmured dawn conspiracies
our telephone calls. She knows—what can she know?
If in my human arrogance I claim to read
her eyes, I find there only my own animal thoughts: 5
that creatures must find each other for bodily comfort,
that voices of the psyche drive through the flesh
further than the dense brain could have foretold,
that the planetary nights are growing cold for those
on the same journey, who want to touch   10
one creature-traveler clear to the end;
that without tenderness, we are in hell.

XI

Every peak is a crater. This is the law of volcanoes,
making them eternally and visibly female.
No height without depth, without a burning core,
though our straw soles shred on the hardened lava.
I want to travel with you to every sacred mountain   5
smoking within like the sibyl stooped over her tripod,
I want to reach for your hand as we scale the path,
to feel your arteries glowing in my clasp,

never failing to note the small, jewel-like flower
unfamiliar to us, nameless till we rename her,   10
that clings to the slowly altering rock—
that detail outside ourselves that brings us to ourselves,
was here before us, knew we would come, and sees beyond us.

XII

Sleeping, turning in turn like planets
rotating in their midnight meadow:
a touch is enough to let us know
we're not alone in the universe, even in sleep:
the dream-ghosts of two worlds   5
walking their ghost-towns, almost address each other.
I've wakened to your muttered words
spoken light- or dark-years away
as if my own voice had spoken.
But we have different voices, even in sleep,   10
and our bodies, so alike, are yet so different
and the past echoing through our bloodstreams
is freighted with different language, different meanings—
though in any chronicle of the world we share
it could be written with new meaning   15
we were two lovers of one gender,
we were two women of one generation.

XIII

The rules break like a thermometer,
quicksilver spills across the charted systems,
we're out in a country that has no language
no laws, we're chasing the raven and the wren
through gorges unexplored since dawn   5
whatever we do together is pure invention
the maps they gave us were out of date
by years . . . we're driving through the desert
wondering if the water will hold out
the hallucinations turn to simple villages   10
the music on the radio comes clear—
neither *Rosenkavalier* nor *Götterdämmerung*[3]
but a woman's voice singing old songs
with new words, with a quiet bass, a flute
plucked and fingered by women outside the law.   15

3. *Der Rosenkavalier* is an opera by the German composer Richard Strauss (1864–1949), famous
for its lilting waltzes; *Götterdämmerung* is the apocalyptic conclusion of a cycle of operas, *The
Ring of the Niebelung*, by the German composer Richard Wagner (1813–83).

XIV

It was your vision of the pilot
confirmed my vision of you: you said, *He keeps
on steering headlong into the waves, on purpose*
while we crouched in the open hatchway
vomiting into plastic bags   5
for three hours between St. Pierre and Miquelon.[4]
I never felt closer to you.
In the close cabin where the honeymoon couples
huddled in each other's laps and arms
I put my hand on your thigh   10
to comfort both of us, your hand came over mine,
we stayed that way, suffering together
in our bodies, as if all suffering
were physical, we touched so in the presence
of strangers who knew nothing and cared less   15
vomiting their private pain
as if all suffering were physical.

(THE FLOATING POEM, UNNUMBERED)

Whatever happens with us, your body
will haunt mine—tender, delicate
your lovemaking, like the half-curled frond
of the fiddlehead fern in forests
just washed by sun. Your traveled, generous thighs   5
between which my whole face has come and come—
the innocence and wisdom of the place my tongue has found there—
the live, insatiate dance of your nipples in my mouth—
your touch on me, firm, protective, searching
me out, your strong tongue and slender fingers   10
reaching where I had been waiting years for you
in my rose-wet cave—whatever happens, this is.

XV

If I lay on that beach with you
white, empty, pure green water warmed by the Gulf Stream
and lying on that beach we could not stay
because the wind drove fine sand against us
as if it were against us   5
if we tried to withstand it and we failed—
if we drove to another place
to sleep in each other's arms

4. Small islands off the coast of Newfoundland.

and the beds were narrow like prisoners' cots
and we were tired and did not sleep together   10
and this was what we found, so this is what we did—
was the failure ours?
If I cling to circumstances I could feel
not responsible. Only she who says
she did not choose, is the loser in the end.   15

XVI

Across a city from you, I'm with you,
just as an August night
moony, inlet-warm, seabathed, I watched you sleep,
the scrubbed, sheenless wood of the dressing-table
cluttered with our brushes, books, vials in the moonlight—   5
or a salt-mist orchard, lying at your side
watching red sunset through the screendoor of the cabin,
G minor Mozart[5] on the tape-recorder,
falling asleep to the music of the sea.
This island of Manhattan is wide enough   10
for both of us, and narrow:
I can hear your breath tonight, I know how your face
lies upturned, the halflight tracing
your generous, delicate mouth
where grief and laughter sleep together.   15

XVII

No one's fated or doomed to love anyone.
The accidents happen, we're not heroines,
they happen in our lives like car crashes,
books that change us, neighborhoods
we move into and come to love.   5
Tristan und Isolde[6] is scarcely the story,
women at least should know the difference
between love and death. No poison cup,
no penance. Merely a notion that the tape-recorder
should have caught some ghost of us: that tape-recorder   10
not merely played but should have listened to us,
and could instruct those after us:
this we were, this is how we tried to love,
and these are the forces they had ranged against us,
and these are the forces we had ranged within us,   15
within us and against us, against us and within us.

5. Symphony no. 40 in G Minor by Wolfgang Amadeus Mozart (1756–91).
6. Opera by Wagner based on the medieval romance about lovers doomed through their drinking
of a love potion.

XVIII

Rain on the West Side Highway,
red light at Riverside:[7]
the more I live the more I think
two people together is a miracle.
You're telling the story of your life   5
for once, a tremor breaks the surface of your words.
The story of our lives becomes our lives.
Now you're in fugue across what some I'm sure
Victorian poet called the *salt estranging sea.*[8]
Those are the words that come to mind.   10
I feel estrangement, yes. As I've felt dawn
pushing toward daybreak. Something: a cleft of light—?
Close between grief and anger, a space opens
where I am Adrienne alone. And growing colder.

XIX

Can it be growing colder when I begin
to touch myself again, adhesions pull away?
When slowly the naked face turns from staring backward
and looks into the present,
the eye of winter, city, anger, poverty, and death   5
and the lips part and say: *I mean to go on living?*
Am I speaking coldly when I tell you in a dream
or in this poem, *There are no miracles?*
(I told you from the first I wanted daily life,
this island of Manhattan was island enough for me.)   10
If I could let you know—
two women together is a work
nothing in civilization has made simple,
two people together is a work
heroic in its ordinariness,   15
the slow-picked, halting traverse of a pitch
where the fiercest attention becomes routine
—look at the faces of those who have chosen it.

XX

That conversation we were always on the edge
of having, runs on in my head,
at night the Hudson trembles in New Jersey light
polluted water yet reflecting even

7. New York City street names.
8. Matthew Arnold, "To Marguerite—Continued," line 24.

sometimes the moon   5
and I discern a woman
I loved, drowning in secrets, fear wound round her throat
and choking her like hair. And this is she
with whom I tried to speak, whose hurt, expressive head
turning aside from pain, is dragged down deeper   10
where it cannot hear me,
and soon I shall know I was talking to my own soul.

XXI

The dark lintels, the blue and foreign stones
of the great round rippled by stone implements
the midsummer night light rising from beneath
the horizon—when I said "a cleft of light"
I meant this. And this is not Stonehenge[9]   5
simply nor any place but the mind
casting back to where her solitude,
shared, could be chosen without loneliness,
not easily nor without pains to stake out
the circle, the heavy shadows, the great light.   10
I choose to be a figure in that light,
half-blotted by darkness, something moving
across that space, the color of stone
greeting the moon, yet more than stone:
a woman. I choose to walk here. And to draw this circle.   15

1974–1976

Transcendental Etude[1]

For Michelle Cliff

This August evening I've been driving
over backroads fringed with queen anne's lace
my car startling young deer in meadows—one
gave a hoarse intake of her breath and all
four fawns sprang after her   5
into the dark maples.
Three months from today they'll be fair game
for the hit-and-run hunters, glorying
in a weekend's destructive power,
triggers fingered by drunken gunmen, sometimes   10
so inept as to leave the shattered animal

9. Prehistoric (1900–1700 B.C.) ceremonial stone circle of upright slabs and lintels on the Salisbury Plain in Wiltshire, England.
1. Study piece of music for the development of a given point of technique.

stunned in her blood. But this evening deep in summer
the deer are still alive and free,
nibbling apples from early-laden boughs
so weighted, so englobed   15
with already yellowing fruit
they seem eternal, Hesperidean
in the clear-tuned, cricket-throbbing air.

Later I stood in the dooryard,
my nerves singing the immense   20
fragility of all this sweetness,
this green world already sentimentalized, photographed,
advertised to death. Yet, it persists
stubbornly beyond the fake Vermont
of antique barnboards glazed into discothèques,   25
artificial snow, the sick Vermont of children
conceived in apathy, grown to winters
of rotgut violence,
poverty gnashing its teeth like a blind cat at their lives.
Still, it persists. Turning off onto a dirt road   30
from the raw cuts bulldozed through a quiet village
for the tourist run to Canada,
I've sat on a stone fence above a great, soft, sloping field
of musing heifers, a farmstead
slanting its planes calmly in the calm light,   35
a dead elm raising bleached arms
above a green so dense with life,
minute, momentary life—slugs, moles, pheasants, gnats,
spiders, moths, hummingbirds, groundhogs, butterflies—
a lifetime is too narrow   40
to understand it all, beginning with the huge
rockshelves that underlie all that life.

No one ever told us we had to study our lives,
make of our lives a study, as if learning natural history
or music, that we should begin   45
with the simple exercises first
and slowly go on trying
the hard ones, practicing till strength
and accuracy became one with the daring
to leap into transcendence, take the chance   50
of breaking down in the wild arpeggio[2]
or faulting the full sentence of the fugue.[3]
    —And in fact we can't live like that: we take on

2. The playing of the tones of a chord in succession rather than simultaneously.
3. Polyphonic musical form in which one or more themes are developed by imitative counter-
   point.

everything at once before we've even begun
to read or mark time, we're forced to begin   55
in the midst of the hardest movement,
the one already sounding as we are born.
At most we're allowed a few months
of simply listening to the simple line
of a woman's voice singing a child   60
against her heart. Everything else is too soon,
too sudden, the wrenching-apart, that woman's heartbeat
heard ever after from a distance,
the loss of that ground-note echoing
whenever we are happy, or in despair.   65

Everything else seems beyond us,
we aren't ready for it, nothing that was said
is true for us, caught naked in the argument,
the counterpoint,[4] trying to sightread
what our fingers can't keep up with, learn by heart   70
what we can't even read. And yet
it *is* this we were born to. We aren't virtuosi[5]
or child prodigies, there are no prodigies
in this realm, only a half-blind, stubborn
cleaving to the timbre, the tones of what we are   75
—even when all the texts describe it differently.

And we're not performers, like Liszt,[6] competing
against the world for speed and brilliance
(the 79-year-old pianist said, when I asked her
What makes a virtuoso?—Competitiveness.)   80
The longer I live the more I mistrust
theatricality, the false glamour cast
by performance, the more I know its poverty beside
the truths we are salvaging from
the splitting-open of our lives.   85
The woman who sits watching, listening,
eyes moving in the darkness
is rehearsing in her body, hearing-out in her blood
a score touched off in her perhaps
by some words, a few chords, from the stage: 90
a tale only she can tell.

But there come times—perhaps this is one of them—
when we have to take ourselves more seriously or die;
when we have to pull back from the incantations,

4. A contrasting but parallel element, item, or musical theme.
5. Musicians with extraordinary ability, technique, or personal style.
6. Franz Liszt (1811–86), Hungarian composer and pianist.

rhythms we've moved to thoughtlessly,   95
and disenthrall ourselves, bestow
ourselves to silence, or a severer listening, cleansed
of oratory, formulas, choruses, laments, static
crowding the wires. We cut the wires,
find ourselves in free-fall, as if   100
our true home were the undimensional
solitudes, the rift
in the Great Nebula.[7]
No one who survives to speak
new language, has avoided this: 105
the cutting-away of an old force that held her
rooted to an old ground
the pitch of utter loneliness
where she herself and all creation
seem equally dispersed, weightless, her being a cry   110
to which no echo comes or can ever come.

But in fact we were always like this,
rootless, dismembered: knowing it makes the difference.
Birth stripped our birthright from us,
tore us from a woman, from women, from ourselves   115
so early on
and the whole chorus throbbing at our ears
like midges, told us nothing, nothing
of origins, nothing we needed
to know, nothing that could re-member us.   120

Only: that it is unnatural,
the homesickness for a woman, for ourselves,
for that acute joy at the shadow her head and arms
cast on a wall, her heavy or slender
thighs on which we lay, flesh against flesh,   125
eyes steady on the face of love; smell of her milk, her sweat,
terror of her disappearance, all fused in this hunger
for the element they have called most dangerous, to be
lifted breathtaken on her breast, to rock within her
—even if beaten back, stranded again, to apprehend   130
in a sudden brine-clear thought
trembling like the tiny, orbed, endangered
egg-sac of a new world:
This is what she was to me, and this
is how I can love myself—
as only a woman can love me.   135

●

7. In the Milky Way clouds of interstellar dust and gas create dark areas called "the Great Nebula" and "the Coalsack."

Homesick for myself, for her—as, after the heatwave
breaks, the clear tones of the world
manifest: cloud, bough, wall, insect, the very soul of light:
homesick as the fluted vault of desire   140
articulates itself: *I am the lover and the loved,*
home and wanderer, she who splits
firewood and she who knocks, a stranger
in the storm, two women, eye to eye
measuring each other's spirit, each other's   145
limitless desire,
                         a whole new poetry beginning here.

Vision begins to happen in such a life
as if a woman quietly walked away
from the argument and jargon in a room
and sitting down in the kitchen, began turning in her lap   150
bits of yarn, calico and velvet scraps,
laying them out absently on the scrubbed boards
in the lamplight, with small rainbow-colored shells
sent in cotton-wool from somewhere far away,
and skeins of milkweed from the nearest meadow—   155
original domestic silk, the finest findings—
and the darkblue petal of the petunia,
and the dry darkbrown lace of seaweed;
not forgotten either, the shed silver
whisker of the cat,   160
the spiral of paper-wasp-nest curling
beside the finch's yellow feather.
Such a composition has nothing to do with eternity,
the striving for greatness, brilliance—
only with the musing of a mind   165
one with her body, experienced fingers quietly pushing
dark against bright, silk against roughness,
pulling the tenets of a life together
with no mere will to mastery,
only care for the many-lived, unending   170
forms in which she finds herself,
becoming now the sherd of broken glass
slicing light in a corner, dangerous
to flesh, now the plentiful, soft leaf
that wrapped round the throbbing finger, soothes the wound;   175
and now the stone foundation, rockshelf further
forming underneath everything that grows.

1977

From *A Wild Patience Has Taken Me This Far: Poems 1978–1981* (1981)

Integrity

The quality or state of being complete; unbroken condition; entirety.
—Webster

A wild patience has taken me this far

as if I had to bring to shore
a boat with a spasmodic outboard motor
old sweaters, nets, spray-mottled books
tossed in the prow
some kind of sun burning my shoulder-blades.   5
Splashing the oarlocks. Burning through.
Your fore-arms can get scalded, licked with pain
in a sun blotted like unspoken anger
behind a casual mist.   10

The length of daylight
this far north, in this
forty-ninth year of my life
is critical.

The light is critical: of me, of this   15
long-dreamed, involuntary landing
on the arm of an inland sea.
The glitter of the shoal
depleting into shadow
I recognize: the stand of pines   20
violet-black really, green in the old postcard
but really I have nothing but myself
to go by; nothing
stands in the realm of pure necessity
except what my hands can hold.   25

●

Nothing but myself? . . . My selves.
After so long, this answer.
As if I had always known
I steer the boat in, simply.
The motor dying on the pebbles   30
cicadas taking up the hum
dropped in the silence.

Anger and tenderness: my selves.
And now I can believe they breathe in me
as angels, not polarities.   35
Anger and tenderness: the spider's genius
to spin and weave in the same action
from her own body, anywhere—
even from a broken web.

The cabin in the stand of pines   40
is still for sale. I know this. Know the print
of the last foot, the hand that slammed and locked that door,
then stopped to wreathe the rain-smashed clematis
back on the trellis
for no one's sake except its own.   45
I know the chart nailed to the wallboards
the icy kettle squatting on the burner.
The hands that hammered in those nails
emptied that kettle one last time
are these two hands   50
and they have caught the baby leaping
from between trembling legs
and they have worked the vacuum aspirator[1]
and stroked the sweated temples
and steered the boat here through this hot   55
misblotted sunlight, critical light
imperceptibly scalding
the skin these hands will also salve.

1978

Transit

When I meet the skier she is always
walking, skis and poles shouldered, toward the mountain

---

1. Device used in performing abortions.

free-swinging in worn boots
over the path new-sifted with fresh snow
her greying dark hair almost hidden by   5
a cap of many colors
her fifty-year-old, strong, impatient body
dressed for cold and speed
her eyes level with mine

And when we pass each other I look into her face   10
wondering what we have in common
where our minds converge
for we do not pass each other, she passes me
as I halt beside the fence tangled in snow,
she passes me as I shall never pass her   15
in this life

Yet I remember us together
climbing Chocorua,[2] summer nineteen-forty-five
details of vegetation beyond the timberline
lichens, wildflowers, birds,   20
amazement when the trail broke out onto the granite ledge
sloped over blue lakes, green pines, giddy air
like dreams of flying

When sisters separate they haunt each other
as she, who I might once have been, haunts me   25
or is it I who do the haunting
halting and watching on the path
how she appears again through lightly-blowing
crystals, how strong her knees carry her,
how unaware she is, how simple   30
this is for her, how without let or hindrance
she travels in her body
until the point of passing, where the skier
and the cripple must decide
to recognize each other?   35

1979

For Memory

Old words: *trust   fidelity*
Nothing new yet to take their place.
●

2. Mountain in New Hampshire.

I rake leaves, clear the lawn, October grass
painfully green beneath the gold
and in this silent labor thoughts of you   5
start up
I hear your voice: *disloyalty   betrayal*
stinging the wires

I stuff the old leaves into sacks
and still they fall and still   10
I see my work undone

One shivering rainswept afternoon
and the whole job to be done over

I can't know what you know
unless you tell me   15
there are gashes in our understandings
of this world
We came together in a common
fury of direction
barely mentioning difference   20
(what drew our finest hairs
to fire
the deep, difficult troughs
unvoiced)
I fell through a basement railing   25
the first day of school and cut my forehead open—
did I ever tell you? More than forty years
and I still remember smelling my own blood
like the smell of a new schoolbook

And did you ever tell me   30
how your mother called you in from play
and from whom? To what? These atoms filmed by ordinary dust
that common life we each and all bent out of orbit from
to which we must return simply to say
this is where I came from   35
this is what I knew

The past is not a husk   yet change goes on

Freedom. It isn't once, to walk out
under the Milky Way,[3] feeling the rivers
of light, the fields of dark—   40
freedom is daily, prose-bound, routine

3. The galaxy in which our solar system is located, visible as a luminous band in the night sky.

remembering. Putting together, inch by inch
the starry worlds. From all the lost collections.

1979

For Ethel Rosenberg

*Convicted, with her husband,
of "conspiracy to commit
espionage"; killed in the
electric chair June 19, 1953*

1.

Europe 1953:
throughout my random sleepwalk
the words

scratched on walls, on pavements
painted over railway arches   5
Liberez les Rosenberg![4]

Escaping from home I found
home everywhere:
the Jewish question, Communism

marriage itself   10
a question of loyalty
or punishment

my Jewish father writing me
letters of seventeen pages
finely inscribed harangues   15

questions of loyalty
and punishment
One week before my wedding

that couple gets the chair
the volts grapple her, don't   20
kill her fast enough

Liberez les Rosenberg!
I hadn't realized
our family arguments were so important

●

4. Free the Rosenbergs!

my narrow understanding   25
of crime   of punishment
no language for this torment

mystery of that marriage
always both faces
on every front page in the world   30

Something so shocking   so
unfathomable
it must be pushed aside

2.

She sank however into my soul   A weight of sadness
I hardly can register how deep   35
her memory has sunk   that wife and mother

like so many
who seemed to get nothing out of any of it
except her children

that daughter   of a family   40
like so many
needing its female monster

she, actually wishing to be   *an artist*
wanting out of poverty
possibly also really wanting   45
                              revolution

that woman   strapped in the chair
no fear and no regrets
charged by posterity

not with selling secrets to the Communists   50
but with wanting   *to distinguish*
herself   being a bad daughter   a bad mother

And I   walking to my wedding
by the same token a bad daughter   a bad sister
my forces focussed   55

on that hardly revolutionary effort
Her life and death   the possible
ranges of disloyalty

●

so painful   so unfathomable
they must be pushed aside
ignored for years   60

                        3.

Her mother testifies against her
Her brother testifies against her
After her death

she becomes a natural prey for pornographers   65
her death itself a scene
her body *sizzling   half-strapped   whipped like a sail*

She becomes the extremest victim
described nonetheless as *rigid of will*
what are her politics by then   no one knows   70

Her figure sinks into my soul
a drowned statue
sealed in lead

For years it has lain there   unabsorbed
first as part of that dead couple   75
on the front pages of the world   the week

I gave myself in marriage
then slowly severing   drifting apart
a separate death   a life unto itself

no longer *the Rosenbergs*   80
no longer the chosen scapegoat
the family monster

till I hear how she sang
a prostitute to sleep
in the Women's House of Detention   85

Ethel Greenglass Rosenberg   would you
have marched to take back the night[5]
collected signatures

for battered women who kill
What would you have to tell us   90
would you have burst the net

5. A rallying cry in the struggle to free women from sexual violence.

4.

Why do I even want to call her up
to console my pain   (she feels no pain at all)
why do I wish to put such questions

to ease myself   (she feels no pain at all   95
she   finally burned to death   like so many)
why all this exercise of hindsight?

since   if I imagine her at all
I have to imagine first
the pain inflicted on her   by women   100

her mother testifies against her
her sister-in-law testifies against her
and how she sees it

not the impersonal forces
not the historical reasons   105
why they might have hated her strength

If I have held her at arm's length till now
if I have still believed it was
my loyalty, my punishment at stake

if I dare imagine her surviving   110
I must be fair to what she must have lived through
I must allow her to be at last

political in her ways   not in mine
her urgencies perhaps   impervious to mine
defining revolution as she defines it   115

or, bored to the marrow of her bones
with "politics"
bored with the vast boredom of long pain

small; tiny in fact; in her late sixties
liking her room   her private life   120
living alone perhaps

no one you could interview
maybe filling a notebook herself
with secrets she has never sold

1980

The Spirit of Place[6]

For Michelle Cliff

v.

Orion[7] plunges like a drunken hunter
over the Mohawk Trail[8]   a parallelogram
slashed with two cuts of steel

A night so clear that every constellation
stands out from an undifferentiated cloud   5
of stars, a kind of aura

All the figures up there look violent to me
as a pogrom on Christmas Eve in some old country
I want our own earth   not the satellites, our

world as it is   if not as it might be   10
then as it is: male dominion, gangrape, lynching, pogrom
the Mohawk wraiths in their tracts of leafless birch

watching: will we do better?
The tests I need to pass are prescribed by the spirits
of place   who understand travel but not amnesia   15

The world as it is: not as her users boast
damaged beyond reclamation by their using
Ourselves as we are   in these painful motions

of staying cognizant: some part of us always
out beyond ourselves   20
knowing   knowing   knowing

Are we all in training for something we don't name?
to exact reparation for things
done long ago to us and to those who did not

survive what was done to them   whom we ought to honor   25
with grief   with fury   with action
On a pure night   on a night when pollution

•

6. The concluding section of a poem arising from Rich's deep identification with the countryside
in western Massachusetts, where she was then living.
7. See above, p. 29, n. 1.
8. A highway across Massachusetts that follows a trail originally blazed by the Mohawks and is a
popular tourist route through the Berkshires.

seems absurdity when the undamaged planet seems to turn
like a bowl of crystal in black ether
they are the piece of us that lies out there   30
knowing   knowing   knowing

1980

Turning the Wheel[9]

8. *Turning the Wheel*

The road to the great canyon always feels
like that road and no other
the highway to a fissure   to the female core
of a continent
Below Flagstaff[1] even   the rock erosions wear   5
a famous handwriting
the river's still prevailing signature

Seeing those rocks   that road   in dreams   I know
it is happening again   as twice while waking
I am travelling to the edge   to meet the face   10
of annihilating and impersonal time
stained in the colors of a woman's genitals
outlasting every transient violation
a face that is strangely intimate to me

Today I turned the wheel   refused that journey   15
I was feeling too alone on the open plateau
of piñon[2] juniper   world beyond time
of rockflank spread around me   too alone
and too filled with you   with whom I talked for hours
driving up from the desert   though you were far away   20
as I talk to you all day   whatever day

1981

9. The concluding section of a poem deriving from an automobile trip Rich took across the desert
in Arizona, including the Grand Canyon.
1. Town in Arizona about one hundred miles from the Grand Canyon.
2. Any of several species of pine trees of the southwestern United States, often growing with
junipers.

From *Your Native Land, Your Life: Poems* (1986)

Sources

For Helen Smelser
—since 1949—

I

Sixteen years.   The narrow, rough-gullied backroads
almost the same.   The farms: almost the same,
a new barn here, a new roof there, a rusting car,
collapsed sugar-house, trailer, new young wife
trying to make a lawn instead of a dooryard,   5
new names, old kinds of names: Rocquette, Desmarais,
Clark, Pierce, Stone.   Gossier.   No names of mine.

The vixen I met at twilight on Route 5
south of Willoughby: long dead.[1] She was an omen
to me, surviving, herding her cubs   10
in the silvery bend of the road
in nineteen sixty-five.

Shapes of things: so much the same
they feel like eternal forms: the house and barn
on the rise above May Pond; the brow of Pisgah;[2]   15
the face of milkweed blooming,
brookwater pleating over slanted granite,
boletus[3] under pine, the half-composted needles
it broke through patterned on its skin.
Shape of queen anne's lace, with the drop of blood.   20
Bladder-campion[4] veined with purple.
Multifoliate heal-all.[5]

1. For an earlier appearance of this fox, see above, pp. 33–34.
2. Named after the mountain range in Jordan that, according to the account in the Bible, Moses
   ascended before his death in order to glimpse the Promised Land (Deuteronomy 34.1).
3. Fungus having an umbrella-shaped cap with spore-bearing tubules on the underside.
4. Plant, *Silene cucubalus*, native to Europe, having white flowers and an inflated calyx.
5. Any of several plants reputed to have healing powers, especially *Prunella vulgaris*.

II

I refuse to become a seeker for cures.
Everything that has ever
helped me has come through what already   25
lay stored in me.   Old things, diffuse, unnamed, lie strong
across my heart.
             This is from where
my strength comes, even when I miss my strength
even when it turns on me   30
like a violent master.

III

From where?   the voice asks coldly.

This is the voice in cold morning air
that pierces dreams.   *From where does your strength come?*

Old things . . .   35
           From where does your strength come, you Southern Jew?
split at the root, raised in a castle of air?

Yes.   I expected this.   I have known for years
the question was coming.   *From where*

(not from these, surely,   40
Protestant separatists, Jew-baiters, nightriders

who fired in Irasburg[6] in nineteen-sixty-eight
on a black family newly settled in these hills)
               From where

the dew grows thick late August on the fierce green grass   45
and on the wooden sill and on the stone

the mountains stand in an extraordinary
point of no return   though still are green

collapsed shed-boards gleam like pewter in the dew
the realms of touch-me-not[7]   fiery with tiny tongues   50

cover the wild ground of the woods

---

6. Vermont town to which a black minister from the South had come, hoping that he and his
    family would have to endure less racism in that location.
7. Any of several plants in the genus *Impatiens*, especially the jewelweed.

IV

With whom do you believe your lot is cast?
From where does your strength come?

I think somehow, somewhere
every poem of mine must repeat those questions   55

which are not the same.   There is a *whom*, a *where*
that is not chosen   that is given   and sometimes falsely given

in the beginning we grasp whatever we can
to survive

V

All during World War II   60
I told myself I had some special destiny:
there had to be a reason
I was not living in a bombed-out house
or cellar   hiding out with rats

there had to be a reason   65
I was growing up safe, American
with sugar rationed in a Mason jar

split at the root   white-skinned social christian
neither gentile nor Jew

through the immense silence   70
of the Holocaust[8]

I had no idea of what I had been spared

still less of the women and men   my kin
the Jews of Vicksburg or Birmingham
whose lives must have been strategies no less   75
than the vixen's on Route 5

VI

If they had played the flute, or chess
I was told   I was not told what they told

8. The mass murder of the Jews by the Nazis before and during World War II.

their children when the Klan [9] rode
how they might have seen themselves   80
              a chosen people [1]

of shopkeepers
clinging by strategy to a way of life
that had its own uses for them

proud of their length of sojourn in America   85
deploring the late-comers   the peasants from Russia

I saw my father building
his rootless ideology

his private castle in air

in that most dangerous place, the family home   90
we were the chosen people

In the beginning we grasp whatever we can

                          VII

    For years I struggled with you: your categories, your theories, your
will, the cruelty which came inextricable from your love.   For years all
arguments I carried on in my head were with you.   I saw myself, the
eldest daughter raised as a son, taught to study but not to pray, taught to
hold reading and writing sacred: the eldest daughter in a house with no
son, she who must overthrow the father, take what he taught her and
use it against him.   All this in a castle of air, the floating world of the
assimilated who know and deny they will always be aliens.
    After your death I met you again as the face of patriarchy, could name
at last precisely the principle you embodied, there was an ideology at
last which let me dispose of you, identify the suffering you caused, hate
you righteously as part of a system, the kingdom of the fathers.   I saw
the power and arrogance of the male as your true watermark; I did not
see beneath it the suffering of the Jew, the alien stamp you bore, because
you had deliberately arranged that it should be invisible to me.   It is
only now, under a powerful, womanly lens, that I can decipher your
suffering and deny no part of my own.

9. Ku Klux Klan, a secret society organized in the South after the Civil War to oppose the civil
   rights of Blacks, Jews, and Catholics with terrorist methods.
1. Phrase used, often specifically of the Jews, to describe those specially elected by God for a
   divine purpose.

VIII

Back there in Maryland the stars   110
showed liquescent,[2] diffuse

in the breathless summer nights
the constellations melted

I thought I was leaving a place of enervation
heading north where the Drinking Gourd[3]   115

stood cold and steady at last
pointing the way

I thought I was following a track of freedom
and for awhile it was

IX

Why has my imagination stayed   120
northeast with the ones who stayed

Are there spirits in me, diaspora-driven[4]
that wanted to lodge somewhere

hooked into the "New" Englanders who hung on
here in this stringent space   125

believing their Biblical language
their harping on righteousness?

And, myself apart, what was this like for them,
this unlikely growing season

after each winter so mean, so mean   130
the tying-down of the spirit

and the endless rocks in the soil, the endless
purifications of self

●

2. Becoming or tending to become liquid.
3. Constellation of seven stars in the region of the north celestial pole, also called the Big Dipper
   and the Great Bear (Ursa Major), which runaway slaves used to guide their journey northward.
4. Driven from native homeland. *Diaspora*, taken from the Greek word for "dispersion," was
   used first to describe the whole body of Jews dispersed among the Gentiles after the Babylonian
   captivity and now can apply more generally to any dispersion of an originally homogeneous
   people.

there being no distance, no space around
to experiment with life?   135

                                    X

These upland farms are the farms
of invaders, these villages

white with rectitude and death
are built on stolen ground

The persecuted, pale with anger   140
know how to persecute

those who feel destined, under god's eye
need never ponder difference

and if they kill others for being who they are
or where they are   145

is this a law of history
or simply, *what must change?*

                                    XI

If I try to conjure their lives
—who are not my people by any definition—

Yankee Puritans, Québec Catholics   150
mingled within sight of the Northern Lights

I am forced to conjure a passion
like the tropism [5] in certain plants

bred of a natural region's
repetitive events   155

beyond the numb of poverty
christian hypocrisy, isolation

—a passion so unexpected
there is no name for it

so quick, fierce, unconditional   160
short growing season is no explanation.

5. The responsive growth or movement of an organism toward or away from an external stimulus.

XII

And has any of this to do with how
Mohawk or Wampanoag knew it?

is the passion I connect with in this air
trace of the original   165

existences that knew this place
is the region still trying to speak with them

is this light a language
the shudder of this aspen-grove a way

of sending messages   170
the white mind barely intercepts

are signals also coming back
from the vast diaspora

of the people who kept their promises
as a way of life?   175

XIII

Coming back after sixteen years
I stare anew at things

that steeple pure and righteous
that clapboard farmhouse

seeing what I hadn't seen before   180
through barnboards, crumbling plaster

decades of old wallpaper roses
clinging to certain studs

—into that dangerous place
the family home: 185

There are verbal brutalities
borne thereafter like any burn or scar

there are words pulled down from the walls
like dogwhips

●

the child backed silent against the wall   190
trying to keep her eyes dry;   haughty;   in panic

I will never let you know
I will never
let you know

XIV

And if my look becomes the bomb that rips   195
the family home apart

is this betrayal, that the walls
slice off, the staircase shows

torn-away above the street
that the closets where the clothes hung   200

hang naked, the room the old
grandmother had to sleep in

the toilet on the landing
the room with the books

where the father walks up and down   205
telling the child to *work, work*

harder than anyone has worked before?
—But I can't stop seeing like this

more and more I see like this everywhere.

XV

It's an oldfashioned, an outrageous thing   210
to believe one has a "destiny"

—a thought often peculiar to those
who possess privilege—

but there is something else: the faith
of those despised and endangered   215

that they are not merely the sum
of damages done to them:

have kept beyond violence the knowledge
arranged in patterns like kente-cloth [6]

●

6. Plaidlike African cloth with interwoven bands of color, usually red, black, green, and gold.

unexpected as in batik[7]   220
recurrent as bitter herbs and unleavened bread

of being a connective link
in a long, continuous way

of ordering hunger, weather, death, desire
and the nearness of chaos.   225

XVI

The Jews I've felt rooted among
are those who were turned to smoke

Reading of the chimneys against the blear air
I think I have seen them myself

the fog of northern Europe licking its way   230
along the railroad tracks

to the place where all tracks end
You told me not to look there

to become
a citizen of the world   235

bound by no tribe or clan
yet dying you followed the Six Day War[8]

with desperate attention
and this summer I lie awake at dawn

sweating the Middle East through my brain   240
wearing the star of David

on a thin chain at my breastbone

XVII

But there was also the other Jew. The one you most feared, the one
from the *shtetl*,[9] from Brooklyn, from the wrong part of history, the

---

7. A process, originated in Indonesia, for creating patterns and pictures on fabric by covering with removable wax those parts of the cloth not intended to be dyed.
8. During this war, June 6–11, 1967, Israel defeated Syria, Jordan, and Egypt, thereby gaining control of the Gaza Strip, all of Jordan's territory west of the Jordan River, the Old City of Jerusalem, and the Golan Heights in Syria.
9. Small Jewish villages in Eastern Europe and Russia.

wrong accent, the wrong class. The one I left you for.   The one both
like and unlike you, who explained you to me for years, who could not
explain himself.   The one who said, as if he had memorized the for-
mula, *There's nothing left now but the food and the humor.*   The one
who, like you, ended isolate, who had tried to move in the floating world
of the assimilated who know and deny they will always be aliens.   Who
drove to Vermont in a rented car at dawn and shot himself.   For so
many years I had thought you and he were in opposition. I needed your
unlikeness then; now it's your likeness that stares me in the face.   There
is something more than food, humor, a turn of phrase, a gesture of the
hands: there is something more.

XVIII

There is something more than self-hatred. That still outlives
these photos of the old Ashkenazi [1] life:
we are gifted children at camp in the country
or orphaned children in kindergarten
we are hurrying along the rare book dealers' street   260
with the sunlight striking one side
we are walking the wards of the Jewish hospital
along diagonal squares   young serious nurses
we are part of a family group
formally taken in 1936   265
with tables, armchairs, ferns
(behind us, in our lives, the muddy street
and the ragged shames [2]
the street-musician, the weavers lined for strike)
we are part of a family wearing white head-bandages   270
we were beaten in a pogrom [3]

The place where all tracks end
is the place where history was meant to stop
but does not stop   where thinking
was meant to stop but does not stop   275
where the pattern was meant to give way at last
                                        but only
becomes a different pattern
                         terrible, threadbare
strained   familiar   on-going   280

1. Referring to the Jews who come from Western Europe, Poland, and Russia, as opposed to
   Sephardic Jews, who come from Spain, Portugal, North Africa, and the Middle East.
2. The beadle in a synagogue.
3. Attack, usually government-inspired, on the Jewish population.

XIX

They say such things are stored
in the genetic code—

half-chances, unresolved
possibilities, the life

passed on because unlived—   285
a mystic biology?—

I think of the women who sailed to Palestine
years before I was born—

halutzot,[4] pioneers
believing in a new life   290

socialists, anarchists, jeered
as excitable, sharp of tongue

too filled with life
wanting equality in the promised land

carrying the broken promises   295
of Zionism in their hearts

along with the broken promises
of communism, anarchism—

makers of miracle who expected miracles
as stubbornly as any housewife does   300

that the life she gives her life to
shall not be cheap

that the life she gives her life to
shall not turn on her

that the life she gives her life to   305
shall want an end to suffering[5]

Zion by itself is not enough.

---

4. Young women who were pioneers in Palestine in the first decades of the twentieth century,
   mostly from Russia and Eastern Europe.
5. The phrase "an end to suffering" was evoked by a sentence in Nadine Gordimer's *Burger's
   Daughter*: "No one knows where the end of suffering will begin" [*Rich's note*].

XX

The faithful drudging child
the child at the oak desk whose penmanship,
hard work, style will win her prizes   310
becomes the woman with a mission, not to win prizes
but to change the laws of history.
How she gets this mission
is not clear, how the boundaries of perfection
explode, leaving her cheekbone grey with smoke   315
a piece of her hair singed off, her shirt
spattered with earth . . . Say that she grew up in a house
with talk of books, ideal societies—
she is gripped by a blue, a foreign air,
a desert absolute: dragged by the roots of her own will   320
into another scene of choices.

XXI

YERUSHALAYIM:[6] a vault of golden heat
hard-pulsing from bare stones

the desert's hard-won, delicate green
the diaspora of the stars   325

thrilling like thousand-year-old locusts
audible yet unheard

a city on a hill[7]
waking with first light to voices

piercing, original, intimate   330
as if my dreams mixed with the cries

of the oldest, earliest birds
and of all whose wrongs and rights

cry out for explication
as the night pales and one more day   335

breaks on this *Zion* of hope and fear
and broken promises
                         this promised land

6. Hebrew name for Jerusalem.
7. Phrase used by John Winthrop (1588–1649) in "A Model of Christian Charity" (1630), a lay
   sermon addressed to the passengers aboard the *Arbella* before the landing in Massachusetts Bay
   Colony. He is describing the Puritan community in New England as a new Zion.

XXII

I have resisted this for years, writing to you as if you could hear me.   It's been different with my father: he and I always had a kind of rhetoric going with each other, a battle between us, it didn't matter if one of us was alive or dead.   But, you, I've had a sense of protecting your existence, not using it merely as a theme for poetry or tragic musings; letting you dwell in the minds of those who have reason to miss you, in your way, or their way, not mine. The living, writers especially, are terrible projectionists.   I hate the way they use the dead.

Yet I can't finish this without speaking to you, not simply of you.   You knew there was more left than food and humor.   Even as you said that in 1953 I knew it was a formula you had found, to stand between you and pain.   The deep crevices of black pumpernickel under the knife, the sweet butter and red onions we ate on those slices; the lox and cream cheese on fresh onion rolls; bowls of sour cream mixed with cut radishes, cucumber, scallions; green tomatoes and kosher dill pickles in half-translucent paper; these, you said, were the remnants of the culture, along with the fresh *challah* [8] which turned stale so fast but looked so beautiful.

That's why I want to speak to you now.   To say: no person, trying to take responsibility for her or his identity, should have to be so alone.   There must be those among whom we can sit down and weep, and still be counted as warriors.   (I make up this strange, angry packet for you, threaded with love.)   I think you thought there was no such place for you, and perhaps there was none then, and perhaps there is none now; but we will have to make it, we who want an end to suffering, who want to change the laws of history, if we are not to *give ourselves away*.

XXIII

Sixteen years ago I sat in this northeast kingdom
reading Gilbert White's *Natural History*
of Selborne [9]   thinking
I can never know this land I walk upon
as that English priest knew his
—a comparable piece of earth—
rockledge   soil   insect   bird   weed   tree

I will never know it so well because . . .

                              ●

8. Braided bread made especially for the Sabbath and for holidays.
9. A book about wildlife and the changing seasons in Selborne, a town in the south of England, where the naturalist White (1720–93) also served as curate.

Because you have chosen
something else: to know other things   375
even the cities which
create of this a myth

Because you grew up in a castle of air
disjunctured

Because without a faith
            you are faithful   380

I have wished I could rest among the beautiful and common weeds I
can name, both here and in other tracts of the globe.   But there is no
finite knowing, no such rest.   Innocent birds, deserts, morning-glories,
point to choices, leading away from the familiar. When I speak of an
end to suffering I don't mean anesthesia. I mean knowing the world,
and my place in it, not in order to stare with bitterness or detachment,
but as a powerful and womanly series of choices: and here I write the
words, in their fullness:
powerful;   womanly.

August t 1981–
August 1982

North American Time

I

When my dreams showed signs
of becoming
politically correct
no unruly images
escaping beyond borders   5
when walking in the street I found my
themes cut out for me
knew what I would not report
for fear of enemies' usage
then I began to wonder   10

II

Everything we write
will be used against us
or against those we love.
These are the terms,

take them or leave them.   15
Poetry never stood a chance
of standing outside history.
One line typed twenty years ago
can be blazed on a wall in spraypaint
to glorify art as detachment   20
or torture of those we
did not love but also
did not want to kill

We move   but our words stand
become responsible   25
for more than we intended

and this is verbal privilege

III

Try sitting at a typewriter
one calm summer evening
at a table by a window   30
in the country, try pretending
your time does not exist
that you are simply you
that the imagination simply strays
like a great moth, unintentional   35
try telling yourself
you are not accountable
to the life of your tribe
the breath of your planet

IV

It doesn't matter what you think.   40
Words are found responsible
all you can do is choose them
or choose
to remain silent.   Or, you never had a choice,
which is why the words that do stand   45
are responsible

and this is verbal privilege

V

Suppose you want to write
of a woman braiding

another woman's hair—   50
straight down, or with beads and shells
in three-strand plaits or corn-rows—
you had better know the thickness
the length   the pattern
why she decides to braid her hair   55
how it is done to her
what country it happens in
what else happens in that country

You have to know these things

                        VI

Poet, sister: words—   60
whether we like it or not—
stand in a time of their own.
No use protesting   *I wrote that*
before Kollontai[1] *was exiled*
Rosa Luxemburg, Malcolm,[2]   65
Anna Mae Aquash,[3] *murdered,*
before Treblinka, Birkenau,[4]
Hiroshima, before Sharpeville,[5]
Biafra, Bangladesh, Boston,[6]
Atlanta, Soweto, Beirut, Assam[7]   70
—those faces, names of places

1. Alexandra Kollontai (1872–1952), important government official in the early years of the Soviet Union; lost favor for her advocacy of women's issues and under Stalin was exiled to Siberia.
2. Malcolm X (1925–65), American Black Muslim leader and activist in the Black Power movement of the 1960s; he was assassinated on February 21, 1965, perhaps by members of a rival faction of Black Muslims. Rosa Luxemburg, Marxist revolutionary and theoretician (1871–1919) and a founder of the German Communist Party; she was imprisoned through much of World War I for her criticism of the war and was killed by soldiers in January 1919, during an antigovernment uprising.
3. Young Micmac woman, active in the American Indian Movement, who was killed in 1976, shot in the back of the head at close range by an unknown assailant. See Joy Harjo, *In Mad Love and War* (Middleton, CT: Wesleyan UP, 1990) 7.
4. Auschwitz-Birkenau is a small town in central Poland. Here and at nearby Treblinka, 2 million inmates, mostly Jews and Poles, were killed in Nazi concentration camps.
5. South African town near Johannesburg; in 1960 a peaceful protest in Sharpeville against apartheid, organized by the Pan-Africanist Congress, ended when police opened fire, killing about 70 protesters and wounding about 190. Hiroshima, city in Japan destroyed by an American atomic bomb on August 6, 1945.
6. Riots over busing to integrate public schools occurred in Boston in the mid-1970s. Biafra, republic proclaimed on May 30, 1967, by the secessionist government of the eastern region of Nigeria; in the ensuing war, hundreds of thousands died, most of them civilians; Biafra capitulated on January 12, 1970. Bangladesh, republic in Asia known as East Bengal until 1955 and as East Pakistan until 1971; in the 1971 struggle for independence from Pakistan 3 million Bengals died.
7. State in northeast India, almost completely separated from India by Bangladesh; in 1959–60 bloody riots occurred when Hindu refugees, fleeing from Muslim East Pakistan, sought refuge there. Atlanta: between mid-1979 and mid-1981, twenty-eight young black Atlantans, most of

sheared from the almanac
of North American time

VII

I am thinking this in a country
where words are stolen out of mouths   75
as bread is stolen out of mouths
where poets don't go to jail
for being poets, but for being
dark-skinned, female, poor.
I am writing this in a time   80
when anything we write
can be used against those we love
where the context is never given
though we try to explain, over and over
For the sake of poetry at least   85
I need to know these things

VIII

Sometimes, gliding at night
in a plane over New York City
I have felt like some messenger
called to enter, called to engage   90
this field of light and darkness.
A grandiose idea, born of flying.
But underneath the grandiose idea
is the thought that what I must engage
after the plane has raged onto the tarmac   95
after climbing my old stairs, sitting down
at my old window
is meant to break my heart and reduce me to silence.

IX

In North America time stumbles on
without moving, only releasing   100

them well under twenty, were murdered; the murderer was apprehended in June 1981, but while the case was unsolved, racial tensions in the city increased sharply. Soweto, black township near Johannesburg, South Africa, where demonstrations that began on July 16, 1976, though bloodily put down, marked the start of a new period of black resistance to apartheid. Beirut, capital of Lebanon and the site of violent conflict between Christians and Muslims, since 1958.

a certain North American pain.
Julia de Burgos[8] wrote:
That my grandfather was a slave
is my grief;   had he been a master
that would have been my shame.   105
A poet's words, hung over a door
in North America, in the year
nineteen-eighty-three.
The almost-full moon rises
timelessly speaking of change   110
out of the Bronx, the Harlem River
the drowned towns of the Quabbin[9]
the pilfered burial mounds
the toxic swamps, the testing-grounds

and I start to speak again   115

1983

Upcountry

The silver shadow   where the line falls grey
and pearly   the unborn villages quivering
under the rock   the snail   travelling the crevice
the furred, flying white insect like a tiny
intelligence lacing the air   5
this woman whose lips lie parted
after long speech
her white hair unrestrained

All that you never paid
or have with difficulty paid   10
attention to

Change and be forgiven!   the roots of the forest
muttered   but you tramped through   guilty
unable to take forgiveness   neither do you
give mercy   15

She is asleep now   dangerous   her mind
slits the air like silk   travels faster than sound
like scissors flung into the next century

●

8. Puerto Rican poet and revolutionary (1917–53), who died on the streets of New York City
[*Rich's note*].
9. Reservoir in western Massachusetts created in 1937 by flooding five towns.

Even as you watch for the trout's hooked stagger
across the lake   the crack of light and the crumpling bear   20
her mind was on them first

               when forgiveness ends

her love means danger

1983

In the Wake of Home

1.

You sleep in a room with bluegreen curtains
posters   a pile of animals on the bed
A woman and a man who love you
and each other   slip the door ajar
you are almost asleep   they crouch in turn   5
to stroke your hair   you never wake

This happens every night for years.
This never happened.

2.

Your lips   steady   never say
It should have been this way   10
That's not what you say
You   so carefully not asking, *Why?*
Your eyes   looking straight in mine
remind me of a woman's
auburn hair   my mother's hair   15
but you never saw that hair

The family coil   so twisted, tight and loose
anyone trying to leave
has to strafe the field
burn the premises down   20

3.

The home houses
mirages   memory fogs the kitchen panes
the rush-hour traffic outside
has the same old ebb and flow
Out on the darkening block   25
somebody calls you home

night after night   then never again
Useless for you to know
they tried to do what they could
before they left for good   30

4.

The voice that used to call you home
has gone off on the wind
beaten into thinnest air
whirling down other streets
or maybe the mouth was burnt to ash   35
maybe the tongue was torn out
brownlung has stolen the breath
or fear has stolen the breath
maybe under another name
it sings on AM radio: 40
And if you knew, what would you know?

5.

But you will be drawn to places
where generations lie
side by side with each other:
fathers, mothers and children   45
in the family prayerbook
or the country burying-ground
You will hack your way through the bush
to the Jodensavanne [1]
where the gravestones are black with mould   50
You will stare at old family albums
with their smiles   their resemblances
You will want to believe that nobody
wandered off   became strange
no woman dropped her baby and ran   55
no father took off for the hills
no axe splintered the door
—that once at least it was all in order
and nobody came to grief

6.

Anytime you go back   60
where absence began

1. The Jodensavanne is an abandoned Jewish settlement in Surinam whose ruins exist in a jungle
   on the Cassipoera River [*Rich's note*].

the kitchen faucet sticks in a way you know
you have to pull the basement door
in before drawing the bolt
the last porch-step is still loose   65
the water from the tap
is the old drink of water
Any time you go back
the familiar underpulse
will start its throbbing: *Home, home!*   70
and the hole torn and patched over
will gape unseen again

7.

Even where love has run thin
the child's soul musters strength
calling on dust-motes   song on the radio   75
closet-floor of galoshes
stray cat   piles of autumn leaves
whatever comes along
—the rush of purpose to make a life
worth living past abandonment   80
building the layers up again
over the torn hole   filling in

8.

And what of the stern and faithful aunt
the fierce grandmother   the anxious sister
the good teacher   the one   85
who stood at the crossing when you had to cross
the woman hired to love you
the skeleton who held out a crust
the breaker of rules   the one
who is neither a man nor a woman   the one   90
who warmed the liquid vein of life
and day after day whatever the need
handed it on to you?
You who did and had to do
so much for yourself   this was done for you   95
by someone who did what they could
when others left for good

9.

You imagine an alley   a little kingdom
where the mother-tongue is spoken

a village of shelters   woven   100
or sewn of hides   in a long-ago way
a shanty standing up
at the edge of sharecropped fields
a tenement where life is seized by the teeth
a farm battened down on snowswept plains   105
a porch with rubber-plant and glider
on a steep city street
You imagine the people would all be there
fathers mothers and children
the ones you were promised would all be there   110
eating   arguing   working
trying to get on with life
you imagine this used to be
for everyone   everywhere

10.

What if I told you your home   115
is this continent of the homeless
of children sold   taken by force
driven from their mothers' land
killed by their mothers to save from capture
—this continent of changed names and mixed-up blood   120
of languages tabooed
diasporas unrecorded
undocumented refugees
underground railroads   trails of tears
What if I tell you your home   125
is this planet of warworn children
women and children standing in line or milling
endlessly calling each others' names
What if I tell you, you are not different
it's the family albums that lie   130
—will any of this comfort you
and how should this comfort you?

11.

The child's soul carries on
in the wake of home
building a complicated house   135
a tree-house without a tree
finding places for everything
the song   the stray cat   the skeleton
The child's soul musters strength
where the holes were torn

but there are no miracles:
even children become exhausted
And how shall they comfort each other
who have come young to grief?
Who will number the grains of loss   145
and what would comfort be?

1983

Poetry: I

Someone at a table under a brown metal lamp
is studying the history of poetry.
Someone in the library at closing-time
has learned to say *modernism,
trope, vatic,*[2] *text.*   5
She is listening for shreds of music.
He is searching for his name
back in the old country.
They cannot learn without teachers.
They are like us   what we were   10
if you remember.

In a corner of night a voice
is crying in a kind of whisper:
More!

Can you remember?   when we thought   15
the poets taught   how to live?
That is not the voice of a critic
nor a common reader
it is someone young   in anger
hardly knowing what to ask   20
who finds our lines   our glosses
wanting   in this world.

1985

Poetry: III

Even if we knew the children were all asleep
and healthy   the ledgers balanced   the water running
clear in the pipes
                    and all the prisoners free
                              •

2. Of or characteristic of a prophet; oracular. Trope, the figurative use of a word or expression.

Even if every word we wrote by then   5
were honest   the sheer heft
of our living behind it

                          not these sometimes
lax, indolent lines
                    these litanies   10

Even if we were told   not just by friends
that this was honest work

Even if each of us didn't wear
a brass locket with a picture
of a strangled woman   a girlchild sewn through the crotch   15

Even if someone had told us, young: *This is not a key*
nor a peacock feather
                    not a kite nor a telephone
This is the kitchen sink   the grinding-stone

would we give ourselves   20
more calmly over   feel less criminal joy
when the thing comes   as it does come
clarifying grammar
and the fixed and mutable stars—?

1984

Yom Kippur 1984 [3]

> *I drew solitude over me, on the long shore.*
> —Robinson Jeffers, "Prelude"

> *For whoever does not afflict his soul throughout*
> *this day, shall be cut off from his people.*
> —*Leviticus* 23:29 [4]

What is a Jew in solitude?
What would it mean not to feel lonely or afraid
far from your own or those you have called your own?
What is a woman in solitude: a queer woman or man?
In the empty street, on the empty beach, in the desert   5
what in this world as it is can solitude mean?

●

3. Yom Kippur is the Day of Atonement, the holiest day of the Jewish calendar, falling in late
September or early October.
4. See below, "The Genesis of 'Yom Kippur 1984' " (hereafter "Genesis"), pp. 252–58.

The glassy, concrete octagon suspended from the cliffs
with its electric gate, its perfected privacy
is not what I mean
the pick-up with a gun parked at a turn-out in Utah or the Golan
            Heights [5]   10
is not what I mean
the poet's tower facing the western ocean, acres of forest planted to
            the east, [6] the woman reading in the cabin, her
            attack dog suddenly risen
is not what I mean

Three thousand miles from what I once called home
I open a book searching for some lines I remember   15
about flowers, something to bind me to this coast as lilacs in the
            dooryard once
bound me back there—yes, lupines on a burnt mountainside,
something that bloomed and faded and was written down
in the poet's book, forever:
Opening the poet's book   20
I find the hatred in the poet's heart: . . . *the hateful-eyed*
and human-bodied are all about me: you that love multitude may
            have them [7]

Robinson Jeffers, multitude
is the blur flung by distinct forms against these landward valleys
and the farms that run down to the sea; the lupines   25
are multitude, and the torched poppies, the grey Pacific unrolling
            its scrolls of surf,
and the separate persons, stooped
over sewing machines in denim dust, bent under the shattering
            skies of harvest
who sleep by shifts in never-empty beds have their various dreams
Hands that pick, pack, steam, stitch, strip, stuff, shell, scrape,
            scour, belong to a brain like no other   30
Must I argue the love of multitude in the blur or defend
a solitude of barbed-wire and searchlights, the survivalist's final
            solution, have I a choice?

To wander far from your own or those you have called your own
to hear strangeness calling you from far away
and walk in that direction, long and far, not calculating risk   35
to go to meet the Stranger without fear or weapon, protection
            nowhere on your mind

5. Annexed from Syria by Israel in 1967 during the Six-Day War.
6. See below, "Genesis," p. 257.
7. The epigraph and quoted lines from Robinson Jeffers come from *The Women at Point Sur and
Other Poems* (New York: Liveright, 1977) [*Rich's note*].

(the Jew on the icy, rutted road on Christmas Eve prays for another
                Jew
    the woman in the ungainly twisting shadows of the street: *Make
                    those be a woman's footsteps*; as if she could believe
                    in a woman's god)

Find someone like yourself.   Find others.
Agree you will never desert each other.   40
Understand that any rift among you
means power to those who want to do you in.
Close to the center, safety; toward the edges, danger.
But I have a nightmare to tell: I am trying to say
that to be with my people is my dearest wish   45
but that I also love strangers
that I crave separateness
I hear myself stuttering these words
to my worst friends and my best enemies
who watch for my mistakes in grammar   50
my mistakes in love.
This is the day of atonement; but do my people forgive me?
If a cloud knew loneliness and fear, I would be that cloud.

To love the Stranger, to love solitude—am I writing merely about
                privilege
about drifting from the center, drawn to edges,   55
a privilege we can't afford in the world that is,
who are hated as being of our kind: faggot kicked into the icy
                river, woman dragged from her stalled car
into the mist-struck mountains, used and hacked to death
young scholar shot at the university gates on a summer evening
                walk, his prizes and studies nothing, nothing
                availing his Blackness
Jew deluded that she's escaped the tribe, the laws of her exclusion,
                the men too holy to touch her hand;   Jew who has
                turned her back   60
on *midrash* and *mitzvah* (yet wears the *chai*[8] on a thong between
                her breasts) hiking alone
found with a swastika carved in her back at the foot of the cliffs
                (did she die as queer or as Jew?)

Solitude, O taboo, endangered species
on the mist-struck spur of the mountain, I want a gun to defend
                you
In the desert, on the deserted street, I want what I can't have: 65

8. The Hebrew word for "alive," often worn as a charm. *Midrash*, legends and stories about the
   Bible. *Mitzvah*, good deeds done as religious duty.

your elder sister, Justice, her great peasant's hand outspread
her eye, half-hooded, sharp and true
And I ask myself, have I thrown courage away?
have I traded off something I don't name?
To what extreme will I go to meet the extremist?   70
What will I do to defend my want or anyone's want to search for
        her spirit-vision
far from the protection of those she has called her own?
Will I find O solitude
your plumes, your breasts, your hair
against my face, as in childhood, your voice like the mockingbird's 75
singing *Yes, you are loved, why else this song?*
in the old places, anywhere?

What is a Jew in solitude?
What is a woman in solitude, a queer woman or man?
When the winter flood-tides wrench the tower from the rock,
        crumble the prophet's headland, and the farms slide
        into the sea   80
when leviathan is endangered and Jonah[9] becomes revenger
when center and edges are crushed together, the extremities
        crushed together on which the world was founded
when our souls crash together, Arab and Jew, howling our
        loneliness within the tribes
when the refugee child and the exile's child re-open the blasted and
        forbidden city
when we who refuse to be women and men as women and men
        are chartered, tell our stories of solitude spent in
        multitude   85
in that world as it may be, newborn and haunted, what will
        solitude mean?

1984–1985

Contradictions: Tracking Poems[1]

3.

My mouth hovers across your breasts
in the short grey winter afternoon
in this bed   we are delicate
and tough   so hot with joy we amaze ourselves

9. See above, p. 18, n. 3, and below, "Genesis," pp. 256–57. Leviathan, a huge aquatic crea-
ture, either mythical or real, often mentioned in Hebrew poetry.
1. This poem of twenty-nine sections (seven of which are printed here) "tracks" the poet's emo-
tional and psychological experience.

tough   and delicate   we play rings   5
around each other   our daytime candle burns
with its peculiar light   and if the snow
begins to fall outside   filling the branches
and if the night falls   without announcement
these are the pleasures of winter   10
sudden, wild and delicate   your fingers
exact   my tongue exact at the same moment
stopping to laugh at a joke
my love   hot on your scent   on the cusp of winter

6.

Dear Adrienne:
                    I'm calling you up tonight
as I might call up a friend   as I might call up a ghost
to ask what you intend to do
with the rest of your life.   Sometimes you act   5
as if you have all the time there is.
I worry about you when I see this.
The prime of life, old age
aren't what they used to be;
making a good death isn't either,   10
now you can walk around the corner of a wall
and see a light
that already has blown your past away.
Somewhere in Boston   beautiful literature
is being read around the clock   15
by writers   to signify
their dislike of this.
I hope you've got something in mind.
I hope you have some idea
about the rest of your life.   20
                              In sisterhood,
                                        Adrienne

7.

Dear Adrienne,
                    I feel signified by pain
from my breastbone through my left shoulder down
through my elbow into my wrist is a thread of pain
I am typing this instead of writing by hand   5
because my wrist on the right side
blooms and rushes with pain
like a neon bulb
You ask me how I'm going to live

the rest of my life   10
Well, nothing is predictable with pain
Did the old poets write of this?
—in its odd spaces, free,
many have sung and battled—
But I'm already living the rest of my life   15
not under conditions of my choosing
wired   into pain
              rider on the slow train

                     Yours, Adrienne

18.

The problem, unstated till now, is how
to live in a damaged body
in a world where pain is meant to be gagged
uncured   un-grieved-over   The problem is
to connect, without hysteria, the pain   5
of any one's body with the pain of the body's world
For it is the body's world
they are trying to destroy forever
The best world is the body's world
filled with creatures   filled with dread   10
misshapen so   yet the best we have
our raft among the abstract worlds
and how I longed to live on this earth
walking her boundaries   never counting the cost

26.

You: air-driven   reft   from the tuber-bitten soil
that was your portion   from the torched-out village
the Marxist study-group   the Zionist cell
café or *cheder*   Zaddik[2] or Freudian   straight or gay
woman or man   O you   5
stripped   bared   appalled
stretched to mere spirit   yet still physical
your irreplaceable knowledge   lost
at the mud-slick bottom of the world
how you held fast   with your bone-meal fingers   10
to yourselves   each other   and strangers
how you touched   held-up from falling
what was already half-cadaver
how your life-cry taunted extinction

2. Holy man. *Cheder*, one-room village school supported by the Jewish community.

with its wild, crude   *so what?*   15
Grief for you has rebellion at its heart
it cannot simply mourn
You: air-driven: reft: are yet our teachers
trying to speak to us in sleep
trying to help us wake   20

28.

This high summer we love will pour its light
the fields grown rich and ragged in one strong moment
then before we're ready will crash into autumn
with a violence we can't accept
a bounty we can't forgive   5
Night frost will strike when the noons are warm
the pumpkins wildly glowing   the green tomatoes
straining huge on the vines
queen anne and blackeyed susan will straggle rusty
as the milkweed stakes her claim   10
she who will stand at last   dark sticks barely rising
up through the snow   her testament of continuation
We'll dream of a longer summer
but this is the one we have:
I lay my sunburnt hand   15
on your table: this is the time we have

29.

You who think I find words for everything
this is enough for now
cut it short   cut loose from my words

You for whom I write this
in the night hours when the wrecked cartilage   5
sifts round the mystical jointure of the bones
when the insect of detritus[3] crawls
from shoulder to elbow to wristbone
remember: the body's pain and the pain on the streets
are not the same   but you can learn   10
from the edges that blur   O you who love clear edges
more than anything   watch the edges that blur

1983–1985

_____

3. Any disintegrated matter; here, specifically, disintegrated bone.

From *Time's Power: Poems* *1985–1988* (1989)

Solfeggietto[1]

1.

Your windfall at fifteen   your Steinway grand
paid for by fire insurance
came to me as birthright   a black cave
with teeth of ebony and ivory
twanging and thundering over the head   5
of the crawling child   until
that child was set on the big book on the chair
to face the keyboard world of black and white
—already knowing the world was black and white
The child's hands   smaller than a sand-dollar   10
set on the keys   wired to their mysteries
the child's wits facing the ruled and ruling staves[2]

2.

For years we battled over music lessons
mine, taught by you   Nor did I wonder
what that keyboard meant to you   15
the hours of solitude   the practising
your life of prize-recitals   lifted hopes
Piatti's[3] nephew praising you at sixteen
scholarships to the North
Or what it was to teach   20
boarding-school girls what won't be used
shelving ambition   beating time
to "On the Ice at Sweet Briar" or

1. "Little study": term used by some composers as the title of a keyboard piece.
2. The horizontal lines and their spaces upon which notes are written or printed.
3. The reference is to Alfred (Carlo) Piatti (1822–1901), renowned Italian cellist and teacher at the Royal Academy of Music in London.

"The Sunken Cathedral" for a child
counting the minutes and the scales to freedom   25

3.

Freedom: what could that mean, for you or me?
—Summers of '36, '37, Europe untuned
what I remember isn't lessons
not Bach or Brahms or Mozart[4]
but the rented upright in the summer rental   30
One Hundred Best-Loved Songs on the piano rack
And so you played, evenings   and so we sang
"Steal Away" and "Swanee River,"
"Swing Low," and most of all
"Mine Eyes Have Seen the Glory of the Coming of the Lord"   35
How we sang out the chorus   how I loved
the watchfires of the hundred circling camps
and *truth is marching on* and *let us die to make men free*

4.

Piano lessons   The mother and the daughter
Their doomed exhaustion   their common mystery   40
worked out in finger-exercises   Czerny, Hanon[5]
The yellow Schirmer[6] albums   quarter-rests   double-holds[7]
glyphs[8] of an astronomy   the mother cannot teach
the daughter because this is not the story
of a mother teaching magic to her daughter   45
Side by side I see us locked
My wrists   your voice   are tightened
Passion lives in old songs   in the kitchen
where another woman cooks   teaches   and sings
He shall feed his flock like a shepherd[9]   50
and in the booklined room
where the Jewish father reads and smokes and teaches
Ecclesiastes, Proverbs, the Song of Songs[1]

4. Wolfgang Amadeus Mozart (1756–91), Austrian composer and pianist. Johann Sebastian Bach
   (1685–1750), German composer and organist. Johannes Brahms (1833–97), German com-
   poser.
5. Charles Louis Hanon (1819–1900), French pianist and pedagogue; next to Czerny the most
   illustrious composer of piano exercises. Karl Czerny (1791–1857), Austrian pianist, teacher,
   and composer.
6. American music publisher founded by Ernest Charles Schirmer (1865–1958) in Boston in
   1921.
7. Musical notation to indicate that a note or a rest is to be prolonged beyond its normal duration.
   Quarter-rests, absence of sound for the intervals taken up by quarter-notes.
8. Symbolic figures, either engraved or incised; here, the notations for a musical composition.
9. Line from a black spiritual.
1. Names of books in the Hebrew Bible.

The daughter struggles with the strange notations
—dark chart of music's ocean   flowers and flags   55
but would rather learn by ear and heart   The mother
says she must learn to read by sight   not ear and heart

5.

Daughter who fought her mother's lessons—
even today a scrip of music balks me—
I feel illiterate in this   60
your mother-tongue   Had it been Greek or Slovak
no more could your native alphabet have baffled
your daughter   whom you taught for years
held by a tether   over the ivory
and ebony teeth of the Steinway   65
                                   It is
the three hundredth anniversary of Johann
Sebastian Bach   My earliest life
woke to his English Suites   under your fingers
I understand a language I can't read   70
Music you played streams on the car radio
in the freeway night
You kept your passions deep   You have them still
I ask you, both of us
—Did you think mine was a virtuoso's hand?   75
Did I see power in yours?
What was worth fighting for?   What did you want?
What did I want from you?

1985–1988

The Desert as Garden of Paradise[2]

1.

Guard the knowledge
from the knowledgeable,
those who gobble:
make it unpalatable.

Stars in this place   5
might look
distant to me as you,
to you as me.

●

2. This poem has eleven sections; we print 1, 4, 9, and 11.

Monotheism. Where it began.
But all the spirits, too.   10
Desert says: What you believe
I can prove. I: amaranth[3] flower,
I: metamorphic rock, I: burrow,
I: water-drop in tilted catchment,
I: vulture, I: driest thorn.   15

Rocks in a trance. Escaped
from the arms of other rocks.
Roads leading to gold and to false gold.

4.

Every drought-resistant plant has its own story
each had to learn to live
with less and less water, each would have loved

to laze in long soft rains, in the quiet drip
after the thunderstorm   5
each could do without deprivation

but where drought is the epic then there must be some
who persist, not by species-betrayal
but by changing themselves

minutely, by a constant study   10
of the price of continuity
a steady bargain with the way things are

9.

Out of a knot of deadwood
on ghostly grey-green stems
the nightblooming cereus opens
On a still night, under Ursa Major
the tallest saguaro[4] cracks with cold   5
The eaters of herbs are eaten
the carnivores' bones fall down
and scavengers pick them clean
This is not for us, or if it is
with whom, and where, is the covenant?   10

3. Any of various, often weedy plants of the genus *Amaranthus*, having clusters of small purplish
or greenish flowers.
4. See above, p. 105, n. 3, for Ursa Major. The saguaro is a very large cactus, *Carnegiea gigan-
tea*, of the southwestern United States and northern Mexico, having up-curving branches,
white flowers, and edible red fruit.

11.

What's sacred is nameless
moves in the eyeflash
holds still in the circle
of the great arid basin
once watered and fertile   5
probes outward through twigbark
a green ghost inhabiting
dormant stick, abstract thorn
What's sacred is singular:
out of this dry fork, this   10
wreck of perspective[5]
what's sacred tries itself
one more time

1987–1988

Delta

If you have taken this rubble for my past
raking through it for fragments you could sell
know that I long ago moved on
deeper into the heart of the matter

If you think you can grasp me, think again: 5
my story flows in more than one direction
a delta springing from the riverbed
with its five fingers spread

1987

6/21

It's June and summer's height
the longest bridge of light
leaps from all the rivets
of the sky
Yet it's of earth   5
and nowhere else I have to speak
Only on earth has this light taken on
these swivelled meanings, only on this earth
where we are dying befouled, gritting our teeth

5. Phrase from John C. van Dyke, *The Desert* (1901).

losing our guiding stars   10
                            has this light
found an alphabet   a mouth

1987

Dreamwood

In the old, scratched, cheap wood of the typing stand
there is a landscape, veined, which only a child can see
or the child's older self,
a woman dreaming when she should be typing
the last report of the day.   If this were a map,   5
she thinks, a map laid down to memorize
because she might be walking it, it shows
ridge upon ridge fading into hazed desert,
here and there a sign of aquifers[6]
and one possible watering-hole.   If this were a map   10
it would be the map of the last age of her life,
not a map of choices but a map of variations
on the one great choice. It would be the map by which
she could see the end of touristic choices,
of distances blued and purpled by romance,   15
by which she would recognize that poetry
isn't revolution but a way of knowing
why it must come.   If this cheap, massproduced
wooden stand from the Brooklyn Union Gas Co.,
massproduced yet durable, being here now,   20
is what it is yet a dream-map
so obdurate, so plain,
she thinks, the material and the dream can join
and that is the poem and that is the late report.

1987

Living Memory

Open the book of tales you knew by heart,
begin driving the old roads again,
repeating the old sentences, which have changed
minutely from the wordings you remembered.
A full moon on the first of May   5
drags silver film on the Winooski River.[7]
The villages are shut

6. Water-bearing rocks, rock formations, or groups of formations.
7. River in Vermont rising east of the Green Mountains and flowing to Lake Champlain.

for the night, the woods are open
and soon you arrive at a crossroads
where late, late in time you recognize   10
part of yourself is buried.   Call it Danville,[8]
village of water-witches.

From here on instinct is uncompromised and clear:
the tales come crowding like the Kalevala[9]
longing to burst from the tongue.   Under the trees   15
of the backroad you rumor the dark
with houses, sheds, the long barn
moored like a barge on the hillside.
Chapter and verse.   A mailbox.   A dooryard.
A drink of springwater from the kitchen tap.   20
An old bed, old wallpaper.   Falling asleep like a child
in the heart of the story.

Reopen the book.   A light mist soaks the page,
blunt naked buds tip the wild lilac scribbled
at the margin of the road, no one knows when.   25
Broken stones of drywall mark the onset
of familiar paragraphs slanting up and away
each with its own version, nothing ever
has looked the same from anywhere.

We came like others to a country of farmers—   30
Puritans, Catholics, Scotch Irish, Québecois:
bought a failed Yankee's empty house and barn
from a prospering Yankee,
Jews following Yankee footprints,
prey to many myths but most of all   35
that Nature makes us free.   That the land can save us.
Pioneer, indigenous; we were neither.

You whose stories these farms secrete,
you whose absence these fields publish,
all you whose lifelong travail   40
took as given this place and weather
who did what you could with the means you had—
it was pick and shovel work
done with a pair of horses, a stone boat

8. Small town in Vermont, home of the International Association of Dowsers, whose members
   are skilled in the art of finding water with the aid of a forked twig.
9. Title of a compilation of Baltic-Finnish poetry first published in 1849 by Elias Lonnrot (1802–
   84).

a strong back, and an iron bar:[1] clearing pasture—   45
Your memories crouched, foreshortened in our text.
Pages torn.   New words crowding the old.

I knew a woman whose clavicle was smashed
inside a white clapboard house with an apple tree
and a row of tulips by the door.   I had a friend   50
with six children and a tumor like a seventh
who drove me to my driver's test and in exchange
wanted to see Goddard College, in Plainfield.   She'd heard
women without diplomas could study there.
I knew a woman who walked   55
straight across cut stubble in her bare feet away,
women who said, *He's a good man*, never
laid a hand to me as living proof.
A man they said fought death
to keep fire for his wife for one more winter, leave   60
a woodpile to outlast him.

I was left the legacy of a pile of stovewood
split by a man in the mute chains of rage.
The land he loved as landscape
could not unchain him.   There are many,   65
Gentile and Jew, it has not saved.   Many hearts have burst
over these rocks, in the shacks
on the failure sides of these hills.   Many guns
turned on brains already splitting
in silence.   Where are those versions?   70
Written-across like nineteenth-century letters
or secrets penned in vinegar, invisible
till the page is held over flame.

I was left the legacy of three sons
—as if in an old legend of three brothers   75
where one changes into a rufous hawk
one into a snowy owl
one into a whistling swan
and each flies to the mother's side
as she travels, bringing something she has lost,   80
and she sees their eyes are the eyes of her children
and speaks their names and they become her sons.
But there is no one legend and one legend only.

●

1. Quoted from *Wally Hunt's Vermont* (Brownington, Vt.: Orleans County Historical Society,
1983) [*Rich's note*].

This month the land still leafless, out from snow
opens in all directions, the transparent woods   85
with sugar-house, pond, cellar-hole unscreened.
Winter and summer cover the closed roads
but for a few weeks they lie exposed,
the old nervous-system of the land.   It's the time
when history speaks in a row of crazy fence-poles   90
a blackened chimney, houseless, a spring
soon to be choked in second growth
a stack of rusting buckets, a rotting sledge.

It's the time when your own living
laid open between seasons   95
ponders clues like the *One Way* sign defaced
to *Bone Way*, the stones
of a graveyard in Vermont, a Jewish cemetery
in Birmingham, Alabama.
How you have needed these places,   100
as a tall gaunt woman used to need to sit
at the knees of bronze-hooded *Grief*[2]
by Clover Adams' grave.
But you will end somewhere else, a sift of ashes
awkwardly flung by hands you have held and loved   105
or, nothing so individual, bones reduced
with, among, other bones, anonymous,
or wherever the Jewish dead
have to be sought in the wild grass overwhelming
the cracked stones.   Hebrew spelled in wilderness.   110

All we can read is life.   Death is invisible.
A yahrzeit candle[3] belongs
to life.   The sugar skulls
eaten on graves for the Day of the Dead[4]
belong to life.   To the living.   The Kaddish[5] is to the living,   115
the Day of the Dead, for the living.   Only the living
invent these plumes, tombs, mounds, funeral ships,
living hands turn the mirrors to the walls,
tear the boughs of yew to lay on the casket,
rip the clothes of mourning.   Only the living   120

2. Monument designed by Augustus Saint-Gaudens for the tomb of Marion Hooper ("Clover")
   Adams, wife of the American historian Henry Adams; Marion Adams committed suicide in
   1885. Eleanor Roosevelt used to visit her grave.
3. Memorial candle lit every year on the anniversary of a person's death.
4. November 2, the Feast of All Souls in the Roman Catholic calendar.
5. Prayer in praise of God, recited in the daily synagogue services and by mourners after the death
   of a close relative.

decide death's color: is it white or black?
The granite bulkhead[6]
incised with names, the quilt of names,[7] were made
by the living, for the living.
                              I have watched   125
films from a Pathé camera,[8] a picnic
in sepia, I have seen my mother
tossing an acorn into the air;
my grandfather, alone in the heart of his family;
my father, young, dark, theatrical;   130
myself, a six-month child.
Watching the dead we see them living
their moments, they were at play, nobody thought
they would be watched so.
                              When Selma threw   135
her husband's ashes into the Hudson
and they blew back on her and on us, her friends,
it was life.   Our blood raced in that gritty wind.

Such details get bunched, packed, stored
in these cellar-holes of memory   140
so little is needed
to call on the power, though you can't name its name:
It has its ways of coming back:
a truck going into gear on the crown of the road
the white-throat sparrow's notes   145
the moon in her fullness standing
right over the concrete steps the way
she stood the night they landed there.
                              From here
nothing has changed, and everything.   150

The scratched and treasured photograph Richard showed me
taken in '29, the year I was born:
it's the same road I saw
strewn with the Perseids[9] one August night,
looking older, steeper than now   155
and rougher, yet I knew it.   Time's

---

6. The Vietnam Veterans Memorial, dedicated in 1982, has walls of black granite on which are
   inscribed the names of over fifty-eight thousand servicemen and -women who died or remain
   missing in Southeast Asia.
7. The quilt whose patches, added over the years, memorialize those who have died of AIDS.
8. Charles Pathé (1873–1957); French motion-picture pioneer, credited with having originated
   the newsreel and film documentary. The French firm Pathé Frères opened a branch in the
   United States in 1904.
9. Annual shower of meteors that appears to originate in the vicinity of the constellation Perseus
   during the second week of August.

power, the only just power—would you
give it away?

1988

Turning

5.[1]

Whatever you are that has tracked us this far,
I never thought you were on our side,
I only thought you did not judge us.

Yet as a cell might hallucinate
the eye—intent, impassioned—   5
behind the lens of the microscope

so I have thought of you,
whatever you are—a mindfulness—
whatever you are: the place beyond all places,

beyond boundaries, green lines,   10
wire-netted walls
the place beyond documents.

Unnameable by choice.
So why am I out here, trying
to read your name in the illegible air?   15

—vowel washed from a stone,
solitude of no absence,
forbidden face-to-face

—trying to hang these wraiths
of syllables, breath   20
without echo, why?

1988

---

1. The last section of a poem that meditates on human history and the possibility of change.

From *An Atlas of the Difficult World: Poems 1988–1991* (1991)

An Atlas of the Difficult World

I

A dark woman, head bent, listening for something
—a woman's voice, a man's voice or
voice of the freeway, night after night, metal streaming downcoast
past eucalyptus, cypress, agribusiness empires
THE SALAD BOWL OF THE WORLD, gurr of small planes   5
dusting the strawberries, each berry picked by a hand
in close communion, strawberry blood on the wrist,
Malathion[1] in the throat, communion,
the hospital at the edge of the fields,
prematures slipping from unsafe wombs,   10
the labor and delivery nurse on her break watching
planes dusting rows of pickers.
Elsewhere declarations are made: at the sink
rinsing strawberries flocked and gleaming, fresh from market
one says: "On the pond this evening is a light   15
finer than my mother's handkerchief
received from her mother, hemmed and initialled
by the nuns in Belgium."
One says: "I can lie for hours
reading and listening to music. But sleep comes hard.   20
I'd rather lie awake and read."   One writes:
"Mosquitoes pour through the cracks
in this cabin's walls, the road
in winter is often impassable,
I live here so I don't have to go out and act,   25
I'm trying to hold onto my life, it feels like nothing."
One says: "I never knew from one day to the next

1. Chemical pesticide.

142

where it was coming from: I had to make my life happen
from day to day.   Every day an emergency.
Now I have a house, a job from year to year.   30
What does that make me?"
In the writing workshop a young man's tears
wet the frugal beard he's grown to go with his poems
hoping they have redemption stored
in their lines, maybe will get him home free.   In the classroom   35
eight-year-old faces are grey.   The teacher knows which children
have not broken fast that day,
remembers the Black Panthers[2] spooning cereal.

I don't want to hear how he beat her after the earthquake,
tore up her writing, threw the kerosene   40
lantern into her face waiting
like an unbearable mirror of his own.   I don't
want to hear how she finally ran from the trailer
how he tore the keys from her hands, jumped into the truck
and backed it into her.   I don't want to think   45
how her guesses betrayed her—that he meant well, that she
was really the stronger and ought not to leave him
to his own apparent devastation.   I don't want to know
wreckage, dreck and waste, but these are the materials
and so are the slow lift of the moon's belly   50
over wreckage, dreck, and waste, wild treefrogs calling in
another season, light and music still pouring over
our fissured, cracked terrain.

Within two miles of the Pacific rounding
this long bay, sheening the light for miles   55
inland, floating its fog through redwood rifts and over
strawberry and artichoke fields, its bottomless mind
returning always to the same rocks, the same cliffs, with
ever-changing words, always the same language
—this is where I live now.   If you had known me   60
once, you'd still know me now though in a different
light and life.   This is no place you ever knew me.
But it would not surprise you
to find me here, walking in fog, the sweep of the great ocean
eluding me, even the curve of the bay, because as always   65
I fix on the land.   I am stuck to earth.   What I love here
is old ranches, leaning seaward, lowroofed spreads between rocks
small canyons running through pitched hillsides
liveoaks twisted on steepness, the eucalyptus avenue leading

2. A militant black party, founded in 1966 in Oakland by Huey P. Newton and Bobby Seale,
   which at first advocated violent revolution and also sponsored programs to feed and support
   the black community.

to the wrecked homestead, the fogwreathed heavy-chested cattle   70
on their blond hills.   I drive inland over roads
closed in wet weather, past shacks hunched in the canyons
roads that crawl down into darkness and wind into light
where trucks have crashed and riders of horses tangled
to death with lowstruck boughs.   These are not the roads   75
you knew me by.   But the woman driving, walking, watching
for life and death, is the same.

II

Here is a map of our country:
here is the Sea of Indifference, glazed with salt
This is the haunted river flowing from brow to groin   80
we dare not taste its water
This is the desert where missiles are planted like corms
This is the breadbasket of foreclosed farms
This is the birthplace of the rockabilly boy
This is the cemetery of the poor   85
who died for democracy   This is a battlefield
from a nineteenth-century war   the shrine is famous
This is the sea-town of myth and story   when the fishing fleets
went bankrupt   here is where the jobs were   on the pier
processing frozen fishsticks   hourly wages and no shares   90
These are other battlefields   Centralia   Detroit[3]
here are the forests primeval   the copper   the silver lodes
These are the suburbs of acquiescence   silence rising fumelike
          from the streets
This is the capital of money and dolor whose spires
flare up through air inversions whose bridges are crumbling   95
whose children are drifting blind alleys pent
between coiled rolls of razor wire
I promised to show you a map you say but this is a mural
then yes let it be   these are small distinctions
where do we see it from is the question   100

III

Two five-pointed star-shaped glass candleholders, bought at the
          Ben Franklin,[4] Barton, twenty-three years ago, one
          chipped
—now they hold half-burnt darkred candles, and in between

3. Michigan city that, since the early decades of this century, has been the site of clashes resulting
   from race and class injustices. Centralia, lumber town in Washington State where, on Novem-
   ber 11, 1919, violence instigated by the Lumbermen's Association against the IWW (Industrial
   Workers of the World; the "Wobblies") led to a number of deaths.
4. Five-and-dime store; here, in Barton, Vermont.

a spider is working, the third point of her filamental passage
a wicker basket-handle.   All afternoon I've sat
at this table in Vermont, reading, writing, cutting an apple in
                    slivers   105
and eating them, but mostly gazing down through the windows
at the long scribble of lake due south
where the wind and weather come from.   There are bottles set in
                    the windows
that children dug up in summer woods or bought for nickels and
                    dimes
in dark shops that are no more, gold-brown, foam-green or cobalt
                    glass, blue that gave way to the cobalt
                    bomb. The woods   110
are still on the hill behind the difficult unknowable
incommensurable barn. The wind's been working itself up
in low gusts gnashing the leaves left chattering on branches
or drifting over still-green grass;   but it's been a warm wind.
An autumn without a killing frost so far, still warm   115
feels like a time of self-deception, a memory of pushing
limits in youth, that intricate losing game of innocence long
                    overdue.
Frost is expected tonight, gardens are gleaned, potplants taken
                    in, there is talk of withering, of wintering-over.

────────────

North of Willoughby the back road to Barton
turns a right-hand corner on a high plateau   120
bitten by wind now and rimed grey-white
—farms of rust and stripping paint, the shortest growing season
south of Quebec, a place of sheer unpretentious hardship, dark
                    pines stretching away
toward Canada.   There was a one-room schoolhouse
by a brook where we used to picnic, summers, a little world   125
of clear bubbling water, cowturds, moss, wild mint, wild mush-
                    rooms under the pines.
One hot afternoon I sat there reading Gaskell's *Life of Charlotte
                    Brontë*[5]—the remote
upland village where snow lay long and late, the deep-rutted
                    roads, the dun and grey moorland
—trying to enfigure such a life, how genius
unfurled in the shortlit days, the meagre means of that house. I
                    never thought   130
of lives at that moment around me, what girl dreamed
and was extinguished in the remote back-country I had come to
                    love,

5. Biography published in 1857 by the British novelist Elizabeth Gaskell (1810–65), about the
   Victorian novelist, author of *Jane Eyre*.

reader reading under a summer tree in the landscape
of the rural working poor.

Now the panes are black and from the south the wind still stag-
          gers, creaking the house: 135
brown milkweeds toss in darkness below but I cannot see them
the room has lost the window and turned into itself: two corner
          shelves of things
both useful and unused, things arrived here by chance or choice,
          two teapots, one broken-spouted, red and blue
came to me with some books from my mother's mother, my
          grandmother Mary
who travelled little, loved the far and strange, bits of India, Asia   140
and this teapot of hers was Chinese or she thought it was
—the other given by a German Jew, a refugee who killed herself:
Midlands flowered ware, and this too cannot be used because
          coated inside—why?—with flaking paint:
"You will always use it for flowers," she instructed when she
          gave it.
In a small frame, under glass, my father's bookplate, engraved in
          his ardent youth, the cleft tree-trunk and the win-
          tering ants: 145
Without labor, no sweetness—motto I breathed in from him and
          learned in grief and rebellion to take and use
—and later learned that not all labor ends in sweetness.
A little handwrought iron candlestick, given by another German
          woman
who hidden survived the Russian soldiers beating the walls in
          1945,
emigrated, married a poet.   I sat many times at their table.
          They are now long apart.   150
Some odd glasses for wine or brandy, from an ignorant, passion-
          ate time—we were in our twenties—
with the father of the children who dug for old medicine bottles
          in the woods
—afternoons listening to records, reading Karl Shapiro's *Poems of
          a Jew* and Auden's "In Sickness and in Health"
          aloud, using the poems to talk to each other
—now it's twenty years since last I heard that intake
of living breath, as if language were too much to bear,   155
that voice overcast like klezmer[6] with echoes, uneven, edged,
          torn, Brooklyn street crowding Harvard Yard
—I'd have known any syllable anywhere.

●

6. Jewish popular music of mixed genres.

Stepped out onto the night-porch.   That wind has changed,
          though still from the south
it's blowing up hard now, no longer close to earth but driving
          high
into the crowns of the maples, into my face   160
almost slamming the stormdoor into me.   But it's warm, warm,
pneumonia wind, death of innocence wind, unwinding wind,
time-hurtling wind.   And it has a voice in the house.   I hear
conversations that can't be happening, overhead in the bedrooms
and I'm not talking of ghosts.   The ghosts are here of course but
          they speak plainly   165
—haven't I offered food and wine, listened well for them all
          these years,
not only those known in life but those before our time
of self-deception, our intricate losing game of innocence long
          overdue?

          _____

The spider's decision is made, her path cast, candle-wick to
          wicker handle to candle,
in the air, under the lamp, she comes swimming toward me   170
(have I been sitting here so long?)   she will use everything,
          nothing comes without labor, she is working so
          hard and I know
nothing all winter can enter this house or this web, not all labor
          ends in sweetness.
But how do I know what she needs?   Maybe simply
to spin herself a house within a house, on her own terms
in cold, in silence.   175

          IV

Late summers, early autumns, you can see something that binds
the map of this country together: the girasol, orange gold-
          petalled
with her black eye, laces the roadsides from Vermont to
          California
runs the edges of orchards, chain-link fences
milo fields and malls, schoolyards and reservations   180
truckstops and quarries, grazing ranges, graveyards
of veterans, graveyards of cars hulked and sunk, her tubers the
          jerusalem artichoke
that has fed the Indians, fed the hobos, could feed us all.
Is there anything in the soil, cross-country, that makes for
a plant so generous?   *Spendthrift* we say, as if   185
accounting nature's waste.   Ours darkens
the states to their strict borders, flushes

down borderless streams, leaches from lakes to the curdled foam
down by the riverside.

Waste.   Waste.   The watcher's eye put out, hands of the
                builder severed, brain of the maker starved   190
those who could bind, join, reweave, cohere, replenish
now at risk in this segregate republic
locked away out of sight and hearing, out of mind, shunted aside
those needed to teach, advise, persuade, weigh arguments
those urgently needed for the work of perception   195
work of the poet, the astronomer, the historian, the architect of
                new streets
work of the speaker who also listens
meticulous delicate work of reaching the heart of the desperate
                woman, the desperate man
—never-to-be-finished, still unbegun work of repair—it cannot
                be done without them
and where are they now?   200

V

Catch if you can your country's moment, begin
where any calendar's ripped-off: Appomattox[7]
Wounded Knee,[8] Los Alamos,[9] Selma,[1] the last airlift from Saigon[2]
the ex-Army nurse hitch-hiking from the debriefing center; medal
                of spit on the veteran's shoulder
—catch if you can this unbound land these states without a cause   205
earth of despoiled graves and grazing these embittered brooks
these pilgrim ants pouring out from the bronze eyes, ears,
                nostrils,
the mouth of Liberty

over the chained bay waters[3]
San Quentin:[4] 210

7. Town in central Virginia where General Robert E. Lee surrendered to General Ulysses S. Grant on April 9, 1865, bringing the Civil War to an end.
8. Wounded Knee Creek, South Dakota, scene of a battle on December 28–29, 1890, the last in the American Indians' centuries-long struggle for autonomy. In 1973 two hundred Sioux, led by members of the American Indian Movement, occupied the town for seventy days to protest the continuing oppression of the Indian peoples by the U.S. government.
9. Town in north-central New Mexico where the atomic bomb was developed.
1. City in Alabama where "Bloody Sunday" occurred on March 7, 1965. Nonviolent demonstrators setting out for Montgomery as part of a voter registration drive were brutally beaten by state troopers.
2. Former capital of South Vietnam and the United States' base of operations during the long and devastating Vietnam War, 1957–75. On April 30, 1975, those Americans left in Vietnam and 150,000 Vietnamese escaped by helicopter from the city in a chaotic and often violent military exodus.
3. From Hart Crane, "To Brooklyn Bridge," in *The Poems of Hart Crane*, ed. Marc Simon (New York and London: Liveright, 1989; poem originally published in 1930) [*Rich's note*].
4. State prison on San Francisco Bay, near the Richmond–San Rafael Bridge.

once we lost our way and drove in under the searchlights to the
        gates
end of visiting hours, women piling into cars
the bleak glare aching over all

                  Where are we moored?   What
                  are the bindings?   What be-
                  hooves us?

Driving the San Francisco–Oakland Bay Bridge   215
no monument's in sight but fog
prowling Angel Island muffling Alcatraz [5]
poems in Cantonese inscribed on fog
no icon lifts a lamp here
history's breath blotting the air   220
over Gold Mountain [6]   a transfer
of patterns like the transfer of African appliqué
to rural Alabama   voices alive in legends, curses
tongue-lashings
                poems on a weary wall   225
And when light swivels off Angel Island and Alcatraz
when the bays leap into life
                    views of the Palace of Fine Arts, [7]
                    TransAmerica [8]
when sunset bathes the three bridges
                    still   230
old ghosts crouch hoarsely whispering
under Gold Mountain

North and east of the romantic headlands there are roads into tule
        fog
places where life is cheap poor quick unmonumented
Rukeyser would have guessed it coming West for the opening   235
of the great red bridge [9]   *There are roads to take* she wrote
when you think of your country [1]   driving south
to West Virginia Gauley Bridge silicon mines [2] the flakes of it
        heaped like snow, death-angel white

---

5. Both Angel Island and Alcatraz are islands in San Francisco Bay. From 1888 to 1946 Angel
    Island, "the Ellis Island of the West," was the site of a quarantine station and an immigration
    facility. Alcatraz was the site of a federal prison until 1963.
6. Name used by Chinese immigrants to refer to California.
7. San Francisco building designed by Bernard Maybeck (1862–1957) for the 1915 Pacific Inter-
    national Exposition.
8. Pryamid-shaped skyscraper in San Francisco topped by a 212-foot spire.
9. The Golden Gate Bridge, between San Francisco and Marin County, opened in 1937.
1. From Muriel Rukeyser, *U.S. 1* (New York: Covici Friede, 1938); see also Muriel Rukeyser,
    The Collected Poems (New York: McGraw-Hill, 1978) [*Rich's note*].
2. In the early 1930s Muriel Rukeyser made a personal investigation of the silicon mines in
    Gauley Bridge, West Virginia, where silicon had killed or disabled over two thousand miners.
    The poetic sequence "The Book of the Dead" in *U.S. 1* describes what she found.

—poet journalist pioneer mother
uncovering her country: *there are roads to take*   240

_____

I don't want to know how he tracked them
along the Appalachian Trail, hid close
by their tent, pitched as they thought in seclusion
killing one woman, the other
dragging herself into town   his defense they had teased his
                    loathing   245
of what they were[3]   I don't want to know
but this is not a bad dream of mine   these are the materials
and so are the smell of wild mint and coursing water remembered
and the sweet salt darkred tissue I lay my face
upon, my tongue within.   250
                    A crosshair against the pupil of an eye
could blow my life from hers
a cell dividing without maps, sliver of ice beneath a wheel
could do the job.   Faithfulness isn't the problem.

VI

A potato explodes in the oven.   Poetry and famine:[4]   255
the poets who never starved, whose names we know
the famished nameless taking ship with their hoard of poetry
Annie Sullivan[5] half-blind in the workhouse enthralling her child-
                    mates
with lore her father had borne in his head from Limerick along
                    with the dream of work
and *hatred of England smouldering like a turf-fire.*[6] But a poetry older
                    than hatred. Poetry   260
in the workhouse, laying of the rails, a potato splattering oven
                    walls
poetry of cursing and silence, bitter and deep, shallow and
                    drunken
poetry of priest-talk, of I.R.A.[7]-talk, kitchen-talk, dream-talk,
                    tongues despised

3. On May 13, 1988, Stephen Roy Carr shot and killed Rebecca Wright, one of two lesbians camping on the Appalachian Trail in Pennsylvania. Her lover, Claudia Brenner, suffered five bullet wounds. She dragged herself two miles along the trail to a road, where she flagged a car to take her to the police. In October of that year, Carr was found guilty of first-degree murder and sentenced to life in prison without parole. During the legal proceedings, it became clear that Carr had attacked the women because they were lesbians. See *Gay Community News* (August 7 and November 11, 1988) [*Rich's note*].
4. The Great Famine of 1845–48, caused by the failure of the Irish potato crop. More than 750,000 Irish died, and more than a million emigrated to America between 1846 and 1851.
5. Anne Sullivan Macy (1866–1936). American teacher and companion of Helen Keller.
6. See Nella Braddy, *Anne Sullivan Macy: The Story Behind Helen Keller* (Garden City, N.Y.: Doubleday, Doran & Company, 1933), p. 13 [*Rich's note*].
7. Irish Republican Army, a guerilla force in Northern Ireland fighting for independence from Britain.

in cities where in a mere fifty years language has rotted to jargon,
    lingua franca of inclusion
from turns of speech ancient as the potato, muttered at the coals
    by women and men   265
rack-rented, harshened, numbed by labor ending
in root-harvest rotted in field. 1847. No relief. No succour.
America. Meat three times a day,[8] they said.   Slaves—You would
    not be that.

VII (THE DREAM-SITE)

Some rooftop, water-tank looming, street-racket strangely quelled
and others known and unknown there, long sweet summer eve-
    ning on the tarred roof: 270
leaned back your head to the nightvault swarming with stars
the Pleiades[9] broken loose, not seven but thousands
every known constellation flinging out fiery threads
and you could distinguish all
—cobwebs, tendrils, anatomies of stars   275
coherently hammocked, blueblack avenues between
—you knew your way among them, knew you were part of them
until, neck aching, you sat straight up and saw:

It was New York, the dream-site
the lost city the city of dreadful light   280
where once as the sacks of garbage rose
like barricades around us we
stood listening to riffs from Pharaoh Sanders'[1] window
on the brownstone steps
went striding the avenues in our fiery hair   285
in our bodies young and ordinary riding the subways reading
or pressed against other bodies
feeling in them the maps of Brooklyn Queens Manhattan
The Bronx unscrolling in the long breakneck
express plunges   290
        as darkly we felt our own blood
streaming   a living city overhead
coherently webbed and knotted   bristling
we and all the others
        known and unknown   295
living its life

8. See Frank Murphy, "The Irish and Afro-Americans in U.S. History," *Freedomways: A Quar-
terly Review of the Freedom Movement* 22, no. 1 (1982): 22 [*Rich's note*].
9. Open star cluster in the constellation Taurus.
1. Sanders is an American jazz tenor saxophonist (1940–).

VIII

He thought there would be a limit and that it would stop him.
            He depended on that:
the cuts would be made by someone else, the direction
come from somewhere else, arrows flashing on the freeway.
That he'd end somewhere gazing   300
straight into It was what he imagined and nothing beyond.
That he'd end facing as limit a thing without limits and so he
            flung
and burned and hacked and bled himself toward that (if I
            understand
this story at all). What he found: FOR SALE: DO NOT
            DISTURB
OCCUPANT on some cliffs;   some ill-marked, ill-kept roads   305
ending in warnings about shellfish in Vietnamese, Spanish and
            English.
But the spray was any color he could have dreamed
—gold, ash, azure, smoke, moonstone—
and from time to time the ocean swirled up through the eye of a
            rock and taught him
limits.   Throwing itself backward, singing and sucking, no
            teacher, only its violent   310
self, the Pacific, dialectical waters rearing
their wild calm constructs, momentary, ancient.

If your voice could overwhelm those waters, what would it say?
What would it cry of the child swept under, the mother
on the beach then, in her black bathing suit, walking straight
            out   315
into the glazed lace as if she never noticed, what would it say of
            the father
facing inland in his shoes and socks at the edge of the tide,
what of the lost necklace glittering twisted in foam?

If your voice could crack in the wind hold its breath still as the
            rocks
what would it say to the daughter searching the tidelines for a
            bottled message   320
from the sunken slaveships?   what of the huge sun slowly de-
            faulting into the clouds
what of the picnic stored in the dunes at high tide, full of the
            moon, the basket
with sandwiches, eggs, paper napkins, can-opener, the meal
packed for a family feast, excavated now by scuttling
ants, sandcrabs, dune-rats, because no one understood   325
all picnics are eaten on the grave?

IX

On this earth, in this life, as I read your story, you're lonely.
Lonely in the bar, on the shore of the coastal river
with your best friend, his wife, and your wife, fishing
lonely in the prairie classroom with all the students who love
                         you. You know some ghosts   330
come everywhere with you yet leave them unaddressed
for years.   You spend weeks in a house
with a drunk, you sober, whom you love, feeling lonely.
You grieve in loneliness, and if I understand you fuck in
                         loneliness.

I wonder if this is a white man's madness.   335
I honor your truth and refuse to leave it at that.

What have I learned from stories of the hunt, of lonely men in
                         gangs?
But there were other stories:
one man riding the Mohave Desert
another man walking the Grand Canyon.   340
I thought those solitary men were happy, as ever they had been.

Indio's long avenues
of Medjool date-palm and lemon sweep to the Salton Sea [2]
in Yucca Flats the high desert reaches higher, bleached and spare
                         of talk.
At Twentynine Palms [3] I found the grave   345
of Maria Eleanor Whallon, eighteen years, dead at the watering-
                         hole in 1903, under the now fire-branded palms
Her mother travelled on alone to cook in the mining camps.

X

Soledad. = f. Solitude, loneliness, homesickness; lonely retreat.
Winter sun in the rosetrees.
An old Mexican with a white moustache prunes them back,
                         spraying   350
the cut branches with dormant oil.   The old paper-bag-brown
                         adobe walls
stretch apart from the rebuilt mission, in their own time.   It is
                         lonely here
in the curve of the road winding through vast brown fields
                         machine-engraved in furrows

2. Artificially formed inland lake below sea level in the desert east of San Diego, California, and
   west of the Colorado River.
3. Indio, Yucca Flats, and Twentynine Palms are towns near Palm Springs, California.

of relentless precision.   In the small chapel[4]
La Nuestra Señora de la Soledad dwells in her shallow arch   355
painted on either side with columns.   She is in black lace crisp
        as cinders
from head to foot.   Alone, solitary, homesick
in her lonely retreat.   Outside black olives fall and smash
littering and staining the beaten path.   The gravestones of the
        padres
are weights pressing down on the Indian artisans.   It is the sixth
        day of another war.[5]   360

Across the freeway stands another structure
from the other side of the mirror   *it destroys*
the logical processes of the mind, a man's thoughts
become completely disorganized, madness streaming from every
        throat
frustrated sounds from the bars, metallic sounds from the walls   365
the steel trays, iron beds bolted to the wall, the smells, the human
        waste.
To determine how men will behave once they enter prison
it is of first importance to know that prison.[6]   (From the freeway
gun-turrets planted like water-towers in another garden, out-
        buildings spaced in winter sun
and the concrete mass beyond: who now writes letters deep in-
        side that cave?)   370

If my instructor tells me that the world and its affairs
are run as well as they possibly can be, that I am governed
by wise and judicious men, that I am free and should be happy,
and if when I leave the instructor's presence and encounter
the exact opposite, if I actually sense or see confusion, war,   375
recession, depression, death and decay, is it not reasonable
that I should become perplexed?

                From eighteen to twenty-eight
                of his years
a young man schools himself, argues,
debates, trains, lectures to himself,   380
teaches himself Swahili, Spanish, learns
five new words of English every day,
chainsmokes, reads, writes letters.
In this college of force he wrestles bitterness,

4. Mission church named in honor of Our Lady of Solitude, in Soledad, California, a town that
   is also the site of a state prison.
5. The Gulf War. In response to Iraq's annexation of oil-rich Kuwait in August 1990, the United
   States, on January 15, 1991, led a military coalition against Iraq, with heavy loss of life and
   property in Kuwait and Iraq.
6. The passages in italics are quoted from *Soledad Brother: The Prison Letters of George Jackson*
   (New York: Bantam, 1970), pp. 24, 26, 93, 245 [*Rich's note*].

self-hatred, sexual anger, cures his own nature.   385
Seven of these years in solitary.   Soledad.

But the significant feature of the desperate man reveals itself
when he meets other desperate men, directly or vicariously;
and he experiences his first kindness, someone to strain with him,
to strain to see him as he strains to see himself,   390
someone to understand, someone to accept the regard,
the love, that desperation forces into hiding.
Those feelings that find no expression in desperate times
store themselves up in great abundance, ripen, strengthen,
and strain the walls of their repository to the utmost;   395
where the kindred spirit touches this wall it crumbles—
no one responds to kindness, no one is more sensitive to it
than the desperate man.

XI

One night on Monterey Bay the death-freeze of the century:
a precise, detached calliper-grip holds the stars and the quarter-
                                        moon   400
in arrest: the hardiest plants crouch shrunken, a "killing frost"
on bougainvillea, Pride of Madeira,[7] roseate black-purple succu-
                                        lents bowed
juices sucked awry in one orgy of freezing
slumped on their stems like old faces evicted from cheap hotels
—into the streets of the universe, now!   405

Earthquake and drought followed by freezing followed by war.[8]
Flags are blossoming now where little else is blossoming
and I am bent on fathoming what it means to love my country.
The history of this earth and the bones within it?
Soils and cities, promises made and mocked, plowed contours of
                                        shame and of hope?   410
Loyalties, symbols, murmurs extinguished and echoing?
Grids of states stretching westward, underground waters?
Minerals, traces, rumors I am made from, morsel, minuscule
                                        fibre, one woman
like and unlike so many, fooled as to her destiny, the scope of
                                        her task?
One citizen like and unlike so many, touched and untouched in
                                        passing   415

---

7. American tropical vine, *Anredera cordifolia*, having small, white fragrant flowers.
8. A devastating earthquake occurred in California on October 17, 1989, at a time when the state
   had already experienced a five-year drought. A record-breaking freeze in December and Jan-
   uary 1990–91 was followed by the outbreak of the Gulf War in mid-January 1991.

—each of us now a driven grain, a nucleus, a city in crisis
some busy constructing enclosures, bunkers, to escape the com-
        mon fate
some trying to revive dead statues to lead us, breathing their
        breath against marble lips
some who try to teach the moment, some who preach the
        moment
some who aggrandize, some who diminish themselves in the face
        of half-grasped events   420
—power and powerlessness run amuck, a tape reeling backward
        in jeering, screeching syllables—
some for whom war is new, others for whom it merely continues
        the old paroxysms of time
some marching for peace who for twenty years did not march for
        justice
some for whom peace is a white man's word and a white man's
        privilege
some who have learned to handle and contemplate the shapes of
        powerlessness and power   425
as the nurse learns hip and thigh and weight of the body he has
        to lift and sponge, day upon day
as she blows with her every skill on the spirit's embers still burn-
        ing by their own laws in the bed of death.
A patriot is not a weapon.   A patriot is one who wrestles for the
        soul of her country
as she wrestles for her own being, for the soul of his country
(gazing through the great circle at Window Rock[9] into the sheen
        of the Viet Nam Wall)[1]   430
as he wrestles for his own being.   A patriot is a citizen trying to
        wake
from the burnt-out dream of innocence, the nightmare
of the white general and the Black general posed in their
        camouflage,[2]
to remember her true country, remember his suffering land:
        remember
that blessing and cursing are born as twins and separated at birth
        to meet again in mourning   435
that the internal emigrant is the most homesick of all women and
        of all men
that every flag that flies today is a cry of pain.
        Where are we moored?
        What are the bindings?
        What behooves us?   440

9. Capitol of the Navajo Nation and sacred ground in Arizona.
1. See above, p. 140, n. 6.
2. General H. Norman Schwarzkopf, U.S. army commander in the Gulf during the Gulf War,
   and General Colin Powell, head of the U.S. Joint Chiefs of Staff.

XII

What homage will be paid to a beauty built to last
from inside out, executing the blueprints of resistance and mercy
drawn up in childhood, in that little girl, round-faced with
                    clenched fists, already acquainted with mourning
in the creased snapshot you gave me?   What homage will be
                    paid to beauty
that insists on speaking truth, knows the two are not always the
                    same,   445
beauty that won't deny, is itself an eye, will not rest under
                    contemplation?
Those low long clouds we were driving under a month ago in
                    New Mexico, clouds an arm's reach away
were beautiful and we spoke of it but I didn't speak then
of your beauty at the wheel beside me, dark head steady, eyes
                    drinking the spaces
of crimson, indigo, Indian distance, Indian presence,   450
your spirit's gaze informing your body, impatient to mark what's
                    possible, impatient to mark
what's lost, deliberately destroyed, can never any way be
                    returned,
your back arched against all icons, simulations, dead letters
your woman's hands turning the wheel or working with shears,
                    torque wrench, knives, with salt pork, onions, ink
                    and fire
your providing sensate hands, your hands of oak and silk, of
                    blackberry juice and drums   455
—I speak of them now.
(FOR M.)

XIII (DEDICATIONS)

I know you are reading this poem
late, before leaving your office
of the one intense yellow lamp-spot and the darkening window
in the lassitude of a building faded to quiet   460
long after rush-hour.   I know you are reading this poem
standing up in a bookstore far from the ocean
on a grey day of early spring, faint flakes driven
across the plains' enormous spaces around you.
I know you are reading this poem   465
in a room where too much has happened for you to bear
where the bedclothes lie in stagnant coils on the bed
and the open valise speaks of flight
but you cannot leave yet.   I know you are reading this poem

as the underground train loses momentum and before running
                    up the stairs   470
toward a new kind of love
your life has never allowed.
I know you are reading this poem by the light
of the television screen where soundless images jerk and slide
while you wait for the newscast from the *intifada*.³   475
I know you are reading this poem in a waiting-room
of eyes met and unmeeting, of identity with strangers.
I know you are reading this poem by fluorescent light
in the boredom and fatigue of the young who are counted out,
count themselves out, at too early an age.   I know   480
you are reading this poem through your failing sight, the thick
lens enlarging these letters beyond all meaning yet you read on
because even the alphabet is precious.
I know you are reading this poem as you pace beside the stove
warming milk, a crying child on your shoulder, a book in your
                    hand   485
because life is short and you too are thirsty.
I know you are reading this poem which is not in your language
guessing at some words while others keep you reading
and I want to know which words they are.
I know you are reading this poem listening for something, torn
                    between bitterness and hope   490
turning back once again to the task you cannot refuse.
I know you are reading this poem because there is nothing else
                    left to read
there where you have landed, stripped as you are.

1990–1991

Eastern War Time

10⁴

Memory says: Want to do right? Don't count on me.
I'm a canal in Europe where bodies are floating
I'm a mass grave   I'm the life that returns
I'm a table set with room for the Stranger⁵
I'm a field with corners left for the landless   5
I'm accused of child-death   of drinking blood
I'm a man-child praising God he's a man
I'm a woman bargaining for a chicken
I'm a woman who sells for a boat ticket

3. Palestinian uprising against Israeli occupation.
4. The last section of a poem arising from Rich's memories of World War II.
5. Jewish custom of leaving an empty seat at the Passover table.

I'm a family dispersed between night and fog   10
I'm an immigrant tailor who says *A coat*
is not a piece of cloth only   I sway
in the learnings of the master-mystics
I have dreamed of Zion   I've dreamed of world revolution
I have dreamed my children could live at last like others   15
I have walked the children of others through ranks of hatred
I'm a corpse dredged from a canal in Berlin
a river in Mississippi   I'm a woman standing
with other women dressed in black
on the streets of Haifa, Tel Aviv, Jerusalem   20
there is spit on my sleeve there are phonecalls in the night
I am a woman standing in line for gasmasks
I stand on a road in Ramallah [6]   with naked face   listening
I am standing here in your poem   unsatisfied
lifting my smoky mirror   25

1989–1990

Tattered Kaddish [7]

Taurean [8] reaper of the wild apple field [9]
messenger from earthmire gleaning
transcripts of fog
in the nineteenth year and the eleventh month
speak your tattered Kaddish for all suicides: 5

Praise to life though it crumbled in like a tunnel
on ones we knew and loved

    Praise to life though its windows blew shut
    on the breathing-room of ones we knew and loved

Praise to life though ones we knew and loved   10
loved it badly, too well, and not enough

    Praise to life though it tightened like a knot
    on the hearts of ones we thought we knew loved us

●

6. Town in West Jordan populated chiefly by Christian Arabs and occupied by Israel since 1967.
7. See above, p. 139, n. 5.
8. See above, p. 39, n. 7.
9. "The Reapers of the Field are the Comrades, masters of this wisdom, because *Mahlkut* is called the Apple Field, and She grows sprouts of secrets and new meanings of Torah. Those who constantly create new interpretations of Torah are the ones who reap Her" (Moses Cordovero, Or ha-Hammah on Zohar III, 106a). See Barry W. Holtz, ed., *Back to the Sources: Reading the Classic Jewish Texts* (New York: Summit, 1984), p. 305 [*Rich's note*].

Praise to life giving room and reason
to ones we knew and loved who felt unpraisable   15

Praise to them, how they loved it, when they could.

1989

Darklight

II[1]

When heat leaves the walls at last
and the breeze comes
or seems to come, off water
or off the half-finished moon
her silver roughened by a darkblue rag   5
this is the ancient hour
between light and dark, work and rest
earthly tracks and star-trails
the last willed act of the day
and the night's first dream   10

If you could have this hour
for the last hour of your life.

1988–1990

Final Notations

it will not be simple, it will not be long
it will take little time, it will take all your thought
it will take all your heart, it will take all your breath
it will be short, it will not be simple

it will touch through your ribs, it will take all your heart   5
it will not be long, it will occupy your thought
as a city is occupied, as a bed is occupied
it will take all your flesh, it will not be simple

You are coming into us who cannot withstand you
you are coming into us who never wanted to withstand you   10

1. The concluding section of a two-part poem.

you are taking parts of us into places never planned
you are going far away with pieces of our lives

it will be short, it will take all your breath
it will not be simple, it will become your will

1991

PROSE

[Poetry and Experience: Statement at a Poetry Reading]
(1964) †

What a poem used to be for me, what it is today.

In the period in which my first two books were written I had a much more absolutist approach to the universe than I now have. I also felt— as many people still feel—that a poem was an arrangement of ideas and feelings, pre-determined, and it said what I had already decided it should say. There were occasional surprises, occasions of happy discovery that an unexpected turn could be taken, but control, technical mastery and intellectual clarity were the real goals, and for many reasons it was satisfying to be able to create this kind of formal order in poems.

Only gradually, within the last five or six years, did I begin to feel that these poems, even the ones I liked best and in which I felt I'd said most, were queerly limited; that in many cases I had suppressed, omitted, falsified even, certain disturbing elements, to gain that perfection of order. Perhaps this feeling began to show itself in a poem like "Rural Reflections," in which there is an awareness already that experience is always greater and more unclassifiable than we give it credit for being.

Today, I have to say that what I know I know through making poems. Like the novelist who finds that his characters begin to have a life of their own and to demand certain experiences, I find that I can no longer go to write a poem with a neat handful of materials and express those materials according to a prior plan: the poem itself engenders new sensations, new awareness in me as it progresses. Without for one moment turning my back on conscious choice and selection, I have been increasingly willing to let the unconscious offer its materials, to listen to more than the one voice of a single idea. Perhaps a simple way of putting it would be to say that instead of poems *about* experiences I am getting poems that *are* experiences, that contribute to my knowledge and my emotional life even while they reflect and assimilate it. In my earlier poems I told you, as precisely and eloquently as I knew how, about something; in the more recent poems something is happening, something has happened to me and, if I have been a good parent to the poem, something will happen to you who read it.

† Quoted in "Adrienne Rich: The Poetics of Change," by Albert Gelpi, in *American Poetry Since 1960*, edited by Robert B. Shaw (Cheadle, Cheshire: Carcanet Press Ltd., 1973), pp. 132–33. Reprinted by permission of the publisher.

When We Dead Awaken: Writing as Re-Vision
(1971) †

The Modern Language Association is both marketplace and funeral parlor
for the professional study of Western literature in North America. Like all
gatherings of the professions, it has been and remains a "procession of the
sons of educated men" (Virginia Woolf): a congeries of old-boys' networks,
academicians rehearsing their numb canons in sessions dedicated to the lit-
erature of white males, junior scholars under the lash of "publish or perish"
delivering papers in the bizarrely lit drawing-rooms of immense hotels: a
ritual competition veering between cynicism and desperation.

However, in the interstices of these gentlemanly rites (or, in Mary Daly's
words, on the boundaries of this patriarchal space),[1] some feminist scholars,
teachers, and graduate students, joined by feminist writers, editors, and pub-
lishers, have for a decade been creating more subversive occasions, chal-
lenging the sacredness of the gentlemanly canon, sharing the rediscovery of
buried works by women, asking women's questions, bringing literary history
and criticism back to life in both senses. The Commission on the Status of
Women in the Profession was formed in 1969, and held its first public event
in 1970. In 1971 the Commission asked Ellen Peck Killoh, Tillie Olsen,
Elaine Reuben, and myself, with Elaine Hedges as moderator, to talk on
"The Woman Writer in the Twentieth Century." The essay that follows was
written for that forum, and later published, along with the other papers from
the forum and workshops, in an issue of *College English* edited by Elaine
Hedges ("Women Writing and Teaching," vol. 34, no. 1, October 1972).
With a few revisions, mainly updating, it was reprinted in *American Poets
in 1976*, edited by William Heyen (New York: Bobbs-Merrill, 1976). That
later text is the one published here.

The challenge flung by feminists at the accepted literary canon, at the
methods of teaching it, and at the biased and astigmatic view of male "lit-
erary scholarship," has not diminished in the decade since the first Women's
Forum; it has become broadened and intensified more recently by the chal-
lenges of black and lesbian feminists pointing out that feminist literary crit-
icism itself has overlooked or held back from examining the work of black
women and lesbians. The dynamic between a political vision and the demand
for a fresh vision of literature is clear: without a growing feminist movement,
the first inroads of feminist scholarship could not have been made; without
the sharpening of a black feminist consciousness, black women's writing
would have been left in limbo between misogynist black male critics and
white feminists still struggling to unearth a white women's tradition; without
an articulate lesbian/feminist movement, lesbian writing would still be lying
in that closet where many of us used to sit reading forbidden books "in a bad
light."

Much, much more is yet to be done; and university curricula have of
course changed very little as a result of all this. What *is* changing is the

---

† Except for cross-references, which have been added by the editors of this volume, notes to this
  essay are Rich's. The introductory paragraphs appeared in Adrienne Rich's *On Lies, Secrets,
  and Silence: Selected Prose, 1966–1978* (New York: Norton, 1979) 31.
1. Mary Daly, *Beyond God the Father* (Boston: Beacon, 1971), pp. 40–41.

availability of knowledge, of vital texts, the visible effects on women's lives
of seeing, hearing our wordless or negated experience affirmed and pursued
further in language.

Ibsen's *When We Dead Awaken* is a play about the use that the male
artist and thinker—in the process of creating culture as we know it—has
made of women, in his life and in his work; and about a woman's slow
struggling awakening to the use to which her life has been put. Bernard
Shaw wrote in 1900 of this play:

> [Ibsen] shows us that no degradation ever devized or permitted is as
> disastrous as this degradation; that through it women can die into
> luxuries for men and yet can kill them; that men and women are
> becoming conscious of this; and that what remains to be seen as
> perhaps the most interesting of all imminent social developments is
> what will happen "when we dead awaken." [2]

It's exhilarating to be alive in a time of awakening consciousness; it
can also be confusing, disorienting, and painful. This awakening of dead
or sleeping consciousness has already affected the lives of millions of
women, even those who don't know it yet. It is also affecting the lives of
men, even those who deny its claims upon them. The argument will go
on whether an oppressive economic class system is responsible for the
oppressive nature of male/female relations, or whether, in fact, patriar-
chy—the domination of males—is the original model of oppression on
which all others are based. But in the last few years the women's move-
ment has drawn inescapable and illuminating connections between our
sexual lives and our political institutions. The sleepwalkers are coming
awake, and for the first time this awakening has a collective reality; it is
no longer such a lonely thing to open one's eyes.

Re-vision—the act of looking back, of seeing with fresh eyes, of enter-
ing an old text from a new critical direction—is for women more than a
chapter in cultural history: it is an act of survival. Until we can under-
stand the assumptions in which we are drenched we cannot know our-
selves. And this drive to self-knowledge, for women, is more than a
search for identity: it is part of our refusal of the self-destructiveness of
male-dominated society. A radical critique of literature, feminist in its
impulse, would take the work first of all as a clue to how we live, how
we have been living, how we have been led to imagine ourselves, how
our language has trapped as well as liberated us, how the very act of
naming has been till now a male prerogative, and how we can begin to
see and name—and therefore live—afresh. A change in the concept of
sexual identity is essential if we are not going to see the old political
order reassert itself in every new revolution. We need to know the writ-

2. G. B. Shaw, *The Quintessence of Ibsenism* (New York: Hill & Wang, 1922), p. 139.

ing of the past, and know it differently than we have ever known it; not to pass on a tradition but to break its hold over us.

For writers, and at this moment for women writers in particular, there is the challenge and promise of a whole new psychic geography to be explored. But there is also a difficult and dangerous walking on the ice, as we try to find language and images for a consciousness we are just coming into, and with little in the past to support us. I want to talk about some aspects of this difficulty and this danger.

Jane Harrison, the great classical anthropologist, wrote in 1914 in a letter to her friend Gilbert Murray:

> By the by, about "Women," it has bothered me often—why do women never want to write poetry about Man as a sex—why is Woman a dream and a terror to man and not the other way around? . . . Is it mere convention and propriety, or something deeper? [3]

I think Jane Harrison's question cuts deep into the myth-making tradition, the romantic tradition; deep into what women and men have been to each other; and deep into the psyche of the woman writer. Thinking about that question, I began thinking of the work of two twentieth-century women poets, Sylvia Plath and Diane Wakoski. It strikes me that in the work of both Man appears as, if not a dream, a fascination and a terror; and that the source of the fascination and the terror is, simply, Man's power—to dominate, tyrannize, choose, or reject the woman. The charisma of Man seems to come purely from his power over her and his control of the world by force, not from anything fertile or life-giving in him. And, in the work of both these poets, it is finally the woman's sense of *herself*—embattled, possessed—that gives the poetry its dynamic charge, its rhythms of struggle, need, will, and female energy. Until recently this female anger and this furious awareness of the Man's power over her were not available materials to the female poet, who tended to write of Love as the source of her suffering, and to view that victimization by Love as an almost inevitable fate. Or, like Marianne Moore and Elizabeth Bishop, she kept sexuality at a measured and chiseled distance in her poems.

One answer to Jane Harrison's question has to be that historically men and women have played very different parts in each others' lives. Where woman has been a luxury for man, and has served as the painter's model and the poet's muse, but also as comforter, nurse, cook, bearer of his seed, secretarial assistant, and copyist of manuscripts, man has played a quite different role for the female artist. Henry James repeats an incident which the writer Prosper Mérimée described, of how, while he was living with George Sand,

3. J. G. Stewart, *Jane Ellen Harrison: A Portrait from Letters* (London: Merlin, 1959), p. 140.

he once opened his eyes, in the raw winter dawn, to see his companion, in a dressing-gown, on her knees before the domestic hearth, a candlestick beside her and a red *madras* round her head, making bravely, with her own hands the fire that was to enable her to sit down betimes to urgent pen and paper. The story represents him as having felt that the spectacle chilled his ardor and tried his taste; her appearance was unfortunate, her occupation an inconsequence, and her industry a reproof—the result of all which was a lively irritation and an early rupture.[4]

The specter of this kind of male judgment, along with the misnaming and thwarting of her needs by a culture controlled by males, has created problems for the woman writer: problems of contact with herself, problems of language and style, problems of energy and survival.

In rereading Virginia Woolf's *A Room of One's Own* (1929) for the first time in some years, I was astonished at the sense of effort, of pains taken, of dogged tentativeness, in the tone of that essay. And I recognized that tone. I had heard it often enough, in myself and in other women. It is the tone of a woman almost in touch with her anger, who is determined not to appear angry, who is *willing* herself to be calm, detached, and even charming in a roomful of men where things have been said which are attacks on her very integrity. Virginia Woolf is addressing an audience of women, but she is acutely conscious—as she always was—of being overheard by men: by Morgan and Lytton and Maynard Keynes and for that matter by her father, Leslie Stephen.[5] She drew the language out into an exacerbated thread in her determination to have her own sensibility yet protect it from those masculine presences. Only at rare moments in that essay do you hear the passion in her voice; she was trying to sound as cool as Jane Austen, as Olympian as Shakespeare, because that is the way the men of the culture thought a writer should sound.

No male writer has written primarily or even largely for women, or with the sense of women's criticism as a consideration when he chooses his materials, his theme, his language. But to a lesser or greater extent, every woman writer has written for men even when, like Virginia Woolf, she was supposed to be addressing women. If we have come to the point when this balance might begin to change, when women can stop being haunted, not only by "convention and propriety" but by internalized

4. Henry James, "Notes on Novelists," in *Selected Literary Criticism of Henry James*, Morris Shapira, ed. (London: Heinemann, 1963), pp. 157–58.
5. A. R., *1978*: This intuition of mine was corroborated when, early in 1978, I read the correspondence between Woolf and Dame Ethel Smyth (Henry W. and Albert A. Berg Collection, The New York Public Library, Astor, Lenox and Tilden Foundations); in a letter dated June 8, 1933, Woolf speaks of having kept her own personality out of *A Room of One's Own* lest she not be taken seriously: ". . . how personal, so will they say, rubbing their hands with glee, women always are; *I even hear them as I write.*" (Italics mine.)

fears of being and saying themselves, then it is an extraordinary moment for the woman writer—and reader.

I have hesitated to do what I am going to do now, which is to use myself as an illustration. For one thing, it's a lot easier and less danger-ous to talk about other women writers. But there is something else. Like Virginia Woolf, I am aware of the women who are not with us here because they are washing the dishes and looking after the children. Nearly fifty years after she spoke, that fact remains largely unchanged. And I am thinking also of women whom she left out of the picture altogether—women who are washing other people's dishes and caring for other peo-ple's children, not to mention women who went on the streets last night in order to feed their children. We seem to be special women here, we have liked to think of ourselves as special, and we have known that men would tolerate, even romanticize us as special, as long as our words and actions didn't threaten their privilege of tolerating or rejecting us and our work according to *their* ideas of what a special woman ought to be. An important insight of the radical women's movement has been how divisive and how ultimately destructive is this myth of the special woman, who is also the token woman. Every one of us here in this room has had great luck—we are teachers, writers, academicians; our own gifts could not have been enough, for we all know women whose gifts are buried or aborted. Our struggles can have meaning and our privileges—however precarious under patriarchy—can be justified only if they can help to change the lives of women whose gifts—and whose very being—con-tinue to be thwarted and silenced.

My own luck was being born white and middle-class into a house full of books, with a father who encouraged me to read and write. So for about twenty years I wrote for a particular man, who criticized and praised me and made me feel I was indeed "special." The obverse side of this, of course, was that I tried for a long time to please him, or rather, not to displease him. And then of course there were other men—writers, teachers—the Man, who was not a terror or a dream but a literary master and a master in other ways less easy to acknowledge. And there were all those poems about women, written by men: it seemed to be a given that men wrote poems and women frequently inhabited them. These women were almost always beautiful, but threatened with the loss of beauty, the loss of youth—the fate worse than death. Or, they were beautiful and died young, like Lucy and Lenore. Or, the woman was like Maud Gonne, cruel and disastrously mistaken, and the poem reproached her because she had refused to become a luxury for the poet.

A lot is being said today about the influence that the myths and images of women have on all of us who are products of culture. I think it has been a peculiar confusion to the girl or woman who tries to write because she is peculiarly susceptible to language. She goes to poetry or fiction looking for *her* way of being in the world, since she too has been putting words and images together; she is looking eagerly for guides, maps, possibilities; and over and over in the "words' masculine persuasive force" of literature she comes up against something that negates everything she is about: she meets the image of Woman in books written by men. She finds a terror and a dream, she finds a beautiful pale face, she finds La Belle Dame Sans Merci, she finds Juliet or Tess or Salomé, but precisely what she does not find is that absorbed, drudging, puzzled, sometimes inspired creature, herself, who sits at a desk trying to put words together.

So what does she do? What did I do? I read the older women poets with their peculiar keenness and ambivalence: Sappho, Christina Rossetti, Emily Dickinson, Elinor Wylie, Edna Millay, H. D. I discovered that the woman poet most admired at the time (by men) was Marianne Moore, who was maidenly, elegant, intellectual, discreet. But even in reading these women I was looking in them for the same things I had found in the poetry of men, because I wanted women poets to be the equals of men, and to be equal was still confused with sounding the same.

I know that my style was formed first by male poets: by the men I was reading as an undergraduate—Frost, Dylan Thomas, Donne, Auden, MacNiece, Stevens, Yeats. What I chiefly learned from them was craft.[6] But poems are like dreams: in them you put what you don't know you know. Looking back at poems I wrote before I was twenty-one, I'm startled because beneath the conscious craft are glimpses of the split I even then experienced between the girl who wrote poems, who defined herself in writing poems, and the girl who was to define herself by her relationships with men. "Aunt Jennifer's Tigers" (1951), written while I was a student, looks with deliberate detachment at this split.[7] In writing this poem, composed and apparently cool as it is, I thought I was creating a portrait of an imaginary woman. But this woman suffers from the opposition of her imagination, worked out in tapestry, and her life-style, "ringed with ordeals she was mastered by." It was important to me that Aunt Jennifer was a person as distinct from myself as possible—distanced by the formalism of the poem, by its objective, observant tone—even by putting the woman in a different generation.

In those years formalism was part of the strategy—like asbestos gloves, it allowed me to handle materials I couldn't pick up barehanded. A later strategy was to use the persona of a man, as I did in "The Loser" (1958):

> A man thinks of the woman he once loved: first, after her wedding, and then nearly a decade later.

6. A. R., 1978: Yet I spent months, at sixteen, memorizing and writing imitations of Millay's sonnets; and in notebooks of that period I find what are obviously attempts to imitate Dickinson's metrics and verbal compression. I knew H. D. only through anthologized lyrics; her epic poetry was not then available to me.
7. In the original essay, "Aunt Jennifer's Tiger" was quoted in full; in this volume it appears on p. 4.

I

I kissed you, bride and lost, and went
home from that bourgeois sacrament,
your cheek still tasting cold upon
my lips that gave you benison
with all the swagger that they knew—
as losers somehow learn to do.

Your wedding made my eyes ache; soon
the world would be worse off for one
more golden apple dropped to ground
without the least protesting sound,
and you would windfall lie, and we
forget your shimmer on the tree.

Beauty is always wasted: if
not Mignon's song sung to the deaf,
at all events to the unmoved.
A face like yours cannot be loved
long or seriously enough.
Almost, we seem to hold it off.

II

Well, you are tougher than I thought.
Now when the wash with ice hangs taut
this morning of St. Valentine,
I see you strip the squeaking line,
your body weighed against the load,
and all my groans can do no good.

Because you are still beautiful,
though squared and stiffened by the pull
of what nine windy years have done.
You have three daughters, lost a son.
I see all your intelligence
flung into that unwearied stance.

My envy is of no avail.
I turn my head and wish him well
who chafed your beauty into use
and lives forever in a house
lit by the friction of your mind.
You stagger in against the wind.

    I finished college, published my first book by a fluke, as it seemed to
me, and broke off a love affair. I took a job, lived alone, went on writing,

fell in love. I was young, full of energy, and the book seemed to mean that others agreed I was a poet. Because I was also determined to prove that as a woman poet I could also have what was then defined as a "full" woman's life, I plunged in my early twenties into marriage and had three children before I was thirty. There was nothing overt in the environment to warn me: these were the fifties, and in reaction to the earlier wave of feminism, middle-class women were making careers of domestic perfection, working to send their husbands through professional schools, then retiring to raise large families. People were moving out to the suburbs, technology was going to be the answer to everything, even sex; the family was in its glory. Life was extremely private; women were isolated from each other by the loyalties of marriage. I have a sense that women didn't talk to each other much in the fifties—not about their secret emptinesses, their frustrations. I went on trying to write; my second book and first child appeared in the same month. But by the time that book came out I was already dissatisfied with those poems, which seemed to me mere exercises for poems I hadn't written. The book was praised, however, for its "gracefulness"; I had a marriage and a child. If there were doubts, if there were periods of null depression or active despairing, these could only mean that I was ungrateful, insatiable, perhaps a monster.

About the time my third child was born, I felt that I had either to consider myself a failed woman and a failed poet, or to try to find some synthesis by which to understand what was happening to me. What frightened me most was the sense of drift, of being pulled along on a current which called itself my destiny, but in which I seemed to be losing touch with whoever I had been, with the girl who had experienced her own will and energy almost ecstatically at times, walking around a city or riding a train at night or typing in a student room. In a poem about my grandmother I wrote (of myself): "A young girl, thought sleeping, is certified dead" ("Halfway").[8] I was writing very little, partly from fatigue, that female fatigue of suppressed anger and loss of contact with my own being; partly from the discontinuity of female life with its attention to small chores, errands, work that others constantly undo, small children's constant needs. What I did write was unconvincing to me; my anger and frustration were hard to acknowledge in or out of poems because in fact I cared a great deal about my husband and my children. Trying to look back and understand that time I have tried to analyze the real nature of the conflict. Most, if not all, human lives are full of fantasy— passive day-dreaming which need not be acted on. But to write poetry or fiction, or even to think well, is not to fantasize, or to put fantasies on paper. For a poem to coalesce, for a character or an action to take shape, there has to be an imaginative transformation of reality which is

8. See *The Fact of a Doorframe*, p. 73.

in no way passive. And a certain freedom of the mind is needed—freedom to press on, to enter the currents of your thought like a glider pilot, knowing that your motion can be sustained, that the buoyancy of your attention will not be suddenly snatched away. Moreover, if the imagination is to transcend and transform experience it has to question, to challenge, to conceive of alternatives, perhaps to the very life you are living at that moment. You have to be free to play around with the notion that day might be night, love might be hate; nothing can be too sacred for the imagination to turn into its opposite or to call experimentally by another name. For writing is re-naming. Now, to be maternally with small children all day in the old way, to be with a man in the old way of marriage, requires a holding-back, a putting-aside of that imaginative activity, and demands instead a kind of conservatism. I want to make it clear that I am *not* saying that in order to write well, or think well, it is necessary to become unavailable to others, or to become a devouring ego. This has been the myth of the masculine artist and thinker; and I do not accept it. But to be a female human being trying to fulfill traditional female functions in a traditional way *is* in direct conflict with the subversive function of the imagination. The word traditional is important here. There must be ways, and we will be finding out more and more about them, in which the energy of creation and the energy of relation can be united. But in those years I always felt the conflict as a failure of love in myself. I had thought I was choosing a full life: the life available to most men, in which sexuality, work, and parenthood could coexist. But I felt, at twenty-nine, guilt toward the people closest to me, and guilty toward my own being.

I wanted, then, more than anything, the one thing of which there was never enough: time to think, time to write. The fifties and early sixties were years of rapid revelations: the sit-ins and marches in the South, the Bay of Pigs, the early antiwar movement, raised large questions—questions for which the masculine world of the academy around me seemed to have expert and fluent answers. But I needed to think for myself—about pacifism and dissent and violence, about poetry and society, and about my own relationship to all these things. For about ten years I was reading in fierce snatches, scribbling in notebooks, writing poetry in fragments; I was looking desperately for clues, because if there were no clues then I thought I might be insane. I wrote in a notebook about this time:

> Paralyzed by the sense that there exists a mesh of relationships—
> e.g., between my anger at the children, my sensual life, pacifism,
> sex (I mean sex in its broadest significance, not merely sexual
> desire)—an interconnectedness which, if I could see it, make it
> valid, would give me back myself, make it possible to function lucidly
> and passionately. Yet I grope in and out among these dark webs.

I think I began at this point to feel that politics was not something "out there" but something "in here" and of the essence of my condition.

In the late fifties I was able to write, for the first time, directly about experiencing myself as a woman. The poem was jotted in fragments during children's naps, brief hours in a library, or at 3:00 A.M. after rising with a wakeful child. I despaired of doing any continuous work at this time. Yet I began to feel that my fragments and scraps had a common consciousness and a common theme, one which I would have been very unwilling to put on paper at an earlier time because I had been taught that poetry should be "universal," which meant, of course, nonfemale. Until then I had tried very much *not* to identify myself as a female poet. Over two years I wrote a ten-part poem called "Snapshots of a Daughter-in-Law" (1958–1960), in a longer looser mode than I'd ever trusted myself with before. It was an extraordinary relief to write that poem. It strikes me now as too literary, too dependent on allusion; I hadn't found the courage yet to do without authorities, or even to use the pronoun "I"—the woman in the poem is always "she." One section of it, No. 2, concerns a woman who thinks she is going mad; she is haunted by voices telling her to resist and rebel, voices which she can hear but not obey.[9]

The poem "Orion," written five years later, is a poem of reconnection with a part of myself I had felt I was losing—the active principle, the energetic imagination, the "half-brother" whom I projected, as I had for many years, into the constellation Orion. It's no accident that the words "cold and egotistical" appear in this poem, and are applied to myself.[1] The choice still seemed to be between "love"—womanly, maternal love, altruistic love—a love defined and ruled by the weight of an entire culture; and egotism—a force directed by men into creation, achievement, ambition, often at the expense of others, but justifiably so. For weren't they men, and wasn't that their destiny as womanly, selfless love was ours? We know now that the alternatives are false ones—that the word "love" is itself in need of re-vision.

There is a companion poem to "Orion," written three years later, in which at last the woman in the poem and the woman writing the poem become the same person. It is called "Planetarium," and it was written after a visit to a real planetarium, where I read an account of the work of Caroline Herschel, the astronomer, who worked with her brother William, but whose name remained obscure, as his did not.[2]

In closing I want to tell you about a dream I had last summer. I

9. In the original essay, section 2 of "Snapshots of a Daughter-in-Law" was quoted in full; in this volume it appears on p. 9.
1. In the original essay, "Orion" was quoted in full; in this volume it appears on pp. 29–30.
2. In the original essay, "Planetarium" was quoted in full; in this volume, it appears on pp. 38–39.

dreamed I was asked to read my poetry at a mass women's meeting, but when I began to read, what came out were the lyrics of a blues song. I share this dream with you because it seemed to me to say something about the problems and the future of the woman writer, and probably of women in general. The awakening of consciousness is not like the crossing of a frontier—one step and you are in another country. Much of woman's poetry has been of the nature of the blues song: a cry of pain, of victimization, or a lyric of seduction.[3] And today, much poetry by women—and prose for that matter—is charged with anger. I think we need to go through that anger, and we will betray our own reality if we try, as Virginia Woolf was trying, for an objectivity, a detachment, that would make us sound more like Jane Austen or Shakespeare. We know more than Jane Austen or Shakespeare knew: more than Jane Austen because our lives are more complex, more than Shakespeare because we know more about the lives of women—Jane Austen and Virginia Woolf included.

Both the victimization and the anger experienced by women are real, and have real sources, everywhere in the environment, built into society, language, the structures of thought. They will go on being tapped and explored by poets, among others. We can neither deny them, nor will we rest there. A new generation of women poets is already working out of the psychic energy released when women begin to move out towards what the feminist philosopher Mary Daly has described as the "new space" on the boundaries of patriarchy.[4] Women are speaking to and of women in these poems, out of a newly released courage to name, to love each other, to share risk and grief and celebration.

To the eye of a feminist, the work of Western male poets now writing reveals a deep, fatalistic pessimism as to the possibilities of change, whether societal or personal, along with a familiar and threadbare use of women (and nature) as redemptive on the one hand, threatening on the other; and a new tide of phallocentric sadism and overt woman-hating which matches the sexual brutality of recent films. "Political" poetry by men remains stranded amid the struggles for power among male groups; in condemning U.S. imperialism or the Chilean junta the poet can claim to speak for the oppressed while remaining, as male, part of a system of sexual oppression. The enemy is always outside the self, the struggle somewhere else. The mood of isolation, self-pity, and self-imitation that pervades "nonpolitical" poetry suggests that a profound change in masculine consciousness will have to precede any new male poetic—or other—inspiration. The creative energy of patriarchy is fast running out;

---

3. A. R. 1978: When I dreamed that dream, was I wholly ignorant of the tradition of Bessie Smith and other women's blues lyrics which transcended victimization to sing of resistance and independence?

4. Mary Daly, *Beyond God the Father: Towards a Philosophy of Women's Liberation* (Boston: Beacon, 1973).

what remains is its self-generating energy for destruction. As women, we
have our work cut out for us.

Vesuvius at Home: The Power of Emily Dickinson (1975) †

This essay was read in its earliest form as a lecture at Brandeis University,
and in its present version as one of the Lucy Martin Donnelley lectures at
Bryn Mawr College. It was first printed in *Parnassus: Poetry in Review*. The
problem of taking Emily Dickinson seriously is still with us today. "The
Belle of Amherst," a specious and reductive "one-woman show" based on
Dickinson's most familiar poems and on the legendary version of her life
and character, was a Broadway and television hit in 1976–77, and is now
being made into a film. There is still almost no adequate criticism of Dick-
inson's poetry. The best scholarly efforts have centered on her life (e.g., Jay
Leyda's *The Days and Hours of Emily Dickinson*; Richard Sewall's respectful
and useful two-volume biography) but most biographers have been conde-
scending, clinical, or sentimental. Virtually all criticism of this poet's work
suffers from the literary and historical silence and secrecy surrounding intense
woman-to-woman relationships—a central element in Dickinson's life and
art; and by the assumption that she was asexual or heterosexually "subli-
mated." [1] As Toni McNaron has written: "I am not waiting to turn Dickin-
son into a practicing lesbian. . . . What I do want is a lesbian-feminist
reading of her poetry and her life as the most accurate way to handle that
otherwise confusing constellation of myth and fact surrounding her." [2] The
distinction made here is a vital one: to "prove" that a woman of the nine-
teenth century did or did not sleep with another woman, or women, is
beside the point. But lesbian/feminist criticism has the power to illuminate
the work of *any* woman artist, beyond proving her a "practicing lesbian" or
not. Such a criticism will ask questions hitherto passed over; will not search
obsessively for heterosexual romance as the key to a woman artist's life and
work; will ask how she came to be for-herself and how she identified with
and was able to use women's culture, a women's tradition; and what the
presence of other women meant in her life. It will thus identify images,
codes, metaphors, strategies, points of stress, unrevealed by conventional
criticism which works from a male/mainstream perspective. And this process
will make women artists of the past—and present—available to us in ways
we cannot yet predict or imagine.

---

† Except where otherwise indicated, notes to this essay are Rich's. The introductory paragraphs
  appeared in Adrienne Rich's *On Lies, Secrets, and Silence: Selected Prose, 1966–1978* (New
  York: Norton, 1979) 157–58. This selection has been edited for publication here; asterisks
  indicate deletions.
1. This includes Albert Gelpi's sensitive, imaginative, and exceptionally sympathetic essay on
  Dickinson in his *The Tenth Muse: The Psyche of the American Poet* (Cambridge, Mass.: Har-
  vard University, 1975).
2. Toni McNaron, "The Necessary Struggle to Name Ourselves," to be included in an anthology
  tentatively entitled *The Lesbian Perspective in Research and Teaching*, edited by Sarah Hoag-
  land and Julia P. Stanley.

I am traveling at the speed of time, along the Massachusetts Turnpike.
For months, for years, for most of my life, I have been hovering like an
insect against the screens of an existence which inhabited Amherst,
Massachusetts, between 1830 and 1886. The methods, the exclusions,
of Emily Dickinson's existence could not have been my own; yet more
and more, as a woman poet finding my own methods, I have come to
understand her necessities, could have been witness in her defense.

"Home is not where the heart is," she wrote in a letter, "but the house
and the adjacent buildings." A statement of New England realism, a
directive to be followed. Probably no poet ever lived so much and so
purposefully in one house; even, in one room. Her niece Martha told
of visiting her in her corner bedroom on the second floor at 280 Main
Street, Amherst, and of how Emily Dickinson made as if to lock the
door with an imaginary key, turned, and said, "Matty: here's freedom."

I am traveling at the speed of time, in the direction of the house and
buildings.

Western Massachusetts: the Connecticut Valley: a countryside still
full of reverberations: scene of Indian uprisings, religious revivals, spiri-
tual confrontations, the blazing-up of the lunatic fringe of the Puritan
coal. How peaceful and how threatened it looks from Route 91, hills
gently curled above the plain, the tobacco barns standing in fields shel-
tered with white gauze from the sun, and the sudden urban sprawl: ARCO,
MacDonald's, shopping plazas. The country that broke the heart of Jon-
athan Edwards, that enclosed the genius of Emily Dickinson. It lies
calmly in the light of May, cloudy skies breaking into warm sunshine,
light-green spring softening the hills, dogwood and wild fruit-trees blos-
soming in the hollows.

From Northampton bypass there's a four-mile stretch of road to
Amherst—Route 9—between fruit farms, steakhouses, supermarkets. The
new University of Massachusetts rears its skyscrapers up from the plain
against the Pelham Hills. There is new money here, real estate, motels.
Amherst succeeds on Hadley almost without notice. Amherst is green,
rich-looking, secure; we're suddenly in the center of town, the crossroads
of the campus, old New England college buildings spread around two
village greens, a scene I remember as almost exactly the same in the dim
past of my undergraduate years when I used to come there for college
weekends.

Left on Seelye Street, right on Main; driveway at the end of a yellow
picket fence. I recognize the high hedge of cedars screening the house,
because twenty-five years ago I walked there, even then drawn toward
the spot, trying to peer over. I pull into the driveway behind a generous
nineteenth-century brick mansion with wings and porches, old trees and
green lawns. I ring at the back door—the door through which Dickin-
son's coffin was carried to the cemetery a block away.

For years I have been not so much envisioning Emily Dickinson as trying to visit, to enter her mind, through her poems and letters, and through my own intimations of what it could have meant to be one of the two mid–nineteenth-century American geniuses, and a woman, living in Amherst, Massachusetts. Of the other genius, Walt Whitman, Dickinson wrote that she had heard his poems were "disgraceful." She knew her own were unacceptable by her world's standards of poetic convention, and of what was appropriate, in particular, for a woman poet. Seven were published in her lifetime, all edited by other hands; more than a thousand were laid away in her bedroom chest, to be discovered after her death. When her sister discovered them, there were decades of struggle over the manuscripts, the manner of their presentation to the world, their suitability for publication, the poet's own final intentions. Narrowed-down by her early editors and anthologists, reduced to quaintness or spinsterish oddity by many of her commentators, sentimentalized, fallen-in-love with like some gnomic Garbo, still unread in the breadth and depth of her full range of work, she was, and is, a wonder to me when I try to imagine myself into that mind.

I have a notion that genius knows itself; that Dickinson chose her seclusion, knowing she was exceptional and knowing what she needed. It was, moreover, no hermetic retreat, but a seclusion which included a wide range of people, of reading and correspondence. Her sister Vinnie said, "Emily is always looking for the rewarding person." And she found, at various periods, both women and men: her sister-in-law Susan Gilbert, Amherst visitors and family friends such as Benjamin Newton, Charles Wadsworth, Samuel Bowles, editor of the Springfield *Republican*, and his wife; her friends Kate Anthon and Helen Hunt Jackson, the distant but significant figures of Elizabeth Barrett, the Brontës, George Eliot. But she carefully selected her society and controlled the disposal of her time. Not only the "gentlewomen in plush" of Amherst were excluded; Emerson visited next door but she did not go to meet him; she did not travel or receive routine visits; she avoided strangers. Given her vocation, she was neither eccentric nor quaint; she was determined to survive, to use her powers, to practice necessary economies.

Suppose Jonathan Edwards had been born a woman; suppose William James, for that matter, had been born a woman? (The invalid seclusion of his sister Alice is suggestive.) Even from men, New England took its psychic toll; many of its geniuses seemed peculiar in one way or another, particularly along the lines of social intercourse. Hawthorne, until he married, took his meals in his bedroom, apart from the family. Thoreau insisted on the values both of solitude and of geographical restriction, boasting that "I have traveled much in Concord." Emily Dickinson— viewed by her bemused contemporary Thomas Higginson as "partially cracked," by the twentieth century as fey or pathological—has increasingly struck me as a practical woman, exercising her gift as she had to, making choices. I have come to imagine her as somehow too strong for her environment, a figure of powerful will, not at all frail or breathless, someone whose personal dimensions would be felt in a household. She was her father's favorite daughter though she professed being afraid of him. Her sister dedicated herself to the everyday domestic labors which would free Dickinson to write. (Dickinson herself baked the bread, made jellies and gingerbread, nursed her mother through a long illness, was a skilled horticulturist who grew pomegranates, calla lilies, and other exotica in her New England greenhouse.)

Upstairs at last: I stand in the room which for Emily Dickinson was "freedom." The best bedroom in the house, a corner room, sunny, overlooking the main street of Amherst in front, the way to her brother Austin's house on the side. Here, at a small table with one drawer, she wrote most of her poems. Here she read Elizabeth Barrett's *Aurora Leigh*, a woman poet's narrative poem of a woman poet's life; also George Eliot; Emerson; Carlyle; Shakespeare; Charlotte and Emily Brontë. Here I become, again, an insect, vibrating at the frames of windows, clinging to panes of glass, trying to connect. The scent here is very powerful. Here in this white-curtained, high-ceilinged room, a red-haired woman with hazel eyes and a contralto voice wrote poems about volcanoes, deserts, eternity, suicide, physical passion, wild beasts, rape, power, madness, separation, the daemon, the grave. Here, with a darning needle, she bound these poems—heavily emended and often in variant versions—into booklets, secured with darning thread, to be found and read after her death. Here she knew "freedom," listening from above-stairs to a visitor's piano-playing, escaping from the pantry where she was mistress of the household bread and puddings, watching, you feel, watching ceaselessly, the life of sober Main Street below. From this room she glided downstairs, her hand on the polished bannister, to meet the complacent magazine editor, Thomas Higginson, unnerve him while claiming she herself was unnerved. "Your scholar," she signed herself in letters to him. But she was an independent scholar, used his criticism selectively, saw him rarely and always on *her* premises. It was a life deliberately organized on her terms. The terms she had been handed by society—Calvinist Protestantism, Romanticism, the nineteenth-century corseting of women's bodies, choices, and sexuality—could spell insanity to a woman genius. What this one had to do was retranslate her own unorthodox, subversive, sometimes volcanic propensities into a dialect called metaphor: her native language. "Tell all the Truth—but tell it Slant—." It is always what is under pressure in us, especially under pressure of concealment—that explodes in poetry.

The women and men in her life she equally converted into metaphor. The masculine pronoun in her poems can refer simultaneously to many aspects of the "masculine" in the patriarchal world—the god she engages in dialogue, again on *her* terms; her own creative powers, unsexing for a woman, the male power-figures in her immediate environment—the lawyer Edward Dickinson, her brother Austin, the preacher Wadsworth, the editor Bowles—it is far too limiting to trace that "He" to some specific lover, although that was the chief obsession of the legend-mongers for more than half a century. Obviously, Dickinson was attracted by and interested in men whose minds had something to offer her; she was, it is by now clear, equally attracted by and interested in women whose minds had something to offer. There are many poems to and about women, and some which exist in two versions with alternate sets of pronouns. Her latest biographer, Richard Sewall, rejecting an earlier Freudian biographer's theory that Dickinson was essentially a psychopathological case, the by-product of which happened to be poetry, creates a context in which the importance, and validity, of Dickinson's attachments to women may now, at last, be seen in full. She was always stirred by the existences of women like George Eliot or Elizabeth Barrett, who possessed strength of mind, articulateness, and energy. (She once characterized Elizabeth Fry and Florence Nightingale as "holy"—one suspects she merely meant, "great.")

But of course Dickinson's relationships with women were more than intellectual. They were deeply charged, and the sources both of passionate joy and pain. We are only beginning to be able to consider them in a social and historical context. The historian Carroll Smith-Rosenberg has shown that there was far less taboo on intense, even passionate and sensual, relationships between women in the American nineteenth-century "female world of love and ritual," as she terms it, than there was later in the twentieth century. Women expressed their attachments to other women both physically and verbally; a marriage did not dilute the strength of a female friendship, in which two women often shared the same bed during long visits, and wrote letters articulate with both physical and emotional longing. The nineteenth-century close woman friend, according to the many diaries and letters Smith-Rosenberg has studied, might be a far more important figure in a woman's life than the nineteenth-century husband. None of this was perceived or condemned as "lesbianism."[3] We will understand Emily Dickinson better, read her poetry more perceptively, when the Freudian imputation of scandal and aberrance in women's love for women has been supplanted by a more informed, less misogynistic attitude toward women's experiences with each other.

But who, if you read through the seventeen hundred and seventy-five poems—who—woman or man—could have passed through that imagination and not come out transmuted? Given the space created by her in that corner room, with its window-light, its potted plants and work-table, given that personality, capable of imposing its terms on a household, on

---

3. "The Female World of Love and Ritual: Relations between Women in Nineteenth-Century America," *Signs*, vol. 1, no. 1.

a whole community, what single theory could hope to contain her, when she'd put it all together in that space?

"Matty: here's freedom," I hear her saying as I speed back to Boston along the turnpike, as I slip the ticket into the toll-collector's hand. I am thinking of a confined space in which the genius of the nineteenth-century female mind in America moved, inventing a language more varied, more compressed, more dense with implications, more complex of syntax, than any American poetic language to date; in the trail of that genius my mind has been moving, and with its language and images my mind still has to reckon, as the mind of a woman poet in America today.

In 1971, a postage stamp was issued in honor of Dickinson; the portrait derives from the one existing daguerrotype of her, with straight, center-parted hair, eyes staring somewhere beyond the camera, hands poised around a nosegay of flowers, in correct nineteenth-century style. On the first-day-of-issue envelope sent me by a friend there is, besides the postage stamp, an engraving of the poet as popular fancy has preferred her, in a white lace ruff and with hair as bouffant as if she had just stepped from a Boston beauty-parlor. The poem chosen to represent her work to the American public is engraved, alongside a dew-gemmed rose, below the portrait:

> If I can stop one heart from breaking
> I shall not live in vain
> If I can ease one life the aching
> Or cool the pain
> Or help one fainting robin
> Unto his nest again
> I shall not live in vain.

Now, this is extremely strange. It is a fact that, in 1864, Emily Dickinson wrote this verse; and it is a verse which a hundred or more nineteenth-century versifiers could have written. In its undistinguished language, as in its conventional sentiment, it is remarkably untypical of the poet. Had she chosen to write many poems like this one we would have no "problem" of nonpublication, of editing, of estimating the poet at her true worth. Certainly the sentiment—a contented and unambiguous altruism—is one which even today might in some quarters be accepted as fitting from a female versifier—a kind of Girl Scout prayer. But we are talking about the woman who wrote

> He fumbles at your Soul
> As Players at the Keys
> Before they drop full Music on—
> He stuns you by degrees—
> Prepares your brittle Nature
> For the Ethereal Blow
> By fainter Hammers—further heard—

Then nearer—Then so slow
Your breath has time to straighten—
Your brain—to bubble Cool—
Deals—One—imperial—Thunderbolt—
That scalps your naked Soul—

When Winds take Forests in their Paws—
The Universe—is still—

(#315)

Much energy has been invested in trying to identify a concrete, flesh-
and-blood male lover whom Dickinson is supposed to have renounced,
and to the loss of whom can be traced the secret of her seclusion and
the vein of much of her poetry. But the real question, given that the art
of poetry is an art of transformation, is how this woman's mind and
imagination may have used the masculine element in the world at large,
or those elements personified as masculine—including the men she knew;
how her relationship to this reveals itself in her images and language. In
a patriarchal culture, specifically the Judeo-Christian, quasi-Puritan
culture of nineteenth-century New England in which Dickinson grew
up, still inflamed with religious revivals, and where the sermon was still
an active, if perishing, literary form, the equation of divinity with male-
ness was so fundamental that it is hardly surprising to find Dickinson,
like many an early mystic, blurring erotic with religious experience and
imagery. The poem I just read has intimations both of seduction and
rape merged with the intense force of a religious experience. But are
these metaphors for each other, or for something more intrinsic to Dick-
inson? Here is another:

He put the Belt around my life—
I heard the Buckle snap—
And turned away, imperial,
My Lifetime folding up—
Deliberate, as a Duke would do
A Kingdom's Title Deed—
Henceforth, a Dedicated sort—
A member of the Cloud.

Yet not too far to come at call—
And do the little Toils
That make the Circuit of the Rest—
And deal occasional smiles
To lives that stoop to notice mine—
And kindly ask it in—
Whose invitation, know you not
For Whom I must decline?

(#273)

These two poems are about possession, and they seem to me a poet's poems—that is, they are about the poet's relationship to her own power, which is exteriorized in masculine form, much as masculine poets have invoked the female Muse. In writing at all—particularly an unorthodox and original poetry like Dickinson's—women have often felt in danger of losing their status as women. And this status has always been defined in terms of relationship to men—as daughter, sister, bride, wife, mother, mistress, Muse. Since the most powerful figures in patriarchal culture have been men, it seems natural that Dickinson would assign a masculine gender to that in herself which did not fit in with the conventional ideology of womanliness. To recognize and acknowledge our own interior power has always been a path mined with risks for women, to acknowledge that power and commit oneself to it as Emily Dickinson did was an immense decision.

Most of us, unfortunately, have been exposed in the schoolroom to Dickinson's "little-girl" poems, her kittenish tones, as in "I'm Nobody! Who Are You?" (a poem whose underlying anger translates itself into archness) or

> I hope the Father in the skies
> Will lift his little girl—
> Old fashioned—naughty—everything—
> Over the stile of "Pearl."
>
> (#70)

or the poems about bees and robins. One critic—Richard Chase—has noted that in the nineteenth century "one of the careers open to women was perpetual childhood." A strain in Dickinson's letters and some—though by far a minority—of her poems was a self-diminutivization, almost as if to offset and deny—or even disguise—her actual dimensions as she must have experienced them. And this emphasis on her own "littleness," along with the deliberate strangeness of her tactics of seclusion, have been, until recently, accepted as the prevailing character of the poet: the fragile poetess in white, sending flowers and poems by messenger to unseen friends, letting down baskets of gingerbread to the neighborhood children from her bedroom window; writing, but somehow naively. John Crowe Ransom, arguing for the editing and standardization of Dickinson's punctuation and typography, calls her "a little home-keeping person" who, "while she had a proper notion of the final destiny of her poems, was not one of those poets who had advanced to that later stage of operations where manuscripts are prepared for the printer, and the poet's diction has to make concessions to the publisher's style-book." (In short, Emily Dickinson did not wholly know her trade, and Ransom believes a "publisher's style-book" to have the last word on poetic diction.) He goes on to print several of her poems, altered by him "with all possible forbearance." What might, in a male writer—a Tho-

reau, let us say, or a Christopher Smart or William Blake—seem a legit-
imate strangeness, a unique intention, has been in one of our two major
poets devalued into a kind of naiveté, girlish ignorance, feminine lack
of professionalism, just as the poet herself has been made into a senti-
mental object. ("Most of us are half in love with this dead girl," con-
fesses Archibald MacLeish. Dickinson was fifty-five when she died.)

It is true that more recent critics, including her most recent biogra-
pher, have gradually begun to approach the poet in terms of her great-
ness rather than her littleness, the decisiveness of her choices instead of
the surface oddities of her life or the romantic crises of her legend. But
unfortunately anthologists continue to plagiarize other anthologies, to
reprint her in edited, even bowdlerized versions; the popular image of
her and of her work lags behind the changing consciousness of scholars
and specialists. There still does not exist a selection from her poems
which depicts her in her fullest range. Dickinson's greatness cannot be
measured in terms of twenty-five or fifty or even five hundred "perfect"
lyrics; it has to be seen as the accumulation it is. Poets, even, are not
always acquainted with the full dimensions of her work, or the sense one
gets, reading in the one-volume complete edition (let alone the three-
volume variorum edition) of a mind engaged in a lifetime's musing on
essential problems of language, identity, separation, relationship, the
integrity of the self; a mind capable of describing psychological states
more accurately than any poet except Shakespeare. I have been surprised
at how narrowly her work, still, is known by women who are writing
poetry, how much her legend has gotten in the way of her being repos-
sessed, as a source and a foremother.

I know that for me, reading her poems as a child and then as a young
girl already seriously writing poetry, she was a problematic figure. I first
read her in the selection heavily edited by her niece which appeared in
1937; a later and fuller edition appeared in 1945 when I was sixteen,
and the complete, unbowdlerized edition by Johnson did not appear
until fifteen years later. The publication of each of these editions was
crucial to me in successive decades of my life. More than any other poet,
Emily Dickinson seemed to tell me that the intense inner event, the
personal and psychological, was inseparable from the universal; that there
was a range for psychological poetry beyond mere self-expression. Yet
the legend of the life was troubling, because it seemed to whisper that a
woman who undertook such explorations must pay with renunciation,
isolation, and incorporeality. With the publication of the *Complete Poems*,
the legend seemed to recede into unimportance beside the unquestion-
able power and importance of the mind revealed there. But taking pos-
session of Emily Dickinson is still no simple matter.

The 1945 edition, entitled *Bolts of Melody*, took its title from a poem
which struck me at the age of sixteen and which still, thirty years later,
arrests my imagination:

I would not paint—a picture—
I'd rather be the One
Its bright impossibility
To dwell—delicious—on—
And wonder how the fingers feel
Whose rare—celestial—stir
Evokes so sweet a Torment—
Such sumptuous—Despair—

I would not talk, like Cornets—
I'd rather be the One
Raised softly to the Ceilings—
And out, and easy on—
Through Villages of Ether
Myself endued Balloon
By but a lip of Metal
The pier to my Pontoon—

Nor would I be a Poet—
It's finer—own the Ear—
Enamored—impotent—content—
The License to revere,
A privilege so awful
What would the Dower be,
Had I the Art to stun myself
With Bolts of Melody!

(#505)

This poem is about choosing an orthodox "feminine" role: the receptive rather than the creative; viewer rather than painter, listener rather than musician; acted-upon rather than active. Yet even while ostensibly choosing this role she wonders "how the fingers feel / whose rare—celestial—stir— / Evokes so sweet a Torment—" and the "feminine" role is praised in a curious sequence of adjectives: "Enamored—*impotent*—content—." The strange paradox of this poem—its exquisite irony—is that it is about choosing not to be a poet, a poem which is gainsaid by no fewer than one thousand seven hundred and seventy-five poems made during the writer's life, including itself. Moreover, the images of the poem rise to a climax (like the Balloon she evokes) but the climax happens as she describes, not what it is to be the receiver, but the maker and receiver at once: "A Privilege so awful / What would the Dower be / Had I the Art to stun myself / With Bolts of Melody!"—a climax which recalls the poem: "He fumbles at your Soul / As Players at the Keys / Before they drop full Music on—" And of course, in writing those lines she possesses herself of that privilege and that Dower. I have said that this is a poem of exquisite ironies. It is, indeed, though in a very different mode, related to Dickinson's "little-girl" strategy. The woman who feels herself to be Vesuvius at home has need of a mask, at least, of innocuousness and of containment.

> On my volcano grows the Grass
> A meditative spot—
> An acre for a Bird to choose
> Would be the General thought—
>
> How red the Fire rocks below—
> How insecure the sod
> Did I disclose
> Would populate with awe my solitude.

(#1677)

Power, even masked, can still be perceived as destructive.

> A still—Volcano—Life—
> That flickered in the night—
> When it was dark enough to do
> Without erasing sight—
>
> A quiet—Earthquake style—
> Too subtle to suspect
> By natures this side Naples—
> The North cannot detect
>
> The Solemn—Torrid—Symbol—
> The lips that never lie—
> Whose hissing Corals part—and shut—
> And Cities—ooze away—

(#601)

Dickinson's biographer and editor Thomas Johnson has said that she often felt herself possessed by a daemonic force, particularly in the years 1861 and 1862 when she was writing at the height of her drive. There are many poems besides "He put the Belt around my Life" which could be read as poems of possession by the daemon—poems which can also be, and have been, read, as poems of possession by the deity, or by a human lover. I suggest that a woman's poetry about her relationship to her daemon—her own active, creative power—has in patriarchal culture used the language of heterosexual love or patriarchal theology. Ted Hughes tells us that

the eruption of [Dickinson's] imagination and poetry followed when she shifted her passion, with the energy of desperation, from [the] lost man onto his only possible substitute,—the Universe in its Divine aspect. . . . Thereafter, the marriage that had been denied in the

real world went forward in the spiritual . . . just as the Universe in
its Divine aspect became the mirror-image of her "husband," so
the whole religious dilemma of New England, at that most critical
moment in history, became the mirror-image of her relationship to
him, of her "marriage" in fact.[4]

This seems to me to miss the point on a grand scale. There are facts we
need to look at. First, Emily Dickinson did not marry. And her non-
marrying was neither a pathological retreat as John Cody sees it,[5] nor
probably even a conscious decision; it was a fact in her life as in her
contemporary Christina Rossetti's; both women had more primary needs.
Second: unlike Rossetti, Dickinson did not become a religiously dedi-
cated woman; she was heretical, heterodox, in her religious opinions,
and stayed away from church and dogma. What, in fact, *did* she allow
to "put the Belt around her Life"—what *did* wholly occupy her mature
years and possess her? For "Whom" did she decline the invitations of
other lives? The writing of poetry. Nearly two thousand poems. Three
hundred and sixty-six poems in the year of her fullest power. What was
it like to be writing poetry you knew (and I am sure she did know) was
of a class by itself—to be fueled by the energy it took first to confront,
then to condense that image of psychic experience into that language;
then to copy out the poems and lay them in a trunk, or send a few here
and there to friends or relatives as occasional verse or as gestures of con-
fidence? I am sure she knew who she was, as she indicates in this poem:

> Myself was formed—a Carpenter—
> An unpretending time
> My Plane—and I, together wrought
> Before a Builder came—
>
> To measure our attainments
> Had we the Art of Boards
> Sufficiently developed—He'd hire us
> At Halves—
>
> My Tools took Human—Faces—
> The Bench, where we had toiled—
> Against the Man—persuaded—
> We—Temples Build—I said—

                                                          (#488)

This is a poem of the great year 1862, the year in which she first sent a
few poems to Thomas Higginson for criticism. Whether it antedates or
postdates that occasion is unimportant; it is a poem of knowing one's
measure, regardless of the judgments of others.

4. Hughes, ed., A *Choice of Emily Dickinson's Verse* (London: Faber & Faber, 1968), p. 11.
5. John Cody, *After Great Pain: The Inner Life of Emily Dickinson* (Cambridge, MA: Harvard
   UP, 1971) [*Editors*].

There are many poems which carry the weight of this knowledge.
Here is another one:

> I'm ceded—I've stopped being Theirs—
> The name They dropped upon my face
> With water, in the country church
> Is finished using, now,
> And they can put it with my Dolls,
> My childhood, and the string of spools,
> I've finished threading—too—
>
> Baptized before, without the choice,
> But this time, consciously, of Grace—
> Unto supremest name—
> Called to my Full—The Crescent dropped—
> Existence's whole arc, filled up,
> With one small Diadem.
>
> My second Rank—too small the first—
> Crowned—Crowing—on my Father's breast—
> A half unconscious Queen—
> But this time—Adequate—Erect—
> With Will to choose, or to reject—
> And I choose, just a Crown—

(#508)

Now, this poem partakes of the imagery of being "twice-born" or, in
Christian liturgy, "confirmed"—and if this poem had been written by
Christina Rossetti I would be inclined to give more weight to a theo-
logical reading. But it was written by Emily Dickinson, who used the
Christian metaphor far more than she let it use her. This is a poem of
great pride—not pridefulness, but *self*-confirmation—and it is curious
how little Dickinson's critics, perhaps misled by her diminutives, have
recognized the will and pride in her poetry. It is a poem of movement
from childhood to womanhood, of transcending the patriarchal con-
dition of bearing her father's name and "Crowing—on my Father's
breast—." She is now a conscious Queen "Adequate—Erect/ With Will
to choose, or to reject—."

There is one poem which is the real "onlie begetter" of my thoughts
here about Dickinson; a poem I have mused over, repeated to myself,
taken into myself over many years. I think it is a poem about possession
by the daemon, about the dangers and risks of such possession if you are
a woman, about the knowledge that power in a woman can seem
destructive, and that you cannot live without the daemon once it has
possessed you. The archetype of the daemon as masculine is beginning
to change, but it has been real for women up until now. But this woman
poet also perceives herself as a lethal weapon:

My life had stood—a Loaded Gun—
In Corners—till a Day
The Owner passed—identified—
And carried Me away—

And now We roam in Sovereign Woods—
And now We hunt the Doe—
And every time I speak for Him—
The Mountains straight reply—

And do I smile, such cordial light
Upon the Valley glow—
It is as a Vesuvian face
Had let its pleasure through—

And when at Night—Our good Day done—
I guard My Master's Head—
'Tis better than the Eider-Duck's
Deep Pillow—to have shared—

To foe of His—I'm deadly foe—
None stir the second time—
On whom I lay a Yellow Eye—
Or an emphatic Thumb—

Though I than He—may longer live
He longer must—than I—
For I have but the power to kill,
Without—the power to die—

(#754)

Here the poet sees herself as split, not between anything so simple as
"masculine" and "feminine" identity but between the hunter, admit-
tedly masculine, but also a human person, an active, willing being, and
the gun—an object, condemned to remain inactive until the hunter—
the *owner*—takes possession of it. The gun contains an energy capable
of rousing echoes in the mountains and lighting up the valleys; it is also
deadly, "Vesuvian"; it is also its owner's defender against the "foe." It is
the gun, furthermore, who *speaks for him*. If there is a female conscious-
ness in this poem it is buried deeper than the images: it exists in the
ambivalence toward power, which is extreme. Active willing and crea-
tion in women are forms of aggression, and aggression is both "the power
to kill" and punishable by death. The union of gun with hunter embod-
ies the danger of identifying and taking hold of her forces, not least that
in so doing she risks defining herself—and being defined—as aggressive,
as unwomanly ("and now we hunt the Doe"), and as potentially lethal.
That which she experiences in herself as energy and potency can also be

experienced as pure destruction. The final stanza, with its precarious balance of phrasing, seems a desperate attempt to resolve the ambivalence; but, I think, it is no resolution, only a further extension of ambivalence.

> Though I than He—may longer live
> He longer must—than I—
> For I have but the power to kill,
> Without—the power to die—

The poet experiences herself as loaded gun, imperious energy; yet without the Owner, the possessor, she is merely lethal. Should that possession abandon her—but the thought is unthinkable: "He longer *must* than I." The pronoun is masculine; the antecedent is what Keats called "The Genius of Poetry."

I do not pretend to have—I don't even wish to have—explained this poem, accounted for its every image; it will reverberate with new tones long after my words about it have ceased to matter. But I think that for us, at this time, it is a central poem in understanding Emily Dickinson, and ourselves, and the condition of the woman artist, particularly in the nineteenth century. It seems likely that the nineteenth-century woman poet, especially, felt the medium of poetry as dangerous, in ways that the woman novelist did not feel the medium of fiction to be. In writing even such a novel of elemental sexuality and anger as *Wuthering Heights*, Emily Brontë could at least theoretically separate herself from her characters; they were, after all, fictitious beings. Moreover, the novel is or can be a construct, planned and organized to deal with human experiences on one level at a time. Poetry is too much rooted in the unconscious; it presses too close against the barriers of repression; and the nineteenth-century woman had much to repress. It is interesting that Elizabeth Barrett tried to fuse poetry and fiction in writing *Aurora Leigh*—perhaps apprehending the need for fictional characters to carry the charge of her experience as a woman artist. But with the exception of *Aurora Leigh* and Christina Rossetti's "Goblin Market"—that extraordinary and little-known poem drenched in oral eroticism—Emily Dickinson's is the only poetry in English by a woman of that century which pierces so far beyond the ideology of the "feminine" and the conventions of womanly feeling. To write it at all, she had to be willing to enter chambers of the self in which

> Ourself behind ourself, concealed—
> Should startle most—

and to relinquish control there, to take those risks, she had to create a relationship to the outer world where she could feel in control.

It is an extremely painful and dangerous way to live—split between a publicly acceptable persona, and a part of yourself that you perceive as the essential, the creative and powerful self, yet also as possibly unacceptable, perhaps even monstrous.

> Much Madness is divinest Sense—
> To a discerning Eye—
> Much Sense—the starkest Madness—
> 'Tis the Majority
> In this, as All, prevail—
> Assent—and you are sane—
> Demur—you're straightway dangerous—
> And handled with a Chain—
>
> (#435)

For many women the stresses of this splitting have led, in a world so ready to assert our innate passivity and to deny our independence and creativity, to extreme consequences: the mental asylum, self-imposed silence, recurrent depression, suicide, and often severe loneliness.

Dickinson is *the* American poet whose work consisted in exploring states of psychic extremity. For a long time, as we have seen, this fact was obscured by the kinds of selections made from her work by timid if well-meaning editors. In fact, Dickinson was a great psychologist, and like every great psychologist, she began with the material she had at hand: herself. She had to possess the courage to enter, through language, states which most people deny or veil with silence.

> The first Day's Night had come—
> And grateful that a thing
> So terrible—had been endured—
> I told my Soul to sing—
>
> She said her Strings were snapt—
> Her Bow—to Atoms blown—
> And so to mend her—gave me work
> Until another Morn—
>
> And then—a Day as huge
> As Yesterdays in pairs,
> Unrolled its horror in my face—
> Until it blocked my eyes—
>
> My Brain—begun to laugh—
> I mumbled—like a fool—
> And tho' 'tis Years ago—that Day—
> My Brain keeps giggling—still.
>
> And Something's odd—within—
> That person that I was—

And this One—do not feel the same—
Could it be Madness—this?

(#410)

Dickinson's letters acknowledge a period of peculiarly intense per-
sonal crisis; her biographers have variously ascribed it to the pangs of
renunciation of an impossible love, or to psychic damage deriving from
her mother's presumed depression and withdrawal after her birth. What
concerns us here is the fact that she chose to probe the nature of this
experience in language:

The Soul has Bandaged moments—
When too appalled to stir—
She feels some ghastly Fright come up
And stop to look at her—

Salute her—with long fingers—
Caress her freezing hair—
Sip, Goblin, from the very lips
The lover—hovered—o'er—
Unworthy, that a thought so mean
Accost a Theme—so—fair—

The soul has moments of Escape—
When bursting all the doors—
She dances like a Bomb, abroad,
And swings upon the Hours. . . .

The Soul's retaken moments—
When, Felon led along,
With shackles on the plumed feet,
And staples, in the Song,

The Horror welcomes her, again,
These, are not brayed of Tongue—

(#512)

In this poem, the word "Bomb" is dropped, almost carelessly, as a cor-
relative for the soul's active, liberated states—it occurs in a context of
apparent euphoria, but its implications are more than euphoric—they
are explosive, destructive. The Horror from which in such moments the
soul escapes has a masculine, "Goblin" form, and suggests the perverse
and terrifying rape of a "Bandaged" and powerless self. In at least one
poem, Dickinson depicts the actual process of suicide:

He scanned it—staggered—
Dropped the Loop
To Past or Period—

Caught helpless at a sense as if
His mind were going blind—

Groped up, to see if God was there—
Groped backward at Himself—
Caressed a Trigger absently
And wandered out of Life.

(#1062)

The precision of knowledge in this brief poem is such that we must assume that Dickinson had, at least in fantasy, drifted close to that state in which the "Loop" that binds us to "Past or Period" is "Dropped" and we grope randomly at what remains of abstract notions of sense, God, or self, before—almost absent-mindedly—reaching for a solution. But it's worth noting that this is a poem in which the suicidal experience has been distanced, refined, transformed through a devastating accuracy of language. It is not suicide that is studied here, but the dissociation of self and mind and world which precedes.

*   *   *

The poet's relationship to her poetry has, it seems to me—and I am not speaking only of Emily Dickinson—a twofold nature. Poetic language—the poem on paper—is a concretization of the poetry of the world at large, the self, and the forces within the self; and those forces are rescued from formlessness, lucidified, and integrated in the act of writing poems. But there is a more ancient concept of the poet, which is that she is endowed to speak for those who do not have the gift of language, or to see for those who—for whatever reasons—are less conscious of what they are living through. It is as though the risks of the poet's existence can be put to some use beyond her own survival.

*   *   *

There are many more Emily Dickinsons than I have tried to call up here. Wherever you take hold of her, she proliferates. I wish I had time here to explore her complex sense of Truth; to follow the thread we unravel when we look at the numerous and passionate poems she wrote to or about women; to probe her ambivalent feelings about fame, a subject pursued by many male poets before her; simply to examine the poems in which she is directly apprehending the natural world. No one since the seventeenth century had reflected more variously or more probingly upon death and dying. What I have tried to do here is follow through some of the origins and consequences of her choice to be, not only a poet but a woman who explored her own mind, without any of the guidelines of orthodoxy. To say "yes" to her powers was not simply a major act of nonconformity in the nineteenth century; even in our own time it has been assumed that Emily Dickinson, not patriarchal society, was "the problem." The more we come to recognize the unwritten and written laws and taboos underpinning patriarchy, the less problematical, surely, will seem the methods she chose.

Women and Honor: Some Notes on Lying (1975) †

These notes were first read at the Hartwick Women Writers' Workshop, founded and directed by Beverly Tanenhaus, at Hartwick College, Oneonta, New York, in June 1975. They were published as a pamphlet by Motheroot Press in Pittsburgh, 1977; in *Heresies: A Feminist Magazine of Art and Politics*, vol. 1, no. 1; and in a French translation by the Québecois feminist press, Les Editions du Remue-Ménage, 1979.

It is clear that among women we need a new ethics; as women, a new morality. The problem of speech, of language, continues to be primary. For if in our speaking we are breaking silences long established, "liberating ourselves from our secrets" in the words of Beverly Tanenhaus, this is in itself a first kind of action. I wrote *Women and Honor* in an effort to make myself more honest, and to understand the terrible negative power of the lie in relationships between women. Since it was published, other women have spoken and written of things I did not include: Michelle Cliff's "Notes on Speechlessness" in *Sinister Wisdom* no. 5 led Catherine Nicolson (in the same issue) to write of the power of "deafness," the frustration of our speech by those who do not want to hear what we have to say. Nelle Morton has written of the act of "hearing each other into speech."[1] How do we listen? How do we make it possible for another to break her silence? These are some of the questions which follow on the ones I have raised here.

(These notes are concerned with relationships between and among women. When "personal relationship" is referred to, I mean a relationship between two women. It will be clear in what follows when I am talking about women's relationships with men.)

The old, male idea of honor. A man's "word" sufficed—to other men—without guarantee.

"Our Land Free, Our Men Honest, Our Women Fruitful"—a popular colonial toast in America.

Male honor also having something to do with killing: *I could not love thee, Dear, so much/ Lov'd I not Honour more,* ("To Lucasta, On Going to the Wars"). Male honor as something needing to be avenged: hence, the duel.

---

† The introductory paragraph appeared in *On Lies, Secrets, and Silence: Selected Prose, 1966–1978* (New York: Norton, 1979) 185.
1. Nelle Morton, "Beloved Image!", paper delivered at the National Conference of the American Academy of Religion, San Francisco, California, December 28, 1977 [*Rich's note*].

Women's honor, something altogether else: virginity, chastity, fidelity to a husband. Honesty in women has not been considered important. We have been depicted as generically whimsical, deceitful, subtle, vacillating. And we have been rewarded for lying.

Men have been expected to tell the truth about facts, not about feelings. They have not been expected to talk about feelings at all.

Yet even about facts they have continually lied.

We assume that politicians are without honor. We read their statements trying to crack the code. The scandals of their politics: not that men in high places lie, only that they do so with such indifference, so endlessly, still expecting to be believed. We are accustomed to the contempt inherent in the political lie.

•   •   •

To discover that one has been lied to in a personal relationship, however, leads one to feel a little crazy.

•   •   •

Lying is done with words, and also with silence.

The woman who tells lies in her personal relationships may or may not plan or invent her lying. She may not even think of what she is doing in a calculated way.

A subject is raised which the liar wishes buried. She has to go downstairs, her parking meter will have run out. Or, there is a telephone call she ought to have made an hour ago.

She is asked, point-blank, a question which may lead into painful talk: "How do you feel about what is happening between us?" Instead of trying to describe her feelings in their ambiguity and confusion, she asks, "How do *you* feel?" The other, because she is trying to establish a ground of openness and trust, begins describing her own feelings. Thus the liar learns more than she tells.

And she may also tell herself a lie: that she is concerned with the other's feelings, not with her own.

But the liar is concerned with her own feelings.

The liar lives in fear of losing control. She cannot even desire a relationship without manipulation, since to be vulnerable to another person means for her the loss of control.

The liar has many friends, and leads an existence of great loneliness.

•   •   •

The liar often suffers from amnesia. Amnesia is the silence of the unconscious.

To lie habitually, as a way of life, is to lose contact with the unconscious. It is like taking sleeping pills, which confer sleep but blot out dreaming. The unconscious wants truth. It ceases to speak to those who want something else more than truth.

In speaking of lies, we come inevitably to the subject of truth. There is nothing simple or easy about this idea. There is no "the truth," "a truth"—truth is not one thing, or even a system. It is an increasing complexity. The pattern of the carpet is a surface. When we look closely, or when we become weavers, we learn of the tiny multiple threads unseen in the overall pattern, the knots on the underside of the carpet.

This is why the effort to speak honestly is so important. Lies are usually attempts to make everything simpler—for the liar—than it really is, or ought to be.

In lying to others we end up lying to ourselves. We deny the importance of an event, or a person, and thus deprive ourselves of a part of our lives. Or we use one piece of the past or present to screen out another. Thus we lose faith even with our own lives.

The unconscious wants truth, as the body does. The complexity and fecundity of dreams come from the complexity and fecundity of the unconscious struggling to fulfill that desire. The complexity and fecundity of poetry come from the same struggle.

•   •   •

An honorable human relationship—that is, one in which two people have the right to use the word "love"—is a process, delicate, violent, often terrifying to both persons involved, a process of refining the truths they can tell each other.

It is important to do this because it breaks down human self-delusion and isolation.

It is important to do this because in so doing we do justice to our own complexity.

It is important to do this because we can count on so few people to go that hard way with us.

•　•　•

I come back to the question of women's honor. Truthfulness has not been considered important for women, as long as we have remained physically faithful to a man, or chaste.

We have been expected to lie with our bodies: to bleach, redden, unkink or curl our hair, pluck eyebrows, shave armpits, wear padding in various places or lace ourselves, take little steps, glaze finger and toe nails, wear clothes that emphasized our helplessness.

We have been required to tell different lies at different times, depending on what the men of the time needed to hear. The Victorian wife or the white southern lady, who were expected to have no sensuality, to "lie still"; the twentieth-century "free" woman who is expected to fake orgasms.

We have had the truth of our bodies withheld from us or distorted; we have been kept in ignorance of our most intimate places. Our instincts have been punished: clitoridectomies for "lustful" nuns or for "difficult" wives. It has been difficult, too, to know the lies of our complicity from the lies we believed.

The lie of the "happy marriage," of domesticity—we have been complicit, have acted out the fiction of a well-lived life, until the day we testify in court of rapes, beatings, psychic cruelties, public and private humiliations.

Patriarchal lying has manipulated women both through falsehood and through silence. Facts we needed have been withheld from us. False witness has been borne against us.

And so we must take seriously the question of truthfulness between women, truthfulness among women. As we cease to lie with our bodies, as we cease to take on faith what men have said about us, is a truly womanly idea of honor in the making?

•　•　•

Women have been forced to lie, for survival, to men. How to unlearn this among other women?

"Women have always lied to each other."
"Women have always whispered the truth to each other."
Both of these axioms are true.

"Women have always been divided against each other."
"Women have always been in secret collusion."
Both of these axioms are true.

In the struggle for survival we tell lies. To bosses, to prison guards, the police, men who have power over us, who legally own us and our children, lovers who need us as proof of their manhood.

There is a danger run by all powerless people: that we forget we are lying, or that lying becomes a weapon we carry over into relationships with people who do not have power over us.

•   •   •

I want to reiterate that when we talk about women and honor, or women and lying, we speak within the context of male lying, the lies of the powerful, the lie as false source of power.

Women have to think whether we want, in our relationships with each other, the kind of power that can be obtained through lying.

Women have been driven mad, "gaslighted," for centuries by the refutation of our experience and our instincts in a culture which validates only male experience. The truth of our bodies and our minds has been mystified to us. We therefore have a primary obligation to each other: not to undermine each others' sense of reality for the sake of expediency; not to gaslight each other.

Women have often felt insane when cleaving to the truth of our experience. Our future depends on the sanity of each of us, and we have a profound stake, beyond the personal, in the project of describing our reality as candidly and fully as we can to each other.

•   •   •

There are phrases which help us not to admit we are lying: "my privacy," "nobody's business but my own." The choices that underlie these phrases may indeed be justified; but we ought to think about the full meaning and consequences of such language.

Women's love for women has been represented almost entirely through silence and lies. The institution of heterosexuality has forced the lesbian to dissemble, or be labeled a pervert, a criminal, a sick or dangerous woman, etc., etc. The lesbian, then, has often been forced to lie, like the prostitute or the married women.

Does a life "in the closet"—lying, perhaps of necessity, about ourselves to bosses, landlords, clients, colleagues, family, because the law and public opinion are founded on a lie—does this, can it, spread into private life, so that lying (described as *discretion*) becomes an easy way to avoid conflict or complication? can it become a strategy so ingrained that it is used even with close friends and lovers?

Heterosexuality as an institution has also drowned in silence the erotic feelings between women. I myself lived half a lifetime in the lie of that denial. That silence makes us all, to some degree, into liars.

When a woman tells the truth she is creating the possibility for more truth around her.

• • •

The liar leads an existence of unutterable loneliness.

The liar is afraid.

But we are all afraid: without fear we become manic, hubristic, self-destructive. What is this particular fear that possesses the liar?

She is afraid that her own truths are not good enough.

She is afraid, not so much of prison guards or bosses, but of something unnamed within her.

The liar fears the void.

The void is not something created by patriarchy, or racism, or capitalism. It will not fade away with any of them. It is part of every woman.

"The dark core," Virginia Woolf named it, writing of her mother. The dark core. It is beyond personality; beyond who loves us or hates us.

We begin out of the void, out of darkness and emptiness. It is part of the cycle understood by the old pagan religions, that materialism denies. Out of death, rebirth; out of nothing, something.

The void is the creatrix, the matrix. It is not mere hollowness and anarchy. But in women it has been identified with lovelessness, barrenness, sterility. We have been urged to fill our "emptiness" with children. We are not supposed to go down into the darkness of the core.

Yet, if we can risk it, the something born of that nothing is the beginning of our truth.

The liar in her terror wants to fill up the void, with anything. Her lies are a denial of her fear; a way of maintaining control.

• • •

Why do we feel slightly crazy when we realize we have been lied to in a relationship?

We take so much of the universe on trust. You tell me: "In 1950 I lived on the north side of Beacon Street in Somerville." You tell me: "She and I were lovers, but for months now we have only been good friends." You tell me: "It is seventy degrees outside and the sun is shining." Because I love you, because there is not even a question of lying between us, I take these accounts of the universe on trust: your address twenty-five years ago, your relationship with someone I know only by sight, this morning's weather. I fling unconscious tendrils of belief, like slender green threads, across statements such as these, statements made so unequivocally, which have no tone or shadow of tentativeness. I build them into the mosaic of my world. I allow my universe to change in minute, significant ways, on the basis of things you have said to me, of my trust in you.

I also have faith that you are telling me things it is important I should know; that you do not conceal facts from me in an effort to spare me, or yourself, pain.

Or, at the very least, that you will say, "There are things I am not telling you."

When we discover that someone we trusted can be trusted no longer, it forces us to reexamine the universe, to question the whole instinct and concept of trust. For awhile, we are thrust back onto some bleak, jutting ledge, in a dark pierced by sheets of fire, swept by sheets of rain, in a world before kinship, or naming, or tenderness exist; we are brought close to formlessness.

• • •

The liar may resist confrontation, denying that she lied. Or she may use other language: forgetfulness, privacy, the protection of someone else. Or, she may bravely declare herself a coward. This allows her to go on lying, since that is what cowards do. She does not say, *I was afraid*, since this would open the question of other ways of handling her fear. It would open the question of what is actually feared.

She may say, *I didn't want to cause pain*. What she really did not want is to have to deal with the other's pain. The lie is a short-cut through another's personality.

•   •   •

Truthfulness, honor, is not something which springs ablaze of itself; it has to be created between people.

This is true in political situations. The quality and depth of the politics evolving from a group depends in very large part on their understanding of honor.

Much of what is narrowly termed "politics" seems to rest on a longing for certainty even at the cost of honesty, for an analysis which, once given, need not be reexamined. Such is the deadendedness—for women—of Marxism in our time.

Truthfulness anywhere means a heightened complexity. But it is a movement into evolution. Women are only beginning to uncover our own truths; many of us would be grateful for some rest in that struggle, would be glad just to lie down with the sherds we have painfully unearthed, and be satisfied with those. Often I feel this like an exhaustion in my own body.

The politics worth having, the relationships worth having, demand that we delve still deeper.

•   •   •

The possibilities that exist between two people, or among a group of people, are a kind of alchemy. They are the most interesting thing in life. The liar is someone who keeps losing sight of these possibilities.

When relationships are determined by manipulation, by the need for control, they may possess a dreary, bickering kind of drama, but they cease to be interesting. They are repetitious; the shock of human possibilities has ceased to reverberate through them.

When someone tells me a piece of the truth which has been withheld from me, and which I needed in order to see my life more clearly, it may bring acute pain, but it can also flood me with a cold, sea-sharp wash of relief. Often such truths come by accident, or from strangers.

It isn't that to have an honorable relationship with you, I have to understand everything, or tell you everything at once, or that I can know, beforehand, everything I need to tell you.

It means that most of the time I am eager, longing for the possibility of telling you. That these possibilities may seem frightening, but not destructive, to me. That I feel strong enough to hear your tentative and groping words. That we both know we are trying, all the time, to extend the possibilities of truth between us.

The possibility of life between us.

Compulsory Heterosexuality and Lesbian Existence (1980) †

FOREWORD (1983)

I want to say a little about the way "Compulsory Heterosexuality" was originally conceived and the context in which we are now living. It was written in part to challenge the erasure of lesbian existence from so much of scholarly feminist literature, an erasure which I felt (and feel) to be not just anti-lesbian, but anti-feminist in its consequences, and to distort the experience of heterosexual women as well. It was not written to widen divisions but to encourage heterosexual feminists to examine heterosexuality as a political institution which disempowers women—and to change it. I also hoped that other lesbians would feel the depth and breadth of woman identification and woman bonding that has run like a continuous though stifled theme through the heterosexual experience, and that this would become increasingly a politically activating impulse, not simply a validation of personal lives. I wanted the essay to suggest new kinds of criticism, to incite new questions in classrooms and academic journals, and to sketch, at least, some bridge over the gap between *lesbian* and *feminist*. I wanted, at the very least, for feminists to find it less possible to read, write, or teach from a perspective of unexamined heterocentricity.

Within the three years since I wrote "Compulsory Heterosexuality"— with this energy of hope and desire—the pressures to conform in a soci-

† Originally written in 1978 for the "Sexuality" issue of *Signs*, this essay was published there in 1980. In 1982 Antelope Publications reprinted it as part of a feminist pamphlet series. The foreword was written for the pamphlet. Notes to this essay are Rich's. This selection has been edited for publication here; asterisks indicate deletions.

ety increasingly conservative in mood have become more intense. The New Right's messages to women have been, precisely, that we are the emotional and sexual property of men, and that the autonomy and equality of women threaten family, religion, and state. The institutions by which women have traditionally been controlled—patriarchal motherhood, economic exploitation, the nuclear family, compulsory heterosexuality—are being strengthened by legislation, religious fiat, media imagery, and efforts at censorship. In a worsening economy, the single mother trying to support her children confronts the feminization of poverty which Joyce Miller of the National Coalition of Labor Union Women has named one of the major issues of the 1980s. The lesbian, unless in disguise, faces discrimination in hiring and harassment and violence in the street. Even within feminist-inspired institutions such as battered-women's shelters and Women's Studies programs, open lesbians are fired and others warned to stay in the closet. The retreat into sameness—assimilation for those who can manage it—is the most passive and debilitating of responses to political repression, economic insecurity, and a renewed open season on difference.

I want to note that documentation of male violence against women—within the home especially—has been accumulating rapidly in this period. At the same time, in the realm of literature which depicts woman bonding and woman identification as essential for female survival, a steady stream of writing and criticism has been coming from women of color in general and lesbians of color in particular—the latter group being even more profoundly erased in academic feminist scholarship by the double bias of racism and homophobia.[1]

There has recently been an intensified debate on female sexuality among feminists and lesbians, with lines often furiously and bitterly drawn, with

1. See, for example, Paula Gunn Allen, *The Sacred Hoop: Recovering the Feminine in American Indian Traditions* (Boston: Beacon, 1986); Beth Brant, ed., *A Gathering of Spirit: Writing and Art by North American Indian Women* (Montpelier, Vt.: Sinister Wisdom Books, 1984); Gloria Anzaldúa and Cherríe Moraga, eds., *This Bridge Called My Back: Writings by Radical Women of Color* (Watertown, Mass.: Persephone, 1981; distributed by Kitchen Table/Women of Color Press, Albany, N.Y.); J. R. Roberts, *Black Lesbians: An Annotated Bibliography* (Tallahassee, Fla.: Naiad, 1981); Barbara Smith, ed., *Home Girls: A Black Feminist Anthology* (Albany, N.Y.: Kitchen Table/Women of Color Press, 1984). As Lorraine Bethel and Barbara Smith pointed out in *Conditions 5: The Black Women's Issue* (1980), a great deal of fiction by Black women depicts primary relationships between women. I would like to cite here the work of Ama Ata Aidoo, Toni Cade Bambara, Buchi Emecheta, Bessie Head, Zora Neale Hurston, Alice Walker. Donna Allegra, Red Jordan Arobateau, Audre Lorde, Ann Allen Shockley, among others, write directly as Black lesbians. For fiction by other lesbians of color, see Elly Bulkin, ed., *Lesbian Fiction: An Anthology* (Watertown, Mass.: Persephone, 1981).

See also, for accounts of contemporary Jewish-lesbian existence, Evelyn Torton Beck, ed., *Nice Jewish Girls: A Lesbian Anthology* (Watertown, Mass.: Persephone, 1982; distributed by Crossing Press, Trumansburg, N.Y. 14886); Alice Bloch, *Lifetime Guarantee* (Watertown, Mass.: Persephone, 1982); and Melanie Kaye-Kantrowitz and Irena Klepfisz, eds., *The Tribe of Dina: a Jewish Women's Anthology* (Montpelier, Vt.: Sinister Wisdom Books, 1986).

The earliest formulation that I know of heterosexuality as an institution was in the lesbian-feminist paper *The Furies*, founded in 1971. For a collection of articles from that paper, see Nancy Myron and Charlotte Bunch, eds., *Lesbianism and the Women's Movement* (Oakland, Calif.: Diana Press, 1975; distributed by Crossing Press, Trumansburg, N.Y. 14886).

sadomasochism and *pornography* as key words which are variously defined according to who is talking. The depth of women's rage and fear regarding sexuality and its relation to power and pain is real, even when the dialogue sounds simplistic, self-righteous, or like parallel monologues.

Because of all these developments, there are parts of this essay that I would word differently, qualify, or expand if I were writing it today. But I continue to think that heterosexual feminists will draw political strength for change from taking a critical stance toward the ideology which *demands* heterosexuality, and that lesbians cannot assume that we are untouched by that ideology and the institutions founded upon it. There is nothing about such a critique that requires us to think of ourselves as victims, as having been brainwashed or totally powerless. Coercion and compulsion are among the conditions in which women have learned to recognize our strength. Resistance is a major theme in this essay and in the study of women's lives, if we know what we are looking for.

I

Biologically men have only one innate orientation—a sexual one that draws them to women,—while women have two innate orientations, sexual toward men and reproductive toward their young.[2]

I was a woman terribly vulnerable, critical, using femaleness as a sort of standard or yardstick to measure and discard men. Yes—something like that. I was an Anna who invited defeat from men without ever being conscious of it. (But I am conscious of it. And being conscious of it means I shall leave it all behind me and become—but what?) I was stuck fast in an emotion common to women of our time, that can turn them bitter, or Lesbian, or solitary. Yes, that Anna during that time was . . .

[Another blank line across the page:][3]

The bias of compulsory heterosexuality, through which lesbian experience is perceived on a scale ranging from deviant to abhorrent or simply rendered invisible, could be illustrated from many texts other than the two just preceding. The assumption made by Rossi, that women are "innately" sexually oriented only toward men, and that made by Lessing, that the lesbian is simply acting out of her bitterness toward men, are by no means theirs alone; these assumptions are widely current in literature and in the social sciences.

I am concerned here with two other matters as well: first, how and why women's choice of women as passionate comrades, life partners, co-workers, lovers, community has been crushed, invalidated, forced

2. Alice Rossi, "Children and Work in the Lives of Women," paper delivered at the University of Arizona, Tuscon, February 1976.
3. Doris Lessing, *The Golden Notebook*, 1962 (New York: Bantam, 1977), p. 480.

into hiding and disguise; and second, the virtual or total neglect of lesbian existence in a wide range of writings, including feminist scholarship. Obviously there is a connection here. I believe that much feminist theory and criticism is stranded on this shoal.

My organizing impulse is the belief that it is not enough for feminist thought that specifically lesbian texts exist. Any theory or cultural/political creation that treats lesbian existence as a marginal or less "natural" phenomenon, as mere "sexual preference," or as the mirror image of either heterosexual or male homosexual relations is profoundly weakened thereby, whatever its other contributions. Feminist theory can no longer afford merely to voice a toleration of "lesbianism" as an "alternative life style" or make token allusion to lesbians. A feminist critique of compulsory heterosexual orientation for women is long overdue. In this exploratory paper, I shall try to show why.

* * *

II

If women are the earliest sources of emotional caring and physical nurture for both female and male children, it would seem logical, from a feminist perspective at least, to pose the following questions: whether the search for love and tenderness in both sexes does not originally lead toward women; *why in fact women would ever redirect that search*; why species survival, the means of impregnation, and emotional/erotic relationships should ever have become so rigidly identified with each other; and why such violent strictures should be found necessary to enforce women's total emotional, erotic loyalty and subservience to men. I doubt that enough feminist scholars and theorists have taken the pains to acknowledge the societal forces which wrench women's emotional and erotic energies away from themselves and other women and from woman-identified values. These forces, as I shall try to show, range from literal physical enslavement to the disguising and distorting of possible options.

I do not assume that mothering by women is a "sufficient cause" of lesbian existence. But the issue of mothering by women has been much in the air of late, usually accompanied by the view that increased parenting by men would minimize antagonism between the sexes and equalize the sexual imbalance of power of males over females. These discussions are carried on without reference to compulsory heterosexuality as a phenomenon, let alone as an ideology. I do not wish to psychologize here, but rather to identify sources of male power. I believe large numbers of men could, in fact, undertake child care on a large scale without radically altering the balance of male power in a male-identified society.

In her essay "The Origin of the Family," Kathleen Gough lists eight characteristics of male power in archaic and contemporary societies which I would like to use as a framework: "men's ability to deny women sexuality or to force it upon them; to command or exploit their labor to control their produce; to control or rob them of their children; to confine them physically and prevent their movement; to use them as objects in male transactions; to cramp their creativeness; or to withhold from them large areas of the society's knowledge and cultural attainments."[4] (Gough does not perceive these power characteristics as specifically enforcing heterosexuality, only as producing sexual inequality.) Below, Gough's words appear in italics; the elaboration of each of her categories, in brackets, is my own.

Characteristics of male power include *the power of men*

1. *to deny women* [their own] *sexuality*—[by means of clitoridectomy and infibulation; chastity belts; punishment, including death, for female adultery; punishment, including death, for lesbian sexuality; psychoanalytic denial of the clitoris; strictures against masturbation; denial of maternal and postmenopausal sensuality; unnecessary hysterectomy; pseudolesbian images in the media and literature; closing of archives and destruction of documents relating to lesbian existence]

2. *or to force it* [male sexuality] *upon them*—[by means of rape (including marital rape) and wife beating; father-daughter, brother-sister incest; the socialization of women to feel that male sexual "drive" amounts to a right;[5] idealization of heterosexual romance in art, literature, the media, advertising, etc.; child marriage; arranged marriage; prostitution; the harem; psychoanalytic doctrines of frigidity and vaginal orgasm; pornographic depictions of women responding pleasurably to sexual violence and humiliation (a subliminal message being that sadistic heterosexuality is more "normal" than sensuality between women)]

3. *to command or exploit their labor to control their produce*—[by means of the institutions of marriage and motherhood as unpaid production; the horizontal segregation of women in paid employment; the decoy of the upwardly mobile token woman; male control of abortion, contraception, sterilization, and childbirth; pimping; female infanticide, which robs mothers of daughters and contributes to generalized devaluation of women]

4. *to control or rob them of their children*—[by means of father right and "legal kidnapping";[6] enforced sterilization; systematized infanticide; seizure of children from lesbian mothers by the courts;

4. Kathleen Gough, "The Origin of the Family," in *Toward an Anthropology of Women*, ed. Rayna [Rapp] Reiter (New York: Monthly Review Press, 1975), pp. 60–70.
5. Kathleen Barry, *Female Sexual Slavery* (Englewood Cliffs, NJ: Prentice-Hall, 1979) pp. 216–219.
6. Anna Demeter, *Legal Kidnapping* (Boston: Beacon, 1977), pp. xx, 126–128.

the malpractice of male obstetrics; use of the mother as "token torturer"[7] in genital mutilation or in binding the daughter's feet (or mind) to fit her for marriage]

5. *to confine them physically and prevent their movement*—[by means of rape as terrorism, keeping women off the streets; purdah; foot binding; atrophying of women's athletic capabilities; high heels and "feminine" dress codes in fashions; the veil; sexual harassment on the streets; horizontal segregation of women in employment; prescriptions for "full-time" mothering at home; enforced economic dependence of wives]

6. *to use them as objects in male transactions*—[use of women as "gifts"; bride price; pimping; arranged marriage; use of women as entertainers to facilitate male deals—e.g., wife-hostess, cocktail waitress required to dress for male sexual titillation, call girls, "bunnies," geisha, *kisaeng* prostitutes, secretaries]

7. *to cramp their creativeness*—[witch persecutions as campaigns against midwives and female healers, and as pogrom against independent, "unassimilated" women;[8] definition of male pursuits as more valuable than female within any culture, so that cultural values become the embodiment of male subjectivity; restriction of female self-fulfillment to marriage and motherhood; sexual exploitation of women by male artists and teachers; the social and economic disruption of women's creative aspirations;[9] erasure of female tradition][1]

8. *to withhold from them large areas of the society's knowledge and cultural attainments*—[by means of noneducation of females; the "Great Silence" regarding women and particularly lesbian existence in history and culture;[2] sex-role tracking which deflects women from science, technology, and other "masculine" pursuits; male social/professional bonding which excludes women; discrimination against women in the professions]

These are some of the methods by which male power is manifested and maintained. Looking at the schema, what surely impresses itself is the fact that we are confronting not a simple maintenance of inequality and property possession, but a pervasive cluster of forces, ranging from

7. Mary Daly, *Gyn/Ecology: The Metaethics of Radical Feminism* (Boston: Beacon, 1978) pp. 139–141, pp. 163–165.
8. Barbara Ehrenreich and Deirdre English, *Witches, Midwives and Nurses: A History of Women Healers* (Old Westbury, N.Y.: Feminist Press, 1973); Andrea Dworkin, *Woman Hating* (New York: Dutton, 1974), pp. 118–154; Daly, pp. 178–222.
9. See Virginia Woolf, *A Room of One's Own* (London: Hogarth, 1929), and *id.*, *Three Guineas* (New York: Harcourt Brace, [1938] 1966); Tillie Olsen, *Silences* (Boston: Delacorte, 1978); Michelle Cliff, "The Resonance of Interruption," *Chrysalis: A Magazine of Women's Culture* 8 (1979): 29–37.
1. Mary Daly, *Beyond God the Father* (Boston: Beacon, 1973), pp. 347–351; Olsen, pp. 22–46.
2. Daly, *Beyond God the Father*, p. 93.

physical brutality to control of consciousness, which suggests that an enormous potential counterforce is having to be restrained.

Some of the forms by which male power manifests itself are more easily recognizable as enforcing heterosexuality on women than are others. Yet each one I have listed adds to the cluster of forces within which women have been convinced that marriage and sexual orientation toward men are inevitable—even if unsatisfying or oppressive—components of their lives. The chastity belt; child marriage; erasure of lesbian existence (except as exotic and perverse) in art, literature, film; idealization of heterosexual romance and marriage—these are some fairly obvious forms of compulsion, the first two exemplifying physical force, the second two control of consciousness. While clitoridectomy has been assailed by feminists as a form of woman torture,[3] Kathleen Barry first pointed out that it is not simply a way of turning the young girl into a "marriageable" woman through brutal surgery. It intends that women in the intimate proximity of polygynous marriage will not form sexual relationships with each other, that—from a male, genital-fetishist perspective—female erotic connections, even in a sex-segregated situation, will be literally excised.[4]

The function of pornography as an influence on consciousness is a major public issue of our time, when a multibillion-dollar industry has the power to disseminate increasingly sadistic, women-degrading visual images. But even so-called soft-core pornography and advertising depict women as objects of sexual appetite devoid of emotional context, without individual meaning or personality—essentially as a sexual commodity to be consumed by males. (So-called lesbian pornography, created for the male voyeuristic eye, is equally devoid of emotional context or individual personality.) The most pernicious message relayed by pornography is that women are natural sexual prey to men and love it, that sexuality and violence are congruent, and that for women sex is essentially masochistic, humiliation pleasurable, physical abuse erotic. But along with this message comes another, not always recognized: that enforced submission and the use of cruelty, if played out in heterosexual pairing, is sexually "normal," while sensuality between women, including erotic mutuality and respect, is "queer," "sick," and either pornographic in itself or not very exciting compared with the sexuality of whips and bondage.[5] Pornography does not simply create a climate in which sex and violence are interchangeable; *it widens the range of behavior*

3. Fran P. Hosken, "The Violence of Power: Genital Mutilation of Females," *Heresies: A Feminist Journal of Art and Politics* 6 (1979): 28–35; Diana Russell and Nicole van de Ven, eds., *Proceedings of the Informational Tribunal of Crimes Against Women* (Millbrae, CA: Les Femmes, 1976) pp. 194–195.

[A.R., 1986: See especially "Circumcision of Girls," in Nawal El Saadawi, *The Hidden Face of Eve: Women in the Arab World* (Boston: Beacon, 1982), pp. 33–43.]
4. Barry, pp. 163–164.
5. The issue of "lesbian sadomasochism" needs to be examined in terms of dominant cultures' teachings about the relation of sex and violence. I believe this to be another example of the "double life" of women.

considered acceptable from men in heterosexual intercourse—behavior which reiteratively strips women of their autonomy, dignity, and sexual potential, including the potential of loving and being loved by women in mutuality and integrity.

In her brilliant study *Sexual Harassment of Working Women: A Case of Sex Discrimination*, Catharine A. MacKinnon delineates the intersection of compulsory heterosexuality and economics. Under capitalism, women are horizontally segregated by gender and occupy a structurally inferior position in the workplace. This is hardly news, but MacKinnon raises the question why, even if capitalism "requires some collection of individuals to occupy low-status, low-paying positions . . . such persons must be biologically female," and goes on to point out that "the fact that male employers often do not hire qualified women, *even when they could pay them less than men* suggests that more than the profit motive is implicated" [emphasis added].[6] She cites a wealth of material documenting the fact that women are not only segregated in low-paying service jobs (as secretaries, domestics, nurses, typists, telephone operators, child-care workers, waitresses), but that "sexualization of the woman" is part of the job. Central and intrinsic to the economic realities of women's lives is the requirement that women will "market sexual attractiveness to men, who tend to hold the economic power and position to enforce their predilections." And MacKinnon documents that "sexual harassment perpetuates the interlocked structure by which women have been kept sexually in thrall to men at the bottom of the labor market. Two forces of American society converge: men's control over women's sexuality and capital's control over employees' work lives."[7] Thus, women in the workplace are at the mercy of sex as power in a vicious circle. Economically disadvantaged, women—whether waitresses or professors—endure sexual harassment to keep their jobs and learn to behave in a complaisantly and ingratiatingly heterosexual manner because they discover this is their true qualification for employment, whatever the job description. And, MacKinnon notes, the woman who too decisively resists sexual overtures in the workplace is accused of being "dried up" and sexless, or lesbian. This raises a specific difference between the experiences of lesbians and homosexual men. A lesbian, closeted on her job because of heterosexist prejudice, is not simply forced into denying the truth of her outside relationships or private life. Her job depends on her pretending to be not merely heterosexual, but a heterosexual *woman* in terms of dressing and playing the feminine, deferential role required of "real" women.

MacKinnon raises radical questions as to the qualitative differences between sexual harassment, rape, and ordinary heterosexual inter-

─Catharine A. MacKinnon, *Sexual Harassment of Working Women: A Case of Sex Discrimi-*
─*tion* (New Haven, Conn.: Yale University Press, 1979), pp. 15–16.
─, p. 174.

course. ("As one accused rapist put it, he hadn't used 'any more force than is usual for males during the preliminaries.' ") She criticizes Susan Brownmiller[8] for separating rape from the mainstream of daily life and for her unexamined premise that "rape is violence, intercourse is sexuality," removing rape from the sexual sphere altogether. Most crucially she argues that "taking rape from the realm of 'the sexual,' placing it in the realm of 'the violent,' allows one to be against it without raising any questions about the extent to which the institution of heterosexuality has defined force as a normal part of 'the preliminaries.' "[9] "Never is it asked whether, under conditions of male supremacy, the notion of 'consent' has any meaning."[1]

The fact is that the workplace, among other social institutions, is a place where women have learned to accept male violation of their psychic and physical boundaries as the price of survival; where women have been educated—no less than by romantic literature or by pornography—to perceive themselves as sexual prey. A woman seeking to escape such casual violations along with economic disadvantage may well turn to marriage as a form of hoped-for protection, while bringing into marriage neither social nor economic power, thus entering that institution also from a disadvantaged position. MacKinnon finally asks:

> What if inequality is built into the social conceptions of male and female sexuality, of masculinity and femininity, of sexiness and heterosexual attractiveness? Incidents of sexual harassment suggest that male sexual desire itself may be aroused by female vulnerability. . . . Men feel they can take advantage, so they want to, so they do. Examination of sexual harassment, precisely because the episodes appear commonplace, forces one to confront the fact that sexual intercourse normally occurs between economic (as well as physical) unequals . . . the apparent legal requirement that violations of women's sexuality appear out of the ordinary before they will be punished helps prevent women from defining the ordinary conditions of their own consent.[2]

Given the nature and extent of heterosexual pressures—the daily "eroticization of women's subordination," as MacKinnon phrases it[3]— I question the more or less psychoanalytic perspective (suggested by such writers as Karen Horney, H. R. Hayes, Wolfgang Lederer, and, most recently, Dorothy Dinnerstein) that the male need to control women

8. Susan Brownmiller, *Against our Will: Men, Women and Rape* (New York: Simon and Schuster, 1975).
9. MacKinnon, p. 219. Susan Schecter writes: "The push for heterosexual union at whatever cost is so intense that . . . it has become a cultural force of its own that creates battering. The ideology of romantic love and its jealous possession of the partner as property provide the masquerade for what can become severe abuse" (*Aegis: Magazine on Ending Violence against Women* [July–August 1979]: 50–51).
1. MacKinnon, p. 298.
2. *Ibid.*, p. 220.
3. *Ibid.*, p. 221.

sexually results from some primal male "fear of women" and of women's sexual insatiability. It seems more probable that men really fear not that they will have women's sexual appetites forced on them or that women want to smother and devour them, but that women could be indifferent to them altogether, that men could be allowed sexual and emotional—therefore economic—access to women *only* on women's terms, otherwise being left on the periphery of the matrix.

The means of assuring male sexual access to women have recently received searching investigation by Kathleen Barry.[4] She documents extensive and appalling evidence for the existence, on a very large scale, of international female slavery, the institution once known as "white slavery" but which in fact has involved, and at this very moment involves, women of every race and class. In the theoretical analysis derived from her research, Barry makes the connection between all enforced conditions under which women live subject to men: prostitution, marital rape, father-daughter and brother-sister incest, wife beating, pornography, bride price, the selling of daughters, purdah, and genital mutilation. She sees the rape paradigm—where the victim of sexual assault is held responsible for her own victimization—as leading to the rationalization and acceptance of other forms of enslavement where the woman is presumed to have "chosen" her fate, to embrace it passively, or to have courted it perversely through rash or unchaste behavior. On the contrary, Barry maintains, "female sexual slavery is present in ALL situations where women or girls cannot change the conditions of their existence; where regardless of how they got into those conditions, e.g., social pressure, economic hardship, misplaced trust or the longing for affection, they cannot get out; and where they are subject to sexual violence and exploitation."[5] She provides a spectrum of concrete examples, not only as to the existence of a widespread international traffic in women, but also as to how this operates—whether in the form of a "Minnesota pipeline" funneling blonde, blue-eyed midwestern runaways to Times Square, or the purchasing of young women out of rural poverty in Latin America or Southeast Asia, or the providing of *maisons d'abattage* for migrant workers in the eighteenth arrondissement of Paris. Instead of "blaming the victim" or trying to diagnose her presumed pathology, Barry turns her floodlights on the pathology of sex colonization itself, the ideology of "cultural sadism" represented by the pornography industry and by the overall identification of women primarily as "sexual beings whose responsibility is the sexual service of men."[6]

Barry delineates what she names a "sexual domination perspective"

4. Barry, *op. cit.*
   [A.R., 1986: See also Kathleen Barry, Charlotte Bunch, and Shirley Castley, eds., *International Feminism: Networking against Female Sexual Slavery* (New York: International Women's Tribune Center, 1984).]

5. Barry, p. 33.
6. *Ibid.*, p. 103.

COMPULSORY HETEROSEXUALITY AND LESBIAN EXISTENCE 213

through whose lens sexual abuse and terrorism of women by men has been rendered almost invisible by treating it as natural and inevitable. From its point of view, women are expendable as long as the sexual and emotional needs of the male can be satisfied. To replace this perspective of domination with a universal standard of basic freedom for women from gender-specific violence, from constraints on movement, and from male right of sexual and emotional access is the political purpose of her book. Like Mary Daly in *Gyn/Ecology*, Barry rejects structuralist and other cultural-relativist rationalizations for sexual torture and anti-woman violence. In her opening chapter, she asks of her readers that they refuse all handy escapes into ignorance and denial. "The only way we can come out of hiding, break through our paralyzing defenses, is to know it all—the full extent of sexual violence and domination of women. . . . In *knowing*, in facing directly, we can learn to chart our course out of this oppression, by envisioning and creating a world which will preclude sexual slavery."[7]

"Until we name the practice, give conceptual definition and form to it, illustrate its life over time and in space, those who are its most obvious victims will also not be able to name it or define their experience."

But women are all, in different ways and to different degrees, its victims; and part of the problem with naming and conceptualizing female sexual slavery is, as Barry clearly sees, compulsory heterosexuality.[8] Compulsory heterosexuality simplifies the task of the procurer and pimp in world-wide prostitution rings and "eros centers," while, in the privacy of the home, it leads the daughter to "accept" incest/rape by her father, the mother to deny that it is happening, the battered wife to stay on with an abusive husband. "Befriending or love" is a major tactic of the procurer, whose job it is to turn the runaway or the confused young girl over to the pimp for seasoning. The ideology of heterosexual romance, beamed at her from childhood out of fairy tales, television, films, advertising, popular songs, wedding pageantry, is a tool ready to the procurer's hand and one which he does not hesitate to use, as Barry documents. Early female indoctrination in "love" as an emotion may be largely a Western concept; but a more universal ideology concerns the primacy and uncontrollability of a male sexual drive. This is one of many insights offered by Barry's work:

> As sexual power is learned by adolescent boys through the social experience of their sex drive, so do girls learn that the locus of sexual power is male. Given the importance placed on the male sex drive in the socialization of girls as well as boys, early adoles-

7. *Ibid.*, p. 5.
8. *Ibid.*, p. 100.
  [A.R., 1986: This statement has been taken as claiming that "all women are victims" purely and simply, or that "all heterosexuality equals sexual slavery." I would say, rather, that all women are affected, though differently, by dehumanizing attitudes and practices directed at women as a group.]

cence is probably the first significant phase of male identification
in a girl's life and development. . . . As a young girl becomes aware
of her own increasing sexual feelings . . . she turns away from her
heretofore primary relationships with girlfriends. As they become
secondary to her, recede in importance in her life, her own identity
also assumes a secondary role and she grows into male identifica-
tion.[9]

We still need to ask why some women never, even temporarily, turn
away from "heretofore primary relationships" with other females. And
why does male identification—the casting of one's social, political, and
intellectual allegiances with men—exist among lifelong sexual lesbians?
Barry's hypothesis throws us among new questions, but it clarifies the
diversity of forms in which compulsory heterosexuality presents itself. In
the mystique of the overpowering, all-conquering male sex drive, the
penis-with-a-life-of-its-own, is rooted the law of male sex right to women,
which justifies prostitution as a universal cultural assumption on the one
hand, while defending sexual slavery within the family on the basis of
"family privacy and cultural uniqueness" on the other.[1] The adolescent
male sex drive, which, as both young women and men are taught, once
triggered cannot take responsibility for itself or take no for an answer,
becomes, according to Barry, the norm and rationale for adult male
sexual behavior: a condition of *arrested sexual development*. Women
learn to accept as natural the inevitability of this "drive" because they
receive it as dogma. Hence, marital rape; hence, the Japanese wife
resignedly packing her husband's suitcase for a weekend in the *kisaeng*
brothels of Taiwan; hence, the psychological as well as economic imbal-
ance of power between husband and wife, male employer and female
worker, father and daughter, male professor and female student.

The effect of male identification means

internalizing the values of the colonizer and actively participating
in carrying out the colonization of one's self and one's sex. . . .
Male identification is the act whereby women place men above
women, including themselves, in credibility, status, and impor-
tance in most situations, regardless of the comparative quality the
women may bring to the situation. . . . Interaction with women is
seen as a lesser form of relating on every level.[2]

What deserves further exploration is the doublethink many women engage
in and from which no woman is permanently and utterly free: However
woman-to-woman relationships, female support networks, a female and
feminist value system are relied on and cherished, indoctrination in male
credibility and status can still create synapses in thought, denial of feel-

9. *Ibid.*, p. 218.
1. *Ibid.*, p. 140.
2. *Ibid.*, p. 172.

ing, wishful thinking, a profound sexual and intellectual confusion.[3] I quote here from a letter I received the day I was writing this passage: "I have had very bad relationships with men—I am now in the midst of a very painful separation. I am trying to find my strength through women—without my friends, I could not survive." How many times a day do women speak words like these or think them or write them, and how often does the synapse reassert itself?

Barry summarizes her findings:

> Considering the arrested sexual development that is understood to be normal in the male population, and considering the numbers of men who are pimps, procurers, members of slavery gangs, corrupt officials participating in this traffic, owners, operators, employees of brothels and lodging and entertainment facilities, pornography purveyors, associated with prostitution, wife beaters, child molesters, incest perpetrators, johns (tricks) and rapists, one cannot but be momentarily stunned by the enormous male population engaging in female sexual slavery. The huge number of men engaged in these practices should be cause for declaration of an international emergency, a crisis in sexual violence. But what should be cause for alarm is instead accepted as normal sexual intercourse.[4]

Susan Cavin, in a rich and provocative, if highly speculative, dissertation, suggests that patriarchy becomes possible when the original female band, which includes children but ejects adolescent males, becomes invaded and outnumbered by males; that not patriarchal marriage, but the rape of the mother by the son, becomes the first act of male domination. The entering wedge, or leverage, which allows this to happen is not just a simple change in sex ratios; it is also the mother-child bond, manipulated by adolescent males in order to remain within the matrix past the age of exclusion. Maternal affection is used to establish male right of sexual access, which, however, must ever after be held by force (or through control of consciousness) since the original deep adult bonding is that of woman for woman.[5] I find this hypothesis extremely suggestive, since one form of false consciousness which serves compulsory heterosexuality is the maintenance of a mother-son relationship between women and men, including the demand that women provide maternal solace, nonjudgmental nurturing, and compassion for their

---

3. Elsewhere I have suggested that male identification has been a powerful source of white women's racism and that it has often been women already seen as "disloyal" to male codes and systems who have actively battled against it (Adrienne Rich, "Disloyal to Civilization: Feminism, Racism, Gynephobia," in *On Lies, Secrets, and Silence: Selected Prose, 1966–1978* [New York: W. W. Norton, 1979]).
4. Barry, p. 220.
5. Susan Cavin, "Lesbian Origins" (Ph.D. diss., Rutgers University, 1978), unpublished, ch. 6. [A.R., 1986: This dissertation was recently published as *Lesbian Origins* (San Francisco: Ism Press, 1986).]

harassers, rapists, and batterers (as well as for men who passively vam-
pirize them).

But whatever its origins, when we look hard and clearly at the extent
and elaboration of measures designed to keep women within a male
sexual purlieu, it becomes an inescapable question whether the issue
feminists have to address is not simple "gender inequality" nor the dom-
ination of culture by males nor mere "taboos against homosexuality,"
but the enforcement of heterosexuality for women as a means of assuring
male right of physical, economic, and emotional access.[6] One of many
means of enforcement is, of course, the rendering invisible of the lesbian
possibility, an engulfed continent which rises fragmentedly into view
from time to time only to become submerged again. Feminist research
and theory that contribute to lesbian invisibility or marginality are actually
working against the liberation and empowerment of women as a group.[7]

The assumption that "most women are innately heterosexual" stands
as a theoretical and political stumbling block for feminism. It remains a
tenable assumption partly because lesbian existence has been written out
of history or catalogued under disease, partly because it has been treated
as exceptional rather than intrinsic, partly because to acknowledge that
for women heterosexuality may not be a "preference" at all but some-
thing that has had to be imposed, managed, organized, propagandized,
and maintained by force is an immense step to take if you consider
yourself freely and "innately" heterosexual. Yet the failure to examine
heterosexuality as an institution is like failing to admit that the economic
system called capitalism or the caste system of racism is maintained by a
variety of forces, including both physical violence and false conscious-
ness. To take the step of questioning heterosexuality as a "preference"
or "choice" for women—and to do the intellectual and emotional work
that follows—will call for a special quality of courage in heterosexually
identified feminists, but I think the rewards will be great: a freeing-up of
thinking, the exploring of new paths, the shattering of another great
silence, new clarity in personal relationships.

6. For my perception of heterosexuality as an economic institution I am indebted to Lisa Leghorn
and Katherine Parker, who allowed me to read the unpublished manuscript of their book
Woman's Worth: Sexual Economics and the World of Women (London and Boston: Routledge
& Kegan Paul, 1981).
7. I would suggest that lesbian existence has been most recognized and tolerated where it has
resembled a "deviant" version of heterosexuality—e.g., where lesbians have, like Stein and
Toklas, played heterosexual roles (or seemed to in public) and have been chiefly identified with
male culture. See also Claude E. Schaeffer, "The Kuterai Female Berdache: Courier, Guide,
Prophetess and Warrior," *Ethnohistory* 12, no. 3 (Summer 1965): 193–236. (Berdache: "an
individual of a definite physiological sex [m. or f.] who assumes the role and status of the
opposite sex and who is viewed by the community as being of one sex physiologically but as
having assumed the role and status of the opposite sex" [Schaeffer, p. 231].) Lesbian existence
has also been relegated to an upper-class phenomenon, an elite decadence (as in the fascina-
tion with Paris salon lesbians such as Renée Vivien and Natalie Clifford Barney), to the obscur-
ing of such "common women" as Judy Grahn depicts in her *The Work of a Common Woman*
(Oakland, Calif: Diana Press, 1978) and *True to Life Adventure Stories* (Oakland, Calif.: Diana
Press, 1978).

III

I have chosen to use the terms *lesbian existence* and *lesbian continuum* because the word *lesbianism* has a clinical and limiting ring. *Lesbian existence* suggests both the fact of the historical presence of lesbians and our continuing creation of the meaning of that existence. I mean the term *lesbian continuum* to include a range—through each woman's life and throughout history—of woman-identified experience, not simply the fact that a woman has had or consciously desired genital sexual experience with another woman. If we expand it to embrace many more forms of primary intensity between and among women, including the sharing of a rich inner life, the bonding against male tyranny, the giving and receiving of practical and political support, if we can also hear it in such associations as *marriage resistance* and the "haggard" behavior identified by Mary Daly (obsolete meanings: "intractable," "willful," "wanton," and "unchaste," "a woman reluctant to yield to wooing"),[8] we begin to grasp breadths of female history and psychology which have lain out of reach as a consequence of limited, mostly clinical, definitions of *lesbianism*.

Lesbian existence comprises both the breaking of a taboo and the rejection of a compulsory way of life. It is also a direct or indirect attack on male right of access to women. But it is more than these, although we may first begin to perceive it as a form of naysaying to patriarchy, an act of resistance. It has, of course, included isolation, self-hatred, breakdown, alcoholism, suicide, and intrawoman violence; we romanticize at our peril what it means to love and act against the grain, and under heavy penalties; and lesbian existence has been lived (unlike, say, Jewish or Catholic existence) without access to any knowledge of a tradition, a continuity, a social underpinning. The destruction of records and memorabilia and letters documenting the realities of lesbian existence must be taken very seriously as a means of keeping heterosexuality compulsory for women, since what has been kept from our knowledge is joy, sensuality, courage, and community, as well as guilt, self-betrayal, and pain.[9]

Lesbians have historically been deprived of a political existence through "inclusion" as female versions of male homosexuality. To equate lesbian existence with male homosexuality because each is stigmatized is to erase female reality once again. Part of the history of lesbian existence is, obviously, to be found where lesbians, lacking a coherent female com-

8. Daly, *Gyn/Ecology*, p. 15.
9. "In a hostile world in which women are not supposed to survive except in relation with and in service to men, entire communities of women are simply erased. History tends to bury what it seeks to reject" (Blanche W. Cook, " 'Women Alone Stir My Imagination': Lesbianism and the Cultural Tradition," *Signs: Journal of Women in Culture and Society* 4, no. 4 [Summer 1979]: 719–720). The Lesbian Herstory Archives in New York City is one attempt to preserve contemporary documents on lesbian existence—a project of enormous value and meaning, working against the continuing censorship and obliteration of relationships, networks, communities in other archives and elsewhere in the culture.

munity, have shared a kind of social life and common cause with homo-
sexual men. But there are differences: women's lack of economic and
cultural privilege relative to men; qualitative differences in female and
male relationships—for example, the patterns of anonymous sex among
male homosexuals, and the pronounced ageism in male homosexual
standards of sexual attractiveness. I perceive the lesbian experience as
being, like motherhood, a profoundly *female* experience, with particular
oppressions, meanings, and potentialities we cannot comprehend as long
as we simply bracket it with other sexually stigmatized existences. Just as
the term *parenting* serves to conceal the particular and significant reality
of being a parent who is actually a mother, the term *gay* may serve the
purpose of blurring the very outlines we need to discern, which are of
crucial value for feminism and for the freedom of women as a group.[1]

As the term *lesbian* has been held to limiting, clinical associations in
its patriarchal definition, female friendship and comradeship have been
set apart from the erotic, thus limiting the erotic itself. But as we deepen
and broaden the range of what we define as lesbian existence, as we
delineate a lesbian continuum, we begin to discover the erotic in female
terms: as that which is unconfined to any single part of the body or solely
to the body itself; as an energy not only diffuse but, as Audre Lorde has
described it, omnipresent in "the sharing of joy, whether physical, emo-
tional, psychic," and in the sharing of work; as the empowering joy
which "makes us less willing to accept powerlessness, or those other
supplied states of being which are not native to me, such as resignation,
despair, self-effacement, depression, self-denial."[2] In another context,
writing of women and work, I quoted the autobiographical passage in
which the poet H.D. described how her friend Bryher supported her in
persisting with the visionary experience which was to shape her mature
work:

> I knew that this experience, this writing-on-the-wall before me, could
> not be shared with anyone except the girl who stood so bravely there
> beside me. This girl said without hestitation, "Go on." It was she
> really who had the detachment and integrity of the Pythoness of
> Delphi. But it was I, battered and dissociated . . . who was seeing
> the pictures, and who was reading the writing or granted the inner
> vision. Or perhaps, in some sense, we were "seeing" it together, for
> without her, admittedly, I could not have gone on.[3]

1. [A.R., 1986: The shared historical and spiritual "crossover" functions of lesbians and gay men
   in cultures past and present are traced by Judy Grahn in *Another Mother Tongue: Gay Words,
   Gay Worlds* (Boston: Beacon, 1984). I now think we have much to learn both from the uniquely
   female aspects of lesbian existence and from the complex "gay" identity we share with gay
   men.]
2. Audre Lorde, "Uses of the Erotic: The Erotic as Power," in *Sister Outsider* (Trumansburg,
   N.Y.: Crossing Press, 1984).
3. Adrienne Rich, "Conditions for Work: The Common World of Women," in *On Lies, Secrets,
   and Silence*, p. 209; H.D., *Tribute to Freud* (Oxford: Carcanet, 1971), pp. 50–54.

If we consider the possibility that all women—from the infant suck-ling at her mother's breast, to the grown woman experiencing orgasmic sensations while suckling her own child, perhaps recalling her mother's milk smell in her own, to two women, like Virginia Woolf's Chloe and Olivia, who share a laboratory,[4] to the woman dying at ninety, touched and handled by women—exist on a lesbian continuum, we can see our-selves as moving in and out of this continuum, whether we identify ourselves as lesbian or not.

We can then connect aspects of woman identification as diverse as the impudent, intimate girl friendships of eight or nine year olds and the banding together of those women of the twelfth and fifteenth centuries known as Beguines who "shared houses, rented to one another, bequeathed houses to their room-mates . . . in cheap subdivided houses in the artisans' area of town," who "practiced Christian virtue on their own, dressing and living simply and not associating with men," who earned their livings as spinsters, bakers, nurses, or ran schools for young girls, and who managed—until the Church forced them to disperse—to live independent both of marriage and of conventual restrictions.[5] It allows us to connect these women with the more celebrated "Lesbians" of the women's school around Sappho of the seventh century B.C., with the secret sororities and economic networks reported among African women, and with the Chinese marriage-resistance sisterhoods—com-munities of women who refused marriage or who, if married, often refused to consummate their marriages and soon left their husbands, the only women in China who were not footbound and who, Agnes Smedley tells us, welcomed the births of daughters and organized successful women's strikes in the silk mills.[6] It allows us to connect and compare disparate individual instances of marriage resistance: for example, the strategies available to Emily Dickinson, a nineteenth-century white woman genius, with the strategies available to Zora Neale Hurston, a twentieth-century Black woman genius. Dickinson never married, had tenuous intellectual friendships with men, lived self-convented in her genteel father's house in Amherst, and wrote a lifetime of passionate letters to her sister-in-law Sue Gilbert and a smaller group of such letters to her friend Kate Scott Anthon. Hurston married twice but soon left each

4. Woolf, A Room of One's Own, p. 126.
5. Gracia Clark, "The Beguines: A Mediaeval Women's Community," Quest: A Feminist Quar-terly 1, no. 4 (1975): 73–80.
6. See Denise Paulmé, ed., Women of Tropical Africa (Berkeley: University of California Press, 1963), pp. 7, 266–267. Some of these sororities are described as "a kind of defensive syndicate against the male element," their aims being "to offer concerted resistance to an oppressive patriarchate," "independence in relation to one's husband and with regard to motherhood, mutual aid, satisfaction of personal revenge." See also Audre Lorde, "Scratching the Surface: Some Notes on Barriers to Women and Loving," in Sister Outsider, pp. 45–52; Marjorie Topley, "Marriage Resistance in Rural Kwangtung," in Women in Chinese Society, ed. M. Wolf and R. Witke (Stanford, Calif.: Stanford University Press, 1978), pp. 67–89; Agnes Smedley, Portraits of Chinese Women in Revolution, ed. J. MacKinnon and S. MacKinnon (Old Westbury, N.Y.: Feminist Press, 1976), pp. 103–110.

husband, scrambled her way from Florida to Harlem to Columbia University to Haiti and finally back to Florida, moved in and out of white patronage and poverty, professional success, and failure; her survival relationships were all with women, beginning with her mother. Both of these women in their vastly different circumstances were marriage resisters, committed to their own work and selfhood, and were later characterized as "apolitical." Both were drawn to men of intellectual quality; for both of them women provided the ongoing fascination and sustenance of life.

If we think of heterosexuality as *the* natural emotional and sexual inclination for women, lives such as these are seen as deviant, as pathological, or as emotionally and sensually deprived. Or, in more recent and permissive jargon, they are banalized as "life styles." And the work of such women, whether merely the daily work of individual or collective survival and resistance or the work of the writer, the activist, the reformer, the anthropologist, or the artist—the work of self-creation—is undervalued, or seen as the bitter fruit of "penis envy" or the sublimation of repressed eroticism or the meaningless rant of a "man-hater." But when we turn the lens of vision and consider the degree to which and the methods whereby heterosexual "preference" has actually been imposed on women, not only can we understand differently the meaning of individual lives and work, but we can begin to recognize a central fact of women's history: that women have always resisted male tyranny. A feminism of action, often though not always without a theory, has constantly re-emerged in every culture and in every period. We can then begin to study women's struggle against powerlessness, women's radical rebellion, not just in male-defined "concrete revolutionary situations"[7] but in all the situations male ideologies have not perceived as revolutionary—for example, the refusal of some women to produce children, aided at great risk by other women;[8] the refusal to produce a higher standard of living and leisure for men (Leghorn and Parker show how both are part of women's unacknowledged, unpaid, and ununionized economic contribution). We can no longer have patience with Dinnerstein's view that women have simply collaborated with men in the "sexual arrangements" of history. We begin to observe behavior, both in history and in individual biography, that has hitherto been invisible or misnamed, behavior which often constitutes, given the limits of the counterforce exerted in a given time and place, radical rebellion. And we can connect these rebellions and the necessity for them with the physical passion of woman for woman which is central to lesbian exis-

---

7. See Rosalind Petchesky, "Dissolving the Hyphen: A Report on Marxist-Feminist Groups 1–5," in *Capitalist Patriarchy and the Case for Socialist Feminism*, ed. Zillah Eisenstein (New York: Monthly Review Press, 1979), p. 387.
8. [A.R., 1986: See Angela Davis, *Women, Race and Class* (New York: Random House, 1981), p. 102; Orlando Patterson, *Slavery and Social Death: A Comparative Study* (Cambridge: Harvard University Press, 1982), p. 133.]

tence: the erotic sensuality which has been, precisely, the most violently erased fact of female experience.

*   *   *

IV

Woman identification is a source of energy, a potential springhead of female power, curtailed and contained under the institution of heterosexuality. The denial of reality and visibility to women's passion for women, women's choice of women as allies, life companions, and community, the forcing of such relationships into dissimulation and their disintegration under intense pressure have meant an incalculable loss to the power of all women *to change the social relations of the sexes, to liberate ourselves and each other.* The lie of compulsory female heterosexuality today afflicts not just feminist scholarship, but every profession, every reference work, every curriculum, every organizing attempt, every relationship or conversation over which it hovers. It creates, specifically, a profound falseness, hypocrisy, and hysteria in the heterosexual dialogue, for every heterosexual relationship is lived in the queasy strobe light of that lie. However we choose to identify ourselves, however we find ourselves labeled, it flickers across and distorts our lives.[9]

The lie keeps numberless women psychologically trapped, trying to fit mind, spirit, and sexuality into a prescribed script because they cannot look beyond the parameters of the acceptable. It pulls on the energy of such women even as it drains the energy of "closeted" lesbians—the energy exhausted in the double life. The lesbian trapped in the "closet," the woman imprisoned in prescriptive ideas of the "normal" share the pain of blocked options, broken connections, lost access to self-definition freely and powerfully assumed.

The lie is many-layered. In Western tradition, one layer—the romantic—asserts that women are inevitably, even if rashly and tragically, drawn to men; that even when that attraction is suicidal (e.g., *Tristan and Isolde,* Kate Chopin's *The Awakening*), it is still an organic imperative. In the tradition of the social sciences it asserts that primary love between the sexes is "normal"; that women *need* men as social and economic protectors, for adult sexuality, and for psychological completion; that the heterosexually constituted family is the basic social unit; that women who do not attach their primary intensity to men must be, in functional terms, condemned to an even more devastating outsiderhood than their outsiderhood as women. Small wonder that lesbians are reported to be a more hidden population than male homosexuals. The Black lesbian-feminist critic Lorraine Bethel, writing on Zora Neale Hurston, remarks

9. See Russell and van de Ven, p. 40: "Few heterosexual women realize their lack of free choice about their sexuality, and few realize how and why compulsory heterosexuality is also a crime against them."

that for a Black woman—already twice an outsider—to choose to assume still another "hated identity" is problematic indeed. Yet the lesbian continuum has been a life line for Black women both in Africa and the United States.

> Black women have a long tradition of bonding together . . . in a Black/women's community that has been a source of vital survival information, psychic and emotional support for us. We have a distinct Black woman-identified folk culture based on our experiences as Black women in this society; symbols, language and modes of expression that are specific to the realities of our lives. . . . Because Black women were rarely among those Blacks and females who gained access to literary and other acknowledged forms of artistic expression, this Black female bonding and Black woman-identification has often been hidden and unrecorded except in the individual lives of Black women through our own memories of our particular Black female tradition.[1]

Another layer of the lie is the frequently encountered implication that women turn to women out of hatred for men. Profound skepticism, caution, and righteous paranoia about men may indeed be part of any healthy woman's response to the misogyny of male-dominated culture, to the forms assumed by "normal" male sexuality, and to *the failure even of "sensitive" or "political" men to perceive or find these troubling.* Lesbian existence is also represented as mere refuge from male abuses, rather than as an electric and empowering charge between women. One of the most frequently quoted literary passages on lesbian relationship is that in which Colette's Renée, in *The Vagabond*, describes "the melancholy and touching image of two weak creatures who have perhaps found shelter in each other's arms, there to sleep and weep, safe from man who is often cruel, and there to taste *better than any pleasure, the bitter happiness of feeling themselves akin, frail and forgotten* [emphasis added]."[2] Colette is often considered a lesbian writer. Her popular reputation has, I think, much to do with the fact that she writes about lesbian existence as if for a male audience; her earliest "lesbian" novels, the Claudine series, were written under compulsion for her husband and published under both their names. At all events, except for her writings on her mother, Colette is a less reliable source on the lesbian continuum than,

---

1. Lorraine Bethel, "This Infinity of Conscious Pain: Zora Neale Hurston and the Black Literary Female Tradition," in *All the Women Are White, All the Blacks Are Men, But Some of Us Are Brave*, eds. Gloria T. Hull, Patricia Bell Scott, and Barbara Smith (Old Westbury, NY: Feminist Press, 1982) 176–88.

2. Dorothy Dinnerstein, the most recent writer to quote this passage, adds ominously: "But what has to be added to her account is that these 'women enlaced' are sheltering each other not just from what men want to do to them, but also from what they want to do to each other" (Dinnerstein, *The Mermaid and the Minotaur: Sexual Arrangements and the Human Malaise* [New York: Harper & Row, 1976], p. 103). The fact is, however, that woman-to-woman violence is a minute grain in the universe of male-against-female violence perpetuated and rationalized in every social institution.

I would think, Charlotte Brontë, who understood that while women may, indeed must, be one another's allies, mentors, and comforters in the female struggle for survival, there is quite extraneous delight in each other's company and attraction to each others' minds and character, which attend a recognition of each others' strengths.

By the same token, we can say that there is a *nascent* feminist political content in the act of choosing a woman lover or life partner in the face of institutionalized heterosexuality.[3] But for lesbian existence to realize this political content in an ultimately liberating form, the erotic choice must deepen and expand into conscious woman identification—into lesbian feminism.

The work that lies ahead, of unearthing and describing what I call here "lesbian existence," is potentially liberating for all women. It is work that must assuredly move beyond the limits of white and middle-class Western Women's Studies to examine women's lives, work, and groupings within every racial, ethnic, and political structure. There are differences, moreover, between "lesbian existence" and the "lesbian continuum," differences we can discern even in the movement of our own lives. The lesbian continuum, I suggest, needs delineation in light of the "double life" of women, not only women self-described as heterosexual but also of self-described lesbians. We need a far more exhaustive account of the forms the double life has assumed. Historians need to ask at every point how heterosexuality as institution has been organized and maintained through the female wage scale, the enforcement of middle-class women's "leisure," the glamorization of so-called sexual liberation, the withholding of education from women, the imagery of "high art" and popular culture, the mystification of the "personal" sphere, and much else. We need an economics which comprehends the institution of heterosexuality, with its doubled workload for women and its sexual divisions of labor, as the most idealized of economic relations.

The question inevitably will arise: Are we then to condemn all heterosexual relationships, including those which are least oppressive? I believe this question, though often heartfelt, is the wrong question here. We have been stalled in a maze of false dichotomies which prevents our apprehending the institution as a whole: "good" versus "bad" marriages; "marriage for love" versus arranged marriage; "liberated" sex versus prostitution; heterosexual intercourse versus rape; *Liebeschmerz* versus humiliation and dependency. Within the institution exist, of course, qualitative differences of experience; but the absence of choice remains the great unacknowledged reality, and in the absence of choice, women will remain dependent upon the chance or luck of particular relationships and will have no collective power to determine the meaning and place of sexuality in their lives. As we address the institution itself, more-

3. Conversation with Blanche W. Cook, New York City, March 1979.

over, we begin to perceive a history of female resistance which has never fully understood itself because it has been so fragmented, miscalled, erased. It will require a courageous grasp of the politics and economics, as well as the cultural propaganda, of heterosexuality to carry us beyond individual cases or diversified group situations into the complex kind of overview needed to undo the power men everywhere wield over women, power which has become a model for every other form of exploitation and illegitimate control.

Split at the Root: An Essay on Jewish Identity (1982) †

For about fifteen minutes I have been sitting chin in hand in front of the typewriter, staring out at the snow. Trying to be honest with myself, trying to figure out why writing this seems to be so dangerous an act, filled with fear and shame, and why it seems so necessary. It comes to me that in order to write this I have to be willing to do two things: I have to claim my father, for I have my Jewishness from him and not from my gentile mother; and I have to break his silence, his taboos; in order to claim him I have in a sense to expose him.

And there is, of course, the third thing: I have to face the sources and the flickering presence of my own ambivalence as a Jew; the daily, mundane anti-Semitisms of my entire life.

These are stories I have never tried to tell before. Why now? Why, I asked myself sometime last year, does this question of Jewish identity float so impalpably, so ungraspably around me, a cloud I can't quite see the outlines of, which feels to me to be without definition?

And yet I've been on the track of this longer than I think.

In a long poem written in 1960, when I was thirty-one years old, I described myself as "Split at the root, neither Gentile nor Jew, / Yankee nor Rebel."[1] I was still trying to have it both ways: to be neither/nor, trying to live (with my Jewish husband and three children more Jewish in ancestry than I) in the predominantly gentile Yankee academic world of Cambridge, Massachusetts.

But this begins, for me, in Baltimore, where I was born in my father's workplace, a hospital in the Black ghetto, whose lobby contained an immense white marble statue of Christ.

---

† I wrote this essay in 1982 for Evelyn Torton Beck's *Nice Jewish Girls: A Lesbian Anthology*. It was later reprinted in *Fathers*, an anthology edited by Ursula Owen for Virago Ltd., in London, and published in the United States by Pantheon. [Notes to this essay are Rich's. This selection has been edited for publication here; asterisks indicate deletions.]

1. Adrienne Rich, "Readings of History," in *Snapshots of a Daughter-in-Law* (New York: W. W. Norton, 1967), pp. 36–40.

My father was then a young teacher and researcher in the department of pathology at the Johns Hopkins Medical School, one of the very few Jews to attend or teach at that institution. He was from Birmingham, Alabama; his father, Samuel, was Ashkenazic, an immigrant from Austria-Hungary and his mother, Hattie Rice, a Sephardic Jew from Vicksburg, Mississippi. My grandfather had had a shoe store in Birmingham, which did well enough to allow him to retire comfortably and to leave my grandmother income on his death. The only souvenirs of my grandfather, Samuel Rich, were his ivory flute, which lay on our living-room mantel and was not to be played with; his thin gold pocket watch, which my father wore; and his Hebrew prayer book, which I discovered among my father's books in the course of reading my way through his library. In this prayer book there was a newspaper clipping about my grandparents' wedding, which took place in a synagogue.

My father, Arnold, was sent in adolescence to a military school in the North Carolina mountains, a place for training white southern Christian gentlemen. I suspect that there were few, if any, other Jewish boys at Colonel Bingham's, or at "Mr. Jefferson's university" in Charlottesville, where he studied as an undergraduate. With whatever conscious forethought, Samuel and Hattie sent their son into the dominant southern WASP culture to become an "exception," to enter the professional class. Never, in describing these experiences, did he speak of having suffered—from loneliness, cultural alienation, or outsiderhood. Never did I hear him use the word *anti-Semitism*.

It was only in college, when I read a poem by Karl Shapiro beginning "To hate the Negro and avoid the Jew / is the curriculum," that it flashed on me that there was an untold side to my father's story of his student years. He looked recognizably Jewish, was short and slender in build with dark wiry hair and deep-set eyes, high forehead and curved nose.

My mother is a gentile. In Jewish law I cannot count myself a Jew. If it is true that "we think back through our mothers if we are women" (Virginia Woolf)—and I myself have affirmed this—then even according to lesbian theory, I cannot (or need not?) count myself a Jew.

The white southern Protestant woman, the gentile, has always been there for me to peel back into. That's a whole piece of history in itself, for my gentile grandmother and my mother were also frustrated artists and intellectuals, a lost writer and a lost composer between them. Readers and annotators of books, note takers, my mother a good pianist still, in her eighties. But there was also the obsession with ancestry, with "background," the southern talk of family, not as people you would necessarily know and depend on, but as heritage, the guarantee of "good breeding." There was the inveterate romantic heterosexual fantasy, the mother telling the daughter how to attract men (my mother often used the word "fascinate"); the assumption that relations between the sexes could only be romantic, that it was in the woman's interest to cultivate "mystery," conceal her actual feelings. Survival tactics of a kind, I think today, knowing what I know about the white woman's sexual role in the southern racist scenario. Heterosexuality as protection, but also drawing white women deeper into collusion with white men.

It would be easy to push away and deny the gentile in me—that white southern woman, that social christian. At different times in my life I have wanted to push away one or the other burden of inheritance, to say merely *I am a woman; I am a lesbian*. If I call myself a Jewish lesbian, do I thereby try to shed some of my southern gentile white woman's culpability? If I call myself only through my mother, is it because I pass more easily through a world where being a lesbian often seems like outsiderhood enough?

According to Nazi logic, my two Jewish grandparents would have made me a *Mischling, first-degree*—nonexempt from the Final Solution.

The social world in which I grew up was christian virtually without needing to say so—christian imagery, music, language, symbols, assumptions everywhere. It was also a genteel, white, middle-class world in which "common" was a term of deep opprobrium. "Common" white people might speak of "niggers"; *we* were taught never to use that word— *we* said "Negroes" (even as we accepted segregation, the eating taboo, the assumption that Black people were simply of a separate species). Our language was more polite, distinguishing us from the "red-necks" or the lynch-mob mentality. But so charged with negative meaning was even the word "Negro" that as children we were taught never to use it in front of Black people. We were taught that any mention of skin color in the presence of colored people was treacherous, forbidden ground. In a parallel way, the word "Jew" was not used by polite gentiles. I sometimes heard my best friend's father, a Presbyterian minister, allude to "the Hebrew people" or "people of the Jewish faith." The world of acceptable folk was white, gentile (christian, really), and had "ideals" (which colored people, white "common" people, were not supposed to have). "Ideals" and "manners" included not hurting someone's feelings by calling her or him a Negro or a Jew—naming the hated identity. This is the mental framework of the 1930s and 1940s in which I was raised.

(Writing this, I feel dimly like the betrayer: of my father, who did not speak the word; of my mother, who must have trained me in the messages; of my caste and class; of my whiteness itself.)

Two memories: I am in a play reading at school of *The Merchant of Venice*. Whatever Jewish law says, I am quite sure I was *seen* as Jewish (with a reassuringly gentile mother) in that double vision that bigotry allows. I am the only Jewish girl in the class, and I am playing Portia. As always, I read my part aloud for my father the night before, and he tells me to convey, with my voice, more scorn and contempt with the word "Jew": "Therefore, Jew . . ." I have to say the word out, and say it loudly. I was encouraged to pretend to be a non-Jewish child acting a non-Jewish character who has to speak the word "Jew" emphatically. Such a child would not have had trouble with the part. But *I* must have had trouble with the part, if only because the word itself was really taboo. I can see that there was a kind of terrible, bitter bravado about my father's way of handling this. And who would not dissociate from Shylock in order to identify with Portia? As a Jewish child who was also a female, I loved Portia—and, like every other Shakespearean heroine, she proved a treacherous role model.

A year or so later I am in another play, *The School for Scandal*, in which a notorious spendthrift is described as having "many excellent friends . . . among the Jews." In neither case was anything explained, either to me or to the class at large, about this scorn for Jews and the disgust surrounding Jews and money. Money, when Jews wanted it, had it, or lent it to others, seemed to take on a peculiar nastiness; Jews and money had some peculiar and unspeakable relation.

At this same school—in which we had Episcopalian hymns and prayers, and read aloud through the Bible morning after morning—I gained the impression that Jews were in the Bible and mentioned in English literature, that they had been persecuted centuries ago by the wicked Inquisition, but that they seemed not to exist in everyday life. These were the 1940s, and we were told a great deal about the Battle of Britain, the noble French Resistance fighters, the brave, starving Dutch—but I did not learn of the resistance of the Warsaw ghetto until I left home.

I was sent to the Episcopal church, baptized and confirmed, and attended it for about five years, though without belief. That religion seemed to have little to do with belief or commitment; it was liturgy that mattered, not spiritual passion. Neither of my parents ever entered that church, and my father would not enter *any* church for any reason— wedding or funeral. Nor did I enter a synagogue until I left Baltimore. When I came home from church, for a while, my father insisted on reading aloud to me from Thomas Paine's *The Age of Reason*—a diatribe against institutional religion. Thus, he explained, I would have a balanced view of these things, a choice. He—they—did not give me the choice to be a Jew. My mother explained to me when I was filling out forms for college that if any question was asked about "religion," I should put down "Episcopalian" rather than "none"—to seem to have no religion was, she implied, dangerous.

But it was white social christianity, rather than any particular christian sect, that the world was founded on. The very word *Christian* was used as a synonym for virtuous, just, peace-loving, generous, etc., etc. [2] The

2. In a similar way the phrase "That's white of you" implied that you were behaving with the superior decency and morality expected of white but not of Black people.

norm was christian: "religion: none" was indeed not acceptable. Anti-Semitism was so intrinsic as not to have a name. I don't recall exactly being taught that the Jews killed Jesus—"Christ killer" seems too strong a term for the bland Episcopal vocabulary—but certainly we got the impression that the Jews had been caught out in a terrible mistake, failing to recognize the true Messiah, and were thereby less advanced in moral and spiritual sensibility. The Jews had actually allowed *moneylenders in the Temple* (again, the unexplained obsession with Jews and money). They were of the past, archaic, primitive, as older (and darker) cultures are supposed to be primitive; christianity was lightness, fairness, peace on earth, and combined the feminine appeal of "The meek shall inherit the earth" with the masculine stride of "Onward, Christian Soldiers."

Sometime in 1946, while still in high school, I read in the newspaper that a theater in Baltimore was showing films of the Allied liberation of the Nazi concentration camps. Alone, I went downtown after school one afternoon and watched the stark, blurry, but unmistakable newsreels. When I try to go back and touch the pulse of that girl of sixteen, growing up in many ways so precocious and so ignorant, I am overwhelmed by a memory of despair, a sense of inevitability more enveloping than any I had every known. Anne Frank's diary and many other personal narratives of the Holocaust were still unknown or unwritten. But it came to me that every one of those piles of corpses, mountains of shoes and clothing had contained, simply, individuals, who had believed, as I now believed of myself, that they were intended to live out a life of some kind of meaning, that the world possessed some kind of sense and order; yet *this* had happened to them. And I, who believed my life was intended to be so interesting and meaningful, was connected to those dead by something—not just mortality but a taboo name, a hated identity. Or was I—did I really have to be? Writing this now, I feel belated rage that I was so impoverished by the family and social worlds I lived in, that I had to try to figure out by myself what this did indeed mean for me. That I had never been taught about resistance, only about passing. That I had no language for anti-Semitism itself.

When I went home and told my parents where I had been, they were not pleased. I felt accused of being morbidly curious, not healthy, sniffing around death for the thrill of it. And since, at sixteen, I was often not sure of the sources of my feelings or of my motives for doing what I did, I probably accused myself as well. One thing was clear: there was nobody in my world with whom I could discuss those films. Probably at the same time, I was reading accounts of the camps in magazines and newspapers; what I remember were the films and having questions that I could not even phrase, such as *Are those men and women "them" or "us"?*

To be able to ask even the child's astonished question *Why do they hate us so?* means knowing how to say "we." The guilt of not knowing, the guilt of perhaps having betrayed my parents or even those victims, those survivors, through mere curiosity—these also froze in me for years the impulse to find out more about the Holocaust.

1947: I left Baltimore to go to college in Cambridge, Massachusetts, left (I thought) the backward, enervating South for the intellectual, vital North. New England also had for me some vibration of higher moral rectitude, of moral passion even, with its seventeenth-century Puritan self-scrutiny, its nineteenth-century literary "flowering," its abolitionist righteousness, Colonel Shaw and his Black Civil War regiment depicted in granite on Boston Common. At the same time, I found myself, at Radcliffe, among Jewish women. I used to sit for hours over coffee with what I thought of as the "real" Jewish students, who told me about middle-class Jewish culture in America. I described my background—for the first time to strangers—and they took me on, some with amusement at my illiteracy, some arguing that I could never marry into a strict Jewish family, some convinced I didn't "look Jewish," others that I did. I learned the names of holidays and foods, which surnames are Jewish and which are "changed names"; about girls who had had their noses "fixed," their hair straightened. For these young Jewish women, students in the late 1940s, it was acceptable, perhaps even necessary, to strive to look as gentile as possible; but they stuck proudly to being Jewish, expected to marry a Jew, have children, keep the holidays, carry on the culture.

I felt I was testing a forbidden current, that there was danger in these revelations. I bought a reproduction of a Chagall portrait of a rabbi in striped prayer shawl and hung it on the wall of my room. I was admittedly young and trying to educate myself, but I was also doing something that *is* dangerous: I was flirting with identity.

One day that year I was in a small shop where I had bought a dress with a too-long skirt. The shop employed a seamstress who did alterations, and she came in to pin up the skirt on me. I am sure that she was a recent immigrant, a survivor. I remember a short, dark woman wearing heavy glasses, with an accent so foreign I could not understand her words. Something about her presence was very powerful and disturbing to me. After marking and pinning up the skirt, she sat back on her knees, looked up at me, and asked in a hurried whisper: "You Jewish?" Eighteen years of training in assimilation sprang into the reflex by which I shook my head, rejecting her, and muttered, "No."

What was I actually saying "no" to? She was poor, older, struggling with a foreign tongue, anxious; she had escaped the death that had been intended for her, but I had no imagination of her possible courage and foresight, her resistance—I did not see in her a heroine who had perhaps saved many lives, including her own. I saw the frightened immigrant, the seamstress hemming the skirts of college girls, the wandering Jew. But I was an American college girl having her skirt hemmed. And I was frightened myself, I think, because she had recognized me ("It takes one to know one," my friend Edie at Radcliffe had said) even if I refused to recognize myself or her, even if her recognition was sharpened by loneliness or the need to feel safe with me.

But why should she have felt safe with me? I myself was living with a false sense of safety.

There are betrayals in my life that I have known at the very moment were betrayals: this was one of them. There are other betrayals committed so repeatedly, so mundanely, that they leave no memory trace behind, only a growing residue of misery, of dull, accreted self-hatred. Often these take the form not of words but of silence. Silence before the joke at which everyone is laughing: the anti-woman joke, the racist joke, the anti-Semitic joke. Silence and then amnesia. Blocking it out when the oppressor's language starts coming from the lips of one we admire, whose courage and eloquence have touched us: *She didn't really mean that; he didn't really say that.* But the accretions build up out of sight, like scale inside a kettle.

1948: I come home from my freshman year at college, flaming with new insights, new information. I am the daughter who has gone out into the world, to the pinnacle of intellectual prestige, Harvard, fulfilling my father's hopes for me, but also exposed to dangerous influences. I have already been reproved for attending a rally for Henry Wallace and the Progressive party. I challenge my father: "Why haven't you told me that I am Jewish? Why do you never talk about being a Jew?" He answers measuredly, "You know that I have never denied that I am a Jew. But it's not important to me. I am a scientist, a deist. I have no use for organized religion. I choose to live in a world of many kinds of people. There are Jews I admire and others whom I despise. I am a person, not simply a Jew." The words are as I remember them, not perhaps exactly as spoken. But that was the message. And it contained enough truth—as all denial drugs itself on partial truth—so that it remained for the time being unanswerable, leaving me high and dry, split at the root, gasping for clarity, for air.

At that time Arnold Rich was living in suspension, waiting to be appointed to the professorship of pathology at Johns Hopkins. The appointment was delayed for years, no Jew ever having held a professional chair in that medical school. And he wanted it badly. It must have been a very bitter time for him, since he had believed so greatly in the redeeming power of excellence, of being the most brilliant, inspired man for the job. With enough excellence, you could presumably make it stop mattering that you were Jewish; you could become the *only* Jew in the gentile world, a Jew so "civilized," so far from "common," so attractively combining southern gentility with European cultural values that no one would ever confuse you with the raw, "pushy" Jews of New York, the "loud, hysterical" refugees from eastern Europe, the "over-dressed" Jews of the urban South.

We—my sister, mother, and I—were constantly urged to speak quietly in public, to dress without ostentation, to repress all vividness or spontaneity, to assimilate with a world which might see us as too flamboyant. I suppose that my mother, pure gentile though she was, could be seen as acting "common" or "Jewish" if she laughed too loudly or spoke aggressively. My father's mother, who lived with us half the year, was a model of circumspect behavior, dressed in dark blue or lavender, retiring in company, ladylike to an extreme, wearing no jewelry except a good gold chain, a narrow brooch, or a string of pearls. A few times, within the family, I saw her anger flare, felt the passion she was repressing. But when Arnold took us out to a restaurant or on a trip, the Rich women were always tuned down to some WASP level my father believed, surely, would protect us all—maybe also make us unrecognizable to the "real Jews" who wanted to seize us, drag us back to the *shtetl*, the ghetto, in its many manifestations.

For, yes, that *was* a message—that some Jews would be after you, once they "knew," to rejoin them, to re-enter a world that was messy, noisy, unpredictable, maybe poor—"even though," as my mother once wrote me, criticizing my largely Jewish choice of friends in college, "some of them will be the most brilliant, fascinating people you'll ever meet." I wonder if that isn't one message of assimilation—of America—that the unlucky or the unachieving want to pull you backward, that to identify with them is to court downward mobility, lose the precious chance of passing, of token existence. There was always within this sense of Jewish identity a strong class discrimination. Jews might be "fascinating" as individuals but came with huge unruly families who "poured chicken soup over everyone's head" (in the phrase of a white southern male poet). Anti-Semitism could thus be justified by the bad behavior of certain Jews; and if you did not effectively deny family and community, there would always be a remote cousin claiming kinship with you who was the "wrong kind" of Jew.

I have always believed his attitude toward other Jews depended on who they were. . . . It was my impression that Jews of this background looked down on Eastern European Jews, including Polish Jews and Russian Jews, who generally were not as well educated. This from a letter written to me recently by a gentile who had worked in my father's department, whom I had asked about anti-Semitism there and in particular regarding my father. This informant also wrote me that it was hard to perceive anti-Semitism in Baltimore because the racism made so much more intense an impression: *I would almost have to think that blacks went to a differ-*

ent heaven than the whites, because the bodies were kept in a separate
morgue, and some white persons did not even want blood transfusions
from black donors. My father's mind was predictably racist and misogyn-
ist; yet as a medical student he noted in his journal that southern male
chivalry stopped at the point of any white man in a streetcar giving his
seat to an old, weary Black woman standing in the aisle. Was this a
Jewish insight—an outsider's insight, even though the outsider was striv-
ing to be on the inside?

Because what isn't named is often more permeating than what is, I
believe that my father's Jewishness profoundly shaped my own identity
and our family existence. They were shaped both by external anti-Sem-
itism and my father's self-hatred, and by his Jewish pride. What Arnold
did, I think, was call his Jewish pride something else: achievement,
aspiration, genius, idealism. Whatever was unacceptable got left back
under the rubric of Jewishness or the "wrong kind" of Jews—unedu-
cated, aggressive, loud. The message I got was that we were really supe-
rior: nobody else's father had collected so many books, had traveled so
far, knew so many languages. Baltimore was a musical city, but for the
most part, in the families of my school friends, culture was for women.
My father was an amateur musician, read poetry, adored encyclopedic
knowledge. He prowled and pounced over my school papers, insisting I
use "grown-up" sources; he criticized my poems for faulty technique and
gave me books on rhyme and meter and form. His investment in my
intellect and talent was egotistical, tyrannical, opinionated, and terribly
wearing. He taught me, nevertheless, to believe in hard work, to mis-
trust easy inspiration, to write and rewrite; to feel that I *was* a person of
the book, even though a woman; to take ideas seriously. He made me
feel, at a very young age, the power of language and that I could share
in it.

The Riches were proud, but we also had to be very careful. Our behavior
had to be more impeccable than other people's. Strangers were not to
be trusted, nor even friends; family issues must never go beyond the
family; the world was full of potential slanderers, betrayers, *people who
could not understand*. Even within the family, I realize that I never in
my whole life knew what my father was really feeling. Yet he spoke—
monologued—with driving intensity. You could grow up in such a house
mesmerized by the local electricity, the crucial meanings assumed by
the merest things. This used to seem to me a sign that we were all living
on some high emotional plane. It was a difficult force field for a favored
daughter to disengage from.

Easy to call that intensity Jewish; and I have no doubt that passion is
one of the qualities required for survival over generations of persecution.
But what happens when passion is rent from its original base, when the
white gentile world is softly saying "Be more like us and you can be
almost one of us"? What happens when survival seems to mean closing

off one emotional artery after another? His forebears in Europe had been forbidden to travel or expelled from one country after another, had special taxes levied on them if they left the city walls, had been forced to wear special clothes and badges, restricted to the poorest neighborhoods. He had wanted to be a "free spirit," to travel widely, among "all kinds of people." Yet in his prime of life he lived in an increasingly withdrawn world, in his house up on a hill in a neighborhood where Jews were not supposed to be able to buy property, depending almost exclusively on interactions with his wife and daughters to provide emotional connectedness. In his home, he created a private defense system so elaborate that even as he was dying, my mother felt unable to talk freely with his colleagues or others who might have helped her. Of course, she acquiesced in this.

The loneliness of the "only," the token, often doesn't feel like loneliness but like a kind of dead echo chamber. Certain things that ought to don't resonate. Somewhere Beverly Smith writes of women of color "inspiring the behavior" in each other. When there's nobody to "inspire the behavior," act out of the culture, there is an atrophy, a dwindling, which is partly invisible.

I was married in 1953, in the Hillel House at Harvard, under a portrait of Albert Einstein. My parents refused to come. I was marrying a Jew of the "wrong kind" from an Orthodox eastern European background. Brooklyn-born, he had gone to Harvard, changed his name, was both indissolubly connected to his childhood world and terribly ambivalent about it. My father saw this marriage as my having fallen prey to the Jewish family, eastern European division.

Like many women I knew in the fifties living under a then-unquestoined heterosexual imperative, I married in part because I knew no better way to disconnect from my first family. I married a "real Jew" who was himself almost equally divided between a troubled yet ingrained Jewish identity, and the pull toward Yankee approval, assimilation. But at least he was not adrift as a single token in a gentile world. We lived in a world where there was much intermarriage and where a certain "Jewish flavor" was accepted within the dominant gentile culture. People talked glibly of "Jewish self-hatred," but anti-Semitism was rarely identified. It was as if you could have it both ways—identity and assimilation—without having to think about it very much.

I was moved and gratefully amazed by the affection and kindliness my husband's parents showed me, the half *shiksa*. I longed to embrace that family, that new and mysterious Jewish world. It was never a question of conversion—my husband had long since ceased being observant—but of a burning desire to do well, please these new parents, heal the split consciousness in which I had been raised, and, of course, to belong. In the big, sunny apartment on Eastern Parkway, the table would be

spread on Saturday afternoons with a white or an embroidered cloth and
plates of coffeecake, spongecake, mohncake, cookies for a family gath-
ering where everyone ate and drank—coffee, milk, cake—and later the
talk still eddied among the women around the table or in the kitchen,
while the men ended up in the living room watching the ball game. I
had never known this kind of family, in which mock insults were cheer-
fully exchanged, secrets whispered in corners among two or three, chil-
dren and grandchildren boasted about, and the new daughter-in-law
openly inspected. I was profoundly attracted by all this, including the
punctilious observance of *kashrut,* the symbolism lurking behind daily
kitchen tasks. I saw it all as quintessentially and authentically Jewish,
and I objectified both the people and the culture. My unexamined anti-
Semitism allowed me to do this. But also, I had not yet recognized that
as a woman I stood in a particular and unexamined relationship to the
Jewish family and to the Jewish culture.

There were several years during which I did not see, and barely com-
municated with, my parents. At the same time, my father's personality
haunted my life. Such had been the force of his will in our household
that for a long time I felt I would have to pay in some terrible way for
having disobeyed him. When finally we were reconciled, and my hus-
band and I and our children began to have some minimal formal contact
with my parents, the obsessional power of Arnold's voice or handwriting
had given way to a dull sense of useless anger and pain. I wanted him to
cherish and approve of me, not as he had when I was a child, but as the
woman I was, who had her own mind and had made her own choices.
This, I finally realized, was not to be; Arnold demanded absolute loy-
alty, absolute submission to his will. In my separation from him, in my
realization at what price that once-intoxicating approval had been bought,
I was learning in concrete ways a great deal about patriarchy, in partic-
ular how the "special" woman, the favored daughter, is controlled and
rewarded.

Arnold Rich died in 1968 after a long, deteriorating illness; his mind
had gone, and he had been losing his sight for years. It was a year of
intensifying political awareness for me: the Martin Luther King and Robert
Kennedy assassinations, the Columbia strike. But it was not that these
events, and the meetings and demonstrations that surrounded them, pre-
empted the time of mourning for my father; I had been mourning a long
time for an early, primary, and intense relationship, by no means always
benign, but in which I had been ceaselessly made to feel that what I did
with my life, the choices I made, the attitudes I held, were of the utmost
consequence.

Sometime in my thirties, on visits to Brooklyn, I sat on Eastern Parkway,
a baby stroller at my feet—one of many rows of young Jewish women
on benches with children in that neighborhood. I used to see the Lubav-

itcher Hasidim—then beginning to move into the Crown Heights neighborhood—walking out on *Shabbes*, the women in their *shaytls* a little behind the men. My father-in-law pointed them out as rather exotic—too old-country, perhaps, too unassimilated even for his devout yet Americanized sense of Jewish identity. It took many years for me to understand—partly because I understood so little about class in America—how in my own family, and in the very different family of my in-laws, there were degrees and hierarchies of assimilation which looked askance upon each other—and also geographic lines of difference, as between southern Jews and New York Jews, whose manners and customs varied along class as well as regional lines.

I had three sons before I was thirty, and during those years I often felt that to be a Jewish woman, a Jewish mother, was to be perceived in the Jewish family as an entirely physical being, a producer and nourisher of children. The experience of motherhood was eventually to radicalize me. But before that, I was encountering the institution of motherhood most directly in a Jewish cultural version; and I felt rebellious, moody, defensive, unable to sort out what was Jewish from what was simply motherhood or female destiny. (I lived in Cambridge, not Brooklyn; but there, too, restless, educated women sat on benches with baby strollers, half-stunned, not by Jewish cultural expectations, but by the middle-class American social expectations of the 1950s.)

My children were taken irregularly to Seders, to bar mizvahs, and to special services in their grandfather's temple. Their father lit Hanukkah candles while I stood by, having rememorized each year the English meaning of the Hebrew blessing. We all celebrated a secular, liberal Christmas. I read aloud from books about Esther and the Maccabees and Moses, and also from books about Norse trolls and Chinese grandmothers and Celtic dragon slayers. Their father told stories of his boyhood in Brooklyn, his grandmother in the Bronx who had to be visited by subway every week, of misdeeds in Hebrew school, of being a bright Jewish kid at Boys' High. In the permissive liberalism of academic Cambridge, you could raise your children to be as vaguely or distinctly Jewish as you would, but Christian myth and calendar organized the year. My sons grew up knowing far more about the existence and concrete meaning of Jewish culture than I had. But I don't recall sitting down with them and telling them that millions of people like themselves, many of them children, had been rounded up and murdered in Europe in their parents' lifetime. Nor was I able to tell them that they came in part out of the rich, thousand-year-old Ashkenazic culture of eastern Europe, which the Holocaust destroyed; or that they came from a people whose traditions, religious and secular, included a hatred of oppression and an imperative to pursue justice and care for the stranger—an anti-racist, a socialist, and even sometimes a feminist vision. I could not tell them these things because these things were still too indistinct in my own mind.

The emergence of the Civil Rights movement in the sixties I remember as lifting me out of a sense of personal frustration and hopelessness. Reading James Baldwin's early essays in the fifties had stirred me with a sense that apparently "given" situations like racism could be analyzed and described and that this could lead to action, to change. Racism had been so utter and implicit a fact of my childhood and adolescence, had felt so central among the silences, negations, cruelties, fears, superstitions of my early life, that somewhere among my feelings must have been the hope that if Black people could become free of the immense political and social burdens they were forced to bear, I, too, could become free of all the ghosts and shadows of my childhood, named and unnamed. When "the movement" began, it felt extremely personal to me. And it was often Jews who spoke up for the justice of the cause, Jewish students and civil rights lawyers who travelled South; it was two young Jews who were found murdered with a young Black man in Mississippi: Schwerner, Goodman, Chaney.

Moving to New York in the mid-sixties meant being plunged almost immediately into the debate over community control of public schools, in which Black and Jewish teachers and parents were often on opposite sides of extremely militant barricades. It was easy as a white liberal to deplore and condemn the racism of middle-class Jewish parents or angry Jewish schoolteachers, many of them older women; to displace our own racism onto them; or to feel it as too painful to think about. The struggle for Black civil rights had such clarity about it for me: I knew that segregation was wrong, that unequal opportunity was wrong; I knew that segregation in particular was more than a set of social and legal rules—it meant that even "decent" white people lived in a network of lies and arrogance and moral collusion. In the world of Jewish assimilationist and liberal politics which I knew best, however, things were far less clear to me, and anti-Semitism went almost unmentioned. It was even possible to view concern about anti-Semitism as a reactionary agenda, a monomania of *Commentary* magazine or, later, the Jewish Defense League. Most of the political work I was doing it the late 1960s was on racial issues, in particular as a teacher in the City University during the struggle for open admissions. The white colleagues I thought of as allies were, I think, mostly Jewish. Yet it was easy to see other New York Jews, who had climbed out of poverty and exploitation through the public-school system and the free city colleges, as now trying to block Black and Puerto Rican students trying to do likewise. I didn't understand then that I was living between two strains of Jewish social identity: the Jew as radical visionary and activist who understands oppression firsthand, and the Jew as part of America's devouring plan in which the persecuted, called to assimilation, learn that the price is to engage in persecution.

And, indeed, there *was* intense racism among Jews as well as white gentiles in the City University, part of the bitter history of Jews and Blacks which James Baldwin had described much earlier, in his 1948 essay "The Harlem Ghetto";[3] part of the divide-and-conquer script still being rehearsed by those of us who have the least to gain from it.

By the time I left my marriage, after seventeen years and three children, I had become identified with the Women's Liberation movement. It was an astonishing time to be a woman of my age. In the 1950s, seeking a way to grasp the pain I seemed to be feeling most of the time, to set it in some larger context, I had read all kinds of things; but it was James Baldwin and Simone de Beauvoir who had described the world—though differently—in terms that made the most sense to me. By the end of the sixties there were two political movements—one already meeting severe repression, one just emerging—which addressed those descriptions of the world.

And there was, of course, a third movement, or a movement-within-a-movement: the early lesbian manifestoes, the new visibility and activism of lesbians everywhere. I had known very early on that the women's movement was not going to be a simple walk across an open field; that it would pull on every fiber of my existence; that it would mean going back and searching the shadows of my consciousness. Reading *The Second Sex* in the 1950s isolation of an academic housewife had felt less dangerous than reading "The Myth of Vaginal Orgasm" or "Woman-identified Woman" in a world where I was in constant debate and discussion with women over every aspect of our lives that we could as yet name. De Beauvoir had placed "The Lesbian" on the margins, and there was little in her book to suggest the power of woman bonding. But the passion of debating ideas with women was an erotic passion for me, and the risking of self with women that was necessary in order to win some truth out of the lies of the past was also erotic. The suppressed lesbian I had been carrying in me since adolescence began to stretch her limbs, and her first full-fledged act was to fall in love with a Jewish woman.

Some time during the early months of that relationship, I dreamed that I was arguing feminist politics with my lover. *Of course,* I said to her in this dream, *if you're going to bring up the Holocaust against me, there's nothing I can do.* If, as I believe, I was both myself and her in this dream, it spoke of the split in my consciousness. I had been, more or less, a Jewish heterosexual woman. But what did it mean to be a Jewish lesbian? What did it mean to feel myself, as I did, both anti-

3. James Baldwin, "The Harlem Ghetto," in *Notes of a Native Son* (Boston: Beacon, 1955).

Semite and Jew? And, as a feminist, how was I charting for myself the
oppressions within oppression?

The earliest feminist papers on Jewish identity that I read were cri-
tiques of the patriarchal and misogynist elements in Judaism, or of the
caricaturing of Jewish women in literature by Jewish men. I remember
hearing Judith Plaskow give a paper called "Can a Woman Be a Jew?"
(Her conclusion was "Yes, but . . .") I was soon after in correspondence
with a former student who had emigrated to Israel, was a passionate
feminist, and wrote to me at length of the legal and social constraints on
women there, the stirrings of contemporary Israeli feminism, and the
contradictions she felt in her daily life. With the new politics, activism,
literature of a tumultous feminist movement around me, a movement
which claimed universality though it had not yet acknowledged its own
racial, class, and ethnic perspectives or its fears of the differences among
women, I pushed aside for one last time thinking further about myself
as a Jewish woman. I saw Judaism simply as another strand of patriarchy.
If asked to choose, I might have said (as my father had said in other
language): *I am a woman, not a Jew.* (But, I always added mentally, if
Jews had to wear yellow stars again, I, too, would wear one—as if I
would have the choice to wear it or not.)

Sometimes I feel I have seen too long from too many disconnected
angles: white, Jewish, anti-Semite, racist, anti-racist, once-married, les-
bian, middle-class, feminist, exmatriate southerner, *split at the root*—
that I will never bring them whole. I would have liked, in this essay, to
bring together the meanings of anti-Semitism and racism as I have expe-
rienced them and as I believe they intersect in the world beyond my life.
But I'm not able to do this yet. I feel the tension as I think, make notes:
If you really look at the one reality, the other will waver and disperse.
Trying in one week to read Angela Davis and Lucy Davidowicz;[4] trying
to hold throughout to a feminist, a lesbian, perspective—what does this
mean? Nothing has trained me for this. And sometimes I feel inadequate
to make any statement as a Jew; I feel the history of denial within me
like an injury, a scar. For assimilation has affected *my* perceptions; those
early lapses in meaning, those blanks, are with me still. My ignorance
can be dangerous to me and to others.

Yet we can't wait for the undamaged to make our connections for us;
we can't wait to speak until we are perfectly clear and righteous. There
is no purity and, in our lifetimes, no end to this process.

This essay, then, has no conclusions: it is another beginning for me.
Not just a way of saying, in 1982 Right Wing America, *I, too, will wear
the yellow star.* It's a moving into accountability, enlarging the range of

---

4. Angela Y. Davis, *Women, Race and Class* (New York: Random House, 1981); Lucy S. Davi-
   dowicz, *The War against the Jews 1933–1945* (1975) (New York: Bantam, 1979).

accountability. I know that in the rest of my life, the next half century or so, every aspect of my identity will have to be engaged. The middle-class white girl taught to trade obedience for privilege. The Jewish lesbian raised to be a heterosexual gentile. The woman who first heard oppression named and analyzed in the Black Civil Rights struggle. The woman with three sons, the feminist who hates male violence. The woman limping with a cane, the woman who has stopped bleeding are also accountable. The poet who knows that beautiful language can lie, that the oppressor's language sometimes sounds beautiful. The woman trying, as part of her resistance, to clean up her act.

Blood, Bread, and Poetry: The Location of the Poet (1984) †

The Miami airport, summer 1983: a North American woman says to me, "You'll love Nicaragua: everyone there is a poet." I've thought many times of that remark, both while there and since returning home. Coming from a culture (North American, white- and male-dominated) which encourages poets to think of ourselves as alienated from the sensibility of the general population, which casually and devastatingly marginalizes us (so far, no slave labor or torture for a political poem—just dead air, the white noise of the media jamming the poet's words)—coming from this North American dominant culture which so confuses us, telling us poetry is neither economically profitable nor politically effective and that political dissidence is destructive to art, coming from this culture that tells me I am destined to be a luxury, a decorative garnish on the buffet table of the university curriculum, the ceremonial occasion, the national celebration—what am I to make, I thought, of that remark? *You'll love Nicaragua: everyone there is a poet.* (Do I love poets in general? I immediately asked myself, thinking of poets I neither love nor would wish to see in charge of my country.) Is being a poet a guarantee that I will love a Marxist-Leninist revolution? Can't I travel simply as an American radical, a lesbian feminist, a citizen who opposes her government's wars against its own people and its intervention in other people's lands? And what effectiveness has the testimony of a poet returning from a revolution where "everyone is a poet" to a country where the possible credibility of poetry is not even seriously discussed?

Clearly, this well-meant remark triggered strong and complex feelings in me. And it provided, in a sense, the text on which I began to build my talk here tonight.

I was born at the brink of the Great Depression; I reached sixteen the

† Talk given for the Institute for the Humanities, University of Massachusetts, Amherst, series "Writers and Social Responsibility," 1983. Originally published in the *Massachusetts Review*. Notes to this essay are Rich's.

year of Nagasaki and Hiroshima. The daughter of a Jewish father and a
Protestant mother, I learned about the Holocaust first from newsreels of
the liberation of the death camps. I was a young white woman who had
never known hunger or homelessness, growing up in the suburbs of a
deeply segregated city in which neighborhoods were also dictated along
religious lines: Christian and Jewish. I lived sixteen years of my life secure
in the belief that though cities could be bombed and civilian populations
killed, the earth stood in its old indestructible way. The process through
which nuclear annihilation was to become a part of all human calcula-
tion had already begun, but we did not live with that knowledge during
the first sixteen years of my life. And a recurrent theme in much poetry
I read was the indestructibility of poetry, the poem as a vehicle for per-
sonal immortality.

I had grown up hearing and reading poems from a very young age,
first as sounds, repeated, musical, rhythmically satisfying in themselves,
and the power of concrete, sensuously compelling images:

> All night long they hunted
>   And nothing did they find
> But a ship a-sailing,
>   A-sailing with the wind.
> One said it was a ship,
>   The other he said, Nay,
> The third said it was a house
>   With the chimney blown away;
> And all the night they hunted
>   And nothing did they find
> But the moon a-gliding
>   A-gliding with the wind. . . .

> Tyger! Tyger! burning bright
>   In the forest of the night,
> What immortal hand or eye
>   Dare frame thy fearful symmetry?

But poetry soon became more than music and images; it was also
revelation, information, a kind of teaching. I believed I could learn from
it—an unusual idea for a United States citizen, even a child. I thought
it could offer clues, intimations, keys to questions that already stalked
me, questions I could not even frame yet: *What is possible in this life?
What does "love" mean, this thing that is so important? What is this
other thing called "freedom" or "liberty"—is it like love, a feeling? What
have human beings lived and suffered in the past? How am I going to
live my life?* The fact that poets contradict themselves and each other
didn't baffle or alarm me. I was avid for everything I could get; my
child's mind did not shut down for the sake of consistency.

> I was angry with my friend,
> I told my wrath, my wrath did end.
> I was angry with my foe,
> I told it not, my wrath did grow.

As an angry child, often urged to "curb my temper," I used to ponder those words of William Blake, but they slid first into my memory through their repetitions of sound, their ominous rhythms.

Another poem that I loved first as music, later pondered for what it could tell me about women and men and marriage, was Edwin Arlington Robinson's "Eros Turannos":

> She fears him, and will always ask
>   What fated her to choose him;
> She meets in his engaging mask
>   All reasons to refuse him;
> But what she meets and what she fears
>   Are less than are the downward years,
> Drawn slowly to the foamless weirs
>   Of age, were she to lose him. . . .

And, of course, I thought that the poets in the anthologies were the only real poets, that their being in the anthologies was proof of this, though some were classified as "great" and others as "minor." I owed much to these anthologies: *Silver Pennies*; the constant outflow of volumes edited by Louis Untermeyer; *The Cambridge Book of Poetry for Children*; Palgrave's *Golden Treasury*; the *Oxford Book of English Verse*. But I had no idea that they reflected the taste of a particular time or of particular kinds of people. I still believed that poets were inspired by some transcendent authority and spoke from some extraordinary height. I thought that the capacity to hook syllables together in a way that heated the blood was the sign of a universal vision.

Because of the attitudes surrounding me, the aesthetic ideology with which I grew up, I came into my twenties believing in poetry, in all art, as the expression of a higher world view, what the critic Edward Said has termed "a quasi-religious wonder, instead of a human sign to be understood in secular and social terms."[1] The poet achieved "universality" and authority through tapping his, or occasionally her, own dreams, longings, fears, desires, and, out of this, "speaking as a man to men," as Wordsworth had phrased it. But my personal world view at sixteen, as at twenty-six, was itself being created by political conditions. I was not a man; I was white in a white-supremacist society; I was being educated from the perspective of a particular class; my father was an "assimilated" Jew in an anti-Semitic world, my mother a white southern Protestant; there were particular historical currents on which my consciousness would

---

1. Edward Said, "Literature As Values," *New York Times Book Review* (September 4, 1983), p. 9.

come together, piece by piece. My personal world view was shaped in
part by the poetry I had read, a poetry written almost entirely by white
Anglo-Saxon men, a few women, Celts and Frenchmen notwithstand-
ing. Thus, no poetry in the Spanish language or from Africa or China
or the Middle East. My personal world view, which like so many young
people I carried as a conviction of my own uniqueness, was not original
with me, but was, rather, my untutored and half-conscious rendering of
the facts of blood and bread, the social and political forces of my time
and place.

I was in college during the late 1940s and early 1950s. The thirties, a
decade of economic desperation, social unrest, war, and also of affirmed
political art, was receding behind the fogs of the Cold War, the selling
of the nuclear family with the mother at home as its core, heightened
activity by the FBI and CIA, a retreat by many artists from so-called
"protest" art, witch-hunting among artists and intellectuals as well as in
the State Department, anti-Semitism, scapegoating of homosexual men
and lesbians, and with a symbolic victory for the Cold War crusade in
the 1953 electrocution of Ethel and Julius Rosenberg.

Francis Otto Matthiessen, a socialist and a homosexual, was teaching
literature at Harvard when I came there. One semester he lectured on
five poets: Blake, Keats, Byron, Yeats, and Stevens. That class perhaps
affected my life as a poet more than anything else that happened to me
in college. Matthiessen had a passion for language, and he read aloud,
made us memorize poems and recite them to him as part of the course.
He also actually alluded to events in the outside world, the hope that
eastern Europe could survive as an independent socialist force between
the United States and the Soviet Union; he spoke of the current Euro-
pean youth movements as if they should matter to us. Poetry, in his
classroom, never remained in the realm of pure textual criticism.
Remember that this was in 1947 or 1948, that it was a rare teacher of
literature at Harvard who referred to a world beyond the text, even though
the classrooms were full of World War II veterans studying on the G.I.
Bill of Rights—men who might otherwise never have gone to college,
let alone Harvard, at all. Matthiessen committed suicide in the spring of
my sophomore year.

Because of Yeats, who by then had become my idea of the Great Poet,
the one who more than others could hook syllables together in a way
that heated my blood, I took a course in Irish history. It was taught by a
Boston Irish professor of Celtic, one of Harvard's tokens, whose father,
it was said, had been a Boston policeman. He read poetry aloud in Gaelic
and in English, sang us political ballads, gave us what amounted to a
mini-education on British racism and imperialism, though the words
were never mentioned. He also slashed at Irish self-romanticizing. Peo-
ple laughed about the Irish history course, said it must be full of football
players. In and out of the Harvard Yard, the racism of Yankee Brahmin

toward Boston Irish was never questioned, laced as it was with equally unquestioned class arrogance. Today, Irish Boston both acts out and takes the weight of New England racism against Black and Hispanic people. It was, strangely enough, through poetry that I first began to try to make sense of these things.

"Strangely enough," I say, because the reading of poetry in an elite academic institution is supposed to lead you—in the 1980s as back there in the early 1950s—not toward a criticism of society, but toward a professional career in which the anatomy of poems is studied dispassionately. Prestige, job security, money, and inclusion in an exclusive fraternity are where the academic study of literature is supposed to lead. Maybe I was lucky because I had started reading poetry so young, and not in school, and because I had been writing poems almost as long as I had been reading them. I should add that I was easily entranced by pure sound and still am, no matter what it is saying; and any poet who mixes the poetry of the actual world with the poetry of sound interests and excites me more than I am able to say. In my student years, it was Yeats who seemed to do this better than anyone else. There were lines of Yeats that were to ring in my head for years:

> Many times man lives and dies
> Between his two eternities,
> That of race and that of soul,
> And ancient Ireland knew it all. . . .

> Did she in touching that lone wing
> Recall the years before her mind
> Became a bitter, an abstract thing
> Her thought some popular enmity:
> Blind and leader of the blind
> Drinking the foul ditch where they lie?

I could hazard the guess that all the most impassioned, seductive arguments against the artist's involvement in politics can be found in Yeats. It was this dialogue between art and politics that excited me in his work, along with the sound of his language—never his elaborate mythological systems. I know I learned two things from his poetry, and those two things were at war with each other. One was that poetry can be "about," can root itself in, politics. Even if it is a defense of privilege, even if it deplores political rebellion and revolution, it can, may have to, account for itself politically, consciously situate itself amid political conditions, without sacrificing intensity of language. The other, that politics leads to "bitterness" and "abstractness" of mind, makes women shrill and hysterical, and is finally a waste of beauty and talent: "Too long a sacrifice / can make a stone of the heart." There was absolutely nothing in the literary canon I knew to counter the second idea. Elizabeth Barrett Browning's anti-slavery and feminist poetry, H.D.'s anti-war and woman-identified poetry, like the radical—yes, revolutionary—work of Langston Hughes and Muriel Rukeyser, were still buried by the academic literary canon. But the first idea was extremely important to me: a poet—one who was apparently certified—could actually write about political themes, could weave the names of political activists into a poem:

> MacDonagh and MacBride
> And Connally and Pearce
> Now and in time to come
> Wherever green is worn
> Are changed, changed utterly:
> A terrible beauty is born.

As we all do when young and searching for what we can't even name yet, I took what I could use where I could find it. When the ideas or forms we need are banished, we seek their residues wherever we can trace them. But there was one major problem with this. I had been born a woman, and I was trying to think and act as if poetry—and the possibility of making poems—were a universal—a gender-neutral—realm. In the universe of the masculine paradigm, I naturally absorbed ideas about women, sexuality, power from the subjectivity of male poets—Yeats not least among them. The dissonance between these images and the daily events of my own life demanded a constant footwork of imagination, a kind of perpetual translation, and an unconscious fragmentation of identity: woman from poet. Every group that lives under the naming and image-making power of a dominant culture is at risk from this mental fragmentation and needs an art which can resist it.

But at the middle of the fifties I had no very clear idea of my positioning in the world or even that such an idea was an important resource for a writer to have. I knew that marriage and motherhood, experiences which were supposed to be truly womanly, often left me feeling unfit, disempowered, adrift. But I had never had to think about bread itself as a primary issue; and what I knew of blood was that mine was white and that white was better off. Much as my parents had worried about questions of social belonging and acceptability, I had never had to swallow rage or humiliation to earn a paycheck. The literature I had read only rarely suggested that for many people it is a common, everyday fact of life to be hungry. I thought I was well educated. In that Cold War atmosphere, which has never really ended, we heard a lot about the "indoctrinating" of people in the Soviet Union, the egregious rewriting of history to conform to Communist dogma. But, like most Americans, I had been taught a particular version of our history, the version of the propertied white male; and in my early twenties I did not even realize this. As a younger and then an older woman, growing up in the white mainstream American culture, I was destined to piece together, for the rest of my life, laboriously and with much in my training against me, the history that really concerned me, on which I was to rely as a poet, the only history upon which, both as a woman and a poet, I could find any grounding at all: the history of the dispossessed.

It was in the pain and confusion of that inward wrenching of the self, which I experienced directly as a young woman in the fifties, that I started to feel my way backward to an earlier splitting, the covert and overt taboos against Black people, which had haunted my earliest childhood. And I began searching for some clue or key to life, not only in poetry but in political writers. The writers I found were Mary Wollstonecraft, Simone de Beauvoir, and James Baldwin. Each of them helped me to realize that what had seemed simply "the way things are" could actually be a social construct, advantageous to some people and detrimental to others, and that these constructs could be criticized and changed. The myths and obsessions of gender, the myths and obsessions of race, the violent exercise of power in these relationships could be identified, their territories could be mapped. They were not simply part of my private turmoil, a secret misery, an individual failure. I did not yet know what I, a white woman, might have to say about the racial obsessions of white consciousness. But I did begin to resist the apparent splitting of poet from woman, thinker from woman, and to write what I feared was political poetry. And in this I had very little encouragement from the literary people I knew, but I did find courage and vindication in words like Baldwin's: "Any real change implies the breakup of the world as one has always known it, the loss of all that gave one an identity, the end of safety." I don't know why I found these words encouraging—perhaps because they made me feel less alone.

Mary Wollstonecraft had seen eighteenth-century middle-class Englishwomen brain-starved and emotionally malnourished through denial of education; her plea was to treat women's minds as respectfully as men's—to admit women as equals into male culture. Simone de Beauvoir showed how the male perception of Woman as Other dominated European culture, keeping "woman" entrapped in myths which robbed her of her independent being and value. James Baldwin insisted that *all* culture was politically significant, and described the complexity of living with integrity as a Black person, an artist in a white-dominated culture, whether as an Afro-American growing up in Harlem, U.S.A., or as an African in a country emerging from a history of colonialism. He also alluded to "that as yet unwritten history of the Negro woman"; and he wrote in 1954 in an essay on Gide that "when men [heterosexual or homosexual] can no longer love women they also cease to love or respect or trust each other, which makes their isolation complete." And he was the first writer I read who suggested that racism was poisonous to white as well as destructive to Black people.

The idea of freedom—so much invoked during World War II—had

become pretty abstract politically in the fifties. Freedom—then as now—was supposed to be what the Western democracies believed in and the "Iron Curtain" Soviet-bloc countries were deprived of. The existentialist philosophers who were beginning to be read and discussed among young American intellectuals spoke of freedom as something connected with revolt. But in reading de Beauvoir and Baldwin, I began to taste the concrete reality of being unfree, how continuous and permeating and corrosive a condition it is, and how it is maintained through culture as much as through the use of force.

I am telling you this from a backward perspective, from where I stand now. At the time I could not have summed up the effect these writers had on me. I only knew that I was reading them with the same passion and need that I brought to poetry, that they were beginning to penetrate my life; I was beginning to feel as never before that I had some foothold, some way of seeing, which helped me to ask the questions I needed to ask.

But there were many voices then, as there are now, warning the North American artist against "mixing politics with art." I have been trying to retrace, to delineate, these arguments, which carry no weight for me now because I recognize them as the political declarations of privilege. There is the falsely mystical view of art that assumes a kind of supernatural inspiration, a possession by universal forces unrelated to questions of power and privilege or the artist's relation to bread and blood. In this view, the channel of art can only become clogged and misdirected by the artist's concern with merely temporary and local disturbances. The song is higher than the struggle, and the artist must choose between politics—here defined as earth-bound factionalism, corrupt power struggles—and art, which exists on some transcendent plane. This view of literature has dominated literary criticism in England and America for nearly a century. In the fifties and early sixties there was much shaking of heads if an artist was found "meddling in politics"; art was mystical and universal, but the artist was also, apparently, irresponsible and emotional and politically naïve.

In North America, moreover, "politics" is mostly a dirty word, associated with low-level wheeling and dealing, with manipulation. (There is nothing North Americans seem to fear so much as manipulation, probably because at some level we know that we belong to a deeply manipulative system.) "Politics" also suggested, certainly in the fifties, the Red Menace, Jewish plots, spies, malcontents conspiring to overthrow democracy, "outside agitators" stirring up perfectly contented Black and/or working people. Such activities were dangerous and punishable, and in the McCarthy era there was a great deal of fear abroad. The writer Meridel LeSueur was blacklisted, hounded by the FBI, her books banned; she was dismissed from job after job—teaching, waitressing—because the FBI intimidated her students and employers. A daughter of Tillie

Olsen recalls going with her mother in the 1950s to the Salvation Army to buy heavy winter clothes because the family had reason to believe that Leftists in the San Francisco Bay Area would be rounded up and taken to detention camps farther north. These are merely two examples of politically committed writers who did survive that particular repression—many never recovered from it.

Perhaps many white North Americans fear an overtly political art because it might persuade us emotionally of what we think we are "rationally" against; it might get to us on a level we have lost touch with, undermine the safety we have built for ourselves, remind us of what is better left forgotten. This fear attributes real power to the voices of passion and of poetry which connect us with all that is not simply white chauvinist/male supremacist/straight/puritanical—with what is "dark," "effeminate," "inverted," "primitive," "volatile," "sinister." Yet we are told that political poetry, for example, is doomed to grind down into mere rhetoric and jargon, to become one-dimensional, simplistic, vituperative; that in writing "protest literature"—that is, writing from a perspective which may not be male, or white, or heterosexual, or middle-class—we sacrifice the "universal"; that in writing of injustice we are limiting our scope, "grinding a political axe." So political poetry is suspected of immense subversive power, yet accused of being, by definition, bad writing, impotent, lacking in breadth. No wonder if the North American poet finds herself or himself slightly crazed by the double messages.

By 1956, I had begun dating each of my poems by year. I did this because I was finished with the idea of a poem as a single, encapsulated event, a work of art complete in itself; I knew my life was changing, my work was changing, and I needed to indicate to readers my sense of being engaged in a long, continuous process. It seems to me now that this was an oblique political statement—a rejection of the dominant critical idea that the poem's text should be read as separate from the poet's everyday life in the world. It was a declaration that placed poetry in a historical continuity, not above or outside history.

In my own case, as soon as I published—in 1963—a book of poems which was informed by any conscious sexual politics, I was told, in print, that this work was "bitter," "personal"; that I had sacrificed the sweetly flowing measures of my earlier books for a ragged line and a coarsened voice. It took me a long time not to hear those voices internally whenever I picked up my pen. But I was writing at the beginning of a decade of political revolt and hope and activism. The external conditions for becoming a consciously, self-affirmingly political poet were there, as they had not been when I had begun to publish a decade earlier. Out of the Black Civil Rights movement, amid the marches and sit-ins in the streets and on campuses, a new generation of Black writers began to speak—and older generations to be reprinted and reread; poetry readings were infused with the spirit of collective rage and hope. As part of the movement against United States militarism and imperialism, white poets also were writing and reading aloud poems addressing the war in Southeast Asia. In many of these poems you sensed the poet's desperation in trying to encompass in words the reality of napalm, the "pacification" of villages, trying to make vivid in poetry what seemed to have minimal effect when shown on television. But there was little location of the self, the poet's own identity as a man or woman. As I wrote in another connection, "The enemy is always outside the self, the struggle somewhere else." I had—perhaps through reading de Beauvoir and Baldwin—some nascent idea that "Vietnam and the lovers' bed," as I phrased it then, were connected; I found myself, in the late sixties, trying to describe those relations in poetry. Even before I called myself a feminist or a lesbian, I felt driven—for my own sanity—to bring together in my poems the political world "out there"—the world of children dynamited or napalmed, of the urban ghetto and militarist violence—and the supposedly private, lyrical world of sex and of male/female relationships.

I began teaching in an urban subway college, in a program intended to compensate ghetto students for the inadequacy of the city's public schools. Among staff and students, and in the larger academic community, there were continual debates over the worth and even the linguistic existence of Black English, the expressive limits and social uses of Standard English—the politics of language. As a poet, I had learned much about both the value and the constraints of convention: the reassurances of traditional structures and the necessity to break from them in recognition of new experience. I felt more and more urgently the dynamic between poetry as language and poetry as a kind of action, probing, burning, stripping, placing itself in dialogue with others out beyond the individual self.

By the end of the 1960s an autonomous movement of women was declaring that "the personal is political." That statement was necessary because in other political movements of that decade the power relation of men to women, the question of women's roles and men's roles, had been dismissed—often contemptuously—as the sphere of personal life. Sex itself was not seen as political, except for interracial sex. Women were now talking about domination, not just in terms of economic exploitation, militarism, colonialism, imperialism, but within the family, in marriage, in child rearing, in the heterosexual act itself. Breaking the mental barrier that separated private from public life felt in itself like an enormous surge toward liberation. For a woman thus engaged, every aspect of her life was on the line. We began naming and acting on issues we had been told were trivial, unworthy of mention: rape by husbands or lovers; the boss's hand groping the employee's breast; the woman beaten in her home with no place to go; the woman sterilized when she sought an abortion; the lesbian penalized for her private life by loss of her child, her lease, her job. We pointed out that women's unpaid work in the home is central to every economy, capitalist or socialist. And in the crossover between personal and political, we were also pushing at the limits of experience reflected in literature, certainly in poetry.

To write directly and overtly as a woman, out of a woman's body and experience, to take women's existence seriously as theme and source for art, was something I had been hungering to do, needing to do, all my writing life. It placed me nakedly face to face with both terror and anger; it did indeed *imply the breakdown of the world as I had always known it, the end of safety*, to paraphrase Baldwin again. But it released tremendous energy in me, as in many other women, to have that way of writing affirmed and validated in a growing political community. I felt for the first time the closing of the gap between poet and woman.

Women have understood that we needed an art of our own: to remind us of our history and what we might be; to show us our true faces—all of them, including the unacceptable; to speak of what has been muffled in code or silence; to make concrete the values our movement was bringing forth out of consciousness raising, speakouts, and activism. But we were—and are—living and writing not only within a women's community. We are trying to build a political and cultural movement in the heart of capitalism, in a country where racism assumes every form of physical, institutional, and psychic violence, and in which more than one person in seven lives below the poverty line. The United States feminist movement is rooted in the United States, a nation with a particular history of hostility both to art and to socialism, where art has been encapsulated as a commodity, a salable artifact, something to be taught in MFA programs, that requires a special staff of "arts administrators"; something you "gotta have" without exactly knowing why. As a lesbian-feminist poet and writer, I need to understand how this *location* affects me, along with the realities of blood and bread within this nation.

"As a woman I have no country. As a woman I want no country. As a woman my country is the whole world." These words, written by Virginia Woolf in her feminist and anti-fascist book *Three Guineas*, we dare not take out of context to justify a false transcendence, an irresponsibility toward the cultures and geopolitical regions in which we are rooted. Woolf was attacking—as a feminist—patriotism, nationalism, the values of the British patriarchal establishment for which so many wars have been fought all over the world. Her feminism led her by the end of her life to anti-imperialism. As women, I think it essential that we admit and explore our cultural identities, our national identities, even as we reject the patriotism, jingoism, nationalism offered to us as "the American way of life." Perhaps the most arrogant and malevolent delusion of North American power—of white Western power—has been the delusion of destiny, that white is at the center, that white is endowed with some right or mission to judge and ransack and assimilate and destroy the values of other peoples. As a white feminist artist in the United States, I do not want to perpetuate that chauvinism, but I still have to struggle with its pervasiveness in culture, its residues in myself.

Working as I do in the context of a movement in which artists are encouraged to address political and ethical questions, I have felt released to a large degree from the old separation of art from politics. But the presence of that separation "out there" in North American life is one of many impoverishing forces of capitalist patriarchy. I began to sense what it might be to live, and to write poetry, as a woman, in a society which took seriously the necessity for poetry, when I read Margaret Randall's anthology of contemporary Cuban women poets *Breaking the Silences*. This book had a powerful effect on me—the consistently high level of poetry, the diversity of voices, the sense of the poets' connections with world and community, and, in their individual statements, the affirmation of an organic relation between poetry and social transformation:

> Things move so much around you.
> Even your country has changed. You yourself have
> changed it.
>
> And the soul, will it change? You must change it.
> Who will tell you otherwise?
> Will it be a desolate journey?
> Will it be tangible, languid
> without a hint of violence?
> As long as you are the person you are today
> being yesterday's person as well,
> you will be tomorrow's . . .
> the one who lives and dies
> to live like this.[2]

It was partly because of that book that I went to Nicaragua. I seized the opportunity when it arose, not because I thought that everyone would be a poet, but because I had been feeling more and more ill informed, betrayed by the coverage of Central America in the United States media. I wanted to know what the Sandinistas believed they stood for, what directions they wanted to take in their very young, imperiled revolution. But I also wanted to get a sense of what art might mean in a society committed to values other than profit and consumerism. What was constantly and tellingly manifested was a *belief* in art, not as commodity, not as luxury, not as suspect activity, but as a precious resource to be made available to all, one necessity for the rebuilding of a scarred, impoverished, and still-bleeding country. And returning home I had to ask myself: What happens to the heart of the artist, here in North Amer-

---

2. Nancy Morejón, "Elogia de la Dialéctica," in *Breaking the Silences: Twentieth-Century Poetry by Cuban Women*, ed. Margaret Randall (1982, Pulp Press, Box 3868 MPO, Vancouver, Canada V6B 3Z3).

ica? What toll is taken of art when it is separated from the social fabric? How is art curbed, how are we made to feel useless and helpless, in a system which so depends on our alienation?

Alienation—not just from the world of material conditions, of power to make things happen or stop happening. Alienation from our own roots, whatever they are, the memories, dreams, stories, the language, history, the sacred materials of art. In *A Gathering of Spirit*, an anthology of writing and art by North American Indian women, a poem by the Chicana/American Indian poet Anita Valerio reasserts the claim to a complex historical and cultural identity, the selves who are both of the past and of tomorrow:

> There is the cab driver root and elevator
> root, there is the water
> root of lies   The root of speech hidden in the secretary's
> marinated tongue   There is the ocean
> root and seeing
> root, heart and belly root, antelope
> roots hidden in hills   There is the root
> of the billy club/beginning with electric drums . . .
>
>   root of hunters   smoky
> ascensions into heaven   trails
>   beat out of ice   There is the root
> of homecoming   The house my grandfather built first   I see
> him   standing in his black
> hat beating the snake with a stick
>   There is the root shaped
> by spirits speaking
> in the lodge   There is the root you don't
> want to hear and the one that hides
> from you under the couch. . . .
>
>   Root of teeth and
> the nape of the goat   oranges,   fog
> written on a camera   There is the carrot owl hunting
> for her hat in the wind   moccasins
>
>   of the blue deer
>   flashing
> in the doorknob. . .
>   There is the root of sex eating
> pound cake in the kitchen   crumbs
>   crumbs
>   alibis
> crumbs
> a convict astroprojects   She is

> picking up her torches, picking up her psalms, her
> necklaces[3]

I write in full knowledge that the majority of the world's illiterates are
women, that I live in a technologically advanced country where 40 per-
cent of the people can barely read and 20 percent are functionally illit-
erate. I believe that these facts are directly connected to the fragmentations
I suffer in myself, that we are all in this together. Because I can write at
all—and I think of all the ways women especially have been prevented
from writing—because my words are read and taken seriously, because
I see my work as part of something larger than my own life or the history
of literature, I feel a responsibility to keep searching for teachers who
can help me widen and deepen the sources and examine the ego that
speaks in my poems—not for political "correctness," but for ignorance,
solipsism, laziness, dishonesty, automatic writing. I look everywhere for
signs of that fusion I have glimpsed in the women's movement, and most
recently in Nicaragua. I turn to Toni Cade Bambara's *The Salt Eaters*
or Ama Ata Aidoo's *Our Sister Killjoy* or James Baldwin's *Just above My
Head*; to paintings by Frida Kahlo or Jacob Lawrence; to poems by Dionne
Brand or Judy Grahn or Audre Lord or Nancy Morejón; to the music of
Nina Simone or Mary Watkins. This kind of art—like the art of so many
others uncanonized in the dominant culture—is not produced as a com-
modity, but as part of a long conversation with the elders and with the
future. (And, yes, I do live and work believing in a future.) Such artists
draw on a tradition in which political struggle and spiritual continuity
are meshed. Nothing need be lost, no beauty sacrificed. The heart does
not turn to a stone.

The Genesis of "Yom Kippur 1984" (1987) †

I want to do something hands-on, about the making of poetry. I want to
talk about the way in which a particular poem came together. I picked
"Yom Kippur 1984" because I have some sense of how it came about. I
don't keep drafts, I don't keep records of the process (maybe sometimes
the briefest of notes in a journal), but I do remember a great deal about
how this poem was written because I was in a kind of struggle with it for
a whole year. I learned a lot in that struggle, some of which I'll try to
tell you about.

There's a tendency to treat poems—at least in certain circles—as a
sort of documentation on the poet's life, as perhaps a kind of autobiog-
raphy, and I want to start by addressing that notion. I feel very strongly

---

3. Anita Valerio, "I Am Listening: A Lyric of Roots," in *A Gathering of Spirit, Sinister Wisdom*
22/23 (1983, ed. Beth Brant): 212–213.
† The text is a transcription of remarks made by Adrienne Rich in New York City in 1987 as
part of an informal discussion of "Yom Kippur 1984." Printed by permission of the author.

with Wallace Stevens that "poetry is the supreme fiction," that a poem is not a slice of the poet's life, although it obviously emerges from intense places in the poet's life and consciousness and experience. But Muriel Rukeyser has a line—she wrote it when she was very young and she already knew this; the line is "Breathe in experience, breathe out poetry." There is a sense of transmutation: something has to happen between the breathing in of experience and the breathing out of poetry. It has been transformed, not only into words but into something new.

At the same time I don't want to present the poem as an aesthetic object unrelated to life and history and social circumstance. When I was an undergraduate in the 1950s, we were taught the New Criticism. The New Critical approach was to examine the poem strictly as text, not to entertain anything from the poet's biography or the historical or social context of the times. But for many of us who had been trained to read that way, and who were poets ourselves, it became more and more apparent that you couldn't read that way: social and historical context were crucial.

And this reaction became coupled with the importance—in the feminist movement of the early 70s—of beginning to find out what in fact had been the *lives* of our artists, what in fact had been the *lives* of our thinkers. What had happened to these women, how had they become the exceptions? What experiences had they been encoding? What concerns me now is whether this has led to a kind of overreading in terms of the autobiographical.

To give you an example, I have a poem written in the 60s called "Women." It begins, "My three sisters are sitting on rocks of black obsidian / For the first time in this light / I can see who they are."[1] I have seen that poem glossed as a poem about Rich's three sisters. On the simplest level such a reading is factually incorrect, since Adrienne Rich has one sister, not three. But more than that, even supposing that Adrienne Rich the individual had three sisters, the poem lives by metaphor. On one level I can look at another woman who is not my blood kin and call her sister, or on another level all three sisters are aspects of the poet's self.

That's a rather straightforward example of what I'm currently concerned about in the reading of poems. The I in a poem, I want to insist, is the consciousness from which the poem comes, but it's not the I to whom I subscribe when I sign an affidavit, when I set forth facts in order to get a driver's license or a passport. It's not *I* as in ID card, not the I of whatever's in my FBI file or *Who's Who*. A poem is not a biographical anecdote. Finally a poem is a construction of language that uses, tries to use everything that language can do, to conjure, to summon up something that's not quite knowable in any other way. Using the tonal and

1. See *The Fact of a Doorframe*, p. 94 [*Editors*].

musical aspects of language, the image-making aspect of language, the associations between words, the merging aspect of language in metaphor where one thing can actually become another and throw light on both.

I will read "Yom Kippur 1984" and then say a little about where these images came from, what they have to do with each other, how they evolve.[2]

Several things literally happened in the summer and fall of 1984. This poem is very clearly located in terms of time. And in terms of place. Yom Kippur, the most solemn day of the Jewish year: a time for fasting, a time for reckoning with one's obligation to God and to one's people, one's community. A time when we attempt to make reconciliation first with our community because it is said that you cannot look to forgiveness from God before you have been forgiven by your people. It is of that day, that time, that *Leviticus* says: *Whoever does not afflict his soul throughout this day shall be cut off from his people.*

Well, shortly before Yom Kippur, 1984, I had crossed the country, leaving the East Coast behind—where I felt I had roots, communities, intense ties—and arrived on the West Coast, in California. That's a fact. Also during that summer I had read of the shooting by police of Edmund Perry, a young Black man who was in fact on his way to Stanford University on a scholarship, shot in the neighborhood of Columbia University. One of many police assaults on Black people during that time and since. I arrived in Santa Cruz, California, which looks like a Dufy landscape or the Italian Riviera. And the first thing that confronted me was a series of murders, in the Santa Cruz Mountains, of women whose cars had broken down or who had been stopped for some reason, had been dragged from their cars and raped and mutilated. The police were sending out warnings that women should not drive alone through the mountains and should only drive with locked windows and doors and a full tank of gas. And the drive through those mountains was going to be my commute to San Jose State University, where I would be teaching that year. And during the time of working on the poem, I read also of the waylaying and beating up of a gay man in Maine who was then dumped into an icy river and who could not swim and died. So all of these are documented facts.

It's also true that as you arrive in a new place and you pull out the book cartons and start shelving the books, you start looking in the books for what you need. At least that happened to me, and I was confronted by the poet Robinson Jeffers. Of course, Jeffers is a California poet known much better on the West Coast than in the east, a poet for whose work I have a great deal of troubled and disturbed admiration. He declared himself an "anti-humanist" because he found the human species so intolerable, so contemptible, so corrupted that he felt that only in the

2. In this volume "Yom Kippur 1984" appears on pp. 124–27 [*Editors*].

natural world was there any surviving innocence and purity. Purity of a certain kind was very important to him, and he passionately loved the natural world and wrote of it in extraordinary poetry.

But even before coming upon the Jeffers lines which I quote in the text of my poem, there was stirring in me the question: what does it mean to take off and go three thousand miles across the country? Yes, we Americans are very mobile people, we move around a lot, we always have. I was following the paths of those who had, and yet . . . what does it mean in terms of roots, of connectedness, of identity? And . . . further, that Jewish sense of what does it mean to be among strangers—the history of a very small persecuted minority—, that Jewish sense overlapping with the sense of threat conjured up or pointed up by these murders of women in this apparently paradisical landscape.

So I just began writing, "What is a Jew in solitude?" Because I did feel cut off from my Jewish world, which had been gradually and in some ways painfully and very richly becoming more and more real to me over the past few years. I had been working in a political group with Jewish women, and now that was behind me, geographically.

However, these were not ideas. They weren't something I could have sat down and written an essay about or even written out in a journal—because they also came to me as rhythms, as scraps of imagery. They were evocations calling for something that could bring images and sound together for me, and therefore hopefully for others. But for a long time I didn't know how to do that. I also really had no idea where all of this was going. It was a poem begun in great need, in the need to understand what in fact was happening to me.

So I put it away and it stayed in the drawer for a number of months. In the course of those months I was reading a lot in the Bible, and I was reading Whitman. When I came back and looked at the poem, I looked at the line-lengths, which were fairly short, and broken up with blank spaces. I realized that this technique, which I do use a lot, was altogether wrong for this poem. And something about living close to the edge of the ocean made the whole rhythm of the poem become clearer to me, what it had to be. It was that, it was also reading in the Hebrew Bible, the Old Testament. And certainly reading Whitman, with whom there turns out to be considerable dialogue. But I didn't set out to have a dialogue with Whitman in this poem. I did know I was having a dialogue with Robinson Jeffers. That was very obvious to me; I had to address Jeffers in this poem, I knew that. I didn't know I was also going to be in dialogue with Whitman.

The dialogue with Whitman begins on the first page: "something to bind me to this coast as lilacs in the dooryard once / bound me back there." That was the epitome of a poem naming something so familiar and so cherished and so beautiful and so necessary: to see those lilacs bloom every year. "When lilacs last in the dooryard bloom'd . . ."; the

measuring of time. . . . But then Whitman comes back again, on the
last page where the mockingbird comes in. Now that mockingbird isn't
there because I thought: "Well, now I'm going to allude to 'Out of the
cradle endlessly rocking, out of the mockingbird's throat, the musical
shuttle.' " There was a real mockingbird singing in the tree outside of
the window where I was working day after day, the most wonderful,
wonderful series of songs, of poetic compositions. But that mockingbird
transplaced into the poem conjures up, by contrast, the America that
Whitman imagined and believed in.

Whitman depicts slavery, depicts hard labor, depicts prostitution, but
although he names those things, his America is very different from the
America of my poem. The America of the kinds of events my poem is
talking about, that makes solitude dangerous for so many people, that
can make it feel really dangerous to walk out beyond your own turf, your
own protected area. Far from your own people, your own kind; that
makes the stranger a threatening figure to us. Howard Beach, Forsythe
County, more recently come to mind. This isn't the America that Whit-
man understood, that he conjures up in his poetry. That series in my
poem—"faggot kicked into the icy river, woman dragged from her stalled
car," and so on—is a kind of Whitmanesque catalogue, naming and
evoking the different kinds of people that make up the American land-
scape, the American city. But these are kinds of situations that our soci-
ety has to reckon with as Whitman himself did not. And did not feel he
had to deal with, despite his homoerotic poems. The America of vio-
lence, the America that humiliates people on the grounds of their dif-
ference. Whitman himself welcomed those differences.

Wordsworth enters the poem too. I must have had somewhere in the
back of my head "I wandered lonely as a cloud / That floats on high o'er
vales and hills"—the ultimate romantic poem in which the poetic vision
comes in a moment of solitude. "The bliss of solitude." No longer is it
possible to assume that bliss: so, in my poem, "If a cloud knew loneliness
and fear, I would be that cloud."

I've been trying to pull together some of the threads that I've found in
the process of writing the poem, retyping the poem, revising the poem,
proofreading the poem, reading the poem aloud. Threads that are all
there, but if you had said to me at the outset, "well, what are you going
to do here?" I couldn't have told you. That process is, and I think truly
has to be, at one and the same time so conscious and so unconscious—
it has to be very conscious finally. There has to be a way of checking
back over all this unconscious work and making sure that it does work,
that finally what your unconscious has produced is going to speak to
someone else. That is very important to me.

One other little gloss I will offer. Out there on the edge of the Pacific
you can sight whales; people go whale watching. You could call it whale
crowding. People go out in boats and try to get friendly with the whales

so that Leviathan is itself in danger. Now Jonah, the man in that very short biblical text, is truly engaged in what Arthur Waskow has called God-wrestling. He has a terribly personal connection with God and he's arguing with God, trying to disobey God as hard as he can, and still so connected with God. I'm using that term—God—as I do use it: meaning whatever it is that gave Jonah a sense of his ultimate destiny and existence and reality. For him it was certainly the God of the Jews, the God of the Hebrew Bible. So Jonah came into the poem, and I then later discovered, much later, to my surprise, that the story of Jonah is very deeply entwined with Yom Kippur. The story is told at Yom Kippur; it's part of the reflecting and searching of the soul that goes on at that time. Well, that's coincidence or a strange given. I just tell you that because such things are always happening in the writing of poetry. One piece of literature speaks to another—not for the sake of scholarly allusion but because you have read and cared about and stored up something. You may have forgotten it in one sense but you remember it in another sense; and sometimes in writing poetry, in that other sense it will come back to you.

Let me end by bringing all this back to Jeffers. The Jeffers epigraph is from the prologue to *The Women at Point Sur.* I was looking in that poem for a passage about the incredible purple of lupines blooming on a fire-scarred mountainside. But literally, on opening the book, I read, "I drew solitude over me on the long shore." That was a tremendously arresting sentence to read at that point. I wasn't totally alone, I was with someone I love; but after the move west I felt the sense of . . . uprooting, of aloneness in a certain way. So I seized onto that. Then I went on and read the rest of the prologue and found the other lines I quoted in the text.

The poet's tower is another direct reference to Jeffers. He got himself trained as a stone mason and built himself a house and a tower in which he wrote on the edge of the Pacific. It's now a monument to Jeffers, and a museum. He built his house on the edge of the Pacific and he deliberately planted acres and acres and acres of trees to the east so that nothing human could encroach from the other side. Where he saw humanity. Encroaching. Well, of course if you know that part of California now—the developments, the condominiums, the suburban sprawl—you can feel a great deal for Jeffers. He certainly saw that coming. But he translated it into an indictment of all humanity.

"The bliss of solitude" again. But one of the core questions in the poem is this: if you reject Jeffers's solitude, if you reject the sort of lofty attitude that says I'm going to keep all of humankind at arm's length except my few chosen ones and I'm going to build myself a tower and dwell in it . . . if you reject that positioning of the poet outside the community, how still do you get the solitude you need for your life and work? That's a problem I'm constantly wrestling with. If you depend very

much on the sense of a community—and I do—you also owe that community. Being part of a community does mean being engaged with it.
Yet at the same time you need solitude in order to write poetry; there's
no question about it. So the poem which began with a sense of solitude
and a longing for community ends up pondering the need for solitude,
pondering two kinds of solitude and the difficult relations between them.

Adrienne Rich: An Interview with David Montenegro (1991)†

DAVID MONTENEGRO: Would you prefer to start with language or politics?
ADRIENNE RICH: We'll get to both, I'm sure; so start wherever you like.
DM: It seems language can be a means of containment—loaded as it is
with tradition—or it can be a means of liberation, if used as a probe.
How do you deal with the double edge of language? What are your
means of *using* language, without being used *by* language?
RICH: Well, I feel that one of the underlying themes of my poetry is that
tension between the possibilities in language for mere containment and
the possibilities for expansion, for liberation. But there is also the fact
that ultimately language alone cannot liberate us. As I said in "Cartographies of Silence," language cannot do everything. There really are
times when, as a poet, I feel I would simply like to be able to create
something like a monumental head, some kind of great unitary visual
image which would possess its own force and power, and stop all this
struggle with words and meanings.

I've written a great deal about that whole issue of dead language, the
oppressor's language, a language that is no longer useful, and the need
to try to find a new language, a common language, if you will. It's the
question of associations with words and of the history of words, and how
they come down to us and how we go on with them. But I'm beginning
to think and talk a lot more again about that which goes along with
language and poetry—which is music, the vibration of a voice. I see that
intonation, that vocal quality, as something that *is* very personal, out of
the self, and then combines with the many traditions, the many histories
that we've been exposed to, that we come out of.

Let me give you an example. I went into a bookstore when I was in
New York—I had been for some weeks thinking about a way of starting
to write poetry again, meaning that I have been writing it less over the
past few months. I was starting to write it again and feeling the necessity
for some new kind of political voice, for myself, but also to keep the

† From *American Poetry Review* 20.1 (January–February 1991): 7–14. Reprinted by permission.
This essay was subsequently reprinted in *Points of Departure: International Writers on Writing
and Politics* (Ann Arbor: U of Michigan P, 1991).

work going on and to keep it fresh. I saw an anthology of Italian poetry since World War Two and I pulled it out just to see what was in it. This book literally opened for me to some poems by Pier Pasolini, the great filmmaker. I hadn't known he was a poet at all. One of them was a long meditation on the ashes of Gramsci, the Italian revolutionary. And it's a very intimate voice, very personal. He's using *terza rima* which is, of course, a grand Italian form and is laden with the history of Italian poetry, Dante in particular. So he's drawing on that tradition, yet the poem has this curiously intimate, grieving, modern quality. And I felt as if it had come to me from somewhere, that I was drawn to pick up this book and open it in this way, to find an example of what I was searching for—an intonation, a quality of speech. It's deeply personal, and yet it *is* public.

DM: The voice within the voice?

RICH: Yes, in a sense. And yet it's important not to lose touch with that, to keep the thread dividing them very clear.

DM: Since you mentioned Pasolini, poet and filmmaker, how is this quality of speech related to imagery? Are there ties between the sound of a voice and the use of an image?

RICH: I think visual images are one of the great sources for refreshment. And the most effective ones come back to something that's very personal and ordinary perhaps, just a glass of water that you're looking at or what have you, not necessarily casting about for images that will be exotic or arresting.

DM: Not sensational.

RICH: No. And that was something those early postwar Italian films did so wonderfully—just took nitty-gritty visual facts of everyday life and played off them.

DM: In the notes to *The Fact of a Doorframe*, you mentioned something about your use of metaphor in your poem "The Diamond Cutters," that after thirty years you were unsure you had taken responsibility when you had used the metaphor of diamond cutting, that you had not taken into account, had not known at the time the actual circumstances of South African diamond miners' lives. Choosing a metaphor, then, has a political responsibility attached to it?

RICH: Yes, to be as aware as possible of the history and politics of the image or metaphor we're choosing. But I think another problem in that poem was that I was going so far afield to get that image. It was *not* something in my own experience; I had this imaginary diamond cutter and these imaginary diamond miners, and some knowledge, some sense of the fact that it was indeed a matter of *travail*.

DM: Travail of craft rather than . . .

RICH: Well, I was equating the travail of craft with a very different kind of labor—virtual enslavement, peonage.

DM: When you choose a metaphor now, do you examine it right away in those political terms or do you live with it and see what emerges after a time before accepting or rejecting it? In other words, do you have a censor or counter-censor going while you're writing now?

RICH: Well, I think you have a censor going if you're—how shall I put it?—in a position of dissent in this country. You need a consciousness alerted about what images you yourself are receiving from outside, what the media are representing, what mainstream art is representing. A lot of critical antennae develop as you become aware of the amount of disinformation that's being purveyed, how little the conditions of our *actual* lives are reported or represented—what's left out as well as what is presented. And I think those censors inevitably also refer to what you yourself are creating. I mean you can't live in a constant state of *checking* everything as it swims to the surface of consciousness. But I think that there is a way in which that process—"what is missing here? how am I using this?"—becomes a part of the creative process. Then there's also the question of how what you write gets used, which I try to talk about in "North American Time."

DM: The vulnerability involved in what you call in that poem "verbal privilege"?

RICH: Yes.

DM: You say there that what we write is sometimes used against us and is out of our control.

RICH: Yes. There really isn't any way to control how it's used. And I think it's probably a waste of energy to try.

DM: It seems that, instead, your impulse is to try to enlarge your awareness of what's happening in the world, your sense of accountability.

RICH: It feels to me that I need to know more than I ever did in order to be a poet, that I need to be conscious of what is happening on this planet in ways that I never used to think about. And it's not that that takes the place of the work of the imagination, but that each of us has an imagination that has itself been created by a set of circumstances, some very nourishing, some very negative in terms of becoming blinders—the *lacunae*, the cartoon-imagery.

DM: You mentioned earlier a quality of speech that's both personal and public. Do you see poetry as still being part of an oral tradition, and as having some responsibility for warding off public amnesia?

RICH: Well, I feel as though poetry has never really ceased being an oral art. It just hasn't been treated as one by critics and in academe and very often by reviewers and *readers*. The idea of the *text* on the page has become such an obsession, and yet it seems to me that as long as I've been a conscious, adult poet, there have been poetry movements which placed a great deal of importance on the reading aloud of poetry, the reciting of poetry. Most of the poets I knew when I was younger—even though they themselves might have thought of their work as very textual and confined to the page—*loved* to recite poetry, people knew reams of poetry by heart. Then later, in the sixties, the public reading or recitation of poetry became a part of political movements, and it's never ceased to be, I think.

DM: In one essay, you said you were slightly suspicious of movements that rely too heavily on the word. Again, is this part of your mixed feeling about the whole operation of language?

RICH: Yes. Well, I guess what I was talking about there was how, specifically in the women's movement, writers have so often been seen and cited as spokespeople and as leaders. My feeling is that it is the *activists* who move the rest of us, and that one may explain, describe, praise, deplore or whatever what is actually happening in the way of action—and that's very important, so I'm not selling the word short either when I say this—but, you don't make a political movement simply out of words.

DM: So activists who are savvy about, say, organizing a strike have a skill that's . . .

RICH: Or I'm thinking about grassroots women's organizations and activists who have sat through hundreds of interviews with battered or raped women telling what happened to them, and helping to empower them, and who have a knowledge about these things which is not metaphorical.

DM: The necessity of ending the general erasure of women's history and of repairing the damage done is a principal focus of your work. Is a transformation occurring as women reclaim their history? Are women now more empowered by having a broad historical base from which to move forward?

RICH: Some. I see it happening in Women's Studies programs in universities, in community colleges. It happens for the women who take those courses, who can avail themselves of them. There is a little revision of the curriculum generally to be found, even some in the high schools. Of course, this is an ignorance that is damaging both to women and to men. Ignorance of the history of more than half the human species. And therefore the history of the entire species is distorted. In some ways we *have* come a long way; in other ways, I think, not at all.

And then outside of the sphere of the kind of education where you would expect to find a certain liberal stance toward feminism, the issue becomes *what* women have any education available to them *at all*. Thinking on a global level, how early do women leave school, if they've gone to school at all? The illiteracy rate among women overall is rapidly on the increase. And so it's not just a question of, do we know our history, but do we know how to *read*, how to write? Do we know that there is such a thing as history, that we can be part of it, makers of it? I don't mean that a sense of history necessarily goes along only with literacy because obviously it doesn't. Women have an oral historical tradition in many cultures, but the disempowerment of women overall, I think, limits very much what those of us who are literate and educated can expect in the way of our history liberating us. It's important; I've argued for it passionately, but I also see the limits of what can be done in an educational system which in itself is so class-bound, so racist, so restrictive.

DM: Would this include Women's Studies programs themselves? Do they create antagonism between Black Studies and Women's Studies?

RICH: Racism in the academy does, and sexism in the academy. Black Studies programs have been and can be very sexist; Women's Studies programs have been and can be very racist. And I think the antagonisms are not peculiar to those programs but are embedded in the whole structure of the society where we live. We don't shed racism or sexism because we're in a liberation movement unless we struggle hard to try to create bridges, to find out where our common base is, to become educated in each other's realities, to search for and document the mistakes of the past so we can stop making them. I'm thinking particularly of the history of the nineteenth-century white suffrage movement, the early North American feminist movement, its visions, and its racist stances, despite its roots in the Abolitionist movement.

DM: How did the Civil Rights movement affect you, your awareness of the women's movement as it was developing, your work as a writer, the growth of your voice as a woman and a poet?

RICH: Well, you have to understand that I grew up in a social and familial world in which there was a great deal of splitting. I've written an essay called "Split at the Root" which actually speaks about my own family roots: Jewish and Gentile. But it was also a world very split by segregation. Baltimore in the thirties and forties was a deeply segregated city. There weren't back-of-the-bus rules, but Black people did not shop in the same department stores as white people, there was the interracial eating taboo, and so on. That kind of thing a child grows up acutely aware of, even if it's never talked about, and of course there was a great deal of pressure not to talk about it. It was a given. And it was a given that, needless to say, white people were extremely tense about. But we learned not to ask questions about it or to discuss it. We did not go to school with Black children. The Black people that I grew up knowing all worked for white people as domestic workers.

So that left a profound impact, in the sense that it was a situation which, I think from a very young age, I felt was so—uncomfortable is hardly the word—almost intolerable. There was so much that wasn't explained, there were codes of behavior that you couldn't question but that you couldn't figure out. They didn't seem to make any sense, and there was this general attitude that, because of being Black, people somehow deserved and needed less in the world. But there was also a great deal of talk about how far Black people had come—you have to remember this was a very southern context—things were said like: "Since the Civil War these people have come a long way," and so on. So that was all very confusing.

When the Civil Rights movement came long in the late fifties, early sixties, and I began to hear Black voices describing and analyzing what were the concrete issues for Black people, like segregation, like racism, it came to me as a great relief. It was like finding language for something that I'd needed a language for all along. That was the first place where I heard a language to name oppression. And it was an enormous relief, even as it threw up a lot of questions for me as to where I stood with all this. Well, I felt I stood with the Civil Rights workers, I understood exactly why they had to do what they were doing. It felt like a completely intuitive knowledge, but I was still very politically ignorant. And that movement, as it grew and became a movement around the country, and as it went through changes and the Black Power movement separated out of it and many white activists became involved in the anti-war movement and various groups against imperialism—groups like SDS—all of that continued to make a great deal of sense to me.

I think that all of that early splitting and fragmentation has made me hungry for connections to be made. Where connections are being made always feels to me like the point of intensest life. So, there was no way that all of that wasn't going to affect me as a poet because the point of intensest life is where I write poetry.

At the same time, I was thinking a lot about something that wasn't being talked about at the time very much. I was thinking about where sexuality belonged in all this. What *is* the connection between Vietnam and the lovers' bed? If this insane violence is being waged against a very small country by this large and powerful country in which I live, what does that have to do with sexuality and with what's going on between men and women, which I felt also as a struggle even then? I was married. I was trying to define myself in a number of ways. I couldn't fit into the . . . I couldn't find a model for the way I wanted to be, either in a relationship with a man or as a woman in the world. So when the women's movement began to crystallize from the Left and the Civil Rights movement, that was another and certainly one of the most powerful connections for me.

DM: Nineteen sixty-eight seems to have been a very important year for you. You wrote a lot of poetry and your essays began to be less literary, more political. Many things happened that year: the Tet offensive, the assassinations of Martin Luther King and Robert Kennedy, student strikes at Berkeley, at Columbia, in Belfast, Prague, Warsaw.

RICH: It was also the year of my father's death. He had been sick a long time, really not present. That loss, of an extremely adversarial relationship, had been happening for some time. I suppose, knowing that there was a real end gave me some sense of relief—as if then I could begin to put it all in order? But it took much longer than I thought it would.

DM: Are you still continuing a conversation with him, in a sense?

RICH: Yes.

DM: Has anything been resolved or has your relationship become more complex?

RICH: I see him more and more as a person. You know, you see your parents first of all as these great looming figures who have no past, no context. They're just *there* and over and against you. Or they're *not* there, which is another kind of looming presence—looming absence. But I've been learning to see my father and to think about his life more and more and more in the context of the social and political world, if you will, that he grew up in, to think about the things that brought him to where he was when I knew him, especially the meaning of his Jewishness. He had been, for me, such an ambiguous figure, so tremendously rewarding, on the one hand, and also such an obstacle. Now, it's much more that there was this person who had his own history and his own family background and parents who had a certain life themselves and who came from certain kinds of families, and that they were Jews in the South in a particular period. I think about him in that field much more than I ever used to be able to.

DM: So you're learning the context of his life?

RICH: Yes, rather than, you know, simply focusing on the relationship itself.

DM: And your mother; she was a pianist and composer?

RICH: Well, she really still is a pianist at eighty-eight. She has her piano—which she's had from the age of fifteen—in her apartment, and she still plays extremely well.

DM: How do you feel about her not having been able to pursue music as a career, perhaps for family reasons? Is that an issue?

RICH: Oh, I think it was a tremendous issue. And very complex. I think, given her context, that she made a choice not to become a professional woman pianist in that musical world which involved the depreciation of women, sexual harassment, which she experienced.

She was fascinated by my father. He had a very powerful personality. She has said that she felt that her life would always be interesting with him, and also that she had no models for living in the world on her own. I think she would have had to come out of a different background and have had a different character and personality to be able to make that decision. Her family were southern people who'd had land but, after the Civil War, little money. My grandmother went to a convent school, which was the best education she could get at that time. My grandfather was a tobacco salesman. I doubt that he'd been to college. There was a lot of struggle for education in that family, but there was not a tradition of women being independent; there was not a tradition of women even being creative. Although my grandmother, I think, would have been a writer if she'd herself come out of another time and place. She did write. And she loved books. She desperately wanted education, and she wanted her children to have education.

But I think that, for me, there was always this question: Is that what happens? You pursue an art, win prizes and scholarships, and then, when you marry, you stop doing it except in the privacy of your living room? That was what I saw, growing up.

DM: My mother, by the way, is a pianist also. She must have gone through a similar conflict between family and music.

RICH: She gave it up?

DM: As a performer, yes. She had five children. It must have been difficult to make that choice.

RICH: Choice is a very loaded word. Choice depends a lot on what you know is possible. There *do* have to be choices indicated. Some people actually seem to invent their choices, but I think that more often we learn about a possibility and think: *I* could do that, or, I don't want to do that, I don't want to be like that.

DM: Do you think there has been a regression during the past ten years from the progress made by the women's movement? Has its momentum slowed, and, if so, will the movement pick up its pace again to what it was in the 1970s? Is there now a sense of exhaustion?

RICH: Well, it very much depends on how you look at the contours of the landscape. An astonishing number of feminist institutions were founded in the seventies. And a lot of movement was going on in existing institutions like universities. But the kind of political retrenchment that began, I think, before Reagan was elected, and in fact led up to his election, inevitably was accompanied by the reassertion of old conservative values about women, and about sexuality. And those attitudes have come down hard.

I think that a couple of things have happened. One is that the economy worsened so much and so fast. And where there used to be bits of funding about here and there—CETA grants, let's say, which could be used to pay someone for a part-time job in a feminist institution—that money disappears. Suddenly there are no grants. Or everybody's competing for these grants because there are no other sources. Women are jobless, or working several poorly paid jobs to survive. So there's a scarcity of resources that were still around at the end of the sixties, just in view of the fact that the economy was still grinding on. And everything that we do at this point, it seems to me, is done with a great deal more effort because those resources are depleted, those *human* energies are spread thinner. People have to put bread on the table and they're trying to do political work as well.

Then there's the fact that the conservatives have been making a lot of work for us with their legislative proposals and their political campaigns.

We have found ourselves fighting back at a level that we were not having to fight on in the seventies. We've found ourselves thrown back on old ground again, not able to push forward as much as one would have hoped.

At the same time, though this is all absorbing a tremendous amount of energy, I think the energy is there. Some people are tired and burnt-out, but I see new women—and men—coming along all the time. And that is very refreshing and very inspiring. It's not as though the same cast of characters that was there in the early seventies still has to be doing it all now. The cast of characters has grown; some have left, some have taken time out and returned, others have come in, many with new understandings, with new contributions.

One of the things that has been growing in the women's movement in this country—and again, in a society like this it can't, it doesn't happen easily, and it doesn't happen overnight—is the consciousness that we aren't a homogeneous movement, that we are a multi-ethnic movement, that women's experiences across the board are different, even though we share common female experiences. There's been a tremendous enrichment through those understandings, and through the visibility, the leadership, of women of color, and the work of Jewish feminists; that has certainly been part of the last few years.

In fall, 1986, the *New York Times* published yet another article about the young white woman of thirty-eight who is an attorney and feels the biological clock ticking. And the last paragraph began: "At a time when the women's movement is virtually invisible . . ." I brought that article to my class in feminist theory. I also brought in an armful of publications that had been lying around my house, from all over the world, from the global women's movement. And I said: "All right: here's this pile of papers, journals, newsletters, pamphlets. It's concrete, it's here, it's visible. And here you have a statement that the women's movement is virtually invisible. Now *to whom* is it invisible? And why? And who is saying that it is invisible? And who benefits if it is?"

An enormous amount is happening globally—different kinds of struggle in different countries, in different societies. When you look at South Africa, there's enormous leadership by women. Black women in South Africa are maintaining and creating a structure. In that violence-ridden society, in the midst of revolution, they are creating childcare centers, soup kitchens, planting gardens, keeping things going on that human level. Now I don't think that's just women doing the service work of the world; those women are also leaders of their communities. We could talk about feminism in the Philippines, in Latin America, in the Caribbean, not a monolithic global movement but many movements, all over the world, contending within and against many different cultures. The United States movement is only a small part of the picture.

DM: As with language in general, your relationship to abstractions, it seems, is a mixed one. What are the dangers of abstractions, whether in poetry—where the risks of their use are fairly clear—or in prose? For example, the "feminization" of poverty, which, in a way, does not reflect at all the realities of a single woman with five children living in an apartment she can't afford where there is lead paint on the ceiling.

RICH: Well, these phrases become a kind of shorthand, a kind of code: "You know what I mean and I know what you mean when we say this." And we may ourselves lose the truth behind it, the concreteness behind it, as well as not being able to communicate that to a third person. All movements have a tendency to in-group language, and that language can become a language of abstraction, a language of stereotype. And yet, it's a powerful thing to talk about your concrete experience in its unique details and then begin to abstract from it. That was really what happened in those early consciousness-raising groups.

DM: To generalize and connect?

RICH: Yes. There has to be abstraction, but we have to keep coming back to the concrete again.

DM: Looking at the evolution of your work, do you see a relationship between the poetry and the prose, and, if so, what do you feel is the connection?

RICH: Well, I first started writing prose about poetry. The first prose I wrote for publication was some book reviews for *Poetry*. I reviewed *The Collected Poetry of D.H. Lawrence,* some anthologies. That was way back—in the early sixties, I think. And then I was asked by the Harvard University Press to write the foreword to an edition of Anne Bradstreet. But I didn't think of myself as an essayist, and I didn't pursue writing prose on my own, except in my journals. I guess that it was finally involvement in politics that got me writing prose more, as a part of life, as a regular part of my writing. And very often it was because somebody asked me to speak or asked for an essay.

So, I feel as if, in some ways, the prose has always been initiated from an exterior point, but it wasn't an exterior point that was irrelevant to what was happening to me, in my life, or even in my poetry. I was writing poems out of a lot of the same things which I discussed in the essay "When We Dead Awaken," and I have a poem with the same title. Certainly a lot of my other essays have points of intersection with poems, probably none so much as "Split at the Root" with "Sources"—which I was writing at about the same time. I was having a lot of difficulty with the poem, and then I wrote the essay and came back to the poem feeling very freed because I'd worked out a great deal in the essay, and then didn't have to spell it out in the poem at all.

DM: In the poem, it was concentrated?

RICH: Yes.

DM: And, in a sense, resolved?

RICH: If such things ever are.

DM: In "Sources" you use prose also.

RICH: Well, I've used blocks of prose in my poetry for some time, actually.

DM: Since the late 1960s?

RICH: Yes.

DM: In one poem written at that time, "The Burning of Paper Instead of Children," you use prose, including a passage in so-called "poor grammar," Black English. Was this written during your years as a teacher at City College in New York?

RICH: Yes.

DM: At the end of that poem, you say: "A language is a map of our failures."

RICH: Well, that was a very specific reference. I was teaching writing in the SEEK program at City College then, and there was, of course, as in all schools, this terrible thing that hung over you—the threat of failure. I mean, that the *student* would fail. Those students were *expected* to fail, they were *intended* to fail, and the SEEK program was trying to show that, no, they don't have to fail. And we teachers used to talk a lot about *who* fails—the teacher or the student—when you have a classroom situation which is rigged entirely against the student, or in which the teacher is too ignorant to teach. Not ignorant of grammar, but ignorant of the students, ignorant of their culture. So, I was thinking very much about *our* failures, the map of *our* failures, we who consider ourselves so possessed of language, so articulate.

DM: The privilege . . .

RICH: To speak so people will listen to you.

DM: In your essay "When We Dead Awaken," published in 1971, you looked back over the span of your work and picked out "Aunt Jennifer's Tigers," "Orion," and then "Planetarium" to show turning points in your poetry. That was sixteen years ago. What poems would you now add to that list, as landmarks of your development?

RICH: Well, after "Planetarium": "The Burning of Paper Instead of Children," "I Dream I'm the Death of Orpheus," "When We Dead Awaken," "The Phenomenology of Anger," "Diving into the Wreck," "Twenty-One Love Poems," "Natural Resources," "A Woman Dead in Her Forties," "For Ethel Rosenberg."

"For Ethel Rosenberg" was a very important poem for me to write. It was like touching the tip of an iceberg. I'm still struggling with a lot of that stuff. When I wrote the poem, I wrote it as best I could, but there's so much more.

Other poems would be: "Frame," "Grandmothers," "In the Wake of Home," "North American Time," "Sources," "Yom Kippur 1984." I guess I'm thinking about poems that were the result of very long struggles to understand what I was writing, why I needed to be writing this at all, and to make it happen—poems that reflect to me some kind of watershed, perhaps.

DM: In the span of your work, one thing that's striking is that, at a certain point, you seem to have had to destroy language, or maybe only structure, or maybe only logic in poems. For example, "Shooting Script," where you do not keep to a logical progression as you did earlier in poems like "Orion" or "The Trees," where the metaphor is developed in a very clear and traditional way. It seems that, in the late 1960s, you broke the language down, you *let* it break down. And then you dove into the wreck—to use your title—and came out the other side with *The Dream of a Common Language*. In this book, it seems, the language is fulfilled. It's wearing its own skin, in a sense. Do you feel that you had to go through that period of destruction of traditional order to go on with your work?

RICH: Well, I certainly had to find an equivalent for the kinds of fragmentation I was feeling, and confusion. One thing that was very helpful to me was working on the translations from the Urdu poet Mirzah Ghalib, which led me to write original *ghazals*. There, I found a structure which allowed for a highly associative field of images. And once I saw how that worked, I felt instinctively, this is exactly what I need, there is no traditional Western order that I have found that will contain all these materials.

And another thing was that, in the 1960s, I was going to the movies more than I ever have in my life, and seeing a vast number of filmic images. I was very much struck by Godard's use of language and image in films. I think I've probably over-referred to him in some of the poems of that era. But that was very helpful to me too. It suggested a way of making images work. So, yes, I feel like that period was essential.

DM: It released certain energies that otherwise would not have been able to express themselves?

RICH: Well, the absolute content of my life. And my times, in so far as I knew them.

DM: One other question about form. In your early poems, you use a very strict meter. For example, "Storm Warnings." Here you have the storm contained within a very tight capsule. What *new* forms—whether it has to do with freeing a personal voice or freeing a woman's tone of voice—are necessary? Does traditional meter—iambic pentameter or whatever—imply a frame of mind? Does it limit content?

RICH: Of course, there's been a lot of argument about that, back and forth, in American poetry for the last many decades since the beginning of the twentieth century, and I was, to a certain extent, involved in that kind of debate in the fifties, when there was considered to be a tremendous divergence between the so-called "Beats" and the "academics." I never really felt I was part of either group. I had started to write in open forms in the fifties, and I felt I would never go back to writing the kind of formal poems that were in *The Diamond Cutters*, or in A *Change of World*. Experience itself had become too much for that.

At the same time, I did not want to "smash the iamb." It seemed to me that iambic pentameter was still a useful line, a line that could also be very elastic, as poets like Wyatt and Hopkins had long before shown. And it has a kind of organic relation to the way Anglo-American is accented, Anglo-American speech-patterns. And so I never wanted to get rid of it.

So, at the time I started writing, that was already set up as a problem. If you were going to be writing a truly new poetry, could you use the old forms? It's a question that is being asked now in a feminist context—for instance, in the work of the Feminist Language poets, a group primarily located on the West Coast. Susan Howe, who wrote a quite provocative book on Emily Dickinson, Kathleen Fraser, Frances Jaffer, and Rachel DuPlessis have a journal called *How(ever)*, which publishes what has always been labeled experimental poetry, in the sense of undercutting traditional syntax, emphasizing typography as part of the statement of the poem, using more open field arrangements on the page.

I have a real question about it though because it feels to me like experimental poetry from the early twenties, or of Black Mountain. It does not feel particularly experimental now. The fact that women are doing it is interesting, but women were doing that kind of thing in the twenties also, people like Mina Loy, for example, Gertrude Stein obviously. I guess what I'm searching for always is a way of staying linked to the past, pulling out of it whatever you can use, and continuing to move on. And I'm not sure that a new textual form creates—it certainly *doesn't* create a new consciousness. It can equally well be said that a new consciousness, a radically divergent one, doesn't necessarily create a new form either. I hate that form/content bifurcation, but sometimes it has to be used, for an attitude, a stance, a positioning of the poet.

I'm trying to think of some examples of the kind of thing I'm talking about. There's a poem by Derek Walcott, in his sequence called *Mid-summer*, (XXIII), which is, in a sense, an expanded sonnet sequence—sprung sonnets, or whatever. He's witnessing a confrontation between skinheads and Blacks, in London. He himself is located in Britain working in the English theatre, a token West Indian in a racist society. The poem moves very rapidly; it's got a strong iambic pentameter base, as they all do, and images fold and collapse into each other very fast. And it ends with this incredible reference, to "an empire/that began with Caedmon's raceless dew, and is ending/in the alleys of Brixton, burning like Turner's ships."

It gives me a great rush, and I think I know why. It's because he is pulling on this contemporary, immediate, and historically powerful image of the riots in Brixton, as a West Indian, with everything that lies behind that—the British colonization of his own country, his own internal colonization. And here is the mother country, and now not only he, but that history, is coming back "home." Then he draws on Caedmon and

Shakespeare and Turner. And underlying the whole is the pulling-together of a consciousness split by colonization and diaspora, through an integrative kind of anger. And it seems to me that that's genuinely *new*. Nobody had done just that, in poetry, until the West Indians did it. It's a fusion of old form and old consciousness with new form and new consciousness that is explosive.

DM: Even visually—by bringing in Turner's paintings.

RICH: Yes. It's the poem that begins with an extraordinary visual image of trees moving in the wind, a tremendous sense of unrest and the storm in the trees. It's a wonderful poem.

DM: And it doesn't matter whether it's in iambic pentameter or not?

RICH: It does matter, especially when he refers to Shakespeare's sonnets.

DM: Poetry is a relationship to language, and language, for a poet, is often an almost physical, sensuous thing. If now women's experience, including lesbianism, is finding a voice, doesn't this or shouldn't this change the sound or feel of language? "Twenty-One Love Poems," for example, expresses a different sensibility and in a changed language.

RICH: Well, a lot of those poems are about looking at sexual passion and, instead of saying: yes, love is like this, it's saying: no, love is not like this. This is something different, a female and lesbian sensuality and sensibility that has not been in poetry before. One of the most sensual and sensuous women poets I can think of is Audre Lorde. She *thinks* in images that are most certainly lesbian images. But also images from Afro-Caribbean culture and from African mythology and experience. And that's a very powerful combination. Because that also has not been available in most poetry in English.

DM: Just a few more questions. Costs—in a word. So much of your work has been a struggle to speak honestly and openly, whether about poetry itself or about social issues, about racism, about lesbianism. What are the costs of doing so, as a poet, as a person?

RICH: What would be the cost of *not* doing it? I feel as though it's for my survival, first and foremost. This is how I cope, this is how I survive. I have learned from my peers that this way of creating can be a way of surviving. I didn't invent that.

DM: You do head for the breaks in the fabric. There's an instinct in your poetry for that spot where the seam's coming apart. Your language goes where the danger is. Do you know why?

RICH: For a very long time, poems were a way of talking about what I couldn't talk about any other way. And why is it that you're not able to talk about certain things? It's because they are the points of danger, you feel that in the social fabric, you feel there are people who don't want you to raise this question, or—if you're a child—to ask this question. That is the threatening place, and of course it becomes a place of great fascination too. I was equipped from a very young age to use language in this way because of how I was brought up, and by whom I was brought up, and the fact that poetry was available to me as a choice, when it might not have been for another seven or ten years if I'd been another child.

If I had become my mother's student—and she did teach me piano from a very young age—if I had really become her student, become a musician, I would have been, I suppose, fulfilling my creative and expressive needs. But it wouldn't have been through language, and language is this medium that we hand back and forth between us in all human relationships all the time, it doesn't really have a privileged place. It's this coinage in which we keep trying to get a hold of each other or make ourselves clear. So, the fact that poetry was available to me for that is very important. I think the fact that it was poetry rather than, say, fiction or some other kind of prose was important because I learned while very young that you could be fairly encoded in poems, and get away with it. Then I began to want to do away with the encoding, or to break the given codes and maybe find another code. But it was a place of a certain degree of control, in which to explore things, in which to start testing the waters.

DM: Then your certainty in language came to be matched by an uncertainty in vision? You had to keep testing, back and forth?

RICH: Oh, tremendous uncertainty, yes.

DM: Is there some feeling of dissatisfaction when you've finished a poem, particularly a poem in which you have resolved or clarified certain issues or made some connections? Do you have the sense that you have to push forward, to move the next step, as if the most recent poem were not enough? Do you ever feel you have actually falsified the experience?

RICH: Experience is always larger than language. And there's always the next poem, yes. Not necessarily because I feel I've falsified something, but because I wrote it as I knew it then, and I'm going to know it differently in six months. Or I'm going to know something else. Or I'm going to *need* to know something else, and the only way I can get to it is by writing that poem.

DM: By choice you would write a poem then, if you were dealing with certain unnameable sensations or experiences? It would be poetry rather than prose that you would go to?

RICH: Increasingly, I feel as if right now I don't want to write any prose, except necessary workmanlike statements. I'll write an ad hoc political manifesto or statement, but for the kind of exploration we've been talking about, I want to be working in poetry more. I feel there are a lot of places that I still need to go—I'm just getting the outlines of certain things.

Swarthmore College Commencement: June 1, 1992†

Hello and congratulations to you, Class of 1992, to your parents, your life-teachers, your friends, your loves.

I want to tell you about a memory I have of teaching at Swarthmore in the spring of 1968, the April of the assassination of Martin Luther King. Dr. King was assassinated at the point when, as a national figure, he was articulating the connections among the Black movement for justice, the self-organizing of poor working people, and the widespread opposition to the Vietnam War. The week after that assassination, I took the train as usual from Penn Station in Manhattan to 30th Street in Philadelphia, boarded the Media local, and got off as usual at the foot of the long walk leading up between daffodil and narcissus beds to the College. I had no idea what to expect here. I noticed that on the lawns were groups of students seated in circles, seemingly in earnest discussion. You were not born yet, but I want you to see this. As I came closer I noticed that in many of the groups of mostly white students, there was one Black student, and it appeared that the Black students had been apportioned out to lend some kind of visual integration to the scene.

I stand here now in 1992, a year of equally deep and shattering national crisis as 1968, alike and different in its social and political configurations. I'm speaking to you who are graduating from Swarthmore, coming into your twenties, out of what the poet W. H. Auden, from another part of history, termed a *low, dishonest decade*. Two decades, in fact, of a public shallowness, lying, greed and heartlessness now falling over themselves as elections approach—which piece of emptiness shall win? Which piece of emptiness, losing, shall ally itself with the winner?

Those of us who came into activism in the sixties and before, who have continued as engaged citizens through the seventies into the nineties—as welfare rights organizers, as feminists, as members of a critical and oppositional press, as community organizers, as lesbian and gay activists, as anti-racism educators, as new and challenging voices in the labor movement, as builders of battered women's shelters and rape crisis centers, as coalition builders among racial and ethnic communities, as creators of socially responsive art—we did not intend for you or any young people to face at your coming-of-age so manipulated and demoralized a society, at once so fearful and so complacement, as this one. But it's not commiseration I feel for you, standing here, but hope. You have had not just educational privilege of a high order, but the privilege of *having* a time of youth, when you could try on different selves, without fear of being locked into any one of them. Most people your age in this country don't have a time of youth. And for those young men and women, who will not stand today or any day soon in academic robes

† Printed by permission of the author.

under a threatening or a clear blue sky, who were early locked by racism and poverty into manhoods and womanhoods they had no time to choose, I also feel, not despair, but hope.

How is it possible, given the enormous social and economic rifts between you and those young people? Because I believe in the potential, both tapped and blocked, within each one of you. I believe that the responses to the Simi Valley verdict[1]—where hundreds of white youth have joined in demonstrations and uprisings in city after city, where citizens of conscience, whatever their, our origins, are being compelled to consider their, our place in all this—I believe that the civil and moral unrest now moving through the inner nervous system of our country, has a chance of catalyzing one of the great shifts in our history. A chance of building not into some hierarchic, monolithic movement, but into many streams of movement, always in touch with and interrogating each other: African American, Arab American, Asian American, Jewish, Latino, white, lesbian, gay and straight: women and men, old and young. My hope, for you and for us all, is that you refuse docility and shallowness and lend your gifts and intelligence to a rising democracy movement here in the United States, sharing power with sisters and brothers at whose expense that power was acquired: learning what can only be taught by those who are not here today.

Dear and cherished graduates: Remember the youth of your generation. Remember all the youths—and the parents—who are not here today nor at any commencement in the land. Remember that our true democracy cannot come to birth without their participation. Nor without yours.

---

1. On April 29, 1992, in suburban Simi Valley, a California Superior Court jury acquitted four white Los Angeles police officers of all but one charge stemming from a March 1991 beating of an unarmed black motorist, Rodney G. King. Riots ensued in Los Angeles and other cities because a videotape of the beating, made by a resident in a nearby apartment, seemed to many clear evidence of police brutality and racism [Editors].

REVIEWS AND CRITICISM

W. H. AUDEN

Foreword to A *Change of World* †

Reading a poem is an experience analogous to that of encountering a person. Just as one can think and speak separately of a person's physical appearance, his mind, and his character, so one can consider the formal aspects of a poem, its contents, and its spirit while knowing that in the latter case no less than in the former these different aspects are not really separate but an indissoluble trinity-in-unity.

We would rather that our friends were handsome than plain, intelligent than stupid, but in the last analysis it is on account of their character as persons that we accept or reject them. Similarly, in poetry we can put up with a good deal, with poems that are structurally defective, with poems that say nothing particularly new or "amusing," with poems that are a bit crazy; but a poem that is dishonest and pretends to be something other than it is, a poem that is, as it were, so obsessed with itself that it ignores or bellows at or goes on relentlessly boring the reader, we avoid if possible. In art as in life, truthfulness is an absolute essential, good manners of enormous importance.

Every age has its characteristic faults, its typical temptation to over-emphasize some virtue at the expense of others, and the typical danger for poets in our age is, perhaps, the desire to be "original." This is natural, for who in his daydreams does not prefer to see himself as a leader rather than a follower, an explorer rather than a cultivator and a settler? Unfortunately, the possibility of realizing such a dream is limited, not only by talent but also by time, and even a superior gift cannot cancel historical priority; he who today climbs the Matterhorn, though he be the greatest climber who ever lived, must tread in Whymper's footsteps.

Radical changes and significant novelty in artistic style can only occur when there has been a radical change in human sensibility to require them. The spectacular events of the present time must not blind us to the fact that we are living not at the beginning but in the middle of a historical epoch; they are not novel but repetitions on a vastly enlarged scale and at a violently accelerated tempo of events which took place long since.

Every poet under fifty-five cherishes, I suspect, a secret grudge against Providence for not getting him born a little earlier. On writing down the

---

† From A *Change of World*, by Adrienne Rich (New Haven: Yale UP, 1951). Reprinted by permission of Adrienne Rich.

obvious names which would occur to everyone as those of the great figures in "modern" poetry, novels, painting, and music, the innovators, the creators of the new style, I find myself with a list of twenty persons: of these, four were born in the sixties, six in the seventies, and ten in the eighties. It was these men who were driven to find a new style which could cope with such changes in our civilization as, to mention only four, the collapse of the liberal hope of peaceful change, of revolution through oratory and literature; the dissolution of the traditional community by industrial urbanization; the exposure of the artist to the styles of every epoch and culture simultaneously; and the skepticism induced by psychology and anthropology as to the face value of any emotion or belief.

Before a similar crop of revolutionary artists can appear again, there will have to be just such another cultural revolution replacing these attitudes with others. So long as the way in which we regard the world and feel about our existence remains in all essentials the same as that of our predecessors we must follow in their tradition; it would be just as dishonest for us to pretend that their style is inadequate to our needs as it would have been for them to be content with the style of the Victorians.

Miss Rich, who is, I understand, twenty-one years old, displays a modesty not so common at that age, which disclaims any extraordinary vision, and a love for her medium, a determination to ensure that whatever she writes shall, at least, not be shoddily made. In a young poet, as T. S. Eliot has observed, the most promising sign is craftsmanship for it is evidence of a capacity for detachment from the self and its emotions without which no art is possible. Craftsmanship includes, of course, not only a talent for versification but also an ear and an intuitive grasp of much subtler and more difficult matters like proportion, consistency of diction and tone, and the matching of these with the subject at hand; Miss Rich's poems rarely fail on any of these counts.

They make no attempt to conceal their family tree: "A Clock in the Square," for instance, is confessedly related to the poetry of Robert Frost, "Design in Living Colors" to the poetry of Yeats; but what they say is not a parrotlike imitation without understanding but the expression of a genuine personal experience.

The emotions which motivate them—the historical apprehension expressed in "Storm Warnings," the conflict between faith and doubt expressed in "For the Conjunction of Two Planets," the feeling of isolation expressed in "By No Means Native"—are not peculiar to Miss Rich but are among the typical experiences of our time; they are none the less for that uniquely felt by her.

I suggested at the beginning of this introduction that poems are analogous to persons; the poems a reader will encounter in this book are neatly and modestly dressed, speak quietly but do not mumble, respect

their elders but are not cowed by them, and do not tell fibs: that, for a
first volume, is a good deal.

JOHN ASHBERY

Tradition and Talent †

Adrienne Rich is a traditional poet, but not a conventional one. She has
made progress since those schoolgirlish days when she would come home
from a Bach concert worried that "A too-compassionate art is half an
art." Such rhetorical questions are now left behind. She speaks in dense,
short lines that suggest the laconic exchanges of a couple who have out-
lived more elaborate forms of communication, and she emerges as a
kind of Emily Dickinson of the suburbs, bleakly eyeing the pullulation
and pollution around her, sometimes being shocked into passionate speech:

> Whatever you are that weeps
> over the blistered riverbeds
> and the cracked skin of cities,
> you are not on our side.
>
> ("Spring Thunder")

or, in this beginning:

> Ailanthus, goldenrod, scrapiron, what makes you flower?
> What burns in the dump today?
>
> ("Open-Air Museum")

In lines like these, where inner and outer reality fuse into a kind of living
fabric, Miss Rich is . . . a metaphysical poet.

Sometimes she does succumb to the mania for overinterpretation that
plagues her contemporaries. (The technical term for this ailment is
objective correlativitis. It attacks poets in their late thirties, and is espe-
cially prevalent in New England; elms are thought to be carriers.) In
"Breakfast in a Bowling Alley in Utica, New York," Miss Rich, appalled
by the crumminess of her surroundings, chews a defrosted sandwich
steak, "thinking of wheatfields—/a gold-beige ceinture—," trying to for-
get about TV aerials and mobile homes until she remembers that in one
of the latter there is "perhaps, a man/alone with his girl/for the first
time." Everybody's hell is different, but a reader conversant with those
of Burroughs, Ginsberg, and Ed Sanders, for instance, is not likely to
be shaken up by Miss Rich's bowling alley, or reassured by the couple
in the trailer.

---

† This review of *Necessities of Life* first appeared in the *New York Herald Tribune Book Week* 4
Sept. 1966. Reprinted by permission of John Ashbery and Georges Borchardt, Inc. Copyright
© 1966.

But it is not often her way to present us with problems which we have to make an effort to take seriously, followed by their imaginary solutions. In this hard and sinewy new poetry she has mastered the art of tacking between alternative resolutions of the poem's tension and of leaving the reader at the right moment, just as meaning is dawning. She does this beautifully in "Mourning Picture," based on Edwin Romanzo Elmer's primitive drawing of parents on a New England lawn watching the spirit of their dead child:

> I tell you, the thread that bound us lies
> faint as a web in the dew.
> Should I make you, world, again,
> could I give back the leaf its skeleton, the air
> its early-summer cloud, the house
> its noonday presence, shadowless,
> and leave *this* out? I am Effie, you were my dream.

MARGARET ATWOOD

Review of *Diving into the Wreck* †

This is Adrienne Rich's seventh book of poems, and it is an extraordinary one. When I first heard the author read from it, I felt as though the top of my head was being attacked, sometimes with an ice pick, sometimes with a blunter instrument: a hatchet or a hammer. The predominant emotions seemed to be anger and hatred, and these are certainly present; but when I read the poems later, they evoked a far more subtle reaction. *Diving into the Wreck* is one of those rare books that forces you to decide not just what you think about it, but what you think about yourself. It is a book that takes risks, and it forces the reader to take them also.

If Adrienne Rich were not a good poet, it would be easy to classify her as just another vocal Women's Libber, substituting polemic for poetry, simplistic messages for complex meanings. But she *is* a good poet, and her book is not a manifesto, though it subsumes manifestoes; nor is it a proclamation, though it makes proclamations. It is instead a book of explorations, of travels. The wreck she is diving into, in the very strong title poem, is the wreck of obsolete myths, particularly myths about men and women. She is journeying to something that is already in the past, in order to discover for herself the reality behind the myth, "the wreck and not the story of the wreck/the thing itself and not the myth." What

† First published in the *New York Times Book Review* 30 Dec. 1973. Copyright © 1973 by The New York Times Company. Reprinted by permission.

she finds is part treasure and part corpse, and she also finds that she herself is part of it, a "half-destroyed instrument." As explorer she is detached; she carries a knife to cut her way in, cut structures apart; a camera to record; and the book of myths itself, a book which has hitherto had no place for explorers like herself.

This quest—the quest for something beyond myths, for the truths about men and women, about the "I" and the "You," the He and the She, or more generally (in the references to wars and persecutions of various kinds) about the powerless and the powerful—is presented throughout the book through a sharp, clear style and through metaphors which become their own myths. At their most successful the poems move like dreams, simultaneously revealing and alluding, disguising and concealing. The truth, it seems, is not just what you find when you open a door: it is itself a door, which the poet is always on the verge of going through.

The landscapes are diverse. The first poem, "Trying to Talk with a Man," occurs in a desert, a desert which is not only deprivation and sterility, the place where everything except the essentials has been discarded, but the place where bombs are tested. The "I" and the "You" have given up all the frivolities of their previous lives, "suicide notes" as well as "love-letters," in order to undertake the risk of changing the desert; but it becomes clear that the "scenery" is already "condemned," that the bombs are not external threats but internal ones. The poet realizes that they are deceiving themselves, "talking of the danger/as if it were not ourselves/as if we were testing anything else."

Like the wreck, the desert is already in the past, beyond salvation though not beyond understanding, as in the landscape of "Waking in the Dark":

> The tragedy of sex
> lies around us, a woodlot
> the axes are sharpened for.
> . . . .
> Nothing will save this. I am alone,
> kicking the last rotting logs
> with their strange smell of life, not death,
> wondering what on earth it all might have become.

Given her view that the wreck, the desert, the woodlot cannot be redeemed, the task of the woman, the She, the powerless, is to concentrate not on fitting into the landscape but on redeeming herself, creating a new landscape, getting herself born:

> your mother dead and you unborn
> your two hands grasping your head
> drawing it down against the blade of life

> your nerves the nerves of a midwife
> learning her trade
>> ("The Mirror in Which Two Are Seen As One")

The difficulty of doing this (the poet is, after all, still surrounded by the old condemned landscape and "the evidence of damage" it has caused) is one of the major concerns of the book. Trying to see clearly and to record what has been seen—the rapes, the wars, the murders, the various kinds of violation and mutilation—is half of the poet's effort; for this she requires a third eye, an eye that can see pain with "clarity." The other half is to respond, and the response is anger; but it is a "visionary anger," which hopefully will precede the ability to love.

These poems convince me most often when they are true to themselves as structures of words and images, when they resist the temptation to sloganize, when they don't preach at me. "The words are purposes./ The words are maps," Rich says, and I like them better when they are maps (though Rich would probably say the two depend on each other and I would probably agree). I respond less fully to poems like "Rape" and references to the Vietnam War—though their truth is undeniable— than I do to poems such as "From a Survivor" and "August" with its terrifying final image:

> His mind is too simple, I cannot go on
> sharing his nightmares
>
> My own are becoming clearer, they open
> into prehistory
>
> which looks like a village lit with blood
> where all the fathers are crying: *My son is mine!*

It is not enough to state the truth; it must be imaged, imagined, and when Rich does this she is irresistible. When she does this she is also most characteristically herself. You feel about her best images, her best myths, that nobody else writes quite like this.

ALBERT GELPI

Adrienne Rich: The Poetics of Change†

The development of a poet's themes, techniques and imagery is an instructive and moving study—if the poet is as compelling as Adrienne

† From *American Poetry Since 1960*, ed. Robert B. Shaw (Cheadle, Cheshire: Carcanet Press Ltd., 1973) 123–43. Reprinted by permission of the publisher. All notes to this essay are the editors'. This selection has been edited for publication here; asterisks indicate deletions.

Rich is. Her first book was published twenty years ago, and she came into her own in the four collections which constitute her poems since the 'sixties; in sequence, the volumes point the drift of American poetry since the Second World War.

The poems which went into A *Change of World*, selected by W. H. Auden for the Yale Younger Poets Series in 1951, were written in the years just after the War, a period dominated by awesome figures: Eliot, Frost, Stevens, and so on. Poets of the generations after theirs—Auden and Tate, for instance, and later Robert Lowell—seemed to be substantiating Eliot's prediction that poetry should take a turn to a stricter formalism than was needed in the 'teens and 'twenties. Dylan Thomas had been a fascinating exotic; Pound was notorious; Williams represented the only major opposing force, but his influence was small compared to the combined presences of Eliot-Tate-Auden. In fact, American poetry was about to take a turn which would make Williams and Pound the presiding eminences for the new poets; the topography of American poetry looked astonishingly different by the end of the fifties, and even more markedly so by the mid-'sixties. But there was little evidence of the impending shift in 1951 when Adrienne Rich, a Radcliffe senior, made a debut as early as it was auspicious.

In his "Foreword" Auden complimented the "younger poet" somewhat condescendingly for not seeking novelty and instead cultivating the "detachment from the self and its emotions" which makes for craftsmanship, as Eliot had observed. Thus the echoes of Frost, Yeats, Stevens, Robinson, Emily Dickinson and Auden himself in these first poems indicated her intelligence and discretion. Auden sums up the virtues of the poems with the statement that they "are neatly and modestly dressed, speak quietly but do not mumble, respect their elders but are not cowed by them, and do not tell fibs." In other words, the stereotype—prim, fussy, and schoolmarmish—that has corseted and strait-laced women-poets into "poetesses" whom men could deprecate with admiration.

Modest and understated as these poems are, they are—the best of them—more interesting than Auden's comments suggest, and the main concerns of the later mature work are adumbrated from the start: the sense of imminent doom in "Storm Warnings," "Eastport to Block Island" and "The Ultimate Act"; the relations between man and woman in "An Unsaid Word" and "Mathilde in Normandy"; the difficulty and necessity of communication in "Stepping Backward"; the metaphysical skepticism of "Air Without Incense" and "For the Conjunction of Two Planets"; the fact of mutability in "A Change of World" and "Walden 1950"; the consequent concentration on the passing moment which almost every one of these pieces exemplifies. Rich's reflex is consistent throughout: she seeks shelter as self-preservation. In "Storm Warnings," the first poem in the book, she prepares against the threats within and without by sealing off a comfortable, weather-proof sanctuary.[1] The only exposure is the keyhole that locks the door. So the finely poised paradoxes of "Afterward" note ruefully that a fond innocence must fall, as it will, to the recognition of limits.[2] Still, acknowledged limits can, *faute de mieux*, raise protective perimeters within which one can learn to operate: not just the walls that enclose the psyche but, by extension, the prosodic and technical conventions that shape the space and time of the poem. Aesthetic form rescues the moment from the flux, as "Designs in Living Colors" says, into a richer and repeated realization; besides, aesthetic form imposes the control that raw emotions demand: "A too-compassionate art is only half an art./Only such proud restraining purity [as Bach has]/Restores the else-betrayed, too-human heart" ("At a Bach Concert").

The poems in A *Change of World* display a variety of meters, rhymes and stanzas, and each piece elaborates its convention symmetrically, as in the balance of unresolved dualities in "For the Conjunction of Two Planets." After a while the reader begins to wonder if the artifice, no matter how skillfully wrought, may serve as a partial evasion of the conflicts which are the subject of the poem. The verbal expression may camouflage a refusal to do what "The Ultimate Act" urges: commit that act "beneath a final sun." Limits which are hard to accept may become, in the end, too easy to accept. The precariousness of one's situation makes for the insistence on remaining unattached and unharmed; hence the decorous reserve of the woman toward the man in "An Unsaid Word," "Mathilde in Normandy" and "Stepping Backward." It's "you and I in our accepted frame," and poetry is itself a frame for viewing at a relatively safe distance a changing world divided from and against itself.

The Diamond Cutters (1955) is filled with travel poems, written on a Guggenheim in Europe and describing famous places and monuments with the acute eye of the tourist. Even such home scenes as Walden and the Charles River take on the detachment of tourist-views. What makes them more than genteel impressions is the developing metaphor which implies that we are all aliens in a fallen world. The first section of the book is called "Letter from the Land of Sinners": Europe littered with the ruins of time which still conjure up an era of greater beauty and order, perhaps even an arcadia when myths seemed true and we "listened to Primavera speaking flowers." But underneath the nostalgia there is the recognition that the fall into history was so original that Primavera is beyond recall, and we visit the ruins without inhabiting them. In "Ideal Landscape": "The human rose to haunt us everywhere,/Raw, flawed, and asking more than we could bear." In "The Celebration in the Plaza," after the balloon has popped and the fireworks fizzed out:

1. In the original essay, "Storm Warnings" was quoted in full; in this volume it appears on p. 3.
2. In the original essay, "Afterward" was quoted in full; in this volume it appears on p. 4.

"But is that all? some little children cry./*All we have left,* their peda-
gogues reply." At the remains of the "Villa Adriana": "His perfect colon-
nades at last attain/The incompleteness of a natural thing."

*   *   *

The last section of the volume recapitulates the major concerns: poems
(such as "The Snow Queen," "A Walk by the Charles," and "The Tree")
in which the individual is the epitome of his mortal and corrupt world;
poems (such as "Love in a Museum," "Colophon," and "The Diamond
Cutters") which commend the demands of art for forcing the moment
to fulfillment in completed form. The poet's continuing attitude toward
the submission of experience to the artistic process is revealed in phrases
like "distance," "imagination's form so sternly wrought," "incisions in
the ice," "tools refined": the hard, cold, clear surface of the engraved
and faceted diamond.

Snapshots of a Daughter-in-Law (1963) is the transitional book in
Adrienne Rich's development. Eight years had intervened between vol-
umes, and they were years of great change, so that the book begins in
one place and ends in another. What happens is the crucial event in the
career of any artist: a penetration into experience which makes for a
distinguishing style. Her themes—the burden of history, the separate-
ness of individuals, the need for relationship where there is no other
transcendence—begin to find their clarifying focus and center: what she
is as woman and poet in late-twentieth-century America. The first poems
in the book are still quite regular; even so striking a piece as "The Knight"
is something of a tour de force in its proportioned elaboration of a con-
ceit. But by the time the reader encounters the title poem, he knows he
is dealing with a sensibility tough, restless, capable of unpredictable leaps
and turns:

> Your mind now, mouldering like wedding-cake, . . .
> crumbling to pieces under the knife-edge
> of mere fact. In the prime of your life.
> . . . .
> A thinking woman sleeps with monsters.
> The beak that grips her, she becomes.
> . . . .
> The argument *ad feminam,* all the old knives
> that have rusted in my back, I drive in yours,
> *ma semblable, ma soeur!*
> . . . .
> *Dulce ridens, dulce loquens,*
> she shaves her legs until they gleam
> like petrified mammoth-tusk.

This thinking woman paraphrases Baudelaire, parodies Horace to regis-
ter the pressures that make the mind moulder. The shock of the imagery

is due not merely to its violence (each of the passages refers to a cutting edge) but to an accuracy so unsparing that the imagination reacts psychosomatically: muscles tighten and nerves twinge. The ten sections of "Snapshots" comprise an album of woman as "daughter-in-law," bound into the set of roles which men have established and which female acquiescence has re-enforced. Women-artists—Emily Dickinson, Mary Wollstonecraft, Simone de Beauvoir—stand out as images of resistance and achievement, and they herald the image of fulfillment in the last lines.[3] The self-image projected here is archetypical, at once individual and collective: a signal of forces which would become a national movement within the decade.

Adrienne Rich's earlier poems were praised for their subtlety of rhythm and tone, and these unmetered lines lose none of their subtlety for being more strongly stressed and more freely paced. But in becoming more concrete, her poetry was becoming primarily visual rather than aural, and she has been increasingly successful at imprinting images so indelibly that they convey the meaning without comment or conclusion. The words "eye" and "see" recur insistently (some thirty times) throughout the *Snapshots* volume, and there can be no mistaking her purpose: to "outstare with truthfulness" each moment in the flux of time and thereby live as keenly as her powers of perception make possible. To be is to see; I am eye. Poetry functions as the vehicle for seeing and for fixing what one comes to see. It is the camera with lens and focus, and poems are snapshots.

Not that art provides a satisfactory alternative to time. Fixing an image dates it, and in the *Snapshots* volume Rich began her custom of dating each poem. The poet outlives the poem, can be dated only on her tombstone; yet each marker points the end. The first section in a sequence called "Readings of History" states her ambivalence about the snapshot-poem by calling the camera "The Evil Eye":

> Your camera stabs me unawares,
> right in my mortal part.
> A womb of celluloid already
> contains my dotage and my total absence.

At the same time the fact of mortality generates the urgency to see: "to know/simply as I know my name/at any given moment, where I stand" ("Double Monologue"); and, with others, to

> spongelike press my gaze
> patiently upon your eyes,
> hold like a photographic plate
> against you my enormous question.
>
> ("Merely to Know")

3. In the original essay, "Snapshots of a Daughter-in-Law," section 10, was quoted in full; in this volume it appears on pp. 12-13.

To see time redeems it as best we can. Through the cultivation of consciousness we can live through time without merely being its victim. Adrienne Rich recognized the risks and responsibilities; "Prospective Immigrants Please Note" warns the reader of the categorical choice: safe security or a dangerous passage.[4] It is indicative that this poem, written in 1962, comes just at that point in Adrienne Rich's life when Jung says that a person in mid-thirties, having accomplished an initial set of goals (career, marriage, family), may be called by an inner necessity to the painful and exacting process of individuation.

"The Roofwalker," the last poem of *Snapshots*, is a redefinition of psychological and poetic perspective. No longer does it seem "worth while to lay—/with infinite exertion—/a roof I can't live under," and the previous stratagems seem "blueprints,/closing of gaps, measurings, calculations"—all useless now that

> A life I didn't choose
> chose me: even
> my tools are the wrong ones
> for what I have to do.

Already she has begun to try out a language more expressive of the uncertainties of a bold conception of selfhood;

> I'm naked, ignorant,
> a naked man fleeing
> across the roofs
> who could with a shade of difference
> be sitting in the lamplight
> against the cream wallpaper
> reading—not with indifference—
> about a naked man
> fleeing across the roofs.

The marvellous pun on "difference/indifference" effects the transition from the literate observer to the roofwalker, "exposed, larger than life,/ and due to break my neck." The phrase "larger than life" suggests not just his heroism but the recognition that, ignorant as he is, he is exposing himself to the dangers and mysteries not just of personal destiny but of existence itself.

The "difference" in perspective calls into question society's assumptions about men and women both separately and in relation to each other. "A Marriage in the 'Sixties" refuses the clichés of conjugal devotion and brings love complicated by intelligence to a separate yet shared existence. "Antinöus: The Diaries" and "Rustication" express, even more viscerally than "Snapshots," a revulsion against the middle-class, sub-

4. In the original essay, "Prospective Immigrants Please Note" was quoted in full; in this volume it appears on p. 17.

urban life which traps women, either willingly or helplessly, in gestures
and postures. In "Antinöus" Rich speaks through the mask of a man;
but as the favorite of the Emperor Hadrian, memorialized in busts for
his sensual beauty, Antinöus becomes the inverted image of the object
of male lust, and so a mirror of a decadent society.

> If what I spew on the tiles at last,
> helpless, disgraced, alone,
> is in part what I've swallowed from glasses, eyes,
> motions of hands, opening and closing mouths,
> isn't it also dead gobbets of myself,
> abortive, murdered, or never willed?

In reaction against the definitions of "woman" allowed by the rules of
the game Rich at first identifies the new possibilities of self-realization
with "masculine" qualities within herself and so with images of men in
several poems near the end of the book. In "Always the Same" Prome-
theus "bleeds to life" and his heroic song is described in a phrase from
Lawrence. In "Likeness" the good man whom the song tells us is hard
to find is "anarchic/as a mountain freshet/and unprotected/by the pro-
tectors." The "larger than life" roofwalker is a naked man. Their mas-
culine strength derives not from mere physical courage but from the
power of mind and will and judgement. "Ghost of a Chance" pits a
man's discriminating intellect against the backward suck of the female
sea, undifferentiated and undifferentiating.[5] The rhythms of the middle
lines imitate the strained effort to emerge into air, and the monosyllable
of the last word-line, climaxing the long drag of the previous line, sug-
gests the satisfaction which comes from the oblivion of the sea's triumph—
a satisfaction which makes resistance all the more urgent. At the end of
"Snapshots" the boy-like woman, cutting through the currents, is linked
with "mind" and "light": "A woman sworn to lucidity," as Adrienne
Rich would later describe herself.

In Jungian psychology the poet is at this point imagining herself in
terms of her "animus," the archetypally "masculine" component in the
woman's psyche which corresponds to the "anima" or archetypally
"female" component in the man's psyche. Each person, man or woman,
is a combination of—or, more accurately, an interaction between—male
and female characteristics; the anima in the man and the animus in the
woman express the dynamism of that interaction, which, if creative, will
open the passage to an accommodation of opposites in an identity. So
for the man the anima is the key to the whole area of feeling and intui-
tion and passion; "she" represents his relationship with matter, with sex-
uality, with the dark and formless unconscious. Correspondingly, for a
woman the animus represents her affinity with light as mind and spirit

---

5. In the original essay, "Ghost of a Chance" was quoted in full; in this volume it appears on pp.
16–17.

and her capacity for intellection and ego-consciousness. In the process of individuation, then, activation of and engagement with the animus or anima is generally the first major, and potentially dangerous, phase; it marks the transition into a fuller realization of one's psychological being and stands as the mediating point—one way or the other—which makes hard-won selfhood possible. Whether initial differences between men and women in psychological character and orientation are inherent or acculturated is a matter for specialists to continue to investigate. Meanwhile Jung's terms provide at least a descriptive, if not prescriptive, frame of reference within which to sort out the different psychological dynamics through which men and women, even sophisticated and aware men and women, struggle towards androgynous wholeness.

One manifestation of this dynamic which neither Jungians nor critics have yet examined is the fact that, with a frequency too regular to be ignored, artists have identified themselves, especially in their capacity as artists, with their anima or animus, as the case may be. One would not want to insist on this connection rigidly, but the tendency is strong enough to suggest a pattern. And the reason would seem to be that the artistic process, a function of the process of self-realization, is thereby a function of the anima or animus in the psyche: the man breaking open the categories of consciousness to the ebb and flow of the unconscious, submitting the light to the darkness; the woman drawing the inchoate into shape, submitting emotion to the discriminating light. Poetry as a function of the anima or of the animus helps to illuminate the difference, for example, between Walt Whitman and Emily Dickinson or, to cite two contemporary poets who have been closely associated with each other, the difference between Robert Duncan and Denise Levertov. The fact that the Muses are women and anima-figures is just a sign that up till now art has been a dominantly masculine domain.

The psychological and artistic point which the *Snapshots* volume dramatizes is Adrienne Rich's rejection of the terms on which society says we must expend our existence and her departure on an inner journey of exploration and discovery. As a woman-poet, she finds herself, perhaps unconsciously to a large extent, making the initial discoveries in the dimension and through the lead of her animus. So in "Face" she finds her reflection in the painting of a man whose "eye glows mockingly from the rainbow-colored flesh." Yet this mirror-image is himself "a fish,/drawn up dripping hugely/from the sea of paint." The metaphor, with the pun on "drawn," establishes the connection between the artistic process and the interaction of consciousness and the unconscious. The unconscious is the reservoir whose elements need to emerge into conscious comprehension and definition, and the artist must draw them up into the "glow" and "flash" of the light "out of the blackness/that is your true element."

Such an attempt at reorientation has inevitably made tremendous differences in the kind of poem Adrienne Rich has been writing. She was herself very aware of the fact that a radical shift had occurred in her conception of the technique and construction of poems. In an introduction to a poetry reading given in 1964, between *Snapshots* and *Necessities of Life*, she summed up the transition. It deserves quotation in full as one of the remarkable statements about contemporary poetry; it describes not just the direction she would increasingly explore but also the controlling impulse of most of the poetry now being written.[6]

In other words, Rich has developed, as a poet, from a single-minded identification with the animus as a controlling consciousness which could secure itself in forms and suppress the threats to that security, to a reliance on the animus as the power within herself through which psychic experience with all its unknown turbulences and depths can emerge into articulation as the images and rhythms of the poem. Anne Bradstreet, our first poet, referred to herself, half playfully, as the mother of her poems; Adrienne Rich gives herself the more comprehensive role of parent. At the same time the animus is only the mediating point within the psyche; no matter how active it is, Adrienne Rich writes as a woman. "The Knight" describes the negative and destructive aspects of identification with the animus: an encasing of the flesh and nerves and even the eye in armor as cold as it is glittering. By contrast, perhaps the most dramatic image in *Snapshots* is the figure of the woman at the climax of the title poem. A 1964 poem published in *Necessities of Life* returns to Emily Dickinson and addresses her almost as the type of the woman-poet:

> you, woman, masculine
> in single-mindedness,
> for whom the word was more
> than a symptom—
>
> a condition of being.
> Till the air buzzing with spoiled language
> sang in your ears
> of Perjury
>
> and in your half-cracked way you chose
> silence for entertainment,
> chose to have it out at last
> on your own premises.

The pun on "premises" makes Dickinson's retreat to the family household a consequence of her resolution to live and write on her own terms in the face of public incomprehension like the critic Higginson's, and

6. In the original essay, "Poetry and Experience" was quoted in full; in this volume it appears on p. 165.

the irony is that her determination only made her seem "half-cracked" to Higginson, complacent in his masculine assumptions about what women and poets are.

Necessities of Life (1966), *Leaflets* (1969) and *The Will to Change* (1971) are better books than *Snapshots*; they move steadily and with growing success towards making a poetry which is not just an activity consonant with life but an act essential to it. "The Trees" is a good example of the development.[7]

Rich has commented on the importance of Williams' example in her learning not to be "self-protective" like Frost and thereby to "take the emotional risk as well as the stylistic risk." But the emotional and psychological quality of her verse is utterly her own, and the prosody shows none of the posturing of much "experimental" verse and none of the halting choppiness which too deliberate a preoccupation with "breath-unit" imposes on some of Williams' followers. In "The Trees," the rhythms trace out the psychic movement, doubling back on itself as it proceeds through a sequence of images. The images, vivid and preter-naturally clear, are not descriptive in the usual sense. That is, they do not paint an actual scene or set up a narrative situation; they compose an internal landscape, eerie but strangely recognizable. Images of "eye" and "camera" persist through *Necessities of Life*, but increasingly in the later volumes dream and dream-imagery occur. And, as in a dream, the details are so present that they convey the poet's involvement with the particulars of experience from which the dream-poem derives.

What, then, does the poem trace out? A movement from within out, so that the empty forest "will be full of trees by morning." The psyche is a house, a structure suggesting now a plantation and now a hospital or sanatorium; but the house is filled with the natural and primitive shapes of trees rooted in the earth beneath the floor-boards and straining with a life of their own. While the conscious ego (the "I" of the poem) conducts its accustomed correspondence, the trees disentangle them-selves and break out under the cover of darkness into the open air, "like newly discharged patients/half-dazed, moving/to the clinic doors." Not that the external world appears merely as the mirror of the individual psyche; the night and moon and forest are out there from the beginning, and "the smell of leaves and lichen" reaching "like a voice into the rooms" seems to have initiated the trees' movement and the internal "whispers/which tomorrow will be silent." The forest is empty to the individual until she realizes it, and the realization involves a distinctly personal and human awareness such as the forest cannot attain in and of itself. The poem ends, as it began, in mystery, and the trees are the exemplification of the mystery—the seemingly related mystery—of the internal and external worlds. One becomes aware of the complexities of

7. In the original essay, "The Trees" was quoted in full; in this volume it appears on pp. 21–22.

one's becoming aware as well as of the complexities of the things perceived. Now the moon that has shone whole in the empty sky "is broken like a mirror,/its pieces flash now in the crown/of the tallest oak." The poem has not unriddled the mind or "reality" but rendered the encounter in a dreamscape for the reader to encounter for himself.

At the same time the entire thrust of the poem is a clarification of the uncomprehended or inadequately comprehended by recreating what *exists* beyond paraphrase or abstraction; in the imagery of several poems in *Necessities* light pierces darkness. Even here the moon, shattered by the branches of the trees, still illuminates the night, and the sun is the source of the rare moments of happiness and release in the book: "In the Woods," "The Corpse-Plant," and "Noon." In "Focus" Rich comes as close as she ever has to an explicitly religious dimension in the perception of things. Caught in the "veridical light," falling on her desk-top through a skylight,

> an empty coffee-cup,
> a whetstone, a handkerchief, take on
>
> their sacramental clarity, fixed by the wand
> of light as the thinker thinks to fix them in the mind.
>
> O secret in the core of the whetstone, in the five
> pencils splayed out like fingers of a hand!
>
> The mind's passion is all for singling out.
> Obscurity has another tale to tell.

The intensity of Rich's poems since the late 'fifties stems precisely from the mind's passion and from the fact that in her mind and passion test and confirm each other. The sacrament is the flash of the mind as it fixes, camera-like, the everyday things caught in this unusual light.

For Rich, however, a deepening subjectivity does not mean withdrawal, as it did for Dickinson, but, on the contrary, a more searching engagement with people and with social forces. "Necessities of Life," the first poem in that volume, notes her re-entry into the world after a time of guarded isolation. A world still marred by mutability ("Autumn Sequence," "Not Like That," "Side by Side," "Moth Hour"), still scarred by the violences of human relationship ("The Parting," "Any Husband to Any Wife," "Face to Face") and by the abuse of the environment ("Open Air Museum," "Breakfast at a Bowling Alley in Utica, N.Y."), increasingly menaced by politics and war ("Spring Thunder"); in short, stained, as "The Knot" tells us, by the blood-spot at the heart of things. *Necessities of Life* is filled with elegies ("After Dark," "Mourning Picture," "Not Like That"), and the title was meant, among other things "to suggest the awareness of death under everything that we are trying to escape from or that is coloring our responses to things, the knowledge that after all time isn't ours." Existence is persistence, but these poems are affirmations, in the extremity of our situation, of the will to persist. "Like This Together," one of the best poems in the book, concludes:

> Dead winter doesn't die,
> it wears away, a piece of carrion
> picked clean at last,
> rained away or burnt dry.
> Our desiring does this,
> make no mistake, I'm speaking
> of fact: through mere indifference
> we could prevent it.
> Only our fierce attention
> get hyacinths out of those
> hard cerebral lumps,
> unwraps the wet buds down
> the whole length of a stem.

Again against "indifference," "our fierce attention": only through that can the world last into the next season; we survive or perish together.

As an expression of this conviction, Rich's politics have taken clearer shape. The rejection of bourgeois mores voiced in *Snapshots* has led to a more radical view of the necessity, for life, of re-ordering social values and structures. But even the political poems in *Leaflets* and *The Will to Change* (for example, "For a Russian Poet," "Implosions," the "Ghazals," "The Burning of Paper Instead of Children") are not, in the end, propaganda leaflets. They remain poems because Rich has too powerful a sense of "original sin" to make the utopian mistake of externalizing evil by projecting it on others. The poems compel us precisely because they record how excruciating it is to live in this time and place; the politics is not abstracted and depersonalized but tested on the nerve-ends. The psychological and political revolutions are interdependent, because personal and public tragedy are linked, as "The Burning of Paper Instead of Children" and "The Photograph of the Unmade Bed," as well as the title poem, declare. Individually and collectively we need not just the will to persist but "the will to change."

As the ultimate challenge to her initial assumptions, Adrienne Rich raises the dreaded question for a poet: the very validity and efficacy of language. Is art the act of clarification and communication that we say it is? As early as "Like This Together" in 1963 she was worrying that "our words misunderstand us." Now in "The Burning of Paper":

> What happens between us
> has happened for centuries
> we know it from literature

> still it happens
> . . . .
>
> there are books that describe all this
> and they are useless

If language has no power to affect the given, then is the resort to lan-
guage an evasion of action, as the revolutionaries charge? The epigraph
to the poem quotes Fr. Daniel Berrigan: "I was in danger of verbalizing
my moral impulses out of existence." Only unsparing honesty permits
an artist to contemplate such a dangerous question, but Rich confronts
it again and again through the last two books. "Shooting Script" speaks
of "the subversion of choice by language." "The Burning of Paper"
imagines "a time of silence / or few words," when touch might be more
immediate, and quotes Antonin Artaud: "*burn the texts.*"

Yet this damning self-examination is conducted in the words of poems
which are urgent, even desperate attempts at clarification and commu-
nication. Not that the questioning has been vain: there must be no blinking
away the dangers of language as escape or the tenuousness of any attempt
at articulation. But in the acknowledgment of all these limits, language
remains a human *act* which makes other actions and choices possible:
"Only where there is language is there world," "We are our words"
("The Demon Lover"); "Our words are jammed in an electric jungle; /
sometimes, though, they rise and wheel croaking above the treetops"
("Ghazals"); "I am thinking how we can use what we have/to invent
what we need" ("Leaflets"); "I wanted to choose words that even you /
would have to be changed by" ("Implosions"). So, even in "The Burn-
ing of Paper," "this is the oppressor's language / yet I need it to talk to
you." The conclusion is not to stop speaking and writing but to make
words penetrate to the will as well as the mind and heart: "the fracture
of order / the repair of speech / to overcome this suffering" ("The Burn-
ing of Paper").

In other words, persistence requires relocation. Much has intervened
between *A Change of World* and *The Will to Change*. In "Storm Warn-
ings" Rich had strategically enclosed herself within protective walls; now
with the apocalypse perhaps about to break over our heads, she insists
that we not merely submit but actively commit ourselves to change, as
persons and as a people.

*   *   *

The imagery associated wth self shifts in the last two books: a sign
from the deeps. The animus is the cross-over point, leading in the direc-
tion of a fuller comprehension and integration of the self; for the male
figure of the animus symbolizes powers of mind and will that have to be
assimilated into her identity as a woman. The poems of *Leaflets* and *The
Will to Change* render the double sense of the animus as self and other.

"Orion," the first piece in *Leaflets*, is an animus poem. In reaction against the entanglements of domestic routine ("Indoors I bruise and blunder") Rich projects her sense of identity on the masculine presence of the constellation Orion, as she had since girlhood: first as her "genius" ("My cast-iron Viking, my helmed / lion-heart king in prison"); then as her "fierce half-brother," weighed down by his phallic sword; now as her mirror-image and apotheosis. Moreover, she is specifically identifying herself as poet with Orion; while writing the poem, she had in mind an essay by the German poet Gottfried Benn on the plight of the modern artist.

But "The Demon Lover," just two years later, presents a more complex analysis. Here "he" is the "other": both the animus and the man who in refusing to recognize her animus compounds her own sense of division; the whole question is whether an accommodation with "him" is possible internally or externally:

> If I give in it won't
> be like the girl the bull rode,
> all Rubens flesh and happy moans.
> But to be wrestled like a boy
> with tongue, hips, knees, nerves, brain . . .
> with language?

Her animus is the sticking-point: for her to insist upon and for the man to negate. Her contention is not to be a man but a whole woman, and as a woman to be taken fully into account. But the circumstances show "him" as adversary; not only does the "man within" appear as "demon lover," but the masculine lover becomes a demon because he clings to the simple opposition between mind and body which makes for the simple distinction between man and woman. In denying her mind and spirit, he must deny his passions and debase his body to lust. The quandary within and without remains unresolved; "he," animus and lover, refuses her his secrets and consigns her to the female element: "Sea-sick, I drop into the sea."

Although to the demon lover she has seized on the terms which make connection most difficult, she has defined the only terms on which relation is possible. Neither man nor woman can be free until each has acknowledged the other. Adrienne Rich's new poems show an absorption of animus-powers into a growing sense of identity as woman and of identification with women, and consciousness is the key. "Women" describes three images of self as "my three sisters," and comments: "For the first time, in this light, I can see who they are." "Planetarium" evokes the astronomer Caroline Herschel, her fame eclipsed by her brother William, as a heroine in the history of women's coming to consciousness, the light of her "virile" eye meeting the stellar light; of herself, Rich concludes:

> I am an instrument in the shape
> of a woman trying to translate pulsations
> into images   for the relief of the body
> and the reconstruction of the mind.

In a hypnotic poem called "I Dream I'm the Death of Orpheus," she adapts imagery from Jean Cocteau's movie about Orpheus to depict herself as a woman whose animus is the archetypal poet.[9] The strong, incantatory rhythms—a significant new development in some of the recent poems—work their magic. What the dream-poem traces out is the resurrection of Orpheus through the woman's determination to resist all depersonalizing forces—psychological, political, sexual—arrayed against the exercise of her powers. The animus-poet comes alive again within the psyche, and his return is a sign of, and a measure of, her ability to "see through" and to move forward on her "mission": not the course laid out by the "authorities" as the safe way to remain intact but the one intimated by "the fulness of her powers" as the only way to deliver herself whole. At this point in her life and in history such a purpose puts her against prevailing conditions and makes for lonely opposition. Orpheus revives within her "on the wrong side of the mirror," "learning to walk backward against the wind."

But the contrary direction is not negative; bent on affirming life's possibilities, it makes the pressure bearable and transfiguring. "We're living through a time / that needs to be lived through us," she writes in "The Will to Change," and that is the reverse of Matthew Arnold's perception of the modern paralysis as the feeling that everything is to be endured and nothing to be done.

The process is not, of course, completed, nor can it be: Selfhood is the motive and end of the journey. But the fact that hers is not merely a private struggle but a summons to us all—at least to all of us who enter the door and cross the threshold into the psyche—informs the poetry with a mythic dimension in a singularly demythologized time. A myth not because her experience has been appended, by literary allusion, to gods and goddesses, but because her experience is rendered so deeply and truly that it reaches common impulses and springs, so that, without gods and goddesses, we can participate in the process of discovery and determination. It is existentialism raised to a mythic power, and the myth has personal and political implications. The result is a restoration to poetry of an ancient and primitive power, lost in the crack-up which the last centuries have documented. The power of the bard in the tribe has long since declined with the power of prophecy. Adrienne Rich's mission is to live out her dream of a society of individual men and women. By challenging us to a more honest realization, she has recovered some-

9. In the original essay, "I Dream I'm the Death of Orpheus" is quoted in full; in this volume it appears on p. 43.

thing of the function of the poet among his people: not by transmitting old legends and tales but by offering herself—without pretensions, with honest hesitations—as the mirror of our consciousness and the medium of our transformation. In effect, her poetry has come to represent a secular and unillusioned vision of the poet as prophet and the prophet as scapegoat living out individually the possibilities of the collective destiny. By long tradition in the patriarchal culture this tribal function has been the prerogative of male poets, but there is something peculiarly clarifying and liberating about confronting ourselves through the mind and imagination of a woman. Equally so for men as for women, because the work of a woman-artist is much more likely than the work of most men to present the counter-image essential to men's wholeness and to activate and call into play that whole area of emotion and intuition within themselves which is the special province of the "woman within."

All this accounts for the centrality of Adrienne Rich's work in the contemporary scene, for the electric immediacy of the reader's or hearer's response, and for the finally healing effect of poems wracked with the pain of awareness and the pain of articulation.

Postscript, 1991

When I wrote this essay on Adrienne Rich's "poetics of change," the "wild impatience" that she was to speak of as the driving power for change had taken her through the 1971 volume *The Will to Change*. In the twenty years since then, there have been decisive developments in her life and work: her commitment to feminism in the early seventies and soon thereafter to lesbian feminism; the life of love and work and commitment she has shared with Michelle Cliff since the late seventies; and, for a poet with so strong a sense of place, the move in 1984, after the years in Cambridge and Manhattan, Vermont and western Massachusetts, to Santa Cruz and the California coast.

These changes are registered in the changing shape and pace of the poems. As I've shown in this essay, the verbal and metaphorical compression and the formal symmetry of the poems from the fifties had given way in the sixties to an unmetered, unrhymed line and an open form which allowed for a searching of her experience on psychological and political terms. In the seventies the stresses came to crisis and breakthrough, and Rich's recognition of the oppressive divisions which within patriarchy rive personal and political relationships made her language more knotted and fragmented: violent images in unpunctuated, jagged lines; line breaks and gaps between lines spacing the pieces in arrested juxtaposition and bold confrontation. But as the eighties brought increasing clarity and assurance and resilience to her life and her feminist vision, she expressed a less embattled, confrontational sense of self and other that could allow differences, ambiguities, questions without foregoing any intensity of purpose and commitment. And in the process the poetry has sought more and more to find a common language of direct communicative statement, shared questioning and shared assertions, inclusive imagery and pronouns, sustained and cumulative rhythms, longer and more capacious lines.

Among other things, my essay of 1973 examined the imagery of the early poems to show that the agent for change in Rich was often felt and presented as what Jung would have called Rich's animus—that is to say, as the dynamism in a woman's psychological, mental, emotional, spiritual, imaginative life which personifies and enacts certain powers and urges and capacities within herself in masculine images. I am aware that the conditions of such imagining in the inner lives of women and men are to a large degree culturally constructed, but the unique form and character of that enactment are the individual's particular psychodrama. Consequently it is not surprising to find that as Rich's changing consciousness fought to reject and reverse her cultural construction under patriarchy, she found animus imagery suspect and subversive. Her feminist poem "Origins and History of Consciousness" takes its title from Erich Neumann's Jungian and masculinist anatomy of the hero archetype, and thereby reclaims the drama of consciousness for women. Dismissing the stereotypes behind notions like anima and animus, Rich would no longer associate her powers of mind and will, language and imagination with male figures, even internalized and imagined male figures, since historically men have been the chief aggressors and their language has been a chief instrument of oppression. Instead the poems of the seventies present men as agents of violent disempowerment and mothers and sisters as agents of empowerment. Rich has even said that she regrets the line "I am the androgyne" in the 1972 poem "The Stranger" and that she won't use the term any more, since androgyny in practice merely masks male appropriation of the feminine.

Nevertheless, the unconscious can prove more elusive and persistent, even more long-sighted than consciousness may will or know. At the prophetic climax of "Diving into the Wreck," written in the same year as "The Stranger," we find this interplay of images and pronouns in a circle of hallucinatory assertions:

> This is the place.
> And I am here, the mermaid whose dark hair
> streams black, the merman in his armored body.
> We circle silently
> about the wreck
> we dive into the hold.
> I am she: I am he

So from its chosen feminist circumference the poetry has continued to circle, in the imagery of "Waking in the Dark," round "the wildwood /

where the split began," instinctively aware that sooner or later, for personal and political reasons, she had to return to that riven center and seek comprehension, perhaps negotiate reconciliation to heal mind and heart and spirit. Even in the initial intensity of her critique of patriarchy, addressing her recently dead husband in "From an Old House in America," Rich insisted: "If they call me man-hater, you / would have known it for a lie."

The important autobiographical poem *Sources* (1981–82) goes back in memory to re-encounter father and husband, the two men crucial to her sense of identity, and she finds that they no longer have any power over her, indeed finds that she can be compassionate and loving because she can now see them too as victims of patriarchy, the individual but related weaknesses that defeated them enmeshed in the circumstances of their lives. Admitting them among her sources, she can assume responsibility for herself. *Sources*, like all Rich's major poems, is an act of consolidation and a transition to a new departure, and "womanly powerful," the final words of the sequence set apart on a separate line, voice her hard-won capacity for reconciliation with the past and resolution for the future.

And yet, without in the least diminishing the force of that feminist vision, I think that it is possible to see the process enacted in *Sources* as bringing the engagement with the animus to a Jungian conclusion. A creative engagement with the animus ends with the empowerment, not the disempowerment, of the woman. Indeed, the purpose of such an engagement, never without dangers of subversion and entrapment nor without necessary resistance to such dangers, is not the negation of the woman's identity but, on the contrary, the integration of her animus powers into a fuller, stronger conviction of herself. A Jungian could see in Rich's continuing emphasis on lucidity of mind, on commitment of will, on choice and empowerment the seal of the integrated animus.

In the essay "The Poetics of Recovery" [1] I present a reading of *Sources*, and the animus poem "Orion" is the linchpin on which the transition from this essay to that later one turns.

HELEN VENDLER

Ghostlier Demarcations, Keener Sounds †

Adrienne Rich's memorable poetry has been given us now, a book at a time, for twenty-two years. Four years after she published her first book,

1. See below, pp. 397–401.
† From *Parnassus: Poetry in Review* 2.1 (Fall–Winter 1973): 5–10, 15–16, 18–24. Reprinted by permission of the author. All notes to this essay are the editors'. This selection has been edited for publication here; asterisks indicate deletions.

I read it in almost disbelieving wonder; someone my age was writing down my life. I felt then, as I feel now, that for each reader there are only a few poets of whom that is true, and by the law of averages, those poets are usually dead or at least far removed in time and space. But here was a poet who seemed, by a miracle, a twin: I had not known till then how much I had wanted a contemporary and a woman as a speaking voice of life:

> Strength came where weakness was not known to be,
> At least not felt; and restoration came
> Like an intruder knocking at the door
> Of unacknowledged weariness.

When I look back now through A *Change of World* (1951), I try to remember which of the pages so held me and why; and I find four sets of poems I greet with the sense of *déja vu*. One set had simply lovely lines, seeming today almost too decorative, too designed, but presenting to me then the poetry of the delicately apprehended and the exquisitely remembered, poetry of "the flecked leaf-gilded boughs," and "paths fern-fringed and delicate,"ornamented with "whisking emerald lizards." I did not mind, in some of these solacing poems, echoes of Auden or Yeats, feeling that what was beautiful was beautiful no matter who invented it; but there was, it was true, an ominous note which kept being interlaced with the poised rhythms.

A second group of poems set the status quo against some threatened future time; yet the danger was contained, and in fact the action of containing danger was gravely obligatory, a sacred trust. The poems articulated their own balance between danger and decorum in imagery of rebellion (which usually lost) against tradition (which usually won, at least tonally). The speaker for tradition in one poem is "the uncle in the drawing room"; gesturing towards "crystal vase and chandelier," knowing the "frailties of glass," he points seriously to the duties of the custodians of culture.[1] The poet-observer creating the uncle may see him ironically in part, but there is no denying the ethical imperative of his last claim. Equally subversive of tradition but yearningly attached to its honor, "For the Felling of a Tree in Harvard Yard" ends ambiguously on a double set of responses:

> The second oldest elm is down.

> The shade where James and Whitehead strolled
> Becomes a litter on the green.
> The young men pause along the paths
> To see the axes glinting bold.

---

1. In the original essay, "The Uncle Speaks in the Drawing Room" was quoted in full; in this volume it appears on p. 4.

> Watching the hewn trunk dragged away,
> Some turn the symbol to their own,
> And some admire the clean dispatch
> With which the aged elm came down.

Though revolution may end this poem, nostalgia rules it, nostalgia for the "roots enormous in their age," for "the great spire . . . overthrown." In 1955 I read this poem purely as elegy (no doubt confusing it in my undiscriminating admiration with "Binsey Poplars" and the spreading chestnut tree) and I was unable as yet, myself, to conceive of revolutionary impatience. But even now its tone seems to contain far more of the pang of elegy than of the briskness of destruction. So the poems played with fire, yet did not burn: I must have liked that.

The third set of poems that moved me then were poems on the identity and lot of women. I had no conscious thoughts on the topic, the natural order of the universe seeming then to be the inequality of man and woman; and yet some strains of discord in the book must have seemed an external documentary to those inarticulate strains in myself. On the one hand, woman was to be Patience on a monument, a Hermione-statue always there when her husband chose to come back.[2] Hard it may be, but learn it she must, says this poem; and it assumes that there is no such "estranged intensity" where *she* could be mentally foraging alone, and whence he might forbear to call *her* back. And yet, in other poems, the imperative of exploration, separation, private discovery, is equally felt:

> Each his own Magellan
> In tropics of sensation. . . .
> These are latitudes revealed
> Separate to each.

("Unsounded")

In still other poems, needlework, that laborious confection of female artistry, becomes the repeated symbol of the ambiguously triumphant womanly lot. While their lords left for "harsher hunting on the opposite coast," Norman ladies

> sat at home
> To the pleasing minor airs of lute and hautbois,
> While the bright sun on the expensive threads
> Glowed in the long windless afternoons.

But what is left of the Anglo-Norman battles but the Bayeux tapestry, which "prove[d] / More than the personal episode, more than all/The little lives" ("Mathilde in Normandy"). And, in spite of the seductive evenings in "The Kursaal at Interlaken," the female speaker, while play-

---

2. In the original essay, "An Unsaid Word" was quoted in full; in this volume it appears on p. 5.

ing her social rôle, nonetheless casts longing eyes toward a solitary virginity:

> Jungfrau, the legendary virgin spire,
> Consumes the mind with mingled snow and fire.

* * *

But most of A *Change of World* is written by a girl in love, a girl "receiving marvels, signs":

> There is a streetcar runs from here to Mars.
> I shall be seeing you, my darling, there,
> Or at the burning bush in Harvard Square.

("Vertigo")

This seems too easy an apotheosis now, but it seemed bold at first reading, and drew me by the same authority as the lines in "For the Conjunction of Two Planets" which imperiously declared for myth against astrophysics:

> Whatever register or law
> Is drawn in digits for these two,
> Venus and Jupiter keep their awe,
> Warders of brilliance, as they do
> Their dual circuit of the west—
> The brightest planet and her guest.

Not only was our feminism only an occasional shadow over our expectation of the ecstatic, our sense of permanent location in our lot was only incipient, too. The fourth set of poems that kept me standing in the library stacks reading this new and revelatory book was the set about Europe. In A *Change of World* Rich struck all the notes of her generation's inchoate responses to Europe: an attachment, a disloyalty; beauty, decadence; the perfect, the tired; art, the artificial. Alienated by a lengthily educated childhood from the American scene, and yet invisibly, visibly, and irrevocably American, the students who went abroad like Rich wandered tranced in the deceptive paradises of the transatlantic escape.

Now, six books later, almost two decades older, Rich's readers encounter her newest book, *Diving into the Wreck*. If we suspend knowledge of what came between, we may ask what has happened to the girl of 1951, that girl who wanted everything suffused by the delicate and the decorative, who questioned her passivity even while exhorting herself to that virtue, who mourned change and yet sensed its coming, who feared her own alienation in her native country, who, above these cares and anxieties, took pains that all her poems should turn out right, that there should be no ragged edges, that chimes should chasten discords—what has become of her? She has forgotten, or repudiated, her dream of Europe: Beethoven makes a fugitive appearance in the new book, but even he is not permitted to represent nineteenth-century European high culture; Rich calls her Beethoven poem "The Ninth Symphony of Beethoven Understood at Last as a Sexual Message." Passivity, too is repudiated in principle, but returns in surreptitious forms, as life is consumed by that which nourished it:

> Time takes hold of us like a draft
> upward, drawing at the heats
> in the belly, in the brain
>   . . . the mirror of the fire
> of my mind, burning as if it could go on
> burning itself, burning down
>
> feeding on everything
> till there is nothing in life
> that has not fed that fire
>
>   ("Burning Oneself Out")

The overtones here come from Williams' "Burning the Christmas Greens," but Williams' poem is about the desire for change which consigns the greens to the fire, while Rich is helplessly suspended in the fires of time and thought. The old decorativeness reappears in the intricate ending, but this time not in the service of a scrim-curtain prettiness. As for the questions of female identity and the rival claims of change and tradition, they have merged into one inextricable and apparently insoluble problem. In the first book, change could be chosen or not; by now, Rich utters ruin (and resurrection) as inevitable law.

*   *   *

There is more to look at in *Diving into the Wreck*, notably its last poem; but first, in order to see the place of this book in Adrienne Rich's continuing writing, writing unflaggingly done through youth, marriage, motherhood, solitude, employment, political engagement, and fame, we must look back to earlier works. Except for youth, any one of these phases, not to speak of all of them, can be destructive of writing: we all recall Jane Austen's years of silence when her father had to give up his house and take the family into lodgings; we remember Sylvia Plath's hectic early-morning sleepless composition before her babies awoke; and there are doubtless other examples. A writer who persists, phase after phase, usually has some intrinsic and compelling self and style demanding expression. If we try to isolate the self and style which appeared in *A Change of World* and which have continued, through age and variation, all the way up to *Diving into the Wreck*, we are asking, really, which are Rich's best poems, how her voice makes itself both remarkable and beautiful.

Rich hit her stride, and wrote her first "perfect" poem (of her voice at that time) in her second volume, *The Diamond Cutters* (1955). The poem in question, "The Middle-Aged," is one of a distinguished group, including "The Tourist and the Town," "Lucifer in the Train," "The Wild Sky," "Villa Adriana," and "Landscape of the Star," which all, in some way, deal with homelessness; and that homelessness, with its accompanying ache of filial nostalgia, is the new theme, coming into the ascendant, which distinctly marks *The Diamond Cutters* as an advance over the first volume. Sometimes the pain of departure and separation is overt and unmediated:

> Imperceptibly
> That landscape altered; now in paler air
> Tree, hill and rock stood out resigned, severe,
> Beside the strangled field, the stream run dry.
>
> ("Lucifer in the Train")

*   *   *

The shape of *The Diamond Cutters* suggests that Rich may need to write explicit *cris du coeur* as sketches, so to speak, for a more contained and disciplined later poem. It is odd that some readers will so placidly receive and even praise such unmediated cries of filial longing, but will become irrationally damning about a single cry of unmediated anger. These hysterias only prove that Rich is touching intense and widely diffused feelings; a poet could hardly ask for more. In her poems, Rich sees more deeply than in her recent prose propaganda; poetry makes her more reflective and more self-corrective, less inflexible, more pained.

In *Snapshots of a Daughter-in-Law* (1963), we find that marriage has turned the earlier filial exile-in-space into something considerably more bitter—separation under the same roof, a sense of separate-and-not-equal lives bequeathed to men and women, with women's only claim that of a more arcane insight into Nature:

> . . . has Nature shown
> her household books to you, daughter-in-law,
> that her sons never saw?

The silent isolation of minds in marriage is followed by a choking, deprived speech. The central poem in this volume is without doubt "A Marriage in the 'Sixties," a poem still hoping for the best and yet unwilling to dissemble the worst.[3] "My words," says Rich, watching those words drop unheard and neglected, "reach you as through a telephone / where some submarine echo of my voice / blurts knowledge you can't use." ("The Lag"). In this volume, Rich's lines loosen up into free verse; we may assume various influences, from Eliot to Lowell to Plath, but since the

---

3. In the original essay, lines of "A Marriage in the 'Sixties" were quoted; in this volume the poem appears on pp. 14–15.

modern movement as a whole was on its way toward dispensing with rhyme, it was inevitable that Rich should forsake her sweetness, cadence, and stanzas once her life began to refuse its earlier arrangements. Nervous, hardened, noting harshly that only cutting onions can provoke her unwept tears into her eyes, she moves under a "load of unexpired purpose, which drains / slowly." Rich's effects now depend only on metaphor, juxtaposition, and adroit lineation; she vomits up "dead gobbets" of herself, "abortive, murdered, or never willed" for new recognition; she crawls out of her cocoon like a fish attempting the grand evolutionary trick of becoming a bird.[4]

If, as Rich's early pattern suggests, blunter poems are followed by subtler ones, *Necessities of Life* derives its power from its absorption of all past phases into its present one. In "Autumn Sequence," Rich forces herself to that generosity toward past selves:

> Generosity is drying out,
>
> it's an act of will to remember
> May's sticky-mouthed buds
> on the provoked magnolias.

But that act of will makes this volume almost an obituary; at least it is the obituary of a whole section of life. The title poem—a second talisman, at least for me, to join with "The Middle-Aged," shows a new self emerging and seeking a new place in the world:

> Piece by piece I seem
> to re-enter the world: I first began
>
> a small, fixed dot, still see
> that old myself, a dark-blue thumbtack
>
> pushed into the scene,
> a hard little head protruding
>
> from the pointillist's buzz and bloom.

We cannot help noticing how free from compulsion Rich's images have become. The early poems were so neat in their useful skeins of imagery; if a color appeared in the upper left of the tapestry, it was sure to reappear, economically but predictably, in the lower right. Now precision of feeling and exactness of recollection govern the correlative, and though the visual reference apparent in the thumbtack and the pointillist is maintained, it is allowed considerable freedom. In adolescence come passion and ambition, melting the pigments:

4. In the original essay, "Ghost of a Chance" was quoted in full; in this volume it appears on pp. 16–17.

After a time the dot

begins to ooze. Certain heats
melt it.
              Now I was hurriedly

blurring into ranges
of burnt red, burning green,

whole biographies swam up and
swallowed me like Jonah.

Jonah! I was Wittgenstein,
Mary Wollstonecraft, the soul

of Louis Jouvet, dead
in a blown-up photograph.

There is a hiatus in the poem at this point, as though the self-devouring of adolescence were nameable, but the other-devouring of marriage and child-rearing were not. The "hard little head" become photograph loses its painterly dimension and becomes a dry bulb waiting out its time of deprivation, "gone underground" like Herbert's flower, through "all the hard weather":

Till, wolfed almost to shreds,
I learned to make myself

unappetizing. Scaly as a dry bulb
thrown into a cellar

I used myself, let nothing use me.
Like being on a private dole,

sometimes more like kneading bricks in Egypt.

In this poverty of slavery—and the comparisons tell us that even the "privileged" life of a Cambridge wife and mother can feel like that—the poem reaches its central minimal state in an exhausted miserliness keeping others at bay:

What life was there, was mine,

now and again to lay
one hand on a warm brick

and touch the sun's ghost
with economical joy,

now and again to name
over the bare necessities.

This beautiful passage, though it could perhaps not have been written
before Stevens' poetry of poverty, has the touch of the physical in it that
Stevens' poetry lacked: that warm brick and its ghostly heat did not inhabit
Stevens' universe. Those "certain heats" of adolescence have dwindled
to this spectral form: passion and ambition alike almost expire in this
daily kneading of the bricks, this being "wolfed almost to shreds" by
others. But the devouring demand has, with time, eased; a tentative
green shoot rises from the root cellar; "Who would have thought my
shrivel'd heart / Could have recover'd greennesse?" asks Herbert under
similar conditions. But Rich's resurrection is not Herbert's cyclical one;
she will never again be a flower. However, she can be a cabbage, an eel,
something sturdy and slippery at once (and female and male at once,
the androgynous imagery suggests):

> So much for those days. Soon
> practice may make me middling perfect, I'll
>
> dare inhabit the world
> trenchant in motion as an eel, solid
>
> as a cabbage-head. I have invitations:
> a curl of mist steams upward
>
> from a field, visible as my breath.

Encouraging, brisk lines: they tell what every depleted mother must feel
when the haze and stumbling of physical and psychic tiredness finally
lift after a decade of babies. But where is the new society to join, when
child-bearing is over? Where but among the old wives?

> houses along a road stand waiting
>
> like old women knitting, breathless
> to tell their tales.

In these lines, acquiescence and rebellion compete: that the little dark-
blue thumbtack should come to this; that the girl who dreamed of being
Wittgenstein should join the garrulous crones. And yet, what else can
the normal lot be; given the submission of the soul in all those years of
Egyptian bondage, given the confines of the root-cellar, is it not enough
to sit on the doorstep and knit?

That was as far ahead as Rich could see in 1962, and, as always, she
told us life as she saw it. It is with an almost desperate vertigo that we
come from this poem and others like it to the poems of violent change
in the later books, when Rich feels picked up and thrown by life into

jangling new positions, unforeseen, unasked-for but welcomed as they
come. The more reproachful of her critics have assumed that her revo-
lutionary stances are chosen and therefore blameworthy; I see them rather
as part of the inexplicable ongoingness of life, to be reported like the
rest. Better a change than the falsely "mature" acceptance of the unac-
ceptable, a stance that Rich falls into off and on in *Necessities of Life*,
notably in the increasingly expedient "literariness" of the poem "After
Dark" on her father's death, and in the forced ending of the fine poem
"Like This Together," where Rich declares that love can be kept alive
by our working at it, that the dry scaly bulb can be pried into life.[5]

*   *   *

The two books preceding *Diving into the Wreck* are waiting out some
murky transition: the most explicit poem in *Leaflets* (1969) jettisons every
past except the residual animal instinct of self-preservation, and every
future except death; comparing herself to "the red fox, the vixen" and
denying any connection to the ascetic New England settlers (like the
Israelites, a "chosen people") with their "instinct mortified in a virgin
forest," Rich says:

> what does she want
> with the dreams of dead vixens,
> the apotheosis of Reynard,
> the literature of fox-hunting?
> Only in her nerves the past
> sings, a thrill of self-preservation. . . .
> and she springs toward her den
> every hair on her pelt alive
> with tidings of the immaculate present. . . .
> She has no archives,
> no heirlooms, no future
> except death
> and I could be more
> her sister than theirs
> who chopped their way across these hills
> —a chosen people.
>
> ("Abnegation")

This vixen ("wise-looking in a sexy way" in Rich's unfortunate descrip-
tion) has none of the vitality of torn-down Cambridge, and so is allegor-
ical rather than convincingly metaphorical, but this rather weak poem
makes the clear point of the book; jettison the past, live in sex and the
present, forget the mind, tradition, and sublimation.

*   *   *

5. In the original essay, "Like This Together, 5" was quoted in full; in this volume it appears on
   pp. 23–24.

[In *The Will to Change*, in a poem called "Shooting Script,"] Rich has abandoned the sentimental fantasy of being a purely animal vixen, but she still wishes for a hypothesized primitive physical human self, like the villagers whose ancestors made the pots:

> Of simple choice they are the villagers; their clothes come
> with them like red clay roads they have been walking.
>
> The sole of the foot is a map, the palm of the hand a letter,
> learned by heart and worn close to the body.

In the new primitivism, the poet must abandon his magic lantern and give up "the temptations of the projector": but in fact the projector itself had come to grief, refusing to move on to the next slide, projecting one image "over & over on empty walls." One must "see instead the web of cracks filtering across the plaster":

> To read there the map of the future, the roads radiating from the
> initial split, the filaments thrown out from that impasse.
>
> To reread the instructions on your palm; to find there how the
> lifeline, broken, keeps its direction.
>
> To read the etched rays of the bullet-hole left years ago in the
> glass; to know in every direction of the light what fracture is.
>
> ("Shooting Script," II, number 14)

Giving up the prism, the lens, the map, and pulling herself up by her own roots, Rich, as *The Will to Change* closes, eats the last meal in her own neighborhood and prepares, deprived of all instruments, to move on, guided only by the fortuitous cracks in the plaster, the innate lifeline, the traumatic rays of the bullet-hole. She could hardly have been more frank; from formalism to—not freedom, but, as always—a new version of truth. If this is a revolution, it is one bound like Ixion on the wheel of the past—environmental past in the plaster, genetic past in the lifeline, traumatic past in the bullet-hole. And if it is revolution, it is one which does not wish to deny the reality of past choices and past modes of life. Putting off in her boat, Rich watches "the lights on the shore I had left for a long time; each one, it seemed to me, was a light I might have lit, in the old days" ("Shooting Script," II, number 13). Houselights and hearthfires, abandoned, remembered, light the departure.

And so, in *Diving into the Wreck*, the old questions are still mining like moles underneath: tradition, civilization, the mind and the body, woman, man, love, writing—and the war added as a metaphor, so far as I can see, for illustration of the war between the sexes rather than for especially political commentary. In the most meditative and searching

9

ꙋ

sides the title poem) in *Diving into the Wreck*,[6] Rich forsakes
s between men and women, for the most part, and sees us all
ppled creatures, scarred by that process of socialization and nurture
which had been, when she began writing, her possession, her treasure;
tapestries, Europe, recorders, Bach—the whole edifice of civilization,
of which she now sees the dark side—war, exploitation, and deadening
of instinct.

* * *

The forcefulness of *Diving into the Wreck* comes from the wish not
to huddle wounded, but to explore the caverns, the scars, the depths of
the wreckage. At first these explorations must reactivate all the old wounds,
inflame all the scar tissue, awaken all the suppressed anger, and inacti-
vate the old language invented for dealing with the older self. But I find
no betrayal of continuity in these later books, only courage in the refusal
to write in forms felt to be outgrown. I hope that the curve into more
complex expression visible in her earlier books will recur as Rich contin-
ues to publish, and that these dispatches from the battlefield will be
assimilated into a more complete poetry. Given Rich's precocious and
sustained gifts, I see no reason to doubt her future. The title poem that
closed *The Diamond Cutters* says that the poetic supply is endless: after
one diamond has been cut, "Africa / Will yield you more to do." When
new books follow, these most recent poems will I think be seen as the
transition to a new generosity and a new self-forgetfulness.

JUDITH McDANIEL

"Reconstituting the World": The Poetry and Vision of Adrienne Rich †

> A life I didn't choose
> chose me . . .
>
> —1961

> Only she who says
> she did not choose, is the loser in the end.
>
> —1976

The will to change dramatically distinguishes the career of Adrienne
Rich from many contemporary artists. Accepting at first the roles assigned

---

6. "Meditations for a Savage Child."
† *Reconstituting the World* was first published as a monograph, © 1978 by Spinsters, Ink. It then appeared in *Reading Adrienne Rich: Reviews and Re-visions, 1951–81*, ed. Jane Roberta Cooper (Ann Arbor: U of Michigan P, 1984). Reprinted by permission of the author. This

by society, Rich moved from dutiful daughter / apprentice to mother / creator, excelling—poetically, at least—within the boundaries of her sex, generation and class. At midlife she began to break out of those boundaries: "Locked in the closet at 4 years old I beat the wall with my body / that act is in me still."[1] Writing poems that were no longer nice, in forms that reflected her mind's straining for new visions, the poet began to challenge, and in recent years her work has reflected her life changes— from daughter-in-law to radical lesbian feminist.[2] The process of this growth is recorded for us in her poetry.

While apparently accepting the traditional female roles in early life, nonetheless feelings of strain and stifled emotion characterize Adrienne Rich's first two volumes.[3] The opening poem in A *Change of World*, "Storm Warnings," sets the tone of both books:

> The glass has been falling all the afternoon,
> And knowing better than the instrument
> What winds are walking overhead, what zone
> Of gray unrest is moving across the land,
> I leave the book upon a pillowed chair
> And walk from window to closed window, watching
> Boughs strain against the sky

The controlled iambic rhythm, broken appropriately in the first, fourth, and sixth lines by an anapest as the wind strains against the glass, contains the threat of violent weather, just as the imagined room protects the poet. The form of the poem is a device, used exactly as the drawn curtains and the hurricane lanterns, as a "defense against the season; / These are the things that we have learned to do / Who live in troubled regions." Another scene of restrained violence follows with "Aunt Jennifer's Tigers" who pace harmlessly across the embroidered tapestry, while her own energy is submerged; she lies "ringed with ordeals she was mastered by." Rich herself was unaware of the tensions her poems illustrate: later she was to write, "In those years formalism was part of the strategy—like asbestos gloves, it allowed me to handle materials I couldn't pick up barehanded."[4] To fill the role of poet, to win the approval of those whom she imitated, Rich had nearly crafted herself out of feeling.

___

selection has been edited for publication here; asterisks indicate deletions. Page references to works by Rich that appear in this Norton Critical Edition are given in brackets after the author's original citation.

1. Adrienne Rich, "Tear Gas," in *Poems: Selected and New 1950–1974* (New York: Norton, 1975), p. 140.
2. By publishing two poems in the anthology *Amazon Poetry*, Rich has included herself in the prefatory note which announces that all of these poems "were written by women who define themselves as lesbians. And who have chosen, by publishing their poetry here, to affirm publicly that identity." *Amazon Poetry*, ed. Joan Larkin and Elly Bulkin (New York: Out & Out Books, 1975), p. 9.
3. *A Change of World* (New Haven: Yale University Press, 1951) and *The Diamond Cutters* (New York: Harper & Brothers, 1955).
4. "When We Dead Awaken: Writing as Re-Vision," *College English* (October 1972): 22 [171].

Like many of the women she described, these early poems seem nearly
suffocated by self-control.

Rich's poetic adaptation was not unique. Barbara Bellow Watson, in
an essay on women and power, reminds us that

> women, like other groups with minority status, adopt various forms
> of accommodation to protect themselves. The most essential form
> of accommodation for the weak is to conceal what power they do
> have and to avoid anything that looks like threat or competition.[5]

Just as these early poems seldom focused specifically on the woman
described, concealing her in metaphors of tapestry, uncharted seas and
skies,[6] so too Rich's first expressed aesthetic accommodated the power of
a masculine school of critical thought. "At a Bach Concert" affirms that
"form is the ultimate gift that love can offer" and admonishes, "A too-
compassionate art is half an art. / Only such proud restraining purity /
Restores the else-betrayed, too-human heart." The self-conscious use
here of the rhymed form, the frequent hyphens, enclose the meaning in
an archaic restraint. The exact meaning of these words must then be
carefully extracted. Form, not the more amorphous "craft," is the pre-
ferred value of this early Rich aesthetic. Only through controlled,
restraining forms can the emotion be communicated safely. The danger
is twofold. Too great a compassion is sentiment, not art; and the artist
may reveal more of herself than is safe for her, or than her critical audi-
ence would wish to read. Rich's essential transformation as an artist was
a movement away from this aesthetic toward an art that allowed a far
more personal expression, allowed her to take risks as a poet and a com-
passionate woman.

Snapshots of a Daughter-in-Law,[7] published eight years after Rich's
second volume, marks a significant change in style and attitude. The
title of the volume is personal; it also emphasizes an awareness of her
role within the forms of marriage. She is no longer the young woman
who could change her world arbitrarily, nor the poet whose craft is com-
pared to that of the diamond cutter.

> The poem was jotted in fragments during children's naps, brief hours
> in a library, or at 3 A.M. after rising with a wakeful child. I despaired
> of doing any continuous work at this time. Yet I began to feel that
> my fragments and scraps had a common consciousness and a com-
> mon theme, one which I would have been very unwilling to put
> on paper at an earlier time because I had been taught that poetry
> should be "universal," which meant, of course, nonfemale.[8]

5. Barbara Bellow Watson, "On Power and the Literary Text," *Signs I* (Autumn 1975): 113.
6. E.g., "Aunt Jennifer's Tigers," "Mathilde in Normandy," "Unsounded," and "For the Con-
   junction of Two Planets" in *A Change of World*.
7. *Snapshots of a Daughter-in-Law* (New York: Harper & Row, 1963).
8. "When We Dead Awaken," p. 24 [175].

Here, the poet is a mother/wife/daughter-in-law whose life is given over to others, and that circumstance significantly affects her subject and, increasingly, the form of her poem. At times, the numbering of the sections within the title poem seems the only controlling factor, argument and syntax giving the reader little direction.

In "Snapshots of a Daughter-in-Law" Rich shows us a young woman who is beginning to realize that her identity is not that of the women she has been given as models: "Nervy, glowering, your daughter / wipes the teaspoons, grows another way." Like Joan of Arc, this protagonist hears voices; but hers bid her not to sacrifice herself: *"Have no patience. / . . . Be insatiable. / . . . Save yourself; others you cannot save."* These are not the voices of angels, but of monsters, the inevitable accompaniment of growing self-awareness and self-involvement for women. And these monsters do not come from another sphere; they are from within: "A thinking woman sleeps with monsters. / The beak that grips her, she becomes."

No specific political connections enlighten the protagonist of this poem. Rich celebrates those several predecessors who remained strong and produced their writing, such as Mary Wollstonecraft and Emily Dickinson, but the future is vague and awkwardly expressed:

> Well,
> she's long about her coming, who must be
> more merciless to herself than history.
> Her mind full to the wind, I see her plunge
> breasted and glancing through the currents,
> taking the light upon her
> at least as beautiful as any boy
> or helicopter,
> poised, still coming,
> her fine blades making the air wince
>
> but her cargo
> no promise then:
> delivered
> palpable
> ours.

The image of the helicopter represents both power and deliverance and its blades are weaponlike. But the ludicrous shape, the emphasis on a technological rather than a natural event, make this leap of the imagination a farfetched one. What we wish to believe is the wistful voice at the poem's end: a promise of selfhood that is "delivered," "palpable" and "ours." The theme of the poem is the role of a woman poet; the problem, in 1960, was one of inadequate models for that mode of female achievement.

While the political perspective of *Snapshots of a Daughter-in-Law* is nebulous, Rich does attempt in this volume to discuss, if not resolve, the problem she must have seen in applying her previously stated aesthetic to this new style of writing. "The Roofwalker" compares the poet to a construction worker balanced precariously on a rafter, "exposed, larger than life,/and due to break my neck." The female poet has labored "with infinite exertion" and succeeded in laying "a roof I can't live under." Her exertions were thwarted because "A life I didn't choose/chose me"— the life this volume depicts of mother, wife and daughter [9]—and thwarted because "even/my tools are the wrong ones/for what I have to do." Rich is not specific, may not be sure herself whether those wrong tools are the problem of gender identification—a woman writing in a man's voice and poetic form—or simply the problem of a formal style which made writing difficult with infants to care for. But both are connected to the use of a language which the poet is finding increasingly awkward. The phenomena Rich wishes to describe—a new female identity, the nuances of a male/female relationship—make impossible demands on a limited and sexist vocabulary. This combination, the wrong tools and the need to build, leave the poet exposed and vulnerable. Taking changes in her writing, the poet sees herself "naked, ignorant,/a naked man fleeing/across the roofs." With only a small difference, however, with a little less existential courage or curiosity, she could reduce these impulses to mere fantasies, daydreams, instead of her own reality.

*   *   *

"The Roofwalker" is dedicated to Denise Levertov and seems to be a response to Levertov's "From the Roof" in which a woman bringing in the wash on her Manhattan rooftop becomes the transformer and the transformed, watching and taking part in the sensuous, teeming life beneath her. And Rich experiences in this volume a problem of voice similar to that which plagued Levertov. In the fifties and sixties it was difficult for a woman to escape the fact that poet was a masculine noun. In Levertov's prose piece, "The Poet in the World," in a grotesque and awkward allegory, the female poet gives birth to a male child who becomes the poet-he, who then goes into the world to experience it. Similarly, in "Snapshots of a Daughter-in-Law" the standard of beauty and achievement is still male. The woman of the future, Rich tells us, will be "at least as beautiful as any boy."

Snapshots of a Daughter-in-Law was a book ignored by the critics, written off, Rich says, as "being too bitter and personal." In her next book she retreated from those earlier insights: ". . . something in me

---

9. "My husband spoke eagerly of the children we would have; my parents-in-law awaited the birth of their grandchild. I had no idea of what *I* wanted, what *I* could or could not choose." Adrienne Rich, *Of Woman Born: Motherhood as Experience and Institution* (New York: Norton, 1976; pb. ed. New York: Bantam, 1977), p. 5.

was saying, 'If my material, my subject matter as a woman is going to be denied me, then there is only *one* other subject for me and that is death.' That's why *Necessities of Life*[1] is a book about death."[2] And it is why *Leaflets*[3] is permeated with anger, diffused nervous tension and unfocused hostility. *Leaflets* opens with "Orion," the you addressed in the poem is the poet herself, "the active principle, the energetic imagination."[4] This aspect of her personality, that energy and self-involvement out of which the poetry is written, is on the defensive and will fight for its life:

> Breathe deep! No hurt, no pardon
> out here in the cold with you
> you with your back to the wall.

That image of defiant extremity recurs and becomes more specific: "Did you think I was talking about my life?/I was trying to drive a tradition up against the wall." And finally, "I can't live at the hems of that tradition—/will I last to try the beginning of the next?" The tradition that is forcing her to the wall, forcing her to live and write on its outskirts, is patriarchy, and this is specifically recognized in Rich's restatement of the theme of Auden's "Musée des Beaux Arts." Auden insisted that "about suffering they were never wrong,/The Old Masters: how well they understood/Its human position." Rich sees that the scenes haven't changed, "We stand in the porch,/two archaic figures: a woman and a man." But her perspective on suffering is unique: "The old masters, the old sources,/haven't a clue what we're about." She is not declaring, as one critic suggested with irritation, that "human experience in general is so radically disparate that even the old masters could fail to intimate our problems, provide us with a clue."[5] She *is* insisting that the old masters, the patriarchy, have cut themselves off from female experience; as her own sense of herself as a woman who has been forced to the edges of male culture becomes more conscious, she realizes how little that culture represents her own needs and desires.

Like the four-year-old flinging herself against the closet door, the images in *Leaflets* strike out against that cultural entombment. Blood, fire and war converge in the repeated identification of the poet with the red fox:

> The fox, panting, fire-eyed,
> gone to earth in my chest.
> How beautiful we are,

1. *Necessities of Life* (New York: Norton, 1966).
2. "Adrienne Rich and Robin Morgan Talk About Poetry and Women's Culture," in *The New Woman's Survival Sourcebook*, ed. Susan Rennie and Kirsten Grimstad (New York: Knopf, 1975), p. 107.
3. *Leaflets* (New York: Norton, 1969).
4. *"When We Dead Awaken,"* p. 24 [175].
5. Robert Boyers, "On Adrienne Rich: Intelligence and Will," *Salmagundi* 22–23 (Spring–Summer 1973): 140.

she and I, with our auburn
pelts, our trails of blood,
our miracle escapes,
our whiplash panic flogging us on
to new miracles!

In "5:30 A.M." Rich is sure that she and the fox will die, the hunters, "inanely single-minded/will have our skins at last." In "Abnegation" the woman poet and the vixen share a common birthright: ". . . no archives,/ no heirlooms, no future/except death."

"No future/except death" is a distinct recognition by Adrienne Rich of the aesthetics expressed by the "confessional poets."[6] But Rich's identification with the confessional poets is not complete. In "On Edges" words appear which indicate that Sylvia Plath is the source of this reverie/nightmare: "dressing-gowns," "monster," "lampshade." Still, Rich is a translator who, taking a "torn letter," cannot "fit these ripped-up flakes together." She recognizes and agrees that "the blades on that machine/could cut you to ribbons." The blades are not the dangerous helicopter blades from "Snapshots of a Daughter-in-Law," but the relentless keys of the poet's typewriter. And the "delicate hooks, scythe-curved intentions/you and I handle," are, in this poem of Rich's, words—in a literal sense, commas, the expression of a hesitation or silence. The last two poems of Sylvia Plath's life were "Edge" and "Words." "Words" are the axe's edge for Plath: "words dry and riderless" take on a life of their own, endangering the poet's life. Rich is willing to acknowledge this danger, to become the renegade:

. . . .I'd rather
taste blood, yours or mine, flowing
from a sudden slash, than cut all day
with blunt scissors on dotted lines
like the teacher told.

Rich echoes Plath's "the blood jet is poetry." But that which differentiates her from the confessional poets is her insistence that poetry/words/ language have a "function" that "is humane." Adrienne Rich will encounter the danger, but her belief in a direction for the future will allow her to survive that encounter.

In *Leaflets*, then, Rich connects the problem of survival to the problem of communication: a primary theme of her mature poetry. *"Tell me what you are going through—,"* the man asks in "Leaflets," "but the attention flickers" and he cannot hear her response, cannot hear her plead, *"Know that I exist!"* The words she tries to write in the "Ghazals" are "vapor-trails of a plane that has vanished" and she implores the reader, "When you read these lines, think of me/and of what I have not written

6. For example, Sylvia Plath, Anne Sexton, John Berryman, Robert Lowell.

here." In the last "Ghazal," dedicated to her husband, she wishes for some magic incantation to protect them from the suffering they will have to endure, and she asks him, speaking "as a woman to a man/ . . . How did we get caught up fighting this forest fire,/we, who were only looking for a still place in the woods?"

Within a year, Rich wrote a poem that begins to analyze politically that question: "how did we get caught?" "Tear Gas" [7] announces:

> The will to change begins in the body not in the mind
> My politics is in my body, accruing and expanding with every
>   act of resistance and each of my failures.

The subjective physical self is now seen as the focus for profound political change. Economically, a woman's body has always been a political object, controlled by a man, a master, a religion or a government. This new war will not be over until the woman can assert control over her own destiny, physical and cultural. To achieve both, she needs

> . . . a language to hear myself with
> to see myself in
> a language like pigment released on the board
> blood-black, sexual green, reds
> veined with contradictions
> bursting under pressure from the tube
> staining the old grain of the wood

The tensions here are palpable and explosive and the language seems inadequate. Rich protests, "but this is not what I mean/these images are not what I mean." It will be years before women find the images they need for this expression; but Rich now knows the direction of the search. She is moving "toward a place where we can no longer be together" as men and women; she is moving toward "another kind of action."

To effect this journey to a new place, a new action, Rich must first create a new language, a new way to express women's experience. The task is enormous, but not impossible; for she means to shape this new language, not through new words, but through new perceptions, so that we may first see ourselves in the new place. The old language causes pain, suffering, and isolation because it does not acknowledge or portray the human situation in a truthful way. One corrective, insists Rich, when "we are confronted with the naked and unabashed failure of patriarchal politics and patriarchal civilization," is to make an accurate record of human feelings by rewriting the stories and myths that purport to represent our deepest reality. And she is determined that "the sexual myths underlying the human condition can and shall be recognized and

7. First published in *Poems: Selected and New 1950–1974* (New York: Norton, 1975) 139.

318   JUDITH McDANIEL

changed."[8] *The Will to Change*[9] and *Diving into the Wreck*[1] represent
a sophisticated and passionate attempt to give us a new vision of our-
selves. These volumes recognize that myths and legends have had a
complex interrelationship with the development of civilization and the
concomitant development of the consciousness of the self. Rich returns
again and again to images of humankind's prehistoric and preconscious
state and then carefully leads us toward a new and altered perception.
The process is one of rebirth and conscious recreation.

The Will to Change opens with a poem that moves us carefully back
into a state where "the last absolutes were torn to pieces." The image of
"November 1968" is an incinerator of autumn leaves, the smoke from
which begins "to float free / . . . the unleafed branches won't hold you /
nor the radar aerials." The smoky essence of the leaves, drifting into the
air and disappearing, becomes a metaphor for the human return to a
preconscious state in which the self and the environment are one, before
the individual begins to differentiate itself from the group or its sur-
roundings. As the poet watches this process—individual leaves merging
into smoke—she wonders:

> How you broke open, what sheathed you
> until this moment
> I know nothing about it
> my ignorance of you amazes me

* * *

"The Burning of Paper Instead of Children" attempts a much more
difficult process of change. It is a poem about language, and once again
we sense a real ambivalence here toward the power of the written word,
which Rich both denies and affirms. The headnote of the poem quotes
Daniel Berrigan, on trial in Baltimore for burning draft records: "I was
in danger of verbalizing my moral impulses out of existence." And the
poem itself is a verbalization of poet's moral impulses about her sense of
her function and purpose in a violent society.

The first section of the poem asserts that the symbolic act (burning a
book) is less important to the poet than the burning of a child, or Joan
of Arc. Yet she learns of Joan's martyrdom in a book, *The Trial of Jeanne
d'Arc*, and is so mesmerized by the telling of the story that "they take the
book away / because I dream of her too often." This irony—the paradox
of the power of words versus the power of action—runs through the
poem. The poet reads the knowledge which allows an identification with
Joan of Arc, and she concludes part one of the poem with the realiza-
tion, "I *know* it hurts to burn" (emphasis mine).

"To imagine a time of silence" is the attempt of the second section,

8. Preface to *Poems: Selected and New 1950–1974*, pp. xv–xvi.
9. *The Will to Change* (New York: Norton, 1971).
1. *Diving into the Wreck* (New York: Norton, 1973).

and the poet proposes communication through touch. Physical love allows a "relief / from this tongue   this slab of limestone / or reinforced concrete." Verbalization is a gravestone, as the Indians discovered who, in the poet's imagination, communicated "in signal of smoke" until "knowledge of the oppressor" gave them language. The ambivalence of the poem is never more profoundly realized than in the terse conclusion of this section: "this is the oppressor's language / yet I need it to talk to you."

The poem does not conclude in the fifth and final section, it ignites. The languages of Frederick Douglass and Jeanne d'Arc were "pure" because their languages and their actions coincided; their languages were their actions: thus, "a language is a map of our failures" and our successes. This is the knowledge that will incite human change. With the realization that "I cannot touch you now," that earlier hope of a personal, physical communication is negated:

> I am in danger. You are in danger. The burning of a book arouses no sensation in me. I know it hurts to burn. There are flames of napalm in Catonsville, Maryland. I know it hurts to burn. The typewriter is overheated, my mouth is burning, I cannot touch you and this is the oppressor's language.

"My politics," Rich had written earlier, "is in my body." When we realize how inextricably related are all of our modes of expression, the lives we live become integrated into new political potential. She shows its complexity to us:

> Trying to tell the doctor where it hurts
> like the Algerian
> who has walked from his village, burning
>
> his whole body a cloud of pain
> and there are no words for this
>
> except himself

In this single image Rich unites the words, the pain, the body, and the politic. A vivid example of her poetic imagination, the precise visualization of an abstraction is a technique she has perfected as a mature poet, and will continue to use.

* * *

In her two most recent books Adrienne Rich explores the potential for women's power. Her prose work, *Of Woman Born: Motherhood as Experience and Institution*, shows that potential interfaced against the dark power of the patriarchy. She writes of women's quest "for models or blueprints of female power which shall be neither replications of male power nor carbon copies of the male stereotype of the powerful, controlling destructive woman."[2] She asks vindication for the belief "that patriarchy is in some ways a degeneration, that women exerting power would use it differently from men: nonpossessively, nonviolently, nondestructively."[3] *The Dream of a Common Language*[4] opens with a poem entitled "Power." The complexities of this power are inherent in the story of Marie Curie, who discovered the vital properties of uranium, and who died from radiation poisoning, "denying / her wounds   came from the same source as her power." Marie Curie did not know—literally—how to handle power. Once again Rich's poetic image—the woman holding in her "suppurating" fingers the test tube of uranium, source of energy and death—unites the abstract and political difficulties of power.

*   *   *

    The center of *The Dream of a Common Language* is a group of lesbian love poems, originally published as a separate booklet[5] and reanthologized here. It is an appropriate choice for continuing the theme of power, for in these poems Rich shows us a glimpse of the power generated by love, specifically the love of women for women:

> You've kissed my hair
> to wake me. *I dreamed you were a poem,*
> I say, *a poem I wanted to show someone . . .*
> and I laugh and fall dreaming again
> of the desire to show you to everyone I love,
> to move openly together
> in the pull of gravity, which is not simple,
> which carries the feathered grass a long way down
>   the upbreathing air.

There is a special recognition in "your small hands, precisely equal to my own," the recognition that "in these hands / I could trust the world. . . ." The strength in these poems is the discovery of the self in another, the range of knowing and identification that seems most possible in same-sex love: the encounter of another's pain, for example, leaves the poet knowing "I was talking to my own soul." Out of that sharing grows the ability to choose solitude "without loneliness," to define one's own sphere of action and growth:

> I choose to be a figure in that light,
> half-blotted by darkness, something moving
> across that space, the color of stone

2. "The Kingdom of the Fathers," *Partisan Review* 43 (Spring 1975): 25. This section appeared in a prepublication excerpt of *Of Woman Born*, but was not included in final publication.
3. *Of Woman Born*, p. 57.
4. *The Dream of a Common Language* (New York: Norton, 1978).
5. *Twenty-One Love Poems* (Emeryville, California: Effie's Press, 1976).

> greeting the moon, yet more than stone:
> a woman. I choose to walk here. And to draw this circle.

The choice, here and in most of Adrienne Rich's poetry, is of a process, a way of becoming, rather than a narrowly defined end.

That emphasis on process can also be found in her frequent images of women creating beautiful quilts out of small pieces of fabric and experience that many women have made, saved and cherished, "piecing our lore in quilted galaxies," as she says in "Sibling Mysteries." In "Natural Resources" she gathers up "these things by women saved,"

> these ribboned letters, snapshots
>
> faithfully glued for years
> onto the scrapbook page
>
> these scraps, turned into patchwork

and the effort is the poet's attempt to give women back the past that has been lost to us, a past of "humble things" without which we have "no memory / no faithfulness, no purpose for the future / no honor to the past." She tells us it is against this knowledge of other women that we must now analyze and test our perceptions and visions for the future.

Adrienne Rich was once accused of "the will to be contemporary," an unhappy influence on her poetry, as she was "neither a radical innovator nor the voice of an age."[6] She is, in fact, both. No poet's voice has spoken as hers has in this period of profound social change in the relations between women and men, among women themselves. In the nearly three decades in which Adrienne Rich has been writing poetry, the quality of her vision and of her poems has been unique. We find again in these poems

> . . . no mere will to mastery,
> only care for the many-lived, unending
> forms in which she finds herself.

Her voice and her work are distinguished by a commitment to "the fibers of actual life" and to change, a commitment that is unmatched in her poetic generation.

> I have to cast my lot with those
> who age after age, perversely,
>
> with no extraordinary power,
> reconstitute the world.

6. Boyers, p. 144.

OLGA BROUMAS

Review of *The Dream of a Common Language* †

> *But this is the saying of a dream*
> *on waking*
> *I wish there were somewhere*
> *actual we could stand*
> *handing the power-glasses back and forth*
> *looking at the earth, the wildwood*
> *where the split began*
>
> —"Waking in the Dark," *Diving into the Wreck*

The Dream of a Common Language is a document, both historical and emotional, of one woman's fierce desire and dedication to actualizing that wish among women and, failing that, to accurately describe the somewhere she finds herself, speechless, standing.

For a poet who has held speech to be synonymous with existence,

> Only where there is language is there world
> ("The Demon Lover," 1966)

and whose identity as a woman, articulate, serious, imperative, has defined and extended the parameters of our collective understanding of identity, the struggle to bring back the dream into the actual is a struggle with, a struggle against death.

This is the most difficult, complex, demanding of Rich's work. Not only is it heroic, as any pitting of the living will against the dark must be; it is, in the midst of the battle, a radical redefinition *of* the heroic

> in its ordinariness
> the slow-picked, halting traverse of a pitch
> where the fiercest attention becomes routine
> —look at the faces of those who have chosen it.
> ("Twenty-One Love Poems," XIX)

Revision, willfulness, change: these are familiar themes in the long work of a poet whose first book, in 1951, was called *A Change of World*. What is unfamiliar about this book is the full focus of those energies being riveted unflinchingly on the nature of interrelationships among women. In previous volumes, largely, though not exclusively, she was addressing men in the name of women; here, the *you* is almost always female, and where it is not, as in "Phantasia for Elvira Shatayev" ("leader of a women's climbing team, all of whom died in a storm on Lenin Peak, August 1974"), in which Rich speaks through Shatayev to her

† This review first appeared in *Chrysalis*, no. 6 (1978). Reprinted by permission of the author. The review has been edited for publication here; asterisks indicate deletions.

husband, it is an abstract *you*, a *you* no longer personal, a being she no longer engages with, only speaks to from afar, from another life, and with no belief or desire in communication.

Everything in Rich's work, both poetry and prose, has prepared the way for this book, in theory, in the mind. The actual book is a shock I've found difficult to recover from. I have felt moved, angry, challenged, betrayed, confronted, comforted. I've had, as a friend reviewing it for another publication said to me the other day, "to come to terms with it, for my own life." I've had to rediscover the original meaning of criticism, *krisis*, the decisive encounter that transforms.

The Dream of a Common Language. The emphasis, grammatical and actual, is not on *common*, which is where I first placed it in my own fierce desire for that reality, but on *dream*. The common language requires another one to hear it, to speak it, to reply. Alone, one dreams of/in it. The commonality of a language, dialogue, implies a tremendous risk for anyone, but certainly for a poet whose voice has matured in

> Isolation, the dream
> of the frontier woman
>
> leveling her rifle along
> the homestead fence
>
> still snares our pride
> —a suicidal leaf
> ("From an Old House in America," 1974)

The risk is so great because one cannot enter dialogue at will; one can only express one's desire, willingness, hunger to do so. It is the giving up of power on faith of another, greater perhaps, certainly different power. It is, for the poet, an ultimate act of faith, not only to understand and speak about the nature of dialogue, but to undertake it, risking, possibly, to fail.

Rich's challenge to men in her last poem before this book:

> *I try to understand*
> he said
>
> *what will you undertake*
> she said
>
> *will you punish me for history*
> he said
>
> *what will you undertake*
> she said
> ("From an Old House in America," 1974)

becomes the challenge she herself has faced—and answered:

> I have to cast my lot with those
> who age after age, perversely,
>
> with no extraordinary power,
> reconstitute the world.
>
> ("Natural Resources," 1977)

The problem, and the complexity, is that Rich has extraordinary powers—of perception, eloquence, rhythm, courage, the rare fusion of vision and action, the ability to suggest not only to others but to herself a course of action in the mind and follow it in the next breath in the world. A few months ago I came across a poem by Wendell Berry, "Healing," and copied these lines from it, inserting them in my copy of *Women and Honor*: "The possible is infinite in the mind, finite in the world. But to fulfill the possible is to enlarge it."

The Dream of a Common Language is, with the exception of one poem ("Nights and Days"), about what has been or is possible among women in the world as we know it. Its limitations constitute the gap between the infinite of the imaginary and the contradictions of the extant; between the force of the single, well-exercised will and voice and the long, hard way toward commonality, of love, of language, of trust.

The core of the book is "Twenty-One Love Poems," which one thousand of us have jealously owned, and a great many more have read, in its beautiful, small edition from Effie's Press. Eight poems precede it in a section called "Power," and ten follow it in a section called "Not Somewhere Else, but Here."

*   *   *

Scrupulous attention to the small and large details of language, a constant reexamination of their function and scope, is as essential to Adrienne Rich's poetry as the uses to which she puts that language. Every volume has been a further exploration of the responsibilities and limits of words as tools. I want to follow this exploration primarily through the poems to the loved one, because they constitute the major part of this volume and because, rooted as they are in the most immediately personal, tangible details of the poet's life, they embody a politics and poetics I most deeply feel.

The sequence I am calling "poems to the loved one" begins with "Origins and History of Consciousness." It is the title-cut: "The dream of a common language" surfaces here.

> No one lives in this room
> without living through some kind of crisis.

No one lives in this room
. . . .

Without contemplating last and late
the true nature of poetry. The drive
to connect. The dream of a common language.

Two women meet, recognize each other, love.

. . . We did this. Conceived
of each other, conceived each other in a darkness
which I remember as drenched in light.
                                    I want to call this, life.

But I can't call it life until we start to move
beyond this secret circle of fire
where our bodies are giant shadows flung on a wall

The secret circle is not enough. Sexuality alone, by which women
have been defined whether we chose to love men or women, whether
we chose at all, is not enough. The gesture of these poems is one of
desire for a totality of living, openness, communication and trust, in the
now, the immediate, the real:

Wherever in this city, screens flicker
with pornography, with science-fiction vampires,
victimized hirelings bending to the lash,
we also have to walk . . . if simply as we walk
through the rainsoaked garbage, the tabloid cruelties
of our own neighborhoods.
We need to grasp our lives inseparable
from those rancid dreams, that blurt of metal, those disgraces,
and the red begonia perilously flashing
from a tenement sill six stories high
                        ("Twenty-One Love Poems," I)

and later, in XIX,

(I told you from the first I wanted daily life,
this island of Manhattan was island enough for me.)

I began "Twenty-One Love Poems" expecting to read twenty-one poems
above love, whatever that has come to mean in my life, but certainly
something of the praiseful, the sexual, the lyric. Instead I found one
long poem, in twenty-two sections, about a deep and anguished prox-
imity of two lives, indeed of love, two lives that only once (in "THE
FLOATING POEM, UNNUMBERED," meaning everywhere, mean-
ing despite) shed their specific realities: of residence, age, politics, beliefs,
limitations. "THE FLOATING POEM" tells not only of a physical inti-

macy, but of the place of physical intimacy in an "honorable human relationship—that is, one in which two people have the right to use the word 'love' " (*Women and Honor.*) It is not the physical which defines this love as lesbian, but the absolute and primary attention directed at the other. Sisterhood—that is, primary and bonding love from women—is, like motherhood, a capacity, not a destiny. It must be chosen, exercised by acts of will; "Twenty-One Love Poems" describes as many instances, acts of the will. The sexual, requiring the least will, floats, unnumbered, informing the sequence the way a canvas is painted in a certain light, but is not about the light.

* * *

The tenderness and restraint of these poems, long after the poet has understood the silence, having tried and tried to break it, are what haunt and teach me most. The animal wild cry of pain, of loss—one of the most evocative and searing articulations of that primal cry—is in the third person, does not involve the loved one in its private grief ("Not Somewhere Else, but Here"). There is no accusation:

> . . . No poison cup,
> no penance. Merely a notion that the tape-recorder
> should have caught some ghost of us: that tape-recorder
> not merely played but should have listened to us,
> and could instruct those after us:
> this we were, this is how we tried to love,
> and these are the forces they had ranged against us,
> and these are the forces we had ranged within us,
> within us and against us, against us and within us.
>
> (XVII)

> When a woman speaks from her heart, when she grounds her words
> in the experience she has lived, when she reads with the full faith
> that she will be heard, understood, she is a wave coming to shore.
> (Ellen Bass)

In the absence of that faith, a woman's voice falters. It is significant that the poems not to or about the loved one are poems in a persona, or to a specific person. They continue the theme of love, as variously defined and possible as there are women, and the theme of power and visionary anger, anger that transforms, wasting no time in complaints. They are acts of vision, demystification, of courage and intelligence ("Sibling Mysteries" encapsulates in six pages the anthropological states of woman), but their poetic voice falters.

> If in this sleep I speak
> it's with a voice no longer personal

says Elvira Shatayev, who, being dead, speaks in fact in the disembodied or many-bodied voice. The impersonal in other poems diminishes their power, their ability to be both symbolic and inextricable from an individual, graspable reality. Often it is a matter of tone, of pacing, difficult to pin down in a few lines. Sometimes the metaphor is far-removed or stereotyped:

> this fraying blanket with its ancient stains
> we pull across the sick child's shoulder
>
> or wrap around the senseless legs
> of the hero trained to kill
>
> ("Natural Resources")

Sometimes the line is prosy, overwritten:

> in a weekend's destructive power,
> triggers fingered by drunken gunmen, sometimes
> so inept as to leave the shattered animal
> stunned in her blood. . . .
>
> ("Transcendental Etude")

These are symptoms of a deeper phenomenon, a voice diminished in its drive to connect, faltering in its faith that it will be heard, understood, a voice that risked extending its certitude beyond the halfway point and was not met. The fragmentation of line is not a stylistic device but a representation of an actual fragmentation:

> Spilt love   seeking its level   flooding other
> lives   that must be lived   not somewhere else
> but here   seeing through blood   nothing is lost
>
> ("Not Somewhere Else, but Here")
>
> I have written so many words
> wanting to live inside you
> to be of use to you
>
> Now I must write for myself . . .
>
> ("Upper Broadway")

The first poem to herself is "Nights and Days," a poem in the imaginary voice, in the infinity of the possible, a poem in the pure language of a dream. The first and last stanzas, identical, are in the rhythm and tense of the future, powerfully lyrical and visionary.

> The stars will come out over and over
> the hyacinths rise like flames
> from the windswept turf down the middle of upper Broadway
> where the desolate take the sun

the days will run together and stream into years
as the rivers freeze and burn
and I ask myself and you, which of our visions will claim us
which will we claim
how will we go on living
how will we touch, what will we know
what will we say to each other.

Pictures form and dissolve in my head

The middle three stanzas begin this way, in the present tense, pictures
in a dream defining in specific ways what/how is possible, how/what she
desires. It may seem paradoxical that the way back toward a common
language begins with a fantasy, a speech to one's self; and yet, common-
ality is an ethics, and as such concerned with value—from the Latin
root *val*, indicating courage, discernment, and praise—which, though
it does not exist until it is manifest and tested in the world, must be
envisioned and revisioned in the mind, the heart, the most private quar-
ters.

"Nights and Days," "Toward the Solstice," and "Transcendental Etude"
are the three poems where Rich does not inhabit

> . . . any place but the mind
> casting back to where her solitude,
> shared, could be chosen without loneliness,
> not easily nor without pains to stake out
> the circle, the heavy shadows, the great light.
>
> (XXI)

The pages of these poems are the most intimate in the book. I feel not
only allowed, but invited into that circle, drawn by the mind of a woman
whose work and life have been an act of becoming conscious against the
established order:

> Every act of becoming conscious
> (it says here in this book)
> is an unnatural act
> ("The Phenomenology of Anger," 1972)

Consciousness, truth, love are becoming synonymous. Truth, Rich
says in *Women and Honor*, is not one thing, or even a system. It is an
increasing complexity. Truth, like poetry, often surprises by an unpre-
dictability that on second look seems obvious, self-evident. The com-
mon language can begin in soliloquy; love is a total and intelligent caring
in which the sexual is a kind of light. The common language may indeed

be *silent*, emblematic, composed of acts of great care, beginning with
the encircled self of each woman

> becoming now the sherd of broken glass
> slicing light in a corner, dangerous
> to flesh, now the plentiful, soft leaf
> that wrapped round the throbbing finger, soothes the wound;
> and now the stone foundation, rockshelf further
> forming underneath everything that grows.

("Transcendental Etude," 1977)

ADRIAN OKTENBERG

"Disloyal to Civilization": The *Twenty-One Love Poems* of Adrienne Rich †

"A man's world. But finished."

From the beginning, in poetry as well as prose, Adrienne Rich has taken
up the questions posed of patriarchy by Virginia Woolf in *Three Guineas*:

> . . . Let us never cease from thinking,—what is this "civilization"
> in which we find ourselves? What are these ceremonies and why
> should we take part in them? What are these professions and why
> should we make money out of them? Where in short is it leading
> us, the procession of the sons of educated men? [1]

From the "respect [for her] elders" (W. H. Auden)[2] and "beautiful lies"
(Rosellen Brown)[3] in her early work, through the troubled evasions,
erasures, zigzag roofwalks later on, to the confrontation "with the naked
and unabashed failure of patriarchal politics and patriarchal civilization"[4]

† From *Reading Adrienne Rich: Reviews and Re-Visions, 1951–81*, ed. Jane Roberta Cooper
(Ann Arbor: U of Michigan P, 1984). © Adrian Oktenberg 1981. Reprinted by permission of
the author. Page references to works that appear in this Norton Critical Edition are given in
brackets after the author's original citation.
1. Virginia Woolf, *Three Guineas* (New York: Harcourt, Brace, 1966), pp. 62–63; first published
1938.
2. "[Rich's poems] . . . are neatly and modestly dressed, speak quietly but do not mumble, respect
their elders but are not cowed by them, and do not tell fibs: that, for a first volume, is a good
deal." W. H. Auden, Foreword to *A Change of World* [278–79].
3. "Rich's poems fall into two major categories, it's necessary but not sufficient to say that: the
beautiful lies, whole and conventional, of the early period; everything that's followed her rec-
ognition that there is nothing apolitical, neither statement nor act. . . ." Rosellen Brown,
"The Notes for the Poem Are the Only Poem," *Parnassus* 4 (Fall/Winter 1975): 50.
4. Adrienne Rich, Foreword to her *Poems: Selected and New 1950–1974* (New York: Norton,
1975), p. xv.

which is the chief necessity of her mature work, Rich has returned to these questions over and again. In the "Twenty-One Love Poems,"[5] Rich confronts "this 'civilization' in which we find ourselves" for perhaps the most concentrated and sustained moment in her poetry, and pronounces herself, more explicitly than ever, disloyal to it.

It is not my purpose to describe the personal, political, or poetical development which led Rich to arrive at these poems, although that development as it is revealed in her work is fascinating and the "Twenty-One Love Poems" are a culminating point in it. The chronicle of tremors and quakes which her work has undergone up to this point, while essential to an understanding of her poetry, will be left to others. I wish to focus instead on what will undoubtedly remain one of the peaks of that development, to offer a reading of the "Twenty-One Love Poems" which, while not ignoring the climb, surveys in some detail the view from the height.

"Every peak is a crater," Rich writes (in poem XI of the series), indicating the dialectical nature of her enterprise. For throughout the "Twenty-One Love Poems" she is concerned with not one but two civilizations; the constant play of her mind is between (and beyond) them. The first is "this still unexcavated hole / called civilization, this act of translation, this half-world" (V) in which we are forced to live; it is the patriarchal peak, the sum or the summit of what men have created. Its apex is the city, the center of industry, commerce, law, culture. It is appropriate, and necessary, that the poems begin there.

> Wherever in this city, screens flicker
> with pornography, with science-fiction vampires,
> victimized hirelings bending to the lash,
> we also have to walk. . . .
>
> (I)

The speaker's disloyalty to this "civilization" is immediately apparent, for the culture of the sons of educated men displays at its apex its most meaningful artifacts: the imagery of violence, human distortion, gynephobia, horror. Woolf's question was, "Where . . . is it leading us . . .?" Sweet Honey in the Rock sang, "B'lieve I'll run on . . . see what the end's gonna be."[6] But they, and Rich, and anyone else who cared to see, saw that the end would be death and destruction. That to avoid disaster, the procession of the sons of educated men must be diverted or halted. That disloyalty to civilization is not a crime (see XIII), but the essence of pragmatism. That disloyalty has become urgent necessity.

5. The "Twenty-One Love Poems" are in Rich, *The Dream of a Common Language, Poems 1974–1977* (New York: Norton, 1978), pp. 25–36. [77–86]. First published as a separate volume by Effie's Press, Emeryville, Calif., in 1976.

6. Bernice Reagan, "B'lieve I'll Run On . . . See What the End's Gonna Be." The song is the title cut of an album by the same name, by the group Sweet Honey in the Rock (Redwood 3500).

But patriarchal civilization is only the starting point, the thesis, for the argument. Rich is equally concerned to grasp and place beside it, as opposition and reproach, another conception of civilization—one that is woman-centered, woman-identified, woman-created. ("To bring forward" or "raise" or "emerge" are perhaps more appropriate verbs for this process, for a civilization which is of use to women is conceived of in the "Twenty-One Love Poems" as having been buried beneath or behind that constructed by men—see V.) While the violence of patriarchal civilization is palpably before us (concrete, assaultive, unavoidable), the struggle to imagine a woman-centered way in the world is of a different character.[7] Because we live, and have lived for centuries, under patriarchy, it must remain in large part the task of the moral imagination; because it is an act of imagination, it is fraught with mistakes, lapses, fears, confusions, setbacks, loops. It sometimes takes on the quality of shadowboxing; our powers of imagination can be weak, dim, or clouded; but the pain of error, fault, or missed connections is intense nevertheless. "No one has imagined us," the poet writes (I). She means that no man, no work of literature, no part of patriarchal culture has taken into account the possibility of two women together, loving each other, and of this as the embryonic beginning of a new, woman-centered civilization. She means that there are no guides or models for this task, so that "whatever we do together is pure invention" (XIII).

The poet also means that the "we" of the "Poems" (two women, lovers; by extension, other women together: "an army of lovers cannot fail") must undertake this essential work of the imagination as individual human beings in the world. In writing, "No one has imagined us," Rich suggests that the lovers of the "Poems" are not only fictive creations, but also, simultaneously, real human beings. The decisions they make have consequences in the actual world, the world of pain and struggle, life and death. Whatever is imagined by them must be created daily, under pressure of events. "A life I didn't choose / chose me . . . ," Rich wrote in an earlier poem,[8] and now she would no longer wish to turn away, but would embrace, the choice. She sees that "we need to grasp our lives inseparable / from those rancid dreams, that blurt of metal, those disgraces" (I).

Necessity requires that the work of the imagination be conducted under conditions by which most women have always worked—without leisure, without space or privacy, without retreating from the immediately pressing and mundane demands of life.[9] Women must grasp their lives whole, and extract beauty ("the red begonia," "the long-legged young girls" of

---

7. "[T]he sea is another story / the sea is not a question of power," from "Diving into the Wreck," in Rich, *Poems: Selected and New*, p. 196 [54].
8. From "The Roofwalker," in Rich, *Poems: Selected and New*, p. 63 [16].
9. See "Conditions for Work: The Common World of Women," in Rich, *On Lies, Secrets and Silence: Selected Prose 1966–1978* (New York: Norton, 1979), p. 203.

poem I) from conditions of ugliness—because other conditions are not available to be chosen. In opposition to patriarchal civilization, Rich attempts to imagine a woman-identified one; the latter remains as yet dim, fragmentary, rough. The "Twenty-One Love Poems" are also a partial documentary record, as if tape-recorded (XVII), of two people engaged in this effort, of their gains and losses, taken at a certain point in the struggle and in their lives.

Rich's procedure is by a method necessarily oxymoronic, paradoxical, contradictory, shocking. Her lovers exist in a patriarchal context, within which they represent, and attempt to create, a way of living profoundly at odds with it. Rich lives among the artifacts and debris of "modern" civilization, yet she knows it is dead ("the unabashed failure . . ."). Its values are dead both in the sense that they no longer hold meaning for us (e.g., patriotism: "*I think that men love wars*," from IV), and that they lead to extinction (the polluted rivers and massacres of VII). The structures and institutions with which she must deal are patriarchal (cities in I, war in IV, culture in V, heterosexism in XIV), yet her true allegiance, and deeper identification, are to modes of thinking and relating which do not subscribe and are fundamentally opposed to patriarchal rules.

The underground life of lovers in the "Poems" is constantly alluded to, and comes from the deeply buried parts of the "primitive" psyche, which continually assert themselves:

> . . . my own animal thoughts:
> that creatures must find each other for bodily comfort,
> that voices of the psyche drive through the flesh
> further than the dense brain could have foretold. . . .
>
> (X)

The speaker's thoughts are "animal" (X), she tells her dreams (II), identifies with "beasts" and "wolverines" (VII), with animals' instinct for physical contact and comfort (X), with planets, dream-ghosts (XII), outlaws and hallucinated transformations (XIII). The lovers feel "animal passion" (I), their lovemaking is described in terms of forest ferns and caves ("THE FLOATING POEM, UNNUMBERED"), the impression they leave is of "some ghost" (XVII), they speak to each other in a dream (XIX), one communicates with the other as "to my own soul" (XX).[1] The *sotto voce* stream, or the subtext, of the "Poems" is the secret life of

---

1. Nor is it an accident that the sequence concludes, in XXI, with the image of a woman walking alone at Stonehenge. The labrys, "the sacred double ax of Crete, symbol of the goddess and of matriarchal rule," appears carved on the stones there. See Elizabeth Gould Davis, *The First Sex* (New York: Putnam, 1971), p. 80.

women—those who are openly disloyal to patriarchal forms are secretly loyal to antipatriarchal ones.

To express paradoxical thoughts, the poet requires a language of paradox. The imagery of the "Poems" is also substantially oxymoronic, and this contributes to the shock of the reader's response. Visionary poetry from Sor Juana Inés de la Cruz to Judy Grahn is oxymoronic in just this way:

> No one has imagined us. We want to live like trees,
> sycamores blazing through the sulfuric air,
> dappled with scars, still exuberantly budding,
> our animal passion rooted in the city.
>
> (I)

> to move openly together
> in the pull of gravity, which is not simple,
> which carries the feathered grass a long way down
>   the upbreathing air.
>
> (II)

> I touch you knowing we weren't born tomorrow,
> and somehow, each of us will help the other live,
> and somewhere, each of us must help the other die.
>
> (III)

> my body still both light and heavy with you
>
> (IV)

> such hands might carry out an unavoidable violence
> with such restraint, with such a grasp
> of the range and limits of violence
> that violence ever after would be obsolete.
>
> (IV)

> Every peak is a crater.
>
> (XI)

> the innocence and wisdom of the place my tongue
>   has found there—
>   (THE FLOATING POEM, UNNUMBERED)

> Across a city from you, I'm with you,
> . . . .
> your generous, delicate mouth
> where grief and laughter sleep together.
>
> (XVI)

two people together is a work
heroic in its ordinariness,
the slow-picked, halting traverse of a pitch
where the fiercest attention becomes routine. . . .

(XIX)

. . . nor any place but the mind
casting back to where her solitude,
shared, could be chosen without loneliness,
not easily nor without pains to stake out
the circle, the heavy shadows, the great light.
I choose to be a figure in that light,
half-blotted by darkness. . . .

(XXI)

Two women who are lovers in heterosexist society live with contradictions embedded in their most intimate thoughts and feelings. What they experience as beautiful, and as absolutely natural, the rest of society views as ugly and perverted. Those who exist in biologically female bodies in a world where only male ones are considered "human" must daily deny the most basic facts about their experience. Feminists who recognize emotional, communal, or political bonds with women as primary, or who assert the centrality of "women's" issues to society as a whole, or who seek to project woman-identified values where masculinist ones hold hegemony, are under no illusions about the ubiquity of patriarchal power. Those who are disloyal to civilization have no reason to obey, or even to recognize, its rules ("we're out in a country that has no language / no laws . . ." from XIII). Living in such a world *is* a paradoxical project for them; they float, unnumbered, in a world of anchored numbers. Why should not their laughter also contain grief, why could not their solitude be shared? And why should not gravity reverse itself, and pull grass up with the "upbreathing air"?

The adoption of antipatriarchal attitudes requires the most clarified vision, the most searching re-vision of received wisdom; nothing in it can be taken for granted. The struggle for clarity is one of the themes of the "Twenty-One Love Poems," as it is of Rich's work in general. This is a poet of celebrated intelligence, "a woman sworn to lucidity,"[2] for whom nothing is simple, to whom nothing is given. She believes in intelligence, which for her carries an active value, as others believe in the redemptive value of grace. In an earlier poem, she wrote:

Only our fierce attention
gets hyacinths out of those
hard cerebral lumps,

---

2. From "I Dream I'm the Death of Orpheus," in Rich, *Poems: Selected and New*, p. 152 [43].

unwraps the wet buds down
the whole length of a stem.[3]

In the "Twenty-One Love Poems," she wrote:

> If I could let you know—
> two women together is a work
> nothing in civilization has made simple,
> two people together is a work
> heroic in its ordinariness,
> the slow-picked, halting traverse of a pitch
> where the fiercest attention becomes routine
> —look at the faces of those who have chosen it.
>
> (XIX)

In the decade between the writing of those two poems, the "fiercest attention" of the focused mind, which seems an effort of supreme will (in the heterosexual context?) in the earlier poem, becomes routine (among women?). Its transformative power has not dissipated over time but has, if anything, increased. The "faces of those who have chosen it" ("it" being "two women together") are beatified not only by love, but also by the intense intellectual work in which they are involved.

But the struggle for clarity cannot be the work solely of the mind, as love cannot be the expression solely of the body. One critic has noted that the intensity of Rich's recent work comes in part from the fact that "mind and passion test and confirm each other,"[4] as they must in any good poetry. But for Rich the test is more rigorous than for most, and the confirmation is by no means assured beforehand. Her quest for intellectual clarity, the naming and placing of it in the larger cultural, historical, or planetary (XII) context, remains "hard," "cerebral," lumped, incomplete, unless passionate linkage can be made—and made to hold. For years, readers have shared her attempt to forge this link (one reason her work holds such fascination), and it is also why there is such relief and joy when she writes, in III: "And you, you move toward me with the same tempo." The lovers *meet*, minds and passions equally joined, as they have not met before in Rich's poetry.[5]

The fully engaged, intellectual and passionate meeting of *these* lovers is unique in the poetry that I know, and I am not speaking of the fact

---

3. From "Like This Together," in Rich, *Poems: Selected and New*, p. 77 [24].
4. Albert Gelpi, "Adrienne Rich: The Poetics of Change," in *Adrienne Rich's Poetry*, ed. Barbara Charlesworth Gelpi and Albert Gelpi (New York: Norton, 1975), p. 141 [292].
5. And more successfully later. ". . . two women, eye to eye / measuring each other's spirit, each other's / limitless desire, / a whole new poetry beginning here." From "Transcendental Etude," in Rich, *The Dream of a Common Language*, p. 76 [90]. Any work published by Rich after this volume is beyond the scope of this essay.

that the lovers are women (though the fact, acknowledged and celebrated, is still so rare in literature that its importance is not to be minimized). The meeting of lovers in the "Twenty-One Love Poems" is unique because it is on terms which are consciously antipatriarchal; lovers who are disloyal to patriarchal civilization strive to free themselves from its attitudes even in their intimate relations, even in themselves. This is a profoundly liberating process, and it is charted in the "Poems." This is what makes the "Twenty-One Love Poems" new, not the fact that the lovers are women. Women have always loved each other, in literature as in life, but they have usually accepted, and done so within, patriarchal forms.

Nothing is given to these lovers—outlaws of patriarchy—neither language nor laws (XIII): "whatever we do together is pure invention." Much of the action of the "Poems" describes the process of trial and error by which the lovers must explore their love. Conventional love, as patriarchy would have them experience it, is useless ("the maps they gave us were out of date/by years . . ." from XIII). They use the only maps available, their own minds and passions. Much "courtly" or "romantic" baggage is jettisoned as so much dead weight.[6] One such item is the notion of lover as subject, beloved as object, and merger as unattainable ideal—one of the characteristic dichotomies of patriarchal thinking. Here are "two lovers of one gender, / . . . two women of one generation" (XII); their lives are seen as merging in a single poem (see II), and "it could be written with new meaning" (XII). The lovers are not human beings divided eternally by rigid categories of difference, but individuals linked by circumstance and choice (XVII).

Indeed, the familiar structure of romantic tragedy is explicitly rejected. Not fate but accident brings the lovers together:

> No one's fated or doomed to love anyone.
> The accidents happen, we're not heroines,
> they happen in our lives like car crashes,
> books that change us, neighborhoods
> we move into and come to love.
>
> (XVII)

No fatal or foredoomed flaw, but mortal choice and responsibility, determines the course of their love:

6. But some, forgotten or unexamined, remains. I have said that the poems are an act of the moral imagination in which confusions, setbacks, and loops are inevitable. One such point of confusion appears in II, in which the speaker desires to show the lover "the poem of my life." A few lines later, it becomes clear that the speaker's life *is* her beloved. "*I dreamed you were a poem,* / I say, *a poem I wanted to show someone. . . .*" The attitude here revealed is a paradigm for the way women are supposed to address the (male) lover in romantic patriarchal literature, on the order of "you are my love, my life, my all." As such, it is a throwback to a way of thinking which the "Poems" as a group reject.

> If I cling to circumstances I could feel
> not responsible. Only she who says
> she did not choose, is the loser in the end.

(XV)

The traditional "choices" for women, self-destruction, suicide, martyr-dom, are recognized for the deathtraps they are:

> Well, that's finished. The woman who cherished
> her suffering is dead. I am her descendant.
> I love the scar-tissue she handed on to me,
> but I want to go on from here with you
> fighting the temptation to make a career of pain.[7]

(VIII)

The climax provides no spectacle of disaster,

> *Tristan und Isolde* is scarcely the story,
> women at least should know the difference
> between love and death. No poison cup,
> no penance. . . .

(XVII)

only the drone of an anticlimactic, analytical voice:

> . . . Merely a notion that the tape-recorder
> should have caught some ghost of us: that tape-recorder
> not merely played but should have listened to us,
> and could instruct those after us:
> this we were, this is how we tried to love,
> and these are the forces they had ranged against us,
> and these are the forces we had ranged within us,
> within us and against us, against us and within us.

(XVII)

For that kind of drama is out of date; its conventions do not, cannot, illuminate the images of these women.

A drama or literary structure that does is still largely unmapped, still in the process of discovery. Like the nineteenth-century feminists who compiled *A History of Woman's Suffrage* while the vote was in the process of being won, we know we must work it out while we are also living it ("—and yet, writing words like these, I'm also living," from VII). The language, the laws, the "charted systems" (XIII) of patriarchy must be transmuted, like the violence of poem VI, into a structure at once recognizable, yet fully expressive of and responsive to, our female passions and minds.

7. The prosaic language of these lines is another lapse—or leak—involving here the poet's effort to translate politics into poetry. "LEAK: There are leaks comparable to water leaks in the consciousness of every person. . . ." Monique Wittig and Sande Zeig, *Lesbian Peoples: Materials for a Dictionary* (London: Virago, 1980), p. 96.

The form of the "Twenty-One Love Poems" also forces a transmutation of more traditional forms for love poems. Many have commented on how Rich's mature work has opened up, her lineation becoming less regular, her syntax more fluid, and so on,[8] and I do not propose to repeat that discussion. But there are two aspects of form in the "Twenty-One Love Poems" on which I feel I can comment.

The first is that, while they *look* like other, perhaps more familiar, love poems, they are in fact dissimilar. It is true that they are a sequence of short, free-verse lyrics; the speaker in the poems is a lover who addresses a beloved; the tone of the poems is intense, passionate, aching, intimate; the poems follow the course of a romantic relation over a relatively short time; the sequence comprises a testament to the beloved, a justification of the lover, and a fictive record of the relationship. In such respects the "Twenty-One Love Poems" do not differ substantially from the sonnets of Shakespeare, Matthew Arnold's "Marguerite" poems, the "Sonnets from the Portuguese," or the love poetry of Emily Dickinson, to all of which they owe a great deal. The "Twenty-One Love Poems" succeed so well in making the leap from the particular to the universal, they are so sensual, swift, and immediate in their impact, that it is possible to read them as if the tantalizing fragments of Sappho had been taken up by a poet of equal stature, and completed at last.

But it would be a mistake to read them that way for the reasons I have outlined. Rich has never been a particularly personal, certainly not a confessional, poet, and it is important to recognize that the "Twenty-One Love Poems" are not an anomaly in her work. They do not represent a private interlude in the work of a poet whose great theme has always been social relations; they are in no sense a departure or retreat from that theme. In fact, they deepen and extend it. While the poems may appear to be the private utterances of the lover to the beloved, while readers may appear to be privileged to eavesdrop on this most intimate relation, we are nevertheless expected to notice and remember the fact that these are only appearances. The "Poems" are political to their roots, and to ignore or minimize this aspect of the matter is to distort them.

Second, the "Twenty-One Love Poems" are constructed in such a way as to open up the whole of Rich's work; they are highly self-referential.[9] More than most contemporary poets, Rich has fashioned a body

---

8. See, e.g., Gelpi, "The Poetics of Change," pp. 142–45 [293–94]; Suzanne Juhasz, *Naked and Fiery Forms, Modern American Poetry by Women: A New Tradition* (New York: Harper Colophon, 1976), pp. 186–200; Helen Vendler, *Part of Nature, Part of Us: Modern American Poets* (Cambridge: Harvard University Press, 1980), p. 251 [304].

9. The "Poems" include references to literature by others as well. The "Victorian poet" of XVIII is Matthew Arnold, whose poem, "To Marguerite, in Returning a Volume of the Letters of

of work rather than an accumulation of poems; the "Twenty-One Love Poems" demand to be read in the context of that work, both poetry and prose. Almost every line reflects on or reverberates off of something Rich has written elsewhere, creating a montage of images and associations. This poet who has been so influenced by film has observed that "the continuity and unity flow from the associations and images playing back and forth. . . ."[1] I have already noted, for example, the "fierce attention" which recurs in poems written years apart; when it resurfaces, the phrase enriches both contexts in which it appears. There are many such examples of recurring words, phrases, images, or ideas which are renewed or expanded each time they appear. The phrase "artist dying in childbirth" (in V) recalls Rich's great poem, "Paula Becker to Clara Westhoff";[2] "neighborhoods / we move into and come to love"(XVII) recaptures the last line of an earlier poem, "Shooting Script";[3] the reference to

---

Ortis," concludes as follows:

> Who order'd that their longing's fire
> Should be, as soon as kindled, cool'd?
> Who renders vain their deep desire?—
> A God, a God their severance rul'd;
> And bade betwixt their shores to be
> The umplumb'd, salt, estranging sea.

From *The Poems of Matthew Arnold, 1849–1867* (London: Oxford University Press, 1922), p. 135. Philoctetes "hurting with an infected foot" in VIII is from the play of the same name by Sophocles, in *The Complete Greek Drama*, vol. I, ed. Whitney J. Oates and Eugene O'Neill, Jr. (New York: Random House, 1938), p. 555. The legend of Tristan and Iseult appears in many places in literature (Beroul, Malory, Tennyson, E. A. Robinson), but Rich's reference in XVII no doubt refers to the music-drama by Richard Wagner, in which the lovers drink from a poisoned wedding cup. She has earlier referred to "Götterdämmerung" (in XIII), the last part of Wagner's tetralogy, "Der Ring des Nibelungen." "Der Rosenkavalier" (XIII) is the opera by Strauss. In V, Swift is seen "loathing the woman's flesh while praising her mind. . . ." Swift praised the minds of the two most important women in his life, to whom he played tutor and mentor: Esther Johnson, of the *Journal to Stella*, and Ester Vanhomrigh, of the long poem *Cadenus and Vanessa*. As for his "loathing the woman's flesh," evidence is abundant in his writing, a single line sufficing: "Celia, Celia, Celia shits." "Goethe's dread of the Mothers" (V) appears in *Faust*, part 2, act 1, scene 5:

Mephistopheles:	Unwilling, I reveal a loftier mystery.—
	In solitude are throned the Goddesses,
	No space around them, Place and Time still less;
	Only to speak of them embarrasses.
	They are THE MOTHERS!
Faust (terrified):	Mothers!
Mephistopheles:	Hast thou dread?
Faust:	The Mother! Mothers!—a strange word is said.

Goethe, *Faust*, trans. Bayard Taylor (Boston: Houghton Mifflin, 1882), pp. 65–66. Eckermann, Goethe's friend, stated that the Mothers are the "creating and sustaining principle, from which everything proceeds that has life and form on the surface of the Earth." See Notes, pp. 352–53. I am unable to locate the reference to Claudel (V), whose vilification of Gide is anyway inherent in the situation. Claudel: devout Catholic and conservative. Gide: anticlerical and radical homosexual. St. Pierre and Miquelon (XIV) are islands in the Atlantic just off the southern coast of Newfoundland. Finally, intuition based on similar experience tells me that the Xerox in the mail (IV) may have come from Amnesty International, the organization that aids prisoners of conscience around the world.

1. Quoted by Albert Gelpi in *Adrienne Rich's Poetry*, p. 144.
2. In Rich, *The Dream of a Common Language*, p. 42.
3. In Rich, *Poems: Selected and New*, p. 182 [47]. The line is: "To pull yourself up by your own roots; to eat the last meal in / your old neighborhood."

midwives' hands, eschewing forceps in the delivery of a child (VI), finds an explanation in *Of Woman Born;*[4] "Every peak is a crater. This is the law of volcanoes . . ." (XI) most directly recalls Rich's essay on Emily Dickinson, "Vesuvius at Home";[5] "the Eleusinian cave" (VI) brings to mind Rich's description of the Eleusinian mysteries in *Of Woman Born;*[6] "the slow-picked, halting traverse of a pitch" (XIX) reminds us of "The Roofwalker," who is "due to break my neck,"[7] and so on.

By inserting external references into the fictive world of the poems, Rich seems to be deliberately blurring the formal distinctions between fictive and natural discourse.[8] Many contemporary writers adopt this procedure; Rich is not alone, or particularly innovative, in this respect. By making reference to extraneous matters, literary or otherwise, the writer's intention is not to set up a bar to comprehension but rather to expand its field. If the reader has encountered nothing else by Rich, the "Twenty-One Love Poems" are of course perfectly comprehensible and moving. But if the reader can also connect the references in these poems to Rich's previous work, then her experience of the "Twenty-One Love Poems" gains in depth and range.

It is a measure of Rich's skill and generosity as a poet that the references do not slacken or degenerate into a private guessing game or code. Only Rich and her friends can identify "Kenneth" in V; the common reader must wonder whether Burke or Koch or Pitchford is involved. By now we know enough of Rich to assume that if Kenneth's full identity would add further dimension to the poem, we would have it, and leave it at that. Contrast Rich with the numerous references to friends in the work of O'Hara, Ginsberg, or Ashbery, and note the difference. Rich's references do not result in an enclosed system or zero-sum game, nor in damage to the poems.

4. Adrienne Rich, *Of Woman Born: Motherhood as Experience and Institution* (New York: Norton, 1976), pp. 142–51.
5. See "Vesuvius at Home: The Power of Emily Dickinson," in Rich, *On Lies, Secrets and Silence,* p. 157 [177]. Volcanoes appear often in Rich's poems. See, e.g., "Re-forming the Crystal," in Rich, *Poems: Selected and New,* pp. 227–28 [61–62].
6. See Rich, *Of Woman Born,* pp. 237–40.
7. See Rich, *Poems: Selected and New,* p. 63 [16].
8. My understanding of such distinctions is derived from Barbara Herrnstein Smith, *On the Margins of Discourse: The Relation of Literature to Language* (Chicago: University of Chicago Press, 1978), esp. pp. 14–40. Natural discourse is essentially historical in character, and is the utterance of a temporal voice which, once having existed, passes from the scene. Conversations, letters, biographies are instances of natural discourse. Fictive discourse is ahistorical; it is the stuff of which poems and novels are made. Because it is ahistorical, we can reenter and reexperience it at will. One of Smith's arguments is that the two modes operate by virtue of characteristics suitable to themselves, and that we confuse them at our peril. When Rich writes, in XVIII, ". . . I am Adrienne alone. And growing colder," the statement is fictive because it is made in a poem. The speaker of it is therefore a fictive "Adrienne." It is *not* the statement of Adrienne Rich, a woman who lives in western Massachusetts, who writes poems, who is feeling cold—because such an understanding of it is appropriate only to natural discourse. My argument here is that Rich does not confuse, but deliberately *merges,* elements of fictive and natural discourse, in order to enlarge her readers' consciousness of the poems. It is a method used by many contemporary poets, whether or not they have been instructed by Smith.

The one extraneous reference we lack is the identity of her lover. I doubt that it matters. Rich has never conspicuously named her husband or sons either, nor is it necessary for her to do so in the important poems in which they figure. Colette: "One is always writing for someone."[9] Whether that someone appears in the work itself, in the flesh as it were and by name, is another question.

The "Poems" remain, then, consummate *fictive* acts; but the fact that Rich blurs the distinction between fictive and natural utterance heightens their intimacy. An impression is thereby achieved of speed, immediacy, and emotional compression. It is as if Rich has so much to say, and her need to say it is so urgent, that she resorts to a kind of emotional speedwriting or shorthand—an abbreviation of associations caused by the pressure of emotion. The "Poems," like Sappho's, become almost transparent and accessible. The result is that the reader is practically vaulted into the "Poems"; the effect is breathtaking.

None of this, however, can explain or do justice to the most striking effect created by the "Twenty-One Love Poems"—they are remarkably appealing. People's reaction to them is visceral, and I have reason to doubt that this response is limited to those readers—lesbian, or feminist, or female—who might be predisposed to favor this particular writer or these particular poems. It would be a sociological, rather than a poetical, enterprise to attempt to "identify" the "factors" which contribute to the appeal of the "Poems," and a futile one. But we can at least speculate on why these particular love poems are so affecting.

I have already suggested some likely reasons, but the most obvious one is that Rich has touched a nerve. We have all understood with Woolf that "the procession of the sons of educated men" is leading us to death and destruction; the evidence for that is everywhere inescapable. In the "Twenty-One Love Poems,"Rich has succeeded, heavily against the odds, in putting us in touch with a powerful counterforce. By rejecting the patriarchal dichotomy between mind and passion, and suggesting instead their unification, she has begun to articulate an idea that it is difficult for most of us even to imagine. The project of the "Poems"— ultimately to unite the Greek concepts of *eros* and *agape*, or in the Gandhian formulation, *satyagraha* and *ahimsa*—is to suggest the regenerative power of knowledge united with love.[1]

9. *Letters from Colette*, ed. Robert Phelps (New York: Farrar, Straus and Giroux, 1980), p. 146.
1. My argument here, perhaps, is somewhat confused by the patriarchal connotations of the words used. The essential component of *eros* is usually identified as physical passion, whereas *agape* represents a more disinterested, sometimes termed "Christian," version of love based on the Golden Rule. *Satyagraha* is inadequately translated as "passive resistance," and *ahimsa*, as "nonviolence." The original meanings, "truth/firmness" for the former, and "the negative of/injury" for the latter, are better, both being more active and less weak. For a useful discussion of the matter, see Joan V. Bondurant, *Conquest of Violence: The Gandhian Philosophy of Conflict*, rev. ed. (Berkeley: University of California Press, 1965), esp. pp. 15–35. Put simply, my claim here is that by breaking down the patriarchal dichotomy between mind and passion, the "Poems" offer a glimpse of what experience would be like if both were free. I have in mind nothing in the least mystical—only visionary.

The "Twenty-One Love Poems" are *feminist* in that they are woman-identified; they acknowledge, define and explore one set of the possibilities of love between women; they recognize the connection, the primary bond, between women as a source of integrity and strength.[2] They are also *radically* feminist in that they constitute a critique, a re-vision, of patriarchal notions of love. "Civilization" has shaped our consciousness of love, and therefore our experience of it, into gynephobic, patriarchal forms; Rich has chosen to "smash the mold straight off."[3] In struggling both to imagine and to live a way of loving which breaks that mold, in transmuting that struggle into art through the medium of poetry, Rich has provided us with a wealth of clues and insights. That the struggle ended in failure—at least in terms of the longevity of the love relationship described in the poems—is also instructive and of use to us. The struggle against patriarchy is an essential one; the "Twenty-One Love Poems" are a new labyris—and a banner of continuing beauty—for all those engaged in it.

CHARLES ALTIERI

Self-Reflection as Action: The Recent Work of Adrienne Rich †

I

If some quantitative measure of self-consciousness were the basic norm for poetry, there would be no question that Ashbery is our most important poet. But my claims about lucidity do not entail such conclusions. Self-consciousness is a means, not an end. And its presence or absence matters less than the particular qualities of it a poet employs. Charles Wright, Hugo, and Merrill are extremely self-conscious poets, but their treatments of self-consciousness tend to weaken their poems. Wright's poems subsume it into craft and subtle sensations, Hugo's revel in reflecting on himself posing in roles he never takes responsibility for, and Merrill's are so conscious of his own position that they offer only attitudes to strike, not significant things to say, with regard to the topics flowing through his mind. Conversely, there are several significant alternatives to Ashbery's way of positioning the self-reflective mind. I think,

2. See Adrienne Rich, "Compulsory Heterosexuality and Lesbian Existence," *Signs* 5 (Summer 1980): 631–60 [203–24].
3. The phrase is from "Snapshots of a Daughter-in-Law," in Rich, *Poems: Selected and New*, p. 50 [12].
† From *Self and Sensibility in Contemporary American Poetry* (Cambridge: Cambridge UP, 1984). Reprinted by permission of the publisher. This selection has been edited for publication here; asterisks indicate deletions. Page references to works by Rich that appear in this Norton Critical Edition are given in brackets after the author's original citation.

for example, of Robert Duncan's recent speculative meditations linking the processes of mind to basic natural forces, of David Antin's experiments in creating a community around a casually self-reflexive narrative voice, of Derek Walcott's penetrating uses of his ambivalence about America, or of younger poets like Charles Hartman, who try to adapt Ashbery to an artful discursive style that echoes High Renaissance lyricism. Nonetheless, for a distinctive imagination, for the power of a style others can adapt, and for engaging many of the basic problems of our culture, the most significant alternative to Ashbery is the recent work of Adrienne Rich.

If Ashbery refines "fence-sitting / raised to the level of an esthetic ideal," [1] Rich shows how poetry can become a challenge to fence-sitting and in large part a redefinition of aesthetic ideals. At her best this "woman sworn to lucidity" [2] develops a discursive lyric speech strong enough to absorb and transform the passive qualities of the scenic style into figures for a poetic will reconstructing the mind and forming a self committed to political identity. Her way of conquering the scenic mode refuses both the defenses of irony and the consolations of craft. Instead she manages to project poetry as a force within social life, a force that literally exemplifies a woman's capacity to integrate subjectivity and community, memory and potential, self-reflexive mediation and believable speech. Such an enterprise risks idealizing itself almost as much as I am idealizing it, but Rich eventually comes to terms with the excesses in her programmatic work and makes that awareness an index of the values one can create as a discursive and political poet. Full of longing and sick of passivity, she makes poetry a way of resisting contemplative states where the collapse of will passes as the triumph of intelligence. Self-consciousness becomes the dramatic vehicle for self-definition.

Rich's concern for exemplary acts of self-definition leads to a critique like Pinsky's of contemporary poetry as enervated romanticism. But her reasons differ from his in much the same way as do her ideas of how poetry must be discursive. For Rich, contemporary poetry fails because it has lost touch with any significant source of energy. Expectations about the medium are less at fault than expectations about life. Poets work in the last stages of a culture characterized by an exhausted, but still dominant egotism that has "misconstrued energy not as Eternal Delight but as pure Will": "I have thought that the sense of doom and resignation to loneliness endemic in much masculine poetry has to do with a sense of *huis clos*, of having come to an end of a certain kind of perception." [3]

Keen as this criticism is, it also betrays some of the most problematic

1. John Ashbery, *The Double Dream of Spring* (New York: Dutton, 1970), p. 18.
2. I quoted from "I Dream I'm the Death of Orpheus," in Rich's *The Will to Change* (New York: Norton, 1971), p. 19 [43].
3. Adrienne Rich, "Poetry, Personality, and Wholeness: A Response to Galway Kinnell," in *A Field Guide to Contemporary Poetry and Poetics*, ed. David Young and Stuart Friebert (New York: Longman, 1980).

elements in Rich's work. Her explanation seems at once too simple and somewhat blind to the nature of her own achievement. If the weaknesses she describes derive largely from an oppressive sense of what counts as lucidity, vague ideals of a feminine source are not likely to restore writers' or readers' confidence in the speculative poetic imagination. And if the main emotional problem is passivity, the logical solution is less a cultivating of sheer delight than a return to using the imagination as an instrument allied with the struggles of will. Most important, Rich seems to me to belie her own greatest strength. Hers is hardly a poetry of "Eternal Delight," but it is a masterful exercise in adapting artistic skill to the processes of defining and taking responsibility for an identity.

As the example of Rich's criticism indicates, it is not always easy to concentrate on her strengths. So a good part of this chapter will be as concerned with how to read Rich as it is with her specific concerns. In my view some of her ideas are little more than slogans, and others seem to me unnecessarily confined to female subjects. On the one hand she can be too general, on the other not general enough. The latter problem is relatively easy to address, although my proposal may prove controversial. If we are to appreciate fully the general import of Rich's poetry—that is, if we are to let males identify with what they overhear—we must read her explicit themes on two levels: as particular responses to woman's plight in our time and as instances of general human concerns for identity and community.

Treating her ideas and the occasional awkward or shrill attitudes they elicit is more difficult, especially since there are already sharp critical dichotomies about her recent work.[4] I think it is clear that we cannot ignore her assertions or treat them as donnés that allow her to create engaging aesthetic objects. Commitment to her ideas is a crucial feature of Rich's poems and, as we shall see, a basic factor in understanding the depth and originality of A *Wild Patience Has Taken Me This Far*. Instead of ignoring the commitment, we must concentrate on the qualities of consciousness and grasp of contemporary experience it produces. This orientation will not justify all her ideas or save all the poems, but it should get us beyond discussions that bog down in overt ideology—hers

4. Several of the best woman critics of contemporary poetry seem embarrassed by the ideological narrowness of Rich's recent work and attack the poetry for what I shall try to show are themselves narrowly aesthetic standards. See Helen Vendler, "All Too Real," *New York Review of Books* (Dec. 16, 1981), pp. 32–5; and, for different, radically modernist aesthetic values, Marjorie Perloff, "Private Lives/Public Images," *Michigan Quarterly Review* 22 (Winter 1983), pp. 130–42. They are in part justified by the largely uncritical adulation that Rich gets from feminist critics. See, for example, the essays by Wendy Martin, Erica Jong, and Nancy Milford in *Adrienne Rich's Poetry*, ed. Barbara Charlesworth Gelpi and Albert Gelpi (New York: Norton, 1975). Even the best reading of Rich, David Kalstone's *Five Temperaments* (New York: Oxford Univ. Press, 1976), cannot satisfactorily bridge the competing frameworks for viewing her work. By concentrating on temperament he gets beyond aesthetic criteria, but he does not provide the contrastive framework that I think necessary for judging her significance to contemporary poetry. I elaborate the model of reading abstractly that I mention here in my "The Idea and Ideal of a Canon," *Critical Inquiry* 10 (1983), pp. 37–60.

or ours. Her positive qualities emerge most clearly, I think, if we treat Rich's ideas not as abstract generalizations about the world but as instruments within a general project of making "the woman in the poem and the woman writing the poem become the same person."[5] The project, then, is primarily ethical, a matter of ethos. Ideas are one of the ways Rich tries to produce and to test a set of character traits exemplifying a woman's power to create an identity in touch with plausible sources of strength and capable of responding forcefully to an oppressive socio-political order. Her poetry is less an assertion of ideas than a quest "to live / in a clearheaded tenderness."[6] Ideas are dialectical features of that quest, as significant for the adjustments in self-understanding they produce as for the general stance toward experience they simultaneously describe and warrant. Finally, this poetic project must be measured not on aesthetic terms but by the existential consequences of poetic craft— by whether or not we can respect the poetic persona produced and the model of community she hopes to produce through the witness she bears.

Describing the poetry in and of this project will not require another tracing of Rich's development from the author of well-made lyrics to radical feminism. We know what she says and the stages in her learning how to say it. We need, nonetheless, ways of describing the force of what she says, especially as it creates an alternative to the dominant mode. Thus I shall concentrate on three basic qualities of her work: its processes of defining and testing personal identity, its capacity to make private states serve as public political testimony, and her elaborating a discursive style that absorbs scenic moments into a dynamic process of self-consciousness capable of linking the poet to her community. For my purposes we need to focus only on her last two volumes, *The Dream of a Common Language* and *A Wild Patience Has Taken Me This Far*. It is here that she fully recognizes how to achieve what her earlier volumes sought. Poetry can become an example of character and the ground of community by making its mode of speech an index of powers of consciousness affording possible stances toward experience. Personal voice can be active, flexible, and compelling in its engagements. Minimally, this model of voice prevents poetry from becoming a delicate instrument for playing nostalgic harmonies. Ideally, personal speech becomes the vehicle for a form of presence that requires no elaborate rhetoric of the numinous. Voice in context is "self-delighting, self-appeasing, self-affrighting" because its energies and permutations are direct, virtually literal expressions of how the poet might encounter experience beyond the text. With Rich we can stress the poetry of and as her politics.

Rich's poetics of the speaking voice has as its basic task a need to overthrow the constructed, illusionistic drama of perceptions one finds

5. Gelpi and Gelpi, *Adrienne Rich's Poetry*, p. 98 [175].
6. Adrienne Rich, *A Wild Patience Has Taken Me This Far: Poems, 1978–81* (New York: Norton, 1981), p. 4.

in the scenic mode. Drama must remain, but now as an image of poetic construction under the constant pressure of the self's need to understand her world and to share that understanding: "There must be ways, and we will be finding out more and more about them, in which the energy of creation and the energy of relation can be united."[7] This is not simply the poetics of process she had worked out by 1969. Then she thought of process largely in epistemological terms, that is, as a means of gaining access to fluid and contradictory feelings that one suppresses if the poem is too consciously controlled. With *The Dream of a Common Language*, she develops a sense of process emphasizing the connection between composition and constructing a responsible self. Writing is more than a process of self-discovery; it is taking a stance as one absorbs a life into linguistic forms and imagines the social roles those forms can play. Instead of providing tactile substitutes for action, Rich wants poems to test what language can achieve in a world made of more (or less) than pure texts:

> If from time to time I envy
> the pure annunciations to the eye
>
> the *visio beatifica*
> if from time to time I long to turn
>
> like the Eleusinian hierophant
> holding up a simple ear of grain
>
> for return to the concrete and everlasting world
> what in fact I keep choosing
>
> are these words, these whispers, conversations
> from which time after time the truth breaks moist and green.[8]

The final metaphor exemplifies the conjunction Rich seeks. Language may seem abstract and mediated in comparison with the other states of vision in the poem. But "these words, these whispers, conversations" in fact recuperate and extend natural powers because they satisfy "the drive to connect," thus fulfilling our deepest natural desires to know and feel that our knowledge is shared. That is why we care about truth. Rich's specific truths also claim to return women to their nature in another, perhaps deeper, sense. Speech is a radical political act cutting through cultural traditions and refusing the self-pity of victimhood that ties women to imposed definitions of their nature. Even their resistance has been appropriated as a mark of frustration and failure. But now Rich hopes to dramatize models for "choosing ourselves   each other   and this life.":

7. Gelpi and Gelpi, *Adrienne Rich's Poetry*, p. 96 [174].
8. Adrienne Rich, *The Dream of a Common Language: Poems, 1974–77* (New York: Norton, 1978), p. 20.

What kind of beast would turn its life into words?
What atonement is this all about?
—and yet, writing words like these, I'm also living.
. . . .

And how have I used rivers, how have I used wars to
escape writing of the worst thing of all—
not the crimes of others, not even our own death,
but the failure to want our freedom passionately enough
so that blighted elms, sick rivers, massacres would seem
mere emblems of that desecration of ourselves?[9]

II

This is poetry of sheer assertion. Its success depends on two sets of factors: internal ones that illustrate the poet's power to control experience by intelligence and external ones that determine the depth and quality of that grasp of experience as she defines her processes of choosing. Will must be able to master language, and the language must give significance to the will it expresses. Readers are likely to demand this interrelationship, and consequently the poet is likely to demand of herself that she continually scrutinize the grounds and consequences of her assertions.

In discussing Rich, then, I shall proceed in three steps. First I want to demonstrate how well she handles the internal factors in her best assertive poem, "Transcendental Etude," which serves as a coda to *The Dream of a Common Language*.[1] Here she gathers the volume's tensions between natural and unnatural (or metaphoric syntheses and metonymic gulfs between emblems and their referents) within a celebration of the power of grounded voice to transform the passive, scenic self into full political identity. After exploring the nature of Rich's achievement in this mode I shall try to provide two kinds of contexts. Assertions are only as good as their capacity to engage problems requiring assertion, so I shall try to indicate how this successful political poem comes to terms with problems basic to Rich's poetry since about 1968. Assertions, however, are not to be appreciated solely by their relation to the past. Part of Rich's greatness is her refusal to be satisfied by such assertions. She makes them points of departure, or the creation of new sites for imaginative inquiry. Indeed, her best work in my view is the process of dialectical self-reflection in *A Wild Patience* through which she tries to understand exactly what her assertions commit her to and the emotional price she must pay in remaining faithful to them. In these reflections she finally wins her battle to subordinate aesthetic questions to simple human con-

9. Ibid., p. 28 [80].
1. Ibid., pp. 72–77 [86–90].

cerns for the ways in which poems might express a life and offer it to a
community.

"Transcendental Etude" begins in the scenic mode, one more foray
in poetic deer hunting. The scene, however, releases energies that can-
not be contained within the meditative lyric mind alone. They require
the speaking voice to become conscious of its powers by adapting private
memory to public contexts. Then memory presents an imperative to
spell out the relation of "the fertility and fragility of all this sweetness,"
won in a moment where nature breaks through a debased language, to
the social problem of women needing to rescue their lives from analo-
gous demonic forces:

> No one ever told us we had to study our lives,
> make of our lives a study, as if learning natural history
> or music, that we should begin
> with the simple exercises first
> and slowly go on trying
> the hard ones, practicing till strength
> and accuracy became one with the daring.

Rich is careful to acknowledge the distinction between nature and cul-
ture Pinsky insists upon, but primarily in order to insist on the possibility
of their complementing one another. Poetic will is woman's way (and, I
insist, a basic human power) of extending natural fertility to cultural
domains:

> No one who survives to speak
> new language, has avoided this:
> the cutting-away of an old force that held her
> rooted to an old ground
> the pitch of utter loneliness
> where she herself and all creation
> seem equally dispersed, weightless, her being a cry
> to which no echo comes or can ever come
>
> But in fact we were always like this,
> rootless, dismembered: knowing it makes the difference.

Such generalized memories build to a final challenge:

> two women, eye to eye
> measuring each other's spirit, each other's
> limitless desire,
> A whole new poetry beginning here.

Rich's response to that challenge mounts slowly, from a quiet sense
that "vision begins to happen in such a life," through a catalogue of the
domestic features of life a woman can will as her own, to a final self-
conscious integration of all the descriptions and metaphors:

Such a composition has nothing to do with eternity,
the striving for greatness, brilliance—
only with the musing of a mind
one with her body, experienced fingers quietly pushing
dark against bright, silk against roughness,
pulling the tenets of a life together
with no mere will to mastery,
only care for the many-lived, unending
forms in which she finds herself,
becoming now the sherd of broken glass
slicing light in a corner, dangerous
to flesh, now the plentiful, soft leaf
that wrapped round the throbbing finger, soothes the wound;
and now the stone foundation, rockshelf further
forming underneath everything that grows.

There are no small want ads here. There is a good deal of Yeatsian idealization, but it is sustained by the flexibility of self and the capacity to treat metaphors as simple, just extensions of natural, descriptive speech. The will to metaphor need not be a will to rhetorical, "poetic" effects, nor must the poet choose between self-consciously parodying her imaginative exuberance or concealing that exuberance by subordinating will to grounds where there reigns only a carefully wrought evocative silence. Metaphor is simply the basic vehicle for composition. It makes available for public thought the many-sidedness of woman's potential, while allowing the poet to recognize the naturalness that moves her to realize her powers. Her mastery does not depend on paralyzing both the self and the lover with Glück's cold control. Mastery for Rich derives directly from the intensity of care, which demands as its expression and fulfillment metaphors responsive to fostering "everything that grows."

III

This relation between natural and cultural orders is more than a thematic ideal. We might say that it is their integration in her speech that gains authority for the poems. She manages to combine rich, rhetorical cadences and public themes with a sense of concrete, personal passions. Such authority is very difficult to maintain. It is threatened on one side by a temptation to heroic self-projection, to Yeats's crowing about the solitary will's triumph over incoherence, and on the other by temptations to valuing the self primarily in terms of the pathos to which its project submits it. It is perhaps only by recognizing how fully she recognizes and addresses her temptations that we learn to relax our suspicions when the poems achieve confident and plausible resolutions. So I want to concentrate here on locating in Rich's political poetry the basic problems that one can say are overcome in poems like "Transcendental

Etude." At the core of these problems is Rich's need to maintain a stance at once realistic and idealized. She must then defend the idealization while locating the authority within concrete encounters. However, the most accessible poetic models for gaining authority in this way in fact contradict her project, deriving emotional intensity and personal integrity from the poet's capacity to register pathos in a dramatic situation. Rich must retain enough of that capacity to engage us in her troubles but not so much that all she offers is another example of noble victimhood. This necessity leaves her with two dangerous options: that she take as her vehicle of poetic emotion a version of the states of pathos by which our culture has trapped women or that she overcompensate for such emotions by strident assertions that in fact undermine the identity she claims. Instead of building a self, such poems appear vehicles for escaping into the fantasized roles of heroine or martyr.

We have seen that for Rich silence is less a means to transcendence than a condition of powerlessness imposed both by the blindness of others and by one's own fears of having nothing of consequence to say or of having too much to say that is all bitterness and invective. Thus she must resist the scenic mode, but clear needs are not necessarily easy to translate into practice. Consequently, many of the most moving poems even in *Diving into the Wreck* are emotionally at odds with the powers they would generate. Their intensity lies in a scenic pathos that often substitutes for images of possible action. For example, "When We Dead Awaken" turns on finding an adequate language for women's social plight. Metonymic details set the scene, but then in summary the poem reaches for metaphors like those of "Transcendental Etude":

> —tell it over and over, the words
> get thick with unmeaning—
> yet never have we been closer to the truth
> of the lies we were living, listen to me:
> the faithfulness I can imagine would be a weed
> flowering in tar, a blue energy piercing
> the marred atoms of a bedrock disbelief.[2]

However, "listen to me" betrays a deep uneasiness. The metaphors are so figurative, so tied to an old language of evasive fantasies, that they in fact call attention to gulfs between the poetic and the true. Rich offers not the truth about lies and a concrete example of fidelity but the transformation of actual problems into figurative solutions that make disbelief harder to dispel. The best one can say for these lines is that the images present an ironic, pathetic state where the imaginary and the effectual prove incompatible. But revealing the temptations of the imaginary is not the truth the poem seeks.

A similar escape to the imaginary becomes even more problematic in

2. Adrienne Rich, *Diving into the Wreck: Poems, 1971–72* (New York: Norton, 1973), p. 6.

the conclusion to "Incipience," a poem about denying the dreams of men and "imagining the existence / of something uncreated / this poem / our lives":

> Outside the frame of their dream we are stumbling up the hill
> hand in hand, stumbling and guiding each other
> Over the scarred volcanic rock.[3]

These images are a long way from new creation. They make me think of the illustrated cover to a cheap paperback romance, *After the Disaster: Love and Freedom in the Wasteland*. The images seek to produce both strength and pathos. But in the lyric mode, without extended dramatic development, and, here, without any form of action except imaginary gestures, those qualities breed only melodrama. And melodrama contradicts all the hopes the poem asserts. The speaker remains, despite her will, trapped in dreams that for centuries men have imposed on the female imagination.

These endings may well be only symptoms of a deeper problem inherent in the style Rich chooses as her vehicle to escape well-made poems and made-to-please psychology. At the end of the sixties her will to change led her to explore a variety of free-verse forms structured by implicit juxtapositions among diverse scenes. This style could capture the fluid, fragmentary aspects of experience while multiple threads of coherence might disclose the unconscious realities and forces relatively free of oppressive patriarchical orders that determine discursive intelligibility. Yet for Rich the style was probably a mistake.[4] It did not give enough play to her remarkably precise intelligence and capacity to control syntax and cadence. (Compare the quotations given here to the state of concentration that is both the subject and the experience of early poems like "An Unsaid Word," where the single sentence and delayed verb dramatize Rich's power to hold in a single thought quite divergent materials.) More important, the juxtapositional, notational style was so successful in capturing the flow of consciousness that it could not produce any of the counterpressure by which one establishes individual identity. The overlapping scenes and reflections present a deep vision of a personal plight; they even give mythic and historical dimensions to the plight. But they do not have the power to transform plight into active personal choices. The style's passivity is part of the poet's lament, not part of her solution.

Because I sound like Yeats on Pound's being only a mirror of the flux

---

3. Ibid., p. 12.
4. Perloff attacks Rich for claiming a radical politics within a thoroughly establishment style that co-opts the assertion. The irony is that when Rich becomes relatively experimental in style, she cannot carry off her vision. Since the core of her politics is a quite traditional notion of self and will, she must use a straightforward style. That becomes radical in itself when, as Gerald Graff argues in *Literature against Itself* (Chicago: Univ. of Chicago Press, 1979, pp. 98–101), experiment has become standard. Rich, in other words, is sustenance for the claims of Lukács and Marcuse against Brecht.

in his mind, I must be cautious. Yeats did not see that Pound's form of juxtaposition was also an attack on scenic self-indulgence or passive submission to events. For Pound, juxtaposition was radical selection, the result of powers of concentration to dwell almost exclusively within luminous details. Rich does not have Pound's options. He could rely on details because he accepted the historical energies and imaginative orders they transferred to the present. There is for her no resonant background not shaped by an oppressor. She must render the scenes and the strength to absorb the scenes into her own definitions of luminous details. Yet her means often fail. Series of scenes become an invitation to contemplative passivity or even to the self-indulgent fantasies of the lines I just quoted. The style will not translate pathos into an effective ethos.

In her most effective renderings of pathos Rich seems to recognize this link between her frustrated powerlessness and the only style available in which she can even render the pain. Consider another concluding segment, this time to "The Burning of Paper Instead of Children:"

> I am composing on the typewriter late at night, thinking of today. How well we all spoke. A language is a map of our failures. Frederick Douglass wrote an English purer than Milton's. People suffer highly in poverty. There are methods but we do not use them. Joan, who could not read, spoke some peasant form of French. Some of the suffering are: it is hard to tell the truth; this is America; I cannot touch you now. In America we have only the present tense. I am in danger. You are in danger. The burning of a book arouses no sensation in me. I know it hurts to burn. There are flames of napalm in Catonsville, Maryland. I know it hurts to burn. The typewriter is overheated, my mouth is burning, I cannot touch you and this is the oppressor's language.[5]

The forces of oppression ultimately reduce the poem to prose and prose to obsessive repetition among associations. Rich becomes Creeley without his self-irony, but with the self-hatred the irony can relieve. Most terrifying is the collapse of all time into the present and hence all community into solipsism. Even the lyric moments within the poem leave only these unconnected traces. The pure present manifests itself as a metonymic perversion of spirit—the composing mind reduced to phrases, scene absorbed into a language divorced from touch, and the self become only an anxious cry trapped in its own needs.

Given such pressures, it should not be surprising that Rich often overcompensates. If passivity continually frustrates, the obvious alternative is to seek some means to project idealizations that at once disclose and justify certain courses of action. Yet, as my brief contrast to Pound indicates, idealization is extremely difficult for someone with Rich's beliefs. She simply has no models. There are no contexts for indirectly giving

5. Rich, Will to Change, p. 18 [42–43].

dignity to the self and no roles into which the self can be subsumed, no mind of Europe that rewards impersonality by embracing its constructions. Even the great women writers found ways to sublimate or ignore their anger, so they provide sustenance but not guidance for Rich's project.[6] So much for her relation to the past. Her relation to the future then becomes extremely problematic. Lacking models yet desiring change, she cannot just do without ideal images. She must turn herself into a representative figure, at once victim of an oppressive history and the necessary emblem of plausible alternatives to it.

But the role of self-created model is a dangerous one, the more so in proportion to her sense of its private as well as public necessity. The features that serve as exemplary are selections from the experiencing self. When one makes such selections while resisting private anxieties, there are obvious and powerful temptations to conceal—from the self as well as others—basic aspects of one's actual emotions. It is all too easy, as Tennyson and Yeats show, to see the self largely in third-person, public terms. There are then numerous possible vacillations between the actual self and the possible selves that one's audience needs (or that the self as audience needs). Conversely, if the model is to have power, it requires a structure of sharp contrasts to other kinds of selves or to blocking social problems (for example, by blanket charges of patriarchy). This need for contrast also intensifies the temptation to exaggerate one's sense of victimhood in order to dramatize the forces oppressing women. Finally, all these existential problems are compounded in Rich's poetry by the desire to unite speaker and writer, for then the actual self is always responsible for its fantasies and projections—a noble moral stance but often a disastrous poetic one, unless one masters techniques of self-irony.

"The Stranger" compresses into a poem brief enough to quote in its entirety the fundamental problems of strained idealization that occur throughout Rich's poetry.[7] This poem acknowledges its status as a pure construct of the imaginary, so one would think that it defuses critical suspiciousness. Yet, in Rich, states of vision must be connected to possible dispositions toward action; this is her great danger and great strength. If we are to take her as seriously as I think she intends to be taken, we must examine the qualities of person the fantasy reveals and hopes to transfer. Here the answers are depressing. The idealized figure who walks the streets could be Ed Dorn's *Gunslinger*. Or perhaps we should think of Gary Cooper suddenly attuned to "the shudder of the caves," as if Westerns could become Cocteau fantasies. Yet Rich cannot treat these associations ironically. She needs a new heroine. In a brief space dignity must be born and must have male and female attributes. The need, however, is all too evident. It is hard not to see the rhetorical strategies

6. Gelpi and Gelpi, *Adrienne Rich's Poetry*, p. 94 [171].
7. In the original essay, "The Stranger" was quoted in full; in this volume it appears on pp. 52–53.

as dictating the mythic elements, rather than the mythic vision requiring the rhetoric. Rich's reach may negate her grasp.

Take the treatment of anger as a first example. Her concept of female anger is deep and precise. Anger cleanses the sight because it brings one to full self-consciousness and frees one from the repressive force of *ressentiment* that blocks full compassion. But must it be visionary? Does it require the androgyne as a figure unifying the anger and the mercy? The mythic reach here tends to make the discursive clarity seem as fantasized as the androgyne figure. This marriage of myth and reality is one where each partner might do better on his or her own.

If the treatment of anger were the only place where the two principles cross, my complaints would be only positivist grumpiness. In fact, though, all the problems get much more severe in the last stanza, ultimately undermining the assertion of identity necessary to Rich's project. Structurally, the second stanza shifts from streets to a room, and from external observation to claims for an identity that cannot be made or understood in the "dead language." But the inside seems terribly impersonal because it is so mystified—as if one could assert identity only in fantasy, in defensive or evasive gestures masking as heroism. The crucial problem is the relation between will and language. Once she must posit her images of value on the other side of language, Rich condemns herself to conditions analogous to those we saw in the scenic modes relying on pregnant silence. There is no determinate content to satisfy an all-too-determinate need. She goes to myth as a way of projecting beyond the dead language some alternative text, some verb that sustains the living "I" and the living mind. But no one can read that text except by self-projections. Otherwise the letters of the name remain illegible, dividing the person into an empirical actor and a fantasized vision of the self as hero. When one's name appears in this language, one can never know if the name read is one's own or an image made up in order to escape the self's actual condition.

IV

Difficulties like these persist in Rich's most recent work. Acute critics like Helen Vendler are correct in virtually all of their specific charges against individual lines. But such accuracy begs the larger question of appropriateness. I suspect that one would be as accurate in making the same charges against Whitman, and as far from the mark. First of all, both poets base their enterprise on rejecting traditional aesthetic criteria. Were Rich not to challenge these criteria, she would risk condemnation on her own terms, because it is crucial to her that women no longer seek to please, or not to displease, what appear to be essentially male cultural demands.[8] Rejection of criteria does not, of course, suffice to

8. Gelpi and Gelpi, *Adrienne Rich's Poetry*, p. 93 [169].

free one from them if the criteria are basic to values one appeals to. Rejection must be accompanied by alternative standards. For Rich, the standards are very simple. Poetry matters to the extent that it makes possible new forms of consciousness that give women "access to their own powers"—whether these be for new styles of poetry or for new ways of representing ourselves in our actions and commitments.[9] Poetry, then, is not different from other modes of discourse except for the focused interrelations it emphasizes and the emotional challenges it poses if the writer is not to appear bathetic or melodramatic. Rich hopes to meet that test by fully elaborating her concern to unite the woman speaking the poem with the woman writing it. Poetry then becomes in part a process of self-criticism, in part a process of adapting these criticisms into plausible idealizations of states of mind and stances. One earns authority not by retrospect but by the way the qualities one's acts exemplify promise an ethos for the future.

We can see Rich implicitly approaching her work with the same critical standards her critics employ, but then interpreting the problems as part of the content she must confront in self-consciousness. Rejecting traditional lyric criteria leads Rich in her recent political poetry to construct standards of self-reflexive lucidity. Poetry matters because of the ways it helps one live one's life. And one demonstrates that conviction by dramatizing the process of trying to understand that life—by recognizing one's blindnesses, by attempting to have one's recognitions lead to worthwhile goals, and by taking full responsibility for the consequences of pursuing the goals. This means, on the one hand, elaborating the ideals of a poem like "Transcendental Etude" and, on the other, idealizing the process of grappling with problems of idealization.

The mode that reaches fulfillment in "Transcendental Etude" gets established at the very beginning of *The Dream of a Common Language*. The title itself carries a strong criticism of much of Rich's earlier political work. The myth that matters is not one beyond language but one of language. The oppressive forces, then, are not ontological features of mediation, the old romantic cry, but political factors that prevent language from fulfilling functions inherent in its potential nature. Rich is to romanticism what Habermas is to Hegel: more restricted and more conceivably effective in leading to changes in our politics.

These implications become explicit in the volume's introductory poem, "Power," whose task is to reverse traditional expectations of the role of myth in poetry. The first lines echo Kore myths as the poet thinks of a bottle of medicine unearthed from a construction site. Rich, however, quickly shifts from medicine to the making of medical cures, from passivity to activity, and hence from mythic associations to a specific historical figure, Madame Curie, whose legacy can take concrete form in

9. Ibid., pp. 114–17.

discursive language. Curie is not quite a model. Instead she establishes a different kind of authority. The poet need not locate single models from the past but can try to construct a sense of community with a variety of women who appear in memory. Even the differences that prevent the past from passing on models become potentially productive by demanding a reciprocal dialogue. Sympathy with another's problems can lead to understanding features of one's own condition, and efforts at self-definition can become instruments for appreciating the problems oppressing others.

In this exchange there is considerable sustenance for Rich's hopes to overcome several dichotomies, especially that between private and public lives.[1] As a community forms with the past, and as sympathy produces self-knowledge, it is possible to imagine poetry as a form of action. In poems one aligns oneself with other women and one tries to dramatize one's capacity to take power through and for them. If Curie died "denying / her wounds   came   from the same source as her power,"[2] then one can use her life to see how the two aspects might be united. And one can use one's sympathy as the contrastive term directing and dignifying the poet's quest to explore her own wounds as potential sources of power. Her project can depend not on a fantasized self but on grounding the imagination in history and then testing oneself against its realities. Once we have this historical consciousness, it is possible to give poetic voice a concrete focus. Instead of a person's being absorbed within scenes, scenes become challenges to the poet to produce a discursive poetic framework adapting them to the concerns of a society. Now Rich's greatest liability becomes an important source of strength. Her obsession with victimhood and her various forms of self-staging become states she can offer within a version of Augustine's confessional community. If she, and we, can understand her intense reactions as states of consciousness to be read dramatically rather than programmatically, they become the wounds within which lie both sources of power and tests of the qualities of a reflective poet to understand and direct her life.

We have seen where this initial project leads. But "Transcendental Etude" cannot be a stopping place because its assertions of identity have yet to meet the very tests of history that sanction figures like Madame Curie. Those tests, in turn, require Rich's articulating the inappropriateness of aesthetic criteria. A *Wild Patience Has Taken Me This Far* is her response to that challenge. Here the single norm for the person speaking the poem is the power she dramatizes that the writer can wield as a historical agent. If we are to appreciate this work fully, we must read it not by aesthetic criteria, but from the inside, as a project for exploring the interconnections between poetry and life. Indeed, how else acknowl-

1. Ibid., pp. 114, 119.
2. Rich, *Dream of a Common Language*, p. 3 [73].

edge the difficulties of change, the slidings and adjustments one must make, and above all, the powers conferred by reflecting on the process, unless we consider individual states as elements of a larger process? In that process, moreover, Rich in effect shows that a political poet need not choose between aesthetic criteria and loose propaganda. She asks us to suspend aesthetic criteria, but only so that we can take a reflective attitude toward her capacity to make language and cadence instruments in understanding, testing, and taking responsibility for the choice of a life.

Making a self worth attending to requires demonstrating power to reflect on the problems that arise from choices, especially problems of oversimplification that breed the excesses I have been discussing. The scenic mode cannot entertain criticism of itself; Rich's recent poetry by contrast depends on a continual self-scrutiny that does not collapse into quiescent self-irony. Thus the power of the poetry resides not in the ideas, which remain somewhat simplistic, but in the poet's grasp of what it is like to try to live in accord with an explicit body of ideals and commitments. Like Yeats in *The Tower* and Lowell in his later poetry, Rich explores a form of poetry in which the work is not primarily a figurative, illusionistic construct that applies to the world as a hypothetical label for possible emotions. Rather, the poems are intended to function as literal examples of living and writing within what history makes possible and necessary. So the greatness of such poems lies less in how they structure experience than in how they dramatize capacities to reflect on and within it as the poets try to keep themselves from hardening into their ideas or using their poetic powers to create alternative worlds. Emphasizing the internal coherence of a volume, then, is not for Rich primarily an aesthetic act but a way of insisting that poems and lives can be continuous, can deepen one another when framed as a single process.

* * *

TERRENCE DES PRES

Adrienne Rich, North America East †

* * *

"Poetry," as Rich says [in "North American Time"] "never stood a chance of standing outside history." One of the more successful illusions of high culture has been the usage of the humanistic "we" in reference, suppos-

† From *Praises and Dispraises: Poetry and Politics, The 20th Century* (New York: Viking) 1988. Copyright © 1988 by The Estate of Terrence Des Pres. Used by permission of Viking Penguin, a division of Penguin Books USA Inc. This selection has been edited for publication here; asterisks indicate deletions. Page references to works by Rich that appear in this Norton Critical Edition are given in brackets after the author's original citation.

edly, to all of us or "man" in general. But this "we" has always been the property of an educated elite, male, white, and eurocentric. Rich escapes this illusion by relying on the forms of "you." If "you" refers to a man the rhetorical slant of the poem might be to blame or curse. If "you" refers to a woman the poem will be informed, most of the time, by praise and blessing. But at all times, in her mature poetry, Rich speaks in her own voice. She has no liking for the ploys of persona. Her voice is responsible to its time and place, and accepts what humanists would rather escape: that even poetry (or especially poetry) is positioned for and against, that the political problem of us-and-them is the poet's limit as well. The poetry of utopia might someday transcend these divisions; here and today, meanwhile, divisions continue in force, and Rich will not be fooled by "humanity" or "the human condition" when such terms are used to mask discord. She stands against an order that is male-governed and that keeps women alien to themselves and each other. She distrusts "revolution" in the old style because after much violence the old patriarchy is replaced by a new patriarchy and women are no better off than they were. Rich sums up this position in an interview:[1]

> I do see saving the lives of women as a priority. The "humanity" trip—not women's liberation, but human liberation—tends to feel too easy to me. Women have always supported every "human" liberation movement, every movement for social change; there have always been women womaning the barricades, but it's never been for us, or about us. I think that women ought to be putting women first now. Which is not to say that we're against the other half of humanity, but just to say that if we don't put ourselves first, we're never going to make it to full humanity.

The political identity that does not limit itself, the movement that goes forward in the name of everyone, can expect to be at odds with itself and exploited by covert interests. Simply to use the term *woman* or *women* is perilously wide, and in fact Rich usually has in mind a more specific tribe, one overtly feminist and antipatriarchal. One might expect, then, that a majority of Rich's readers will be offended to some degree when, in fact, some are and some are not. One doesn't have to be a woman to see the decency of feminist concerns. Men enjoying a measure of male privilege can see the damage done by patriarchal claims. Being female is not in itself the criterion for valuing Rich's poems against males, like "Trying to Talk with a Man," for example, which integrates nuclear and patriarchal orders, or the merciless "Ghost of a Chance," with men like beached fish, or—to my mind one of the best—the pained and somber "August," in which the poet's curse is pitted against what might be called the primal curse of the fathers. The poem develops

1. Barbara Charlesworth Gelpi and Albert Gelpi, *Adrienne Rich's Poetry* (New York: Norton, 1975), pp. 120–121.

mythical time, beginning with the collapse of Eden in the first four
stanzas:

> Two horses in yellow light
> eating windfall apples under a tree
>
> as summer tears apart   milkweeds stagger
> and grasses grow more ragged
>
> They say there are ions in the sun
> neutralizing magnetic fields on earth
>
> Some way to explain
> what this week has been, and the one before it!

To "explain" the sullen days of late summer, we can point to electro-
magnetic goings-on in the heavens. And if it were only the "yellow light"
of dog-day afternoons, the scientists might be right. But for Rich the
seasons correspond to spiritual conditions, with oppressive heat signal-
ling the pain of political intrusion. In "Burning Oneself In," written
along with "August" in 1972, the summer "heat-wave" lifts at last but
awful news from the war in Vietnam "has settled in" and "a dull heat
permeates the ground / of the mind." In "August," something similar is
tearing things apart and "neutralizing" the earth's "magnetic" powers, a
force that throws eros (the binding power of life itself) into ragged con-
fusion. And "it," whatever it is, goes on and on; this week was bad, but
"the one before it!"—the one before was worse. As we enter the rest of
the poem we see the poet torn by, and struggling to confront, her own
recognitions:

> If I am flesh sunning on rock
> if I am brain burning in fluorescent light
>
> if I am dream like a wire with fire
> throbbing along it
>
> if I am death to a man
> I have to know it
>
> His mind is too simple, I cannot go on
> sharing his nightmares
>
> My own are becoming clearer, they open
> into prehistory
>
> which looks like a village lit with blood
> where all the fathers are crying: *My son is mine!*

A merciless poem, hard-edged and honed to its purpose—which is to confront the curse of the fathers—and a poem that cuts to the quick of its painful occasion. As the summer devolves toward its ruin, so the poet begins to see how men imagine women, a recognition that forces a further terrible knowledge, impossible now to avoid or rationalize further. She beholds, that is, the curse of the fathers in its blood-lit origin, while off in the background Mister Kurtz is whispering "the horror, the horror."

"August" and "Diving into the Wreck" were written at about the same time. Both are poems of confrontation. Having seen through the book of myths, the poet is face to face with the thing itself. What to *do* has become a question of what to *be*. The "I am" of the middle stanzas asserts self-possession by confronting the monster in male nightmare, which is to say that the poem makes little sense until we grasp its threshold image, in this case a reptilian thing that suns itself on a rock and that, like the Medusa, is believed by men to be death to him who beholds it. We are back to the sleeping man of "Incipience," dreaming of female monsters while women talk of "how to live." In "August," the mind of the dreaming man is "too simple" because as victor and beneficiary he can be satisfied with myths. He does not *need* to contemplate complexity, nor does he *wish* to acknowledge the ancient cry of the fathers. Meanwhile, the patriarchal curse resounds through the poem, and once heard it opens on awful truth: the male child is separated from the life-serving body-world of women and inducted into the warrior cult of men, the moment when mother-right is defeated. That is the horror implicit in "My son is mine!" The fathers claim the son for themselves. They raise him to scorn life and women. They ready him—*Pro patria!*—for the wars they will declare. Women are "given" in marriage, men in battle.

But how is it that someone like myself, or any man, reads Rich's work with care and benefit? The question isn't only how men enter into and enjoy poems by women who are feminists, but how any of us, male or female, enter into the world of any poet who is actively for and against; how we come to value Brecht blasting the Nazis, or Breytenbach cursing his native tongue while blessing the cause of blacks in South Africa. I am not of the tribe to whom these poets speak, yet I join in and feel involved. In the presence of the poet's voice I willingly suspend disbelief in my own exclusion. How is that?

The problem of belonging is extended by recalling the age-old obligation of poetry to give, with so much else, pleasure; and then to consider what pleasure can be found in poems as filed and tuned to pain, or as merciless, as those by Rich when she is least lyrical, least reconciled. If the politics of her work can be off-putting, so can the splintlike diction and edgy imagery that give her art its feel, and then the unrelieved attention to torment that keeps this poet from solace and joy. If, for example, we have been trained to take delight in language, its music and its elegance, what are we to make of Rich's poem called "A Woman Dead in Her Forties," which begins with this stanza:

> —Your breasts/   sliced off   The scars
> dimmed   as they would have to be
> years later[.]

No lyricism or lifting rhythm sustains that language; phrasing is bland or even banal except for the startling intimacy of its occasion. Yet the poem with its ungainly lines and fractured stanzas turns out to be an elegy intense with female travail, a declaration of love complete with the scars and wounds that, in Rich's art generally, attend her praises of women's selves. The lines above, moreover, help suggest why Rich is not like other poets cited in this study. Working with her art does not yield the same enjoyment got from working with Yeats or Brecht or McGrath. Only with Breytenbach has the case been similar. He, like Rich, is wild with the burden of injustice, is often angry and feels besides that his art must go forward, *if* it goes forward, against a language that is grossly patriarchal. But he is not as resolute as Rich, not as starkly willful, nor does he pass up small consolations, humor among them. Rich stands alone. And her poetry takes its tribe into poetic-political terrain so unknown and newly entered that we might speak, as Rich does, of "a whole new poetry beginning here."[2]

Rich stands up to the world. She takes place as a poet and a woman, with poetic conduct and the conduct of life informing each other. Language is held accountable to history, to women's collective experience first of all. And insofar as her poetry and her politics share a common vision, her example has about it a "nobility" such as Stevens might point to, a moral symmetry that is cause in itself for delight. In the following section from "Natural Resources," poetry becomes a *vita activa* and the way itself a communal continuum:

> There are words I cannot choose again:
> *Humanism   androgyny*
>
> Such words have no shame in them, no diffidence
> before the raging stoic grandmothers:
>
> their glint is too shallow, like a dye
> that does not permeate
>
> the fibers of actual life
> as we live it, now;

2. Rich, "Transcendental Etude," *The Dream of a Common Language* (New York: Norton, 1978), p. 76 [90].

this fraying blanket with its ancient stains
we pull across the sick child's shoulder

or wrap around the senseless legs
of the hero trained to kill

this weaving, ragged because incomplete
we turn our hands to, interrupted

over and over, handed down
unfinished, found in the drawer

of an old dresser in the barn,
her vanished pride and care

still urging us, urging on
our works, to close the gap

in the Great Nebula,
to help the earth deliver.

Rich's art arises immediately out of history, out of life's embattled
moments day by day, and with the added sense that where "I" am there
also "we" are. This tribal construct has a firm grip on the actual, but it
also extends the poem's occasion to include readers outside the tribal
exclusivity at issue, and allows any one of us, finally, to join in and
"help the earth deliver." That something like this occurs I cannot doubt,
given my own attention to, and pleasure in, the poetry of a feminist like
Rich. Her work offers an alternative vision, one that curses the sins of
patriarchal order and goes on to praise strengths and virtues basic to
everyone, precisely the life-reclaiming strengths and virtues of women
through the ages.

For all the radicalness of Rich's feminism, her work has about it a
radicalism that goes even deeper, a way of life that men can no longer
scorn or despise, a *vita activa* that anyone might find worth having in
this, the twilight era of nuclear politics. The poet, therefore, summons
a tribe, and we—men and women—respond to the call. The situation
is startling, perhaps, but only at first. For if poets in times of political
upheaval tend to revive bardic practices, might not the case be likewise
that we, as readers in a time of political strain, tend to fall back on the
older relation to poetry and take up our role in the bardic situation? In
adversity the bard emerges. So, it would seem, does the tribe.

The feminist poetics that Rich has worked to realize depends on
capacities essential to women, including alertness to the pain of others,
a fierce attention to relationships of all kinds and, along with these, a
sense of self with boundaries less rigid and guarded, more flexible and

embracing, than most men's. Women do not wear armor, do not go
panoplied with weapons, do not automatically see people as challengers
and, in consequence, do not reify the world of selves into a wall of
otherness. This, in part, is Rich's sense of female powers, a view she
praises in the following lines:

> And I think of those lives we tried to live
> in our globed helmets, self-enclosed
> bodies self-illumined gliding
> safe from the turbulence

> and how, miraculously, we failed[.]

The failure of the self to shut down and close off, the refusal of poetry
to turn in contempt from the earth—these "failings" are part of women's
strength in Rich's view, and they provide her feminist poetics with a
crucial element. For her the virtues of reception and response are pri-
mary. She wants to mobilize empathy, compassion, the imaginative
capacity for suffering with—a seeing *beyond* the self *into* the world; or,
a seeing *through* the self, an entrance into the experience of others via
one's own self-knowledge. In "Hunger," Rich responds to the spectacle
of African famine in terms that are more actual than metaphoric:

> I know I'm partly somewhere else—
> huts strung across a drought-stretched land
> not mine, dried breasts, mine and not mine, a mother
> watching my children shrink with hunger.
> I live in my Western skin,
> my Western vision, torn
> and flung to what I can't control or even fathom.

To reduce these lines to a poetics of guilt is to forget the power of
anger to override indulgence. It would also be to ignore Rich's consistent
melding of self and world, private grief and public pain, insisting that
between the two no demarcation exists except, of course, the false divi-
sion of experience into separate categories as a stratagem of evasion. The
following lines are often quoted, but not always with sufficient care for
the actualization of metaphor that takes place:

> In the bed the pieces fly together
> and the rifts fill   or else
> my body is a list of   wounds
> symmetrically placed
> a village
> blown open by planes
> that did not finish   the job[.]

The reference is to Vietnam, and the poem in which these lines occur
is "Nightbreak," written in 1968 at the peak of the war when the horror

has reached such a pitch that the poet, so to say, is cracking up. The poem goes on to encircle napalm with anger, then devolves into the following characteristic (for Rich) stanza:

> Time is quiet   doesn't break things
> or even wound   Things are in danger
> from people   The frail clay lamps
> of Mesopotamia
> row on row under glass
> in the ethnological section
> little hollows of dried-
> up oil   The refugees
> with their identical
> tales of escape   I don't
> collect what I can't use   I need
> what can be broken.

The "dried- / up oil" of the ancient lamps, which once afforded sacred light, is played against the "oildrum" of napalm that balls into fire over an Asian village. The clay lamps, now useless, are preserved with great care when, meanwhile, the breaking of vessels elsewhere goes without notice. In the last stanza of "Nightbreak," the night itself seems to shatter, and the pieces, which are also the bits of the shattered self, at dawn "move / dumbly back / toward each other." The theme of this poem is the shattering impact of political intrusion on a self that feels shockingly continuous with the suffering of children in a distant place. The poem's threshold image is the earthen vessel (signalled by the clay lamps) that Rich links to the creative powers of women. Rich argues, in *Of Woman Born*, that "the woman potter molded, not simply vessels, but images of herself, the vessel of life, the transformer of blood into life and milk." She goes on to say that "the pot, vessel, urn, pitcher, was not an ornament or a casual container; it made possible the longterm storage of oils and grains, the transforming of raw food into cooked; it was also sometimes used to store the bones or ashes of the dead." The earthen vessel, then, "is anything but a 'passive' receptacle; it is *transformative*—active, powerful."[3]

"Nightbreak" is an angry probe into the experience of political intrusion. The poet's openness to the world makes her vulnerable to the world's horror, especially the violence her own nation visits upon helpless children elsewhere, a violence Rich apprehends as a citizen and as a woman acquainted with the pain of motherhood. The outcome is devastating. Even sleep is "cracked and flaking," and the dawn feels like a "white / scar splitting / over the east." If we follow "the woman/vessel association," as Rich calls it, we see that the poem is about the breakup of self, including the self's poetic capacity, under the ruinous press of the real.

3. Rich, *Of Woman Born*, pp. 97–98.

This sounds extreme, but the crisis portrayed in "Nightbreak" is not, I think, overdone. To an open imagination the Vietnam war was everywhere. Its atrocities and ravaged faces—chiefly of women and children—filled the news and haunted the places of sleep. We in America were always safe, unless of an age and a class to be drafted, but not, after a certain point of horror's surfeit, immune.

What happens in the world happens over in the heart, not in an exact equivalent way, of course, but as suffering transformed by imagination; pain is pain however we know it, and can be called the ground (and cost) of alertness to life. Speaking of feminism and the "connection between inner and outer," Rich says:[4]

> We are attempting, in fact, to break down that fragmentation of inner and outer in every possible realm. The psyche and the world out there are being acted on and interacting intensely all the time. There is no such thing as the private psyche, whether you're a woman—or a man, for that matter.

Rich praises acts of extended awareness. Unfortunately, this opening outward of self, and the vulnerability that must follow, are often criticized as a fault which men avoid and women fall prey to. Rich thinks of it as a "source of power" and therefore a hopeful gift. She says: "the so-called 'weak ego boundaries' of women . . . might be a negative way of describing the fact that women have tremendous powers of intuitive identification and sympathy with other people."[5] That is the point, of course; and if it should be considered a fault—if empathetic imagination is thought unmanly, or if care for life beyond one's own is discounted as "feminine" and therefore weak—then masculine preference for detachment and "objectivity" is more vicious than we usually admit. In patriarchal culture, transcendence has meant "rising above it all"; in Rich's feminist ethos, on the other hand, transcendence means reaching beyond oneself in sympathy with the plight of others. Male transcendence negates and masters; female transcendence moves to acknowledge and interact. There are easy formulations, of course, but even so one sees the benefit to a poetics incorporating female *virtu* of this kind. A truly *political* imagination moves beyond the self and into the world. The kind of political experience I've called political intrusion becomes, in Rich's poetry, more than historical torment. It becomes her art's occasion.

Adrienne Rich bears witness to pain that is shared and unnecessary. She curses those who ignore the suffering they create and sustain. She praises those who absorb the impact and survive. In "Hunger," the closing image stares back at us indelibly:

4. Gelpi & Gelpi, *Adrienne Rich's Poetry*, p. 114.
5. *Ibid.*, p. 115.

>   Swathed in exhaustion, on the trampled newsprint,
>   a woman shields a dead child from the camera.
>   The passion to be inscribes her body.

An image of African famine got from a photograph, its import resides in its political dimension. "The decision to feed the world," Rich says earlier in the poem, "is the real decision. No revolution / has chosen it." That, I take it, is the plain shocking truth of the matter. And at its heart is the victim's lack of public existence—a "passion to be" that fails to be acknowledged. Those who suffer have neither a name nor a voice, a condition that makes their lives easy to ignore and dispose of, and reminds us that worldly power controls people by controlling names. If she could, Rich would praise the mothers and children in "Hunger" by lamenting their lives and cruel lot. She would, that is, restore them to their name. To create a public existence, however, requires a revelation of private being. In extremity private being is often inaccessible to anyone outside the circle of suffering. It's here, too often, that "political" poetry gives way to propaganda and falls back on ideology.

In "Hunger" Rich returns repeatedly to the image of mothers and children; as a woman and a mother, she trusts maternal anger to guide her art. In "Integrity" she praises "anger and tenderness: my selves," and in "From an Old House in America" rage and compassion are united with the will to bear witness:

>   Who is here. The Erinyes.
>   One to sit in judgment.
>
>   One to speak tenderness.
>   One to inscribe the verdict on the canyon wall.

These lines announce a feminist poetics. Rich's defense of poetry rests on the moral and imaginative power of maternal anger and female care. Not everyone, however, can or would wish to invoke the Furies. There are several ways to stand *in relation* to suffering not directly our own— the kind of disturbance that photojournalism is capable of causing, for example. In representations of suffering it's the experience of relation— the submerged connectedness of self to other selves—that poets like Rich explore. We might even define poetic imagination, in this case, as willing suspension of disbelief in other people's pain. Rich has spelled out the relation of poetry to political distress this way:[6]

> No true political poetry can be written with propaganda as an aim to persuade others "out there" of some atrocity or injustice (hence the failure, as poetry, of so much anti-Vietnam poetry of the sixties). As *poetry*, it can come only from the poet's need to identify

6. Rich, *On Lies, Secrets, and Silence*, p. 251.

her relationship to atrocities and injustice, the sources of her pain, fear, and anger, the meaning of her resistance.

In "Hunger," Rich explores her relationship to disaster. She faces the experience of political intrusion, in this case the impact of catastrophe abroad upon moral awareness at home. But here also she envisions the solidarity of all women whose pain is shared and unnecessary:

> Is death by famine worse than death by suicide,
> than a life of famine and suicide, if a black lesbian dies,
> if a white prostitute dies, if a woman of genius
> starves herself to feed others,
> self-hatred battening on her body?
> Something that kills us or leaves us half-alive
> is raging under the name of an "act of god"
> in Chad, in Niger, in the Upper Volta—
> yes, that male god that acts on us and on our children,
> that male State that acts on us and on our children
> till our brains are blunted by malnutrition,
> yet sharpened by the passion for survival,
> our powers expended daily on the struggle
> to hand a kind of life on to our children,
> to change reality for our lovers
> even in a single trembling drop of water.

Rich offers a global summary of suffering anchored in famine, then curses its political cause, and then with small praises goes on to the ordeal of women surviving. What this poem blesses, grim though it may be, is a state of mind generous enough to grasp the underlying oneness of victims. What it curses is the claim that some kinds of suffering are less (or more) terrible than others. Rich abhors the notion that "pain belongs to some order." She would bless all cases with equal urgency, as if victimization were the basis of tribal union. But if the solidarity of political victims exists de facto it remains to be recognized and acted upon. Hence the poem's end: "Until we find each other, we are alone."

*   *   *

A rare poetic confidence has kept Rich sane and creative through a lifetime of combat. At the end of "Transcendental Etude," she presents us with an emblem of womanly art as she discovers it—the woman "turning in her lap" the scraps and rags of her life—then goes on to close the poem with a poetics that reaches beyond will or anger merely, to a clemency or gentleness without which "the passion to be" could not take place:

> Such a composition has nothing to do with eternity,
> the striving for greatness, brilliance—

only with the musing of a mind
one with her body, experienced fingers quietly pushing
dark against bright, silk against roughness,
pulling the tenets of a life together
with no mere will to mastery,
only care for the many-lived, unending
forms in which she finds herself,
becoming now the sherd of broken glass
slicing light in a corner, dangerous
to flesh, now the plentiful, soft leaf
that wrapped round the throbbing finger, soothes the wound:
and now the stone foundation, rockshelf further
forming underneath everything that grows.

"Transcendental Etude" is the closing poem in *The Dream of a Common Language*, and the book's last section, in turn, is called "Not Somewhere Else, But Here." Exactly what "dream of a common language" means has provoked much critical debate. Usually the several meanings of "common" are stressed—plain and ordinary on the one hand, accessible and shared on the other—but the sense of "dream" is also important, suggesting a goal, the visionary state of poetic thinking, maybe also a *second* language, preconscious and unbroken, like a rock-shelf of linguistic resource underlying poetry in general. For a feminist poet, in any case, the condition of language as she finds it will be a vexing problem, "a knot of lies / eating at itself to get undone." How shall the integrity of female experience be kept intact once "rendered into the oppressor's language"?

Rich's solution is implicit in her sense that "Only where there is language is there world." This notion has been formulated most succinctly by Wittgenstein in his *Philosophical Investigations*, where he says, for example, that "to imagine a language means to imagine a form of life."[7] To imagine a language befitting a feminist form of life is, I take it, Rich's "dream." Wittgenstein also says that "the *speaking* of language is part of an activity," a specific way of taking place in the world. He adds that "only those hope who can talk." That the basic scene in a Rich poem is two women talking—the poet speaking to and with a woman like herself—suggests the kind of language, and the form of life, Rich works to imagine. Language and world together make up "the weave of our life," as Wittgenstein puts it. And when, finally, he observes that the totality of our linguistic milieu consists "of language and the actions into which it is woven," he endorses Rich's fundamental belief as an activist-poet: "Poetry never stood a chance / of standing outside history."

This, finally, is where Rich stands: inside her own body's sorrow and deeply settled into time—"not somewhere else, but here." Her language

---

7. Ludwig Wittgenstein, *Philosophical Investigations*, tr. G. E. M. Anscombe (New York: The Macmillan Co., 1969), pp. 8e, 11e, 174e.

is time's stark vernacular, the idiom of being-in-the-world where "being" is female and "the world," as ever, is still a kingdom of the fathers. Against the patriarchal order she sets her art and her life because, as things now stand, it's an order given to conquest and illusions of mastery, hostile to earth and the flesh. In the tradition of bardic practice, her poetry announces communal identity, calls for courage and fortitude in battle, keeps a language (and a lore) by which members of the tribe can stand up, take place, and together realize their collective "passion to be." In Rich's case, moreover, it's not difficult to say when she took up her political station. It began when she "was finished with the idea of a poem as a single, encapsulated event, a work of art complete in itself."[8] It began, that is, when she started appending dates to her poems, beginning with those that make up *Snapshots of a Daughter-in-Law*, her volume of 1963 in which she breaks free to imagine herself as "long about her coming, who must be / more merciless to herself than history." To herself she has been merciless, and often to her enemies as well, but with tenderness to temper her anger, and always with "care for the many-lived, unending / forms in which she finds herself."

WILLARD SPIEGELMAN

"Driving to the Limits of the City of Words": The Poetry of Adrienne Rich†

Polemic has its own natural claims to recognition in any discussion of didacticism, but it is neither for her political programs nor for her visionary anger that Adrienne Rich most warrants attention. Rather, it is her intelligent, insistent exploration of the grounds and possibilities of language itself that earns her a place in this book. She has seldom received the *literary* criticism she most deserves; understandably, her defenders usually take a feminist line, discussing and approving her poetry mostly in terms of its political content or in relation to her prose explorations, and her hostile critics simply adjust their sights in the same way but with an aim to destroy rather than to praise. Considerably less has been said about Rich as a poet; in their anxious desire to have their say about radical politics, lesbianism, female hysteria, patriarchal structures (the list could be extended), most critics have ignored the real innovations and the intelligent accommodation in Rich's poetry to linguistic con-

8. Adrienne Rich, *Blood, Bread, and Poetry: Selected Prose 1979–1985* (New York: Norton, 1986), p. 180.
† From *The Didactic Muse*, copyright © 1989 by Princeton University Press. Reprinted by permission of the publisher. This section has been edited for publication here; asterisks indicate deletions. Page references to works by Rich that appear in this Norton Critical Edition are given in brackets after the author's original citation.

cerns.[1] For her, diving into the wreck of civilization or consciousness always means moving into some untrodden region of her mind (Keats's description of his poetic program in the "Ode to Psyche") and exploring language itself.

This chapter's title comes from "Images for Godard," Rich's 1970 homage to the most political of film directors. The poem's opening images derive from Wittgenstein's speculation about the inevitably organic and constructed, one might say the civilized and urban, force of language as a defining, limiting place: "Our language can be seen as an ancient city: a maze of little streets and squares, of old and new houses with additions from various periods; and this surrounded by a multitude of new boroughs with straight regular streets and uniform houses."[2] Exploring the city of language, any poet risks entrapment within it because it offers itself as both maze and salvation; the poet must discover a map for the city that is inevitably identical to it. The inadequacy of language to experience is a subject shared by a majority of the poets I have labeled didactic, but Rich goes even further, emphasizing language's political horrors and its falseness. In an increasingly bourgeois society, language consists of translations and fibs, lists of things desperately strung together to make a necklace of shabby desires. And, although "every existence speaks a language of its own"[3] Rich wishes to discover in language a map not only for herself but also for the larger community—often a community

1. A representative, early attack (but intelligent nonetheless) on Rich came from Robert Boyers, disappointed by her political stridency in the late 1960s: see "On Adrienne Rich," in Robert Boyers, ed., *Contemporary Poetry in America* (New York: Schocken Books, 1974), 157–73. Frank Lentricchia has recently done battle with Sandra Gilbert and Susan Gubar on the matter of feminist stances and what he has regarded as their too-easy dichotomies: see Lentricchia, "Patriarchy Against Itself—The Young Manhood of Wallace Stevens," *Critical Inquiry* 13 (1987): 742–86; Gilbert and Gubar, "The Man on the Dump versus the United Dames of America; or, What Does Frank Lentricchia Want?" *Critical Inquiry* 14 (1988): 386–406; and Lentricchia, "Andiamo," ibid., 407–13. Paula Bennett, *My Life a Loaded Gun: Female Creativity and Feminist Poetics* (Boston: Beacon Press, 1986), is the most recent book to treat Rich, as well as other women poets, but with a primary emphasis on political rather than linguistic issues. An exception to the general rule of treating Rich primarily for her political value is Charles Altieri, *Self and Sensibility in Contemporary American Poetry* (Cambridge: Cambridge University Press, 1984), 165–90, who presents Rich as an alternative to Ashbery, and as one who transcends what he calls the scenic mode. He defends Rich for, among other reasons, having developed a "discursive lyric speech" (166) in an age that needs discursiveness in its poetry: "In a critical age we cannot do without discursiveness. Indeed, the contemporary poetry most aware of the issues . . . tends to meet demands for lucidity by incorporating a good deal of discursiveness within the poetic experience" (26). [Altieri's essay is reprinted on pp. 342–57 of this volume—*Editors*.] A new, Arnoldian tack—poetry as a criticism of life—seems inevitable as we round toward the end of the twentieth century. Alicia Ostriker, "Dancing at the Devil's Party: Some Notes on Politics and Poetry," *Critical Inquiry* 13 (1987): 579–96, distinguishes between the need for aesthetic discriminations and the political efficacy of the poetry by women that she discusses.
2. *Adrienne Rich's Poetry*, ed. Barbara Charlesworth Gelpi and Albert Gelpi (New York: W. W. Norton, 1975), 51n. Hereafter cited as ARP.
3. "Ghazals: Homage to Ghalib," in *The Fact of a Doorframe: Poems Selected and New, 1950–1984* (New York: W. W. Norton, 1984), 109. Rich's work will frustrate future scholars because, like Robert Lowell and all other self-revising American poets since Whitman, she is an inveterate fusser. This means that poems appear, disappear, and reappear in various volumes. All references are to *The Fact of a Doorframe*, hereafter *FD*; *Poems Selected and New, 1950–1974* (New York: W. W. Norton, 1974, hereinafter, *PSN*); and the Gelpis' *ARP*.

of women, sometimes one that includes both sexes—of which she is a part. The adequacy of language versus its inadequacy and the attempt to assert commonality in the face of the knowledge of individuality are her constant themes.

Another poem from her most politically assertive period (from *The Will to Change* and dated 1969) offers a miniaturized version of these issues. "Our Whole Life" both dramatizes and proposes a relationship between language and political status:

> Our whole life a translation
> the permissible fibs
>
> and now a knot of lies
> eating at itself to get undone
>
> Words bitten thru words
>
> meanings burnt-off like paint
> under the blowtorch
>
> All those dead letters
> rendered into the oppressor's language
>
> Trying to tell the doctor where it hurts
> like the Algerian
> who walked from his village, burning
>
> his whole body a cloud of pain
> and there are no words for this
>
> except himself
>
>   *(FD, 133)* [43–44]

The seeming randomness of the technique—the absence of punctuation, the participial nature of phrases, the infrequent verbs—makes the poem, like so much else in Rich's work, seem entirely provisional. In the whole poem there are but two real predicates, appearing in subordinate clauses, and, at the end, a deliberately weak copulative. The horror of pain is its permanence: it takes no verbs. Any translation is like a photograph, immortalizing a reality of which its form is an inadequate imitation and that its articulating can hardly hope to cure. The fecklessness of articulation is a dangerous recognition for a poet who claimed earlier that "only where there is language is there world" ("The Demon Lover," *FD*, 84) [32].

The search for integrity or wholeness may be doomed to failure, and closure itself an illusion. Our lives are broken; the wasteland offers little consolation or totality. As maps of wholes (and like lists, a form Rich favors), poems themselves are also like wire photos whose essence is division and particularity: an accumulation of dots amounting to only the appearance of an image. In "Waking in the Dark" Rich wonders:

> The thing that arrests me is
>> how we are composed of molecules
>
> (he showed me the figure in the paving stones)
>
> arranged without our knowledge and consent
>
>> like the wirephoto composed
>> of millions of dots
>
>> in which the man from Bangladesh
>> walks starving
>>> on the front page
>>> knowing nothing about it
>
>> which is his presence for the world
>
> $\qquad\qquad\qquad\qquad$ (*FD*, 152) [49]

Presence and representation, the relationship of reality to a linguistic understanding of it—these subjects have obsessed Rich since her third volume, *Snapshots of a Daughter-in-Law* (1963), in which she finally broke the bonds of conventional form and of conventional female roles as well. It was in the title poem that she first acknowledged those "permissible fibs" in her own life, which "Our Whole Life" raises to a communal, political level.

What to do with inadequate tools and how to find the right ones: these are Rich's early, breakthrough motifs. In "The Roofwalker" (1961), she portrays a life of daring self-exposure that is, at the same time, unchosen and therefore a passive submission to rules not of her own making. Again, she questions not only the adequacy of maps as guides to truth but also the purposefulness of any daring that is *merely* apparent. The poem treats poetry itself as a vehicle for the poet's life; work is never selected but somehow dictated. The poet tries to break free from passivity only to succumb to another, less terrifying passiveness. Her choice is not a real one, her vocabulary limited by the rules of others: after identifying with the builders, she questions the worth of her own metaphor:

> Was it worth while to lay—
> with infinite exertion—
> a roof I can't live under?
> —All those blueprints,
> closings of gaps,
> measurings, calculations?

A life I didn't choose
chose me: even
my tools are the wrong ones
for what I have to do.
I'm naked, ignorant,
a naked man fleeing
across the roofs
who could with a shade of difference
be sitting in the lamplight
against the cream wallpaper
reading—not with indifference—
about a naked man
fleeing across the roofs.

(*FD*, 49–50) [16]

The poems of the sixties express discontent, sometimes without a clear vision of alternatives: does the dangerous exertion of the roofwalker's life outweigh the passivity of his or her not having chosen it? Would she prefer reading about the experience to enacting a life of danger? The balancing act required of both worker and speaker in the poem is terrible, tenuous, and ultimately unfulfilling. But this has been all along the condition of the speakers and characters in Rich's early poems, the ones praised by Auden and other early reviewers for their good manners and their formal proprieties. Self-exploration comes to mean, in Rich's career as in that of any major poet, a quest for an adequate language, and "The Roofwalker," with its own vaguenesses, exemplifies her difficulties during this period.

Rich's work appears, at first glance, to have moved away from the graceful elegance of two early volumes to the more spare, jagged, and free forms of the past two decades, and from poems about lovely things and scenes to those about war, torture, and oppression. But with the omniscience of hindsight one can see how the beginning contained all that followed. The characteristic early themes, presented with mature prosodic assurance, are suffocation, alienation, and entombment. The poems constitute defenses against outer threats and inner doubts. In "Storm Warnings," a girl shuns the fluctuations in the external and internal climates, her "sole defense" to "draw the curtains" (*FD*, 3 [3]; in "The Uncle Speaks in the Drawing Room," a bastion of refined order fears in troubled times "for crystal vase and chandelier" (*ARP*, 2–3) [5]. Aunt Jennifer, embroiderer of elegant tigers, is restrained by "the massive weight of Uncle's wedding band": the pride and strength of her tigers complement her life of frustrated confinement. At the awful price of her own freedom, sublimation has produced art: "When Aunt is dead, her terrified hands will lie / Still ringed with ordeals she was mastered by. / The tigers in the panel that she made / Will go on prancing, proud and unafraid" (*FD*, 4) [4].

The people in *A Change of World* (1951) and *The Diamond Cutters* (1955) are elegant, passive, and will-less. The Griselda-like woman in "An Unsaid Word" "has power to call her man / From that estranged intensity / Where his mind forages alone, / Yet keeps her peace and leaves him free" (*FD*, 5) [5]. But she does not go foraging herself. A professor's wife can only begin to articulate her discontent: "I thought that life was different than it is" ("Autumn Equinox," *PSN*, 25). The tourists in those poems composed during a year in Europe are essentially out of place and barely in control: "We had to take the world as it was given / . . . And always time was rushing like a tram / Through streets of a foreign city" ("Ideal Landscape," *FD*, 13). "Lucifer in the Train" wittily invokes the first traveler to an alien land for guidance:

> O foundered angel, first and loneliest
> To turn this bitter sand beneath your hoe,
> Teach us, the newly-landed, what you know;
> After our weary transit, find us rest.
>
> (*PSN*, 18)

The alienation in these poems is neither painful nor merely fashionable; rather, it inspires creativity and a set of formalist values: "Art requires a distance: let me be / Always the connoisseur of your perfection" ("Love in the Museum," *ARP*, 5); "Form is the ultimate gift that love can offer— / The vital union of necessity / With all that we desire, all that we suffer" ("At a Bach Concert," *FD*, 6). The human heart requires "proud restraining purity" to repair itself in a world of inevitable imperfection and disappointment. Art defends against invasions from without and threats from within. This youthful stoicism half-accepts the reality of human weakness yet holds out for an ideal landscape and an ideal form for poetry, however distanced. In poems like "The Roofwalker," Rich begins to abandon this last infirmity of the Romantic mind, because she increasingly refuses to take the world as it is given. Her distaste for lapidary forms and for the calm betrayals and falsehoods of language gives way to her later, far from adolescent, rebellion against tradition. Just as she began to realize in her late twenties that the rules by which she was living a privileged life as a model Cambridge mother and faculty wife were false, that she *was* Aunt Jennifer, so to speak, so did she disavow the rules for poetry that enabled her to tell fibs in her first two books: "I had suppressed . . . certain disturbing elements to gain that perfection of order" (*ARP*, 89) [165], she later admitted.

No wonder, then, that Rich's poetry became increasingly didactic and overtly concerned with the power of language to hide and to distort. One's whole life-as-translation necessitates an attempt, however arduous, to speak in the original tongue and to authenticate the true self. But how can the poet do this when language itself works against her?—her tools are the wrong ones. Even Gabriel, the eponymous angel of a 1968 poem, speaks no language and makes his annunciation with only his body. Silence has replaced such artful proclamations as older generations of poets or painters might have construed, and the relationship between speaker and listener reduces itself to a pitiful, desperate request:

> It's true   there are moments
> close and closer together
> when words stick   in my throat
> *the art of love*
> *the art of words*
> I get your message Gabriel
> just   will you stay looking
> straight at me
> awhile longer

> (*PSN*, 115–16)

The dangers of language painfully assert themselves in the failures of love, as (autobiographically) Rich recounts the breakdown of her marriage and the gradual avowal of her lesbianism; these linguistic traps are also connected, in the political poems of the Vietnam era, to more public forms of oppression. Increasingly in Rich's work, public and private spheres cease to have opposite meanings. Rather, they complement one another; Rich's feminist politics is condensed in one of the two epigraphs to *Diving into the Wreck* (1973), from George Eliot: "There is no private life which is not determined by a wider public life."

* * *

Although she seems to disavow it, a delicate humanism has infused Rich's work at least since "A Valediction Forbidding Mourning" (1970), beneath the rage and anger that also inform the more thoroughly political poems. It is a humanism intimately connected to concerns for discovering truth in language and language as the proper vehicle for truth. In that earlier poem, two initial phrases open into a complete sentence, which significantly introduces a linguistic motif: "My swirling wants. Your frozen lips. / The grammar turned and attacked me" (*FD*, 136) [44]. Language assaults as well as corrupts, but the woman wants to control, rather than submit to, the only power she may own:

> A last attempt: the language is a dialect called metaphor.
> These images go unglossed: hair, glacier, flashlight.
> When I think of a landscape I am thinking of a time.
> When I talk of taking a trip I mean forever.
> I could say: those mountains have a meaning
> but further than that I could not say.
>
> To do something very common, in my own way.

> (137) [44–45]

Making a last attempt to break through language to meaning, she resigns herself to, and in, an infinitive of expectation. The very "common"ness of the goal surpasses the assertion of individuality ("in my own way") as the single voice asks to speak for others.

This is the emotional tenor of many of her recent poems. Tenderness replaces terror; speaking for others allows her to speak for herself. The course of public life—the end of Vietnam, the gains of the women's movement—as well as the frank coming-to-terms-with her own homosexuality, may account for this new maturity. But the wisdom of middle age does not signal complacency. On the contrary, as the very fact as well as the content of *Twenty-One Love Poems* attests, patience is matched by the urgent desire to make up for lost time ("At forty-five, I want to know even our limits," *FD*, 237 [78]) and by future reckonings:

> and we still have to stare into the absence
> of men who would not, women who could not, speak
> to our life—this still unexcavated hole
> called civilization, this act of translation, this half-world.
>
> (239) [79]

Rich would agree with Robert Frost's adage that poetry is what gets lost in translation; she has sought for a poetry that will not betray its sources but will accommodate the truths of silence through articulation. As she acknowledges in her *Love Poems*, "I fear this silence, / this inarticulate life," and her lover helps make "the unnameable / nameable" (240) [81]. Poetry begins, like politics, in the body, but Rich is able to "start to speak again," as she claims in a recent poem ("North American Time," *FD*, 324–28) [118], precisely because, as for any post-Romantic poet, the powers of articulation must incorporate the truths and combat the delusions of muteness. She states her credo most forcefully at the end of "Cartographies of Silence," as much a map to the contours of her speech as a blueprint of the forms of rigorous silence:

> If from time to time I envy
> the pure annunciations to the eye
>
> the *visio beatifica*
> if from time to time I long to turn
>
> like the Eleusinian hierophant
> holding up a simple ear of grain
>
> for return to the concrete and everlasting world
> what in fact I keep choosing
>
> are these words, these whispers, conversations
> from which time after time the truth breaks moist and green.
>
> (*FD*, 236)

Although she complains obsessively that "in the matrix of need and anger" "the words / get thick with unmeaning" ("When We Dead Awaken," *FD*, 151), only language offers the sustaining, magical power to present and to animate: truth opens up, green and living, not through the unknown ceremonies of the mysteries but more mysteriously through the agency of metaphor and its appropriations.

Like any poet, of course, Rich relies largely on the various categories of figurative language, however one chooses to label them, to contain and then to augment her statements. More striking, though, is her ability to make out of imagery a discursive technique. As in "Waking in the Dark," part of which is quoted above, she realizes the differences between selfhood and "presence for the world" as versions of the contrast between integrity and partiality, pain and knowledge, and, most important, truth and its signifiers. Occasionally, Rich will develop an image into a conventional vehicle to convey discursive truths symbolically. Owing to its confusions, "The Roofwalker" is a relatively unsuccessful attempt at this, while the famous "Diving into the Wreck" (*FD*, 162–64) [53–55] more strongly encapsulates in a narrative framework the motifs of exploration and submergence in what Conrad termed the "destructive element." Although she is not especially playful with language—her didacticism would scorn the ingenious wit of Nemerov and Merrill as unreliable or duplicitous—Rich occasionally employs a central device (as in "The Burning of Paper") with an ironic sense of its dimensions or, as in "Tear Gas" and "Storm Warnings" and the more recent "Frame," submits the image of her title to various examinations."[4]

Rich is, however, seldom comfortable with this strategy, the kind of thing seen more frequently in Howard Nemerov or Richard Wilbur. Instead, relying on an associationism the roots of which extend from Wordsworth and native English empiricism through surrealism and "deep image" poetics, Rich develops poems along strands of connection provided by imagistic contexts. Thus, the image serves a didactic purpose, if by "didactic" one understands the lessons that the poet both encloses and discovers through her associative structures. Rich's middle period offers the most frequent use of such discursive images. The occasional literalness of her procedure marks these images as the tool of an intellectual more than of a lyricist. I have already given examples of an obsession with words, usually unacceptable ones, that occupy the speaker's consciousness; the beginning of the title poem in *Leaflets* exemplifies this procedure:

> The big star, and that other
> lonely on black glass
> overgrown with frozen

4. Rich could be mistaken for Howard Nemerov or Auden when she remarks that "poetry is a way of expressing unclear feelings," in her interview with Joyce Greenberg, "By Woman Taught," *Parnassus* 7 (1979): 103.

lesions, endless night
the Coal Sack gaping
black veins of ice on the pane
spelling a word:

> *Insomnia*
> not manic but ordinary
> to start out of sleep
> turning off and on
> this seasick neon
> vision, this
> division

(*FD*, 99–100)

From the obliquities of phrasing and unpunctuated syntax, a word comes clear as the result of a waking consciousness and a pulling together of individual particles in a nocturnal scene. Not until the climactic seventh line does one hear a phrase without major assonance or alliteration, as if Rich is suggesting that insomnia stands alone, visually and aurally, as the insomniac herself lies alone amid the eternal silence of infinite spaces.

* * *

"Anger," Rich once remarked in conversation, "can be a kind of genius if it's acted on" (*ARP*, 111), and it is as a poet of and for anger that Rich has acted out her genius. Acting on anger establishes the necessary grounds for identity—emotional and poetic—from which other, gentler emotions may pour. In her earlier poetry, notably *Necessities of Life*, Rich duplicates the process outlined by Julia Kristeva in *Powers of Horror:* "I expel *myself*, I spit *myself* out, I abject *myself*, within the same motion through which 'I' claim to establish *myself*."[5] Rich has discovered an appropriate form, not a mere outlet, for her anger; in so doing, she creates a *self*, expelling and establishing simultaneously.

Aristotle calls anger the emotion closest to reason; the anger that gives birth to polemic should provide a strong basis for didactic poetry.[6] But most of us would agree experientially that anger frequently inhibits or prevents articulation: it may dam the wells of speech, or erupt with a fury that overflows all boundaries, but we seldom associate it with the formal control demanded by poetry. Rich herself, recognizing the ironic frustrations of working out of such an emotional impasse, has allowed this truth. Can the poet speak "words thick with unmeaning" in order to clarify, to reduce, and clearly to propound? Moreover, in performing

5. Julia Kristeva, *Powers of Horror*, trans. Leon S. Roudiez (New York: Columbia University Press, 1982), 3.
6. Aristotle, *Rhetoric*, 2.2; *Nichomachean Ethics*, book 7. Jane Marcus, "Art and Anger," *Feminist Studies* 4 (1978): 94, calls anger "a primary source of creative energy," and follows Freud in understanding anger as the ego's narcissistic defense against threats to its integrity. Like many feminist critics, she regards this narcissism as a healthy self-preservation by Rich in the late 1960s.

their maneuvers, other great poetic haters like Blake and Pound usually work in forms more capacious than lyric, which give free rein to their emotions and counsels. Within the condensation of lyric, with its abbreviations of thought, intimacies of address, and suggestiveness of feeling, a poet seldom confines political advice, let alone full programs. Of the major political poets of our half of this century, Allen Ginsberg has followed the path pioneered by Blake and Whitman, while Robert Lowell developed out of his revised lyrics an extended commentary on the mirroring realms of public and private lives. But only Rich has radically redefined the scope and province of lyric, remaking it into a vessel solid enough to contain anger without bursting, and lucid enough to adduce political themes rationally. Emotions—rage, despair, hatred—that almost occupy the far side of articulation become an instrument as well as a subject.

The remainder of this chapter explores the poetic strategies, both the larger formal structures and the habits of syntax and style, that Rich has made her own. Three main tactics for organizing thought seem to have become comfortable for her, starting with her middle volumes. I label these list making, antiphony, and weaving; looking at them enables us to understand her particular brand of poetic teaching. The list is the technique of obsession, antiphony that of dialectic, weaving that of harmonious synthesis. Since critics have paid scant attention to Rich's methods, preferring to see her in the light of her political programs or their own, it may come as a surprise to discover that she is one of the most formally adept poets since Wallace Stevens.

Stevens might seem an unlikely name to utter in an essay that stresses Rich's turning aside from the strictly formalist lessons she learned from Auden, Frost, and Yeats, but she has herself given an explicit clue to her feelings for him in one of the "Blue Ghazals" from *The Will to Change* (1971), which is not included in her two *Selected Poems*. "You were our poet of revolution all along," she declares, and goes on to notice the "gaieties of anarchy," the disorder one finds in parades of political protest: "Disorder is natural, these leaves absently blowing / in the drinking fountain, filling the statue's crevice."[7] This homage to the poet of anarchy is juxtaposed with a reference to "the use of force in public architecture: / nothing, not even the honeycomb, manifests such control." As a connoisseur of chaos herself, Rich often takes a cue from Stevens in the very titles of poems: her "Script," "Snapshots," "Images," "Pieces," "Photograph," "Letters," and "Postcard" all betray a careful debt to the poet of "Prologues to What Is Possible," "Questions Are Remarks," "Asides on the Oboe," "Sketch of the Ultimate Politician," "Pieces," "A Postcard from the Volcano," "Extracts from Addresses to

---

7. *The Will to Change* (New York: W. W. Norton, 1971), 21.

the Academy of Fine Ideas," "Prelude to Objects," and, above all, *Notes Toward a Supreme Fiction.*

Listing is a favorite form in contemporary American poetry.[8] Whitman, of course, is the seigneurial lister, with his exclamations, his resounding anaphora, greetings, collections of mementos and experiences, his use of inventory as the sole suitable mode for detailing the richness of the nation and the fullness of the self: "How can I but here chanting, invite you for yourself to collect bouquets of the incomparable feuillage of these States?" ("Our Old Feuillage"). From him have descended Williams, whose Dr. Paterson assembles the things of his world in book I of *Paterson*, and Ginsberg, with his breathy, impelling chants, apostrophes, and descriptions. But even Stevens reminds us in his titles, as in his techniques, of the need for notes, and of the two sorts of them: something elementary, in preparation for something else, and something tentative, experiential, and on-the-run. Like *The Prelude*, *Notes Toward a Supreme Fiction* in one way constitutes the whole of that fiction: it makes the very statement for which it was intended to prepare poet and reader. Lists, like notes, are provisional in two ways: they offer fodder, nourishment, what is required; and they may be temporary and, because forward looking, never adequate.

This provisional nature accounts for the frequency of lists in Rich's work. Wholeness, completion—of self or world—are unreal possibilities in our lives. And, especially after *Snapshots*, Rich's poetry adheres to the tentativeness of experience; her poems become ampler and more provisional as their lists duplicate the frustrated questioning from which they stem. "What burns in the dump today?" she asks in "Open-Air Museum" (*FD*, 63), casting a cold eye on the lapidary perfection of Richard Wilbur's "art" poems, or early Rich, or on the abstruseness of Stevens's "The Man on the Dump." The title poem of *Leaflets* defines the transitory nature of poems as political statements, testimonies to involvement, presence, and evanescence. They disintegrate like leaves, impermanent in a frenzied world. A leaflet is "merely something / to leave behind, a little leaf / in the drawer of a sublet room" (*FD*, 103).

Like others among her contemporaries, Rich relies on naming to identify the enemy: it is the first step in a political/poetic assault on norms that have failed. Obsession, hard to account for in any manifestation, may have been for a long time her prime impulse. Like a photograph, a list may represent an ever-changing reality, a vision always focusing on different arcs of a circumference. A list keeps vivid the horrors, as well as the lessons, of the past: to enumerate is to remind others of defilement and desertion, lest they forget: "These stays of tooled whalebone in the Salem museum— / erotic scrimshaw, practical even in lust." The questions of history, centering on reminders of its objects, reopen the wounds.

> The body has been exhumed from the burnt-out bunker;
> the teeth counted, the contents of the stomach told over.

> And you, Custer, the Squaw-killer, hero of primitive
>   schoolrooms—
> where are you buried, what is the condition of your bones?
>
> ("Ghazals," *FD*, 108)

During her radical middle years, listing served Rich as a means of detailing lessons of history, accumulations within bourgeois society, and the fundamental ambivalence the poet feels when accounting for all the presences and absences in her world:

> What we've had to give up to get here—
> whole LP collections, films we've starred in
> playing in the neighborhoods, bakery windows
> full of dry, chocolate-filled Jewish cookies,
> the language of love-letters, of suicide notes,
> afternoons on the riverbank
> pretending to be children
>
> ("Trying to Talk with a Man," *FD*, 149) [48]

One of the ironies of radical feminism is that after rejecting patriarchal stereotypes of female domesticity, the clichés of housekeeping-as-fulfillment, many women return to similar motifs—in their lived lives and in their literary work—with renewed and altered enthusiasms. Rich's recent poetry is filled with lists of what might have been condescendingly called in earlier days "women's subjects"—domestic life, indoors and out, attention to natural conditions of flora and fauna, a focus on traditional women's work, cooking and sewing—"a universe of humble things," she calls it in "Natural Resources," in which she adduces with touching simplicity the poet's role as archaeologist and builder:

> These things by women saved
> are all we have of them

> or of those dear to them
> these ribboned letters, snapshots

> faithfully glued for years
> onto the scrapbook page

> these scraps, turned into patchwork,
> doll-gowns, clean white rags

for stanching blood
the bride's tea-yellow handkerchief

the child's height penciled on the cellar door
In this cold barn we dream

a universe of humble things—
and without these, no memory

no faithfulness, no purpose for the future
no honor to the past

                                                    (FD, 262)

Ordinariness has always made its claims on Rich's attention, but nowhere more effectively than in these recent poems. Precisely because patriarchal society demands individual striving, and because power inevitably torments, she has increasingly seen social life as a collective stay against individual assertions, and personal life as itself a collective experience.

                    *   *   *

Listing or enumeration, the trope of obsession, is one kind of didactic habit; antiphony, question and answer, the trope of dialectical exploration, is another. Rich often maintains a double allegiance; even at her angriest, as feminist critics have observed, her dream of burning the male enemy is a charitable one, directed not at murder but at transformation (see "The Phenomenology of Anger," FD, 165–69 [55–59]. Not even John Ashbery's double-columned poems manifest so strong a didactic stance, insistent on doubleness, as Rich's stichomythia, her passages resembling Socratic dialogues that go nowhere. Part 14 of "From an Old House in America" (FD, 220) [70–71] is a naked conversation, "he said" versus "she said," questions without answers, rendering human relationships into a stalemated battle with no advancement. Conversation with no place to go, no resolution, appears once again in "Natural Resources" (FD, 258) in a reconstructed interview between a male correspondent and a female poet. "Can you imagine . . ." [x or y] he inquires, to which she "wearily" answers, "yes," she can imagine separate worlds of men and women. In both of these cases, Rich alights on the oldest technique out of Greek drama to portray irresolvable conflict. The nakedness of confrontation, so perennial a subject in Rich's work ("A Marriage in the Sixties," "Trying to Talk with a Man," "A Valediction Forbidding Mourning," "Leaflets," "The Phenomenology of Anger," "Rape," "Re-Forming the Crystal") demands its appropriate form for presentation. These mock catechisms, especially when leading to no resolution, convey the frustrations as well as the imaginative reachings out, in Rich's effort to confront, learn from, and teach the opposition.

Only two ways out are possible, and one is unlikely: a synthetic resolution to such dialectic maneuvers or confrontations. On rare occasions, in the hallucinated conjugations ("I am she, I am he . . .") that begin to coin a new language, Rich's speaker may construct a new idiom that breaks the bonds of gender and consequently the bondage of sexual exploitation. But another way, implicit in the forms of her longer poems, is more sympathetic: what I have labeled the technique of weaving, a way of interlacing voices, echoes, or motifs in poetry, creates a whole from distinct and separate elements. Individual readers will decide whether the resulting fabric is an organic unity or a crazy quilt of bits and patches, joined only by Rich's indomitable will. The medley, a genre Rich hit upon in the breakthrough title poem in *Snapshots of a Daughter-in-Law*, allows her to build for, or in, a poem a composite identity comparable to the composite selves that she accumulates in her pictures of the new woman she writes about and becomes. The recent poem "Culture and Anarchy" (*FD*, 275–80) proceeds chunk by chunk, verse paragraphs sprawled on the left- and right-hand margins, a first person voice interspersed with italicized fragments from nineteenth-century women's letters and diaries. It significantly opens at a rural house, as a descriptive poem echoing "Tintern Abbey" ("Daylilies / run wild, 'escaped' the botanists call it / from dooryard to meadow to roadside") before spreading open a list of accumulated objects:

> Rainy days at the kitchen table typing,
> heaped up letters, a dry moth's
> perfectly mosaiced wings, pamphlets on rape,
> forced sterilization, snapshots in color
> of an Alabama woman still quilting in her nineties,
> *The Life and Work of Susan B. Anthony*. . . .
>
> (275)

Naming, stitching, quilting—these activities continue throughout the poem, as if to account for, duplicate, and counter what she calls the "anarchy of August," but culture and anarchy often look complementary rather than antagonistic:

> Anarchy of August: as if already
> autumnal gases glowed in darkness underground
> the meadows roughen, grow guttural
> with goldenrod, milkweed's late-summer lilac,
> cat-tails, the wild lily brazening,
> dooryards overflowing in late, rough-headed
> bloom: bushes of orange daisies, purple mallow,
> the thistle blazing in her clump of knives,
> and the great SUNFLOWER turns
>
> (276–77)

The luscious elements are gorgeously presented, and flow trippingly from the tongue, now in perfect iambs ("autumnal gases," and so on), now cemented by alliteration ("grow guttural / with goldenrod") and slant or internal rhymes (milkweed . . . lilac . . . wild lily; brazening . . . late . . . daisies). Rich has focused her diction as well as her energy, aligning quotations from women's history against a natural foreground of her own detailing and against the implied contrast in her title borrowed from Matthew Arnold.

This doubleness proves, as it were, the unity suggested in the poem's last citation, a letter from Elizabeth Cady Stanton to Susan B. Anthony: "*I should miss you more than any other / living being from this earth . . . / Yes, our work is one, / we are one in aim and sympathy / and we should be together*" (280). Human identity is plural, collective, and although Rich's primary interest is in woman's identity, one can make the legitimate leap from gender to species since Rich herself had done so in "Diving into the Wreck" and "The Stranger." Boundaries blur, as she suggested in the title poem of *Necessities of Life*; even prose and poetry sit squarely together or, rather, inhabit one another's realms. In "The Burning of Paper," prose assumed the rhythms and condensation of lyric, and in "Culture and Anarchy" the very decision to print prose excerpts in poetic lineation, as above, forces readers to hear in those triple-stressed lines a rhythm appropriate to formal, public, and lyric pronouncement instead of to private address. Public-private, outer-inner, prose-poetry, self-other: all the old dichotomies break down, no longer through mere fiat but through the weaving of filaments of language into a unity.

Weaving and listing are sometimes alternatives to one another; the obsessive, hallucinated naming of enemies or victims makes for a monolithic, toneless articulation, whereas the interlacing of figures naturally embeds would-be opposites in one another's limits. But like the woman in "Transcendental Etude" "who survives to speak / new language," Rich has from her middle years onward absorbed the lessons of Penelope, sequentially weaving and unweaving, accumulating through lists that she then proceeds to unravel, trying to bring meaning and language, which she opposed to one another in "Tear Gas," into new coordinations with one another. The 1967 poem "Postcard" (*PSN*, 137), with its Stevensesque title, opposes the "dream of language / unlived behind the clouds" to the "hacked" bronze image of Rodin's Orpheus, paralyzed in silent pain. The perfect, because frozen, sculpture, a summary of all the works of art that appeared in Rich's early volumes, represents the primal poet as if petrified by the horrible force of his own song. Language kills, but it can also release, as her later work reveals. Even "Tear Gas," in the same volume, uses tears as a leitmotiv to balance desire and the inadequacy of desire in a search for sufficiency. The tears of the title, provoked during a political demonstration, combine with "tears of fear" and "tears of relief" on the public and private fronts as the speaker seeks "a way of saying" that will include, as well as cure her of, her laments. Once again, a strettolike conclusion picks up the earlier strands:

> things I have said which in a few years will be forgotten
> matter more to me than this or any poem
> and I want you to listen
> when I speak badly
> not in poems but in tears
> not my best but my worst
> that these repetitions are beating their way
> toward a place where we can no longer be together
> where my body no longer will demonstrate outside your stockade
> and wheeling through its blind tears will make for the open air
> of another kind of action
>
> (I am afraid.)
> It's not the worst way to live.

(FD, 200)

The simplicity of declaration acknowledges the usefulness of fear and counters the parenthetical, sotto voce statement made in shame or embarrassment. From an aside to a full articulation, from a muttered, private grief to a public conversion of fear to bravery, Rich's poetry produces a program for the discovery of sufficiency.

*   *   *

Antiphony is an easy means to structure provocation and response. The 1983 "Education of a Novelist" (*FD*, 314–17), like "Meditations for a Savage Child" and "Culture and Anarchy," offers a meditation on italicized lines from Ellen Glasgow's autobiography, but by the end the poet acknowledges her own resemblance to the novelist. Quotation becomes a linguistic appropriation, as one self merges with another that originally seemed merely a reflection. This dialectic—thesis and antithesis synthesized through an absorption of one voice into another—has been an American habit at least since William Carlos Williams's Dr. Paterson, and owes something to the more fractured, spasmodic medleys of voices in *The Cantos* and *The Waste Land*. But Rich differs from her male predecessors in committing herself to a personal merging of identities instead of focusing on vaster, communal voices. She would not say with Whitman, "I am great. I contain multitudes," but rather "I am contained by them." Like the speaker in the 1968 "Planetarium," thinking of Caroline Herschel, she might say: "I am bombarded yet   I stand," where bombardment includes the "direct path of a battery of signals" (*FD*, 116) [39] and the more indirect (or, in her subsequent label, "untranslatable") pulsations that she attempts first to absorb, then to translate, then to retransmit.

If all this sounds curiously like the male stereotypes of woman as first the absorber, then the deliverer of life, it shows only that Rich has succeeded as much in rethinking and reformulating the clichés of identity as she has in employing domestic activity and details from rural life as the new ground for woman's identity. New presbyter may be only old priest writ large, but in Rich's case intelligence and artistic variety empower those images to teach an audience to see this woman as a renovated chameleon poet. "I am an American woman," she announced in "From an Old House in America" (1974), by which she means also all women, and just as "any woman's death diminshes" the composite speaker, so does she gain strength from the union of others: "I never chose this place / yet I am of it now" (*FD*, 216) [66] echoes Rich's earlier passivity and her fortitude. The artistic weaving of strands becomes equivalent to the psychological and political solidarity with the miners and "raging stoic grandmothers" in "Natural Resources" (1977), but its roots lie deep in Rich's earlier work.

Unlike Stevens, progressively contenting himself with less, Rich in many ways affirms Blake's proverb that nothing less than *all* will satisfy. Her demands for sufficiency increase proportionately with her battle for self-realization and political change, via an expansion of her own person to include those of others. The early poem "Double Monologue" poses the problem succinctly:

> To live illusionless, in the abandoned mine-
>   shaft of doubt, and still
> mime illusions for others? A puzzle
>   for the maker who has thought
> once too often too coldly.
>
> Since I was more than a child
>   trying on a thousand faces
> I have wanted one thing: to know
>   simply as I know my name
> at any given moment, where I stand.
>
>   (*PSN*, 55)

Defining the self by withdrawing and fixing limits is one way, but Rich chooses the other way, of pushing beyond the boundaries and participating in other lives. To transform the enemy for his rebirth, to identify the enemy within: the goal is one of Keatsian empathy, hard won with pain and struggle. The title poem of *Necessities of Life* states the dilemma: either the self has a rigid identity, in which case it is a "small, fixed dot," "a dark-blue thumbtack / pushed into the scene," or else it loses itself under the onrush of other lives:

After a time the dot

begins to ooze. Certain heats
melt it

Now I was hurriedly

blurring into ranges
of burnt red, burning green,

whole biographies swam up and
swallowed me like Jonah.

(FD, 55) [18]

Involving and absorbing such various presences as Wollstonecraft, Wittgenstein, Godard, Louis Jouvet, and Caroline Herschel in the poems of the late sixties, Rich confronts the challenge of the past to identify foreign elements within herself, to share female weakness and strength, and to teach us—this is her stunningly original theme—the dangers as well as the solaces of empathy. Reaching beyond the sexes in an effort to understand sexuality, her poetry urges readers to accept the bisexuality of the psyche. Animus and anima, as yolk and white of the one shell, are interwoven: all identity is shared. The theme that I have called "original" is so, really, only for lyric poetry; it is a staple of modernism, especially within the longer and more congenial forms that Eliot, Woolf, and Joyce mastered. As Calvin Bedient has recently noted in his study of *The Waste Land*, "one of the assumptions of modernism is that every individual contains the blueprints of all the rest. 'We have other lives,' says wispy Lucy Swithin in Virginia Woolf's *Between the Acts.*"[9]

Of her recent poems, perhaps "Transcendental Etude" best demonstrates Rich's techniques for teaching us the worth of multiple selves. Starting with the title, which prepares us for music as subject and formal principle, the poem works its weavings into a resonant whole, always so naturally as to seem inevitable. Concluding with [a] list of objets trouvés the poem retains firm control at the same time that it consciously abjures all "mere will to mastery" (words with special consequence throughout Rich's work) in favor of communal identity. But throughout, the poet nimbly offers assurances that oppositions can in fact yield to deeper syntheses. These polarities—beginning and ending, love gained and love lost, study and mastery, fragility and endurance, flying up and sinking down—all exist, in the words of the 1978 "Integrity," a poem about the uneasy truce between anger and tenderness, "as angels, not polarities" (FD, 274) [92].

Like a Romantic nature lyric, according to the classic formula of

9. Calvin Bedient, *He Do the Police in Different Voices* (Chicago: University of Chicago Press, 1986), 113.

M. H. Abrams,[1] "Transcendental Etude" begins with a specific situation in time and place, moves to a long, meditative, and thoroughly didactic middle part concerning women's love, and ends with the catalogue as a trope appropriate to "vision" and "a whole new poetry." What most impresses is the continuity between and within the individual sections, which are both seamless and cut off from one another by the conventional signs of lineation and spacing. The musical title must be taken as a clue to the poem's method and to its central image, one that is ironically invoked and shunned at the same time.

The opening description—of late summer in Vermont—establishes a scene and a rhetoric of dialectic. The poet watches deer run frightened from her car, and then thinks ahead to autumn's hunting season when "they'll be fair game for the hit-and-run hunters." Above the apparent contrast between the observed and the envisioned scenes, however, lies an uneasy resemblance, since the poet already has startled the deer with her own vehicle. The paragraph ends with an implicit reworking of "To Autumn" and "Sunday Morning":

> But this evening deep in summer
> the deer are still alive and free,
> nibbling apples from early-laden boughs
> so weighted, so englobed
> with already yellowing fruit
> they seem eternal, Hesperidean
> in the clear-tuned, cricket-throbbing air.

(FD, 264) [87]

Nowhere else does Rich so easily capture Keats's sense of nature's inevitable process, of boughs early-laden but seemingly eternal, and of our own deception, like that of the bees who think warm days will never cease.

Having established the polarities and conplementarities—twin scenes of humans and deer, an apparently eternal summer moment already absorbed by its own "yellowing"—the poem proceeds to contrast the "fragility of all this sweetness" in the "green world" with both the "fake Vermont" that has been sentimentalized, photographed, and developed, and the "sick Vermont" of poverty and violence, which tourists never see. What "persists," in other words, is the very fragility of nature, whereas human desecration, abrupt and transforming, may turn out, after all, to be superficial. And once more suggesting Keats, she ends this paragraph with a section bringing into focus the eternal beneficence of natural foison:

> I've sat on a stone fence above a great, soft, sloping field
> of musing heifers, a farmstead

1. M. H. Abrams, "Structure and Style in the Greater Romantic Nature Lyric," in Frederick W. Hilles and Harold Bloom, eds., *From Sensibility to Romanticism* (New York: Oxford University Press, 1965), 527–60.

slanting its planes calmly in the calm light,
a dead elm raising bleached arms
above a green so dense with life,
minute, momentary life—slugs, moles, pheasants, gnats,
spiders, moths, hummingbirds, groundhogs, butterflies—
a lifetime is too narrow
to understand it all, beginning with the huge
rockshelves that underlie all that life.

(265) [87]

Death and life, the minute and the expansive, the "dense" and the "momentary," stone and light, a narrow lifetime and the "huge rock-shelves" underlying everything mingle in neo-Romantic lushness.

These sensuous oppositions, observed through a landscape, prepare the poet for her more overt didacticism, the human application of her perceptions, in the middle section, which wonders about the relationship between study or practice and transcendence or perfection: the title comes to refer to more than music. Humans do not have the luxury of choice: "No one ever told us we had to study our lives, / make of our lives a study, as if learning natural history / or music" . . . "And in fact we can't live like that: we take on / everything at once before we've even begun / to read or mark time." Birth dislocates woman from mother, and loss, a wrenching apart, becomes the ground note of existence. So what we have, her metaphor continues, is a text as "counterpoint": "trying to sightread / what our fingers can't keep up with, learn by heart / what we can't even read. And yet / it *is* this we were born to" (266) [88].

Turning away from virtuoso performers (her version of Prufrock's rejection of heroism), mistrusting the false glamour of theatricality, the poet allies herself instead with the quiet, anonymous audience, responding to the music, "hearing-out in her blood / a score touched off in her perhaps / by some words, a few chords, from the stage" (266) [88]. Just when it seems, however, that she is reaffirming the old stereotypes of the passive, responsive nature of woman, Rich steps back to consider the moment of a new kind of daring, a "severer listening, cleansed / of oratory," the unavoidable detachment (a repetition, within the poem, of the earlier traumatic "wrenching-apart" from the mother) from old solaces:

No one who survives to speak
new language, has avoided this:
the cutting-away of an old force that held her
rooted to an old ground
the pitch of utter loneliness
where she herself and all creation
seem equally dispersed, weightless, her being a cry
to which no echo comes or can ever come.

(267) [89]

The language of music ("ground," "pitch," "echo") interweaves itself with the images from nature with which the poem began ("cutting-away," "rooted") to expand and extend the figurative base of the poem.

Turning from the moment of loss, the poet continues to mingle the languages of nature and music as she ecstatically claims the joys of women's love as "a sudden brine-clear thought / trembling like the tiny, orbed, endangered / egg-sac of a new world." From this recognition comes a new birth, a new music, a new nature ("as, after the heatwave / breaks, the clear tones of the world / manifest: cloud, bough, wall, insect, the very soul of light"), a "whole new poetry" (268) [90].

Such is the list of the "finest findings" that ends the poem; although *assemblage* has replaced music as the primary metaphor, the actual and implicit terms of the rest of the poem continue through its didactic conclusion, quoted earlier. The "sherd of broken glass" recalls the helicopter's wings at the end of "Snapshots of a Daughter-in-Law"; the contrast of danger and salving repeats the end of "Necessities of Life," where the speaker faces the daring invitation of the world and goes out "trenchant in motion as an eel, solid / as a cabbage-head" (*FD*, 56) [19]. Taking her cue from objects of the world, the woman here "becomes" what she finds, complementing the world and becoming herself a complementary principle that reconciles oppositions like danger and safety: various, ephemeral, but also solid and enduring, she becomes the stone foundation, itself an echo of the "rockshelves that underlie all life," with which the poem had begun.

*   *   *

The 1973 "Re-Forming the Crystal" exhibits all the poetic-didactic gestures I've suggested throughout this chapter, and deserves quotation in full.[2] The alternation of poetry and prose is not surprising, but as in "The Burning of Paper Instead of Children," the prose itself resonates with strong rhythms that repeat and expand single images and motifs within the poem. The alternation calls attention to itself—what, one might ask, are the reasons for printing part of this as lineated poetry, part as prose with justified margins? For one thing, the "poetic" segments deal with present issues, while the first prose passage recollects past time and the second anticipates the future. I discuss further the importance of fragmentation, ellipsis, and verblessness later in these pages: poetry means "presence" and the present tense is Rich's vehicle for wonder, as in the unpunctuated opening, which gives a perpetually hallucinated quality to her "imagining," and in her turning away from all "images" of the represented self in the third section (e.g., the photo, the name, the reminder).

2. In the original essay, "Re-forming the Crystal" was quoted in full; in this volume it appears on pp. 61–62 [*Editors*].

A personal reformation requires an imaginative re-forming and a formal response to the demands of empathy: sexuality and imagination inhabit the same field of energy in the first section (desire "focused like a burning-glass" is the first image of crystallization) and in the second, where "the sudden knowledge . . . that the body is sexual" opens a sequence from knowledge to "fantasizing" to the energy of anticipation. Each of the prose sections builds from simpler to more complex structures, as the listing of possibilities shows the workings of the imagination. Additionally, where the first prose chunk works largely with fragments, the second deploys complex sentences, which culminate in the aggressive listing of possible outlets for imaginative energy. As an experiment in reformation, the poem builds itself up from an initial act of wonder through a contemplation of past eagerness, possibility, and daring to a commitment to self-exposure. As part of a personal and poetic program it occupies (along with the stylistically more conventional "Diving into the Wreck") in Rich's oeuvre a place similar to that of the odes to Psyche and Melancholy in Keats's. Imagining an act of daring—in poetry—is equivalent to performing it. The final image invoking the ancient priestess and her victim-votary certainly recalls the goddess Melancholy, who admits her suitor to her temple only to have him hung among her cloudy trophies through a comparably suicidal act of imaginative adventure. The poem's various crystals—the burning-glass, the telephone, thin ice, frozen spiderweb—all give way to the one implied, unmentioned crystal: the ball for predicting the future that becomes the prophet's medium as the poem is that of the energized poet.

"Re-Forming the Crystal" exemplifies Rich's technique as well as her ideology. It combines the tropes of listing and weaving that I have already mentioned. Its hallucinated quality is presented more variously than the comparable obsessions of "I Dream I'm the Death of Orpheus" (*FD*, 119–20) [43] with its anaphoric "I am a woman . . . a woman . . . a woman" threading through the imaginary occupation of a movie script. Its concision matches the more narrative organization of "Diving into the Wreck," which also relies on anaphora as a structural principle and an equivalent of mental attention, and the insistent choral quality of the end of "Tear Gas," with its prayerful reiteration of need and fear building to the relief of a conclusion: "(I am afraid.) / It's not the worst way to live." Rich's poetry is a poetry of repetition: its assertive verbs express the demands of self on the world, as in "Splittings" (1974), with its antiphonal strands "I choose" and "I choose not" woven into the refusal of division and separation implied by the title. Here, in fact, the language of choosing, in its insistent repetition, is made part of a specifically educational program ("Yet if I could instruct / myself, if we could learn to learn from pain," [*FD*, 228] [76]). Rich's lessons to her implied and actual audiences always derive from an effort of self-instruction: "I choose to love   this time   for once / with all my intelligence," she announces at the end, her self-admonitions having been rehearsed, heeded, and cured.

* * *

Infinitives, fragments, grammatically incomplete units that nevertheless encourage full apprehension, have become virtual signatures in Rich's work. Significantly, these fragments, bits, or shards tend to cluster at the opening or close of a poem. It is as if we have caught a speaker in midthought or, rather, as if she has taken us by surprise, demanding our attention. The arresting opening of "The Phenomenology of Anger" could easily be rewritten, and is certainly to be understood in part, as a simple statement: "The freedom of *x* is not the freedom of *y*." Instead, Rich gives us the following:

> The freedom of the wholly mad
> to smear & play with her madness
> write with her fingers dipped in it
> the length of a room
>
> which is not, of course, the freedom
> you have, walking on Broadway
> to stop & turn back or go on
> 10 blocks; 20 blocks
>
> but feels enviable maybe
> to the compromised
>
> curled in the placenta of the real
> which was to feed & which is strangling her.
>
> (FD, 165) [55–56]

The phrasal nature of this stanza, relegating its metaphor to a subordinate clause while withholding an independent clause, and its unpunctuated lineation both arrest and deceive us: this is especially true of the dramatically ambiguous "which," guarding the pass between the confined patient and the ambulatory, sane addressee, but also bringing the two into an uncomfortable resemblance while keeping them apart. Since the entire poem both constructs and undermines logical oppositions, the apparent randomness of the form of the opening definition prepares us for the speculations that follow.

I take this stylistic tactic as a synecdoche for the job of the entire poem. Poetry, addressed in and symbolized by "The Fact of a Doorframe," the 1974 poem that stands as the title piece in the latest selection from Rich's complete work, serves, according to its central image, to support, to build, to divide:

> Now, again, poetry,
> violent, arcane, common,

hewn of the commonest living substance
into archway, portal, frame
I grasp for you, your bloodstained splinters, your
ancient and stubborn poise
—as the earth trembles—
burning out from the grain

(iv)[62–63]

The poem, which starts with an ellipsis from title to first line ("The Fact of a Doorframe . . . means there is something to hold"), bears witness to the fear that Rich explains in her foreword to the latest anthology—"that the walls cannot be broken down, that these words will fail to enter another soul"—the fear that lies behind the fractured utterances in poems like "The Phenomenology of Anger." She has concerned herself for more than twenty years with images about building and joining:

I long to create something
that can't be used to keep us passive:
I want to write
a script about plumbing, how every pipe
is joined
to every other

("Essential Resources," FD, 202)

And I think of those lives we tried to live
in our globed helmets, self-enclosed
bodies self-illumined gliding
safe from the turbulence

and how, miraculously, we failed

("The Wave," FD, 205)

A city waits at the back of my skull
eating its heart out to be born:
how design the first
city of the moon? how shall I see it
for all of us who are done
with enclosed spaces, purdah, the salon, the sweatshop loft,
the ingenuity of the cloister?

("The Fourth Month of the Landscape Architect," PSN, 225)

It is not, therefore, inappropriate for Rich to focus her readers' attention onto syntactic and grammatical arrangements that bolster those images. Words fail, words support: a doorframe steadies and also gives one leave to thrust one's "forehead against the wood." The implicit doubleness of the infinitive (the very idea of action without temporal specificity) and the ambivalence of her expressive means justify Rich's hopefulness, the part of her disposition encouraged to think of radical change as the complement to her frustrations, conscious as she is of the pitfalls, dangers, and failures of all attempts to communicate.

Rich is predominantly a poet of the present tense: even her infinitives, suggesting purpose or futurity, ring with present determination. And the present tense typically provides the time and language of instruction. Direct or implied address demands the immediacy of lyric; presence is actual, even when represented by the wire-dot photograph of a man in pain. Temporal continuity may be an equivalent to personal integrity, something hoped for but difficult to know, and some of Rich's most touching poems admit a preference for small moments to anything grander. The teacher, when addressing her students or audience, is still mostly addressing herself; the lessons of the past encourage a reformed faith for the future, as in the touching "From a Survivor," addressed to her husband shortly after his death. If the arts of teaching and learning demand an absorption of the past as preparation for the future, this delicate, unembellished piece may stand as a paradigm of educational technique.

It, too, is a poem of statement:

> The pact that we made was the ordinary pact
> of men & women in those days
>
> I don't know who we thought we were
> that our personalities
> could resist the failures of the race
>
> Lucky or unlucky, we didn't know
> the race had failures of that order
> and that we were going to share them
>
> Like everybody else, we thought of ourselves as special
>
> Your body is as vivid to me
> as it ever was: even more
>
> since my feeling for it is clearer:
> I know what it could and could not do
>
> it is no longer
> the body of a god
> or anything with power over my life
>
> Next year it would have been 20 years
> and you are wastefully dead
> who might have made the leap
> we talked, too late, of making

which I live now
not as a leap
but a succession of brief, amazing movements

each one making possible the next.

(FD, 176–77)[59–60]

Figurative language is reserved for the lines about the dead man's body and the final simile comparing life to a leap and a succession of moments, but even these sections barely rise to the level of poetic revelation. As in so many of Rich's poems the appearance of the lines, separated, grouped, isolated on the page, adds an emotional frisson that calls attention to single lines or clusters; these poems would lose much of their effect if printed as simple, justified prose. And yet in spite of such bareness, its relative flatness, its seemingly unpoetic structure, "From a Survivor" movingly exemplifies the didacticism to which Rich has laid claim. Its progress is a temporal one, its three sections neatly focused on past, present, and future. The survivor is also a surveyor, examining a temporal terrain and commenting rationally but sympathetically on the eagerness of youth, in its self-deceiving confidence, to "resist the failures of the race," then coolly appraising the legacy of the past to the present, and finally looking hopefully forward to a conditional future that includes the present, but that looks backward just as the first section treated the past in terms of the couple's youthful expectations for future successes. The temporal configurations provide the poem with both a formal organization and a controlling hope: they are Rich's equivalent of the string of days embodied in Wordsworth's "My Heart Leaps Up" that stand as epigraph to the Intimations ode: "And I could wish my days to be / Bound each to each in natural piety."

As the time changes through the poem, so does the social or human focus: the first third places the young marrieds ("we") ironically against a background of the race to whom they mistakenly feel themselves superior; the second section makes the first and only extended apostrophe to the dead husband; the third part, just as it resurveys past and present ("we talked," "I live") in terms of the future ("next year"), also reconsiders the pronominal terms of the past two parts ("we," "you") before settling squarely into a final clause depicting the woman alone, accommodating herself to solitude, middle age, and all the compromises that define what we call maturity.

Emotionally, at least, the lessons of the poem have neatly progressed from the ironies of youthful illusions overturned, through an acceptance of a realistic commitment to another person that is possible only because of his death and her growth, to a confident statement of forward progress. Gradually stripping herself of imagined superiority, of a godlike husband and her own inflated sense of his powers, of the larger community ("race") and the smaller unit of the marriage, the speaker finds surest confidence and happiness through deprivation and loss. Knowing what to make of a diminished thing, she has learned to profit from disaster. The act of self-instruction is all the more delicate for gradually eliminating the very verbs of knowledge at the moment of clearest insight: after "I don't know . . . we thought . . . we didn't know . . . I know," the final eight lines present their lessons unobtrusively and confidently, doing away with the apparatus of instruction and thinking, and relying instead on the sure knowledge implicit in a direct statement, all the more powerful for coming late.

In her early poem, "The Middle-aged," observing the phenomenon proleptically, Rich concludes an evaluation of the lessons and compromises of age touchingly: "All to be understood by us, returning / Late, in our own time—how that peace was made, / Upon what terms, with how much left unsaid" (FD, 15). In "From a Survivor" Rich revises her earlier poem, as she depicts her own private arrangements in public (the later "pact" echoes the earlier "peace" and "terms"). She makes a truce with a dead man and her own dead, past self and attends to future arrangements. She learns, because she has earned them, the satisfactions of difficult ordinary happiness: happiness ordinary in and because of its difficulties. And what she learns she teaches, through the clarity of simple speech in "From a Survivor" as well as through the more complex structures of later poems like "Transcendental Etude." For a poet normally thought of as political and polemical, even recklessly uncontrolled, Rich teaches gently: her best poems seldom hector or lecture. Like any good teacher she resorts to an arsenal of instructional weapons that includes a larger percentage of patience, even when wild, than aggressiveness. As a poet, she has forged a technique out of simple speech as well as more ornate figurations. Her recent long poem, Sources (1983), a retrieval and replanting of her own roots, ends with a moving definition of the knowledge she seeks, and a defense of the methods of articulation that she long ago wielded:

> But there is no finite knowing, no such rest. Innocent birds, deserts, morning-glories, point to choices, leading away from the familiar. When I speak of an end to suffering I don't mean anesthesia. I mean knowing the world, and my place in it, not in order to stare with bitterness or detachment, but as a powerful and womanly series of choices: and here I write the words, in their fullness: powerful; womanly.[3]

3. Sources (Woodside, Calif.: Heyeck Press, 1983), 23 [114]. See also Blood, Bread, and Poetry, Selected Prose, 1979–1985 (New York: W. W. Norton, 1986) for Rich's prose meditations on her sense of her own Jewishness, a late but significant part of her poetic/political program [224–39].

ALBERT GELPI

The Poetics of Recovery: A Reading of Adrienne Rich's *Sources* †

Autogenesis, birthing one's self, is a theme in Rich's poetry from as far back as *Snapshots of a Daughter-in-Law* (1958–60) and *Necessities of Life* (1962), which begins: "Piece by piece I seem / to re-enter the world." The second section of *Sources* begins by cautioning against any recourse to magic ("I refuse to become a seeker for cures"), but projects the poem as a self-birthing:

> Everything that has ever
> helped me has come through what already
> lay stored in me. Old things, diffuse, unnamed, lie strong
> across my heart.

Sources evolved in twenty-three sections between August 1981 and August of the following year; the sections are of varying length, written often in pairs of unmetered lines (like H. D.'s *Trilogy*), sometimes in verse paragraphs, occasionally in prose. Again as in *Trilogy*, the progress of the poem, drawing up, defining and naming the sources of identity "already . . . stored in me" is not linear but looping and circular. It expands to contract, it focuses to open out; its revelations are at once cumulative and climactic; its returns make the point of origin a full circle.

"Sixteen years," the first phrase of the first section, indicates the first turning back and turning in. She is returning to the Vermont house which occupies a special place in her life and has served in the past as an imaginative matrix—last time in the long poem "From an Old House in America," written in 1974. So it has not been literally sixteen years since she has been back to Vermont. What period, then, is she demarcating so self-consciously? As we shall see, without reverting to magic, the poem achieves an unexpected mandala, circling back to the squaring of square. Sixteen years from the composition of the poem in 1981–82 takes her back to 1965–66, back to what stands now as a decisive turning point in her life: her departure from New England—a poet not yet forty but already acclaimed, wife of the economist Alfred Conrad, mother of three sons—to live with her family in New York. The intervening years had brought change and trauma, both public and private, political and psychological: the Vietnam War and New Left politics, the struggle for civil rights, the Conrads' involvement in demonstrations of protest and

---

† Reprinted from *The Southern Review* 26.2 (April 1990), where it appeared as part of the essay "Two Ways of Spelling It Out: An Archetypal-Feminist Reading of H. D.'s *Trilogy* and Adrienne Rich's *Sources*." Copyright © 1990 by Albert Gelpi. *Sources* appears on pp. 101–14.

solidarity, her husband's suicide, her sons' adolescence, her teaching in the open-admissions program at the City University of New York, her radicalization as a feminist and a lesbian. Where did those changes leave her as woman and poet?

The imagery of the first section also indicates a submersion in her earlier poetry as well as her life. The New England landscape recalls such poems as "Autumn Sequence" (1964), "From an Old House in America" (1974), and "The Spirit of Place" (1980); the vixen in the second verse paragraph is carried forward from "5:30 A.M." (1967) and "Abnegation" (1968); the queen anne's lace in the third verse paragraph repeats the description of the flower in "The Knot" (1965). Allusions from the earlier poetry thread through the text, reinforcing our awareness that Rich is concentrating her previous life towards a new clarification. She had begun dating her poems in the fifties in order to track the progress of her consciousness. In "Planetarium" (1968) she had written "seeing is changing," and in "Images for Godard" (1970), "the moment of change is the only poem." And she summed up the purpose of her poetry when she gave the autobiographical essay "When We Dead Awaken" the subtitle "Writing As Re-vision"—that is, as change and metamorphosis.

So now it has been sixteen years since she saw the vixen in 1965 as "an omen / to me, surviving, herding her cubs," but that vixen is now "long dead." That phrase begins to reverberate, initiating the principal drama of *Sources*: the poet's confrontation with the two men, both dead, who shaped her life as a woman and a poet—her father and her husband. A pair of poems from 1972 addressing her husband after his suicide are called "For the Dead" and "From a Survivor." The "twilight" world of the vixen may even recall the "twilight" in which the poet bids farewell to her dying father in "After Dark" (1964). The vixen raises the question of the poet's plight: survival or death. In the end, can the dead awaken? They are beyond metamorphosis. Since the course of her life has been bound to the dead, can she survive them and re-vise?

The essay "When We Dead Awaken," in *On Lies, Secrets, and Silence*, tells of her being reared by Dr. Rich as a prodigy and educated by him from the books in his library to be a poet: "So for about twenty years I wrote for a particular man, who criticized and praised me and made me feel I was indeed 'special.' " By the time she returned to him in *Sources*, she had for years identified as patriarchal oppression the paternal authority she learned from and learned to resist: "I saw myself, the eldest daughter raised as a son, taught to study but not to pray, taught to hold reading and writing sacred: the eldest daughter in the house with no son, she who must overthrow the father, take what he taught her and use it against him." Marrying Conrad soon after graduation from Radcliffe, against her father's vehement opposition, liberated Rich from "that most dangerous place, the family home." And if she soon found herself at the center of her own "family home" (also described in "When We Dead Awaken" and in *Of Woman Born*), Conrad encouraged her career and sought to help her open spaces in the domestic routine for poetry. In turn she addressed him as spousal partner in poems like "A Marriage in the 'Sixties" (1961)—"Dear fellow–particle" and "twin"—and "Like This Together" (1963)—"Sometimes at night / you are my mother . . . Sometimes / you're the wave of birth. . . ." Moreover, the poets who influenced her development even after she left her father's library were principally men. Echoes of Yeats, Frost, Stevens, Auden punctuate the early poems; Auden chose her first book for the Yale Younger Poet's Award; Robert Lowell, Randall Jarrell, and John Berryman became admiring peers.

Rich's sense of intelligence and verbal mastery as masculine qualities had strong autobiographical reenforcement, as it did for H. D., and expressed itself in a number of dialogues with her animus as the source of her identity and poetic power. "Orion" (1965, sixteen years before *Sources*) sums up an identification with her animus.[1] In the early stanzas Rich treats Orion with ironic humor—the Viking in cast-iron armor, Richard the Lion-Heart imprisoned in the night sky, the swaggering adolescent with his phallicized sword—but there can be no doubt about her envious empathy. Orion is both other and self: her "genius" and "half-brother," invulnerable to such soft "feminine" virtues as pity; and Rich's note to the poem, indicating that a few phrases echo Gottfried Benn's essay on the plight of the modern artist, underscores the fact that the animus-figure represents her capacity as poet.

"Indoors" is the domestic setting for the wife-mother to "bruise and blunder," for breaking faith with herself, for emptiness (the man finding her eyes vacant) and alienation (the woman turning away from her image in the mirror) and fragmentation (the children "eating crumbs of my life"). Her own sense of being walled into the house may make her see Orion with his back to the celestial wall; nevertheless, she chooses, in her imagination and for the sake of her imagination, his situation over hers. She escapes the house and opens herself to receive the "transfusion" of her twin's ego, more potent than "divine astronomy." His masculine privilege still laces her empathy with irony ("You take it all for granted"), but her incandescent identification with him gives her a "star-like eye" (a transcendent perspective and insight as well as identity). By the end of the poem her potent glance matches his, spear for sword, as she finds words for her "speechless pirate."

So now, sixteen years later, casting back to see whence she has come in order to see where she stands, Rich must confront the masculine again. In the third and fourth sections of the poem, a voice that seems hers but speaks in italics with her father's challenging and rebuking tone,

1. In the original essay, "Orion" was quoted in full; in this volume it appears on pp. 29–30.

presses on her the question of sources: *"From where does your strength come, you Southern Jew? / split at the root, raised in a castle of air?";* *"With whom do you believe your lot is cast?"* The psychology and politics of gender are inseparable from the psychology and politics of race and class, of historical and geographical circumstance. Split at the root between a father Jewish in name but not in faith and a nominally Christian mother, alienated from both southern and New England values, Rich ponders the dilemma of her identity in the widening historical gyre: the oppression of women by men, of the poor by the privileged, of blacks by Klansmen, of Indians by Yankees, of the Jews by the Nazis.

Rich's Jewishness, particularly in the shadow of the Holocaust, poses the problem of identity most acutely. What is it for a woman, a radical feminist and lesbian, to be a Jew? Can she separate Jewish culture, Jewish history from traditional Jewish faith? What is it for a nonbelieving Jew to participate in secular, patriarchal WASP culture? How can she weigh the oppression of Jewish patriarchalism towards women against the anti-Semitism which caused the Holocaust, continues to oppress Jews, men and women alike, and makes deracination the price of assimilation into WASP society? In her husband she found a Jew of a different kind and social class from her father, but no more a believing and observing Jew than her father: in fact, in the end, a man whose alienation led to his death. So now she sees the two of them, whom she used to think antagonists, tragically kin: both deracinated Jews whose sense of identity as men was defined and compromised by the anti-Semitism of their culture.

As the poem tells us, she had been brooding over her Jewishness since adolescence, and the issue presses in now insisting on clarification. The phrase "split at the root," which sounds like a knell throughout *Sources*, echoes her statement of the dilemma in the 1960 poem "Readings of History":

> Split at the root, neither Gentile nor Jew
> Yankee nor Rebel, born
> in the face of two ancient cults,
> I'm a good reader of histories.

Simultaneously with the writing of *Sources*, Rich was also exploring her Jewishness in an essay entitled "Split at the Root," written for the lesbian-feminist collection *Nice Jewish Girls*.[2] Where the essay fills in the autobiographical narrative behind the poem, the poem seeks to push beyond the irresolution at the end of the essay. Through the course of the poem Rich's identity begins to take root, paradoxically, in her admission of and separation from both father and husband, and specifically in her rejection of their deracination. She does not think but *feels* her way

2. See above, pp. 224–39.

past the paradoxes and contradictions of her situation. Her psychological probe reaches past paradox, past the empowering and constricting contention with the masculine, to a founding sense of self as a Jewish woman. From the integrity of that perspective, "now, under a powerful, womanly lens . . . I can decipher your suffering and deny no part of my own." The acknowledgment of suffering, and the cause of the suffering, with an unsparing love, attains a searing, healing clarity in the three prose sections of *Sources*, beyond the formal decorum of verse: the direct address to her dead father in Section VII, and to her dead husband in Sections XVII and the penultimate XXII.

No discursive commentary can convey the concentrated catharsis of those encounters in the space opened by the ruminations of the surrounding verse passages. But those recognitions and relinquishments and self-recognitions ground Rich sufficiently to enable her to move on: "without faith" but "faithful," convinced at least that there is "something more" to being a Jew than custom, and so "wearing the star of David / / on a thin chain at my breastbone."

The painful recovery and redefinition allows the poem to speak more and more distinctly with the accents of a "woman with a mission, not to win prizes," as her ambitious father intended for her poetic career, "but to change the laws of history." This daunting ambition makes her describe herself in Section XX in the transpersonal, archetypal third person: "she is gripped by a blue, a foreign air, / a desert absolute: dragged by the roots of her own will / into another scene of choices." But the archetypal energies of the self which Rich is drawing on here enable her to conclude forcefully, even prophetically, in the first person. From that vantage she looks backward and forward in the last lines and locates her self in the sources and resources she intuited at the beginning "already / lay stored in me" embryonically; acknowledging her dead husband at the end of the poem's gestation she stands free. The prose passage that ends *Sources* indicates not a conclusion but a renewed commitment to the difficult process of definition and construction:

> When I speak of an end to suffering I don't mean anesthesia. I mean knowing the world, and my place in it, not in order to stare with bitterness or detachment, but as a powerful and womanly series of choices: and here I write the words, in their fullness:
> powerful;   womanly.

Through the power of womanhood she assumes responsibility to and for "your native land, your life"; the open pronoun in that title of a recent volume includes us all in the responsibility for self and society.

JOANNE FEIT DIEHL

"Of Woman Born": Adrienne Rich and the Feminist Sublime †

Every age has its characteristic faults, its typical temptation to over-emphasize some virtue at the expense of others, and the typical danger for poets in our age is, perhaps, the desire to be "original." This is natural, for who in his daydreams does not prefer to see himself as a leader rather than a follower, an explorer rather than a cultivator and a settler? Unfortunately, the possibility of realizing such a dream is limited, not only by talent but also by time, and even a superior gift cannot cancel historical priority; he who today climbs the Matterhorn, though he be the greatest climber who ever lived, must tread in Whymper's footsteps.

Radical changes and significant novelty in artistic style can only occur when there has been a radical change in human sensibility to require them. The spectacular events of the present time must not blind us to the fact that we are living not at the beginning but in the middle of a historical epoch; they are not novel but repetitions on a vastly enlarged scale and at a violently accelerated tempo of events which took place long since.

—W. H. Auden, "Foreword" to Adrienne Rich's *A Change of World* (1951)[1]

I

The "radical change in human sensibility" W. H. Auden finds essential to poetic originality is at once documented and created in the overarching shape of Adrienne Rich's poetic career. That career may best be summarized as a move away from painstaking imitation, through encoded representations of women's experience, to a radical poetics that seeks to reimagine the relationship among writing, eros, and sexual identity.[2] In

---

† From *Women Poets and the American Sublime* (Bloomington, Indiana: Indiana UP, 1990). Reprinted by permission of the publisher. This selection has been edited for publication here; asterisks indicate deletions. Page references to works that appear in this Norton Critical Edition are given in brackets after the author's original citation.

1. In her essay "When We Dead Awaken: Writing as Re-Vision," Adrienne Rich comments on the predicament of patriarchal poetry in this "historical epoch": "To the eye of a feminist, the work of Western male poets now writing reveals a deep, fatalistic pessimism as to the possibilities of change, whether societal or personal, along with a familiar and threadbare use of women (and nature) as redemptive on the one hand, threatening on the other; . . . [See "When We Dead Awaken: Writing as Re-Vision," in *On Lies, Secrets, and Silence: Selected Prose 1966–1978* (New York: W. W. Norton & Co., 1979), p. 49 [176].

2. Of Rich's early work, Judith McDaniel notes, "To fill the role of poet, to win the approval of those whom she imitated, Rich had nearly crafted herself out of feeling." Judith McDaniel, "Reconstituting the World: The Poetry and Vision of Adrienne Rich," in *Reading Adrienne Rich: Reviews and Re-Visions, 1951–1981*, ed. Jane Roberta Cooper (Ann Arbor: The University of Michigan Press, 1984), p. 4 [311].

its devotion to both Whitman and Dickinson (as well as to the American literary tradition more generally), Rich's work enacts the revisionary project of merging Whitmanian power with the legacy of Dickinson's alternative Sublime. The interplay between Rich's sources underlies the discussion that follows, an evaluation of Rich's attempt to construct a single-sex, feminist poetics and her subsequent repudiation of the exclusionary aspects of that poetics in favor of a more inclusive yet specifically female-identified vision.[3] I begin with *The Dream of a Common Language*, for it is in this volume that Rich most fully elaborates a gender-based poetics. And it is here as well that Rich describes the dream of finding a language with the capacity to release itself from its own history, the power to escape the lengthening shadows of the patriarchal poetic tradition. That such a vision carries with it a risk—the danger of silencing the poetic or linguistic imagination—is neither surprising nor new, for the woman poet's need to find her own language in order to assume the prerogatives of an originating voice has been the central challenge facing all ambitious nineteenth- and twentieth-century women poets. In the wake of the Romantics' self-conscious identification of the male poet as quester and poetry as the language of desire, women who wish to write repeatedly strive for ways to appropriate language, to claim it for female experience. If the title of Rich's volume acknowledges the visionary character of such an enterprise, it also names its audience, for what Rich hopes to discover is a language that, while freeing itself from the exclusionary dominance of patriarchy, establishes a new, antithetical commonality of readers, a language spoken by and for other women. Rich's title contains an allusion to Virginia Woolf's sense of commonality as Woolf described it in her introductory essay to *The Common Reader*. Here Woolf quotes a sentence from Dr. Johnson's "Life of Gray": ". . . I rejoice to concur with the common reader; for by the common sense of readers, uncorrupted by literary prejudices, after all the refinements of subtlety and the dogmatism of learning, must be finally decided all claim to poetical honours."[4] Rich makes clear that she shares with Woolf the desire to speak not to an exclusive, educated audience but to those who share the concerns, desires, and burdens that define them as being excluded from the tradition of patriarchy, the lineage of male writers that has dominated literature in the West. Rich aims, moreover, to reach beyond the "exceptional" women who have developed an awareness of their situation, and who have the means to articulate their burden, to reach those

---

3. Albert Gelpi astutely isolates Rich's early concern with the possibilities and limitations of language: "As the ultimate challenge to her initial assumptions, Adrienne Rich raises the dreaded question for a poet: the very validity and efficacy of language. . . ." "As early as 'Like This Together,' " Gelpi notes, "in 1963 she was worrying that 'our words misunderstand us.' " For a thorough and insightful reading of Rich's poetic development, see Gelpi, "Adrienne Rich: The Poetics of Change," in *American Poetry Since 1960: Some Critical Perspectives*, ed. Robert B. Shaw (Cheshire: Carcanet, 1973) [282–99].

4. Virginia Woolf, *The Common Reader: First Series* (New York: A Harvest Book, Harcourt, Brace & World, Inc., 1953), p. 1.

deprived of such opportunities. It is from her sense of audience and the
politics that determines such a sense that the literary method of her
poems develops. The desire to convert ordinariness into a new mythos
leads Rich to explore the conversational aspects of a language close to
speech, in which secrets are laid open and wishes, too long silent, find
their voice.

How can woman, that perpetual "other" of male consciousness, his
object of desire, create either the linguistic and/or social conditions that
establish *her* not as the mediator of inspiration, the maculate whore-
mother-muse of tradition, but as the predominant, shaping conscious-
ness, inventor of relationships that inform art? Although Rich's major
nineteenth-century predecessors, Elizabeth Barrett Browning, Christina
Rossetti, and Emily Dickinson, did find ways of breaking through the
male dominance of language to discover new possibilities for the word,
the difficulty of their search for imaginative priority does not, of course,
fade with time. There can be no "final solution" for a woman who faces
the cumulative force of a tradition that has its origins in the Homeric
voice and echoes with renewed strength in our post-Miltonic assump-
tions about the nature of language and the patriarchal perceptions of
image-making itself.[5] It is just this need to find a way of piercing the
web of traditional discourse to open and extend her dialogue with the
predominant culture that Rich explores. Her search for a shared mythol-
ogy becomes a means of reclaiming a communal experience for women
that takes them into history, on an archaeological dig for lost possibilities
of metaphor. In an essay on Levertov, Rich, and Rukeyser, Rachel Blau
DuPlesis remarks on this remythologizing process in Rich's "Diving into
the Wreck":

> In this poem of journey and transformation Rich is tapping the
> energies and plots of myth, while re-envisioning the content. While
> there is a hero, a quest, and a buried treasure, the hero is a woman;
> the quest is a critique of old myths; the treasure is knowledge: the
> whole buried knowledge of the personal and cultural foundering of
> the relations between the sexes, and a self-knowledge that can be
> won only through the act of criticism.[6]

The opening poem in *The Dream of a Common Language* describes
a similar revision of myth—again, the hero is a woman, and the treasure
is not simply scientific knowledge but also knowledge of self, as the poet
describes an attempt to reach into the earth for the sources of woman's

5. For an insightful discussion of women readers' and writers' responses to Milton, specifically to
Paradise Lost, see Sandra M. Gilbert, "Patriarchal Poetry and Women Readers: Reflections
on Milton's Bogey," *PMLA*, vol. 93, no. 3 (May 1978), p. 368–82.
6. Rachel Blau DuPlessis, "The Critique of Consciousness and Myth in Levertov, Rich, and
Rukeyser," in *Shakespeare's Sisters: Feminist Essays on Women Poets* (Bloomington and Lon-
don: Indiana University Press, 1979), p. 295.

distinctive power.[7] Rich first combs through the earth deposits of "our" (female) experience of history to discover the amber bottle with its bogus palliative that will not ease the pain "for living on this earth   in the winters of this climate." The second gesture of the poem is toward a text and model: the story of Marie Curie, a woman who seeks a "cure," denying that the "element she had purified" causes her fatal illness. Her refusal to confront the crippling force of her success and recognize the deadly implications of original discovery enables Curie to continue her work at the cost of her life. Denying the reality of the flesh, "the cracked and suppurating skin   of her finger-ends," she presses on to death:

> She died   a famous woman   denying
> her wounds
> denying
> her wounds   came   from the same source as her power

Here, in the poem's closing lines, Rich uses physical space and the absence of punctuation (an extension of Dickinson's use of dashes) to loosen the deliberate, syntactic connections between words and thus introduce ambiguities that disrupt normative forms. The separation between words determines through the movement of the reader's eye—the movement past the "wounds" where it had rested the first time—the emphasis on the activity of denial and its necessary violation. The second "denying" carries the reader past the initial negativity of a woman's denying self-destruction by extending the phrase "denying her wounds" into "denying her wounds came from the same source as her power." Denial is an essential precondition for the woman inventor's continuing to succeed; what she is denying, of course, is the inevitable sacrifice of self in work as well as the knowledge that her power and her wounds share a common source. Like Curie, this book's later poems inform us, the woman poet must recognize a similar repression of her knowledge that what she is doing involves a deliberate rejection of the borrowed power of the tradition, the necessity of incurring the self-inflicted wounds that mark the birth of an individuated poetic voice.

Why should the process of image-making, using language for one's own ends, be, in Rich's words, "mined with risks" for women?[8] And how are these pressures different from those confronting men? The poems respond directly to these issues and suggest that women are not only secondary in status but also latecomers to a patriarchal world of images. In a culture where words are formed and assigned their dominant asso-

7. The poem is entitled "Power" [73]. For another treatment of Marie Curie's story within the context of an extended poetic discussion of women and creativity, see William Carlos Williams' *Paterson*, Book 4, II.
8. The phrase "mined with risks" appears in Rich's essay "Vesuvius at Home: The Power of Emily Dickinson," first published in *Parnassus: Poetry in Review* 5, no. 1 (Fall–Winter 1976), p. 57 [184].

ciations by men, women, in order to speak at all, either must subvert their own speech by using the patriarchal tongue or seek for themselves experiences available only to women—what it means to be a daughter, the emotions of a lesbian relationship, the process of childbirth—experiences that would serve to free women poets through their choice of subject from the history of patriarchal associations. Thus Rich insists upon the authority of, as well as the necessity for, solely female experience.[9] Other women poets, of course (Sylvia Plath, Anne Sexton, and their contemporaries), have written of this need and described it. Each, in her own way, asserts that the power of language depends upon the originary capacity of the woman poet, her ability to create a linguistic context freed from the prescriptive tradition of male-dominated images. Rich's "Phantasia for Elvira Shatayev," for example, attempts to replace the received image of the male adventurer, the rugged masculinity of the climber, with the woman hero. In this poem, which speaks through the voice of the leader of a women's climbing team whose members died in a storm on Lenin Peak, Rich provides a narrative that supports the need to climb to a fresh place, to discover a ground where emotions stifled for years can be expressed. Describing an experience customarily associated with men and showing instead the physical courage of women demonstrates how female consciousness can transgress and repossess male territory. The newness of the possibility for free expression depends upon an isolation complete and uncompromised, a quest that demands the sacrifice of life itself to reach it. In the courageous spirit of Dickinson's "If your Nerve, deny you—Go above your Nerve—" the climbers adjust to a cold matched only by the blood's will to turn still colder. In a dream, Elvira Shatayev voices her intent—to speak not as an individual but with a language shared by this team of women climbers, a voice that achieves authority through the heroic and fatal struggle to the summit. But what these women learn transcends (thus calling into question) the power of language itself. Leaving behind the separation that exists between women on the earth below, the climbers discover that

> What we were to learn   was simply   what we had
> up here   as out of all words   that *yes*   gathered
> its forces   fused itself   and only just in time
> to meet a   *No* of no degrees
> the black hole   sucking the world in

9. Susan Stanford Friedman traces the impact of "H. D." on *The Dream of a Common Language*. Friedman emphasizes the importance each poet associates with mother-daughter relationships. She tellingly addresses not only the specific grounds for comparison but also the character of Rich's understanding of influence relations among women. "Rich's stance toward women writers is distinctly compassionate and noncompetitive. It embodies a feminist theory of reading in which the underlying receptivity inevitable in any literary influence overlaps with her desire to build a tangible women's culture," Cooper, p. 172. One might contrast this stance with Rich's initial overdependence upon male modernists and her subsequent break with them.

Only through a rejection of tainted or "grounded" language, in this will to confront physical challenge, can the "yes" be fulfilled. Although the voice we hear is triumphant in its achieved independence, it is that of a dead woman. Yet even after death, Shatayev guards against her husband's powers of appropriation as he pursues the team to discover their fate. If in the past, his wife has trailed him through the Caucasus, she escapes this secondariness in death:

> Now I am further
> ahead   than either of us dreamed   anyone would be

Her "self" merges with the land:

> I have become
> the white snow packed like asphalt by the wind

And death completes the commonality of the climbers:

> the women I love   lightly flung   against the mountain
> that blue sky
> our frozen eyes unribboned   through the storm
> we could have stitched that blueness   together   like a quilt

After her husband finds the bodies and tells his story, Shatayev insists that the women's experiences does not end; their death engenders a physical metamorphosis into the world's being that continues the internal transformation of their climb. But this union of mind and spirit, this sharing of love, grows only as the women leave the world; in the diary, which must be "torn" from the dead climber's fingers (as if, even in death, she were still insisting that the words belonged to her alone), Shatayev had written:

> *What does love mean*
> *what does it mean   "to survive"*
> *A cable of blue fire ropes our bodies*
> *burning together in the snow   We will not live*
> *to settle for less   We have dreamed of this*
> *all of our lives*

The burning, ice-blue cable of connection holds the climbers, enforcing as it symbolizes the symbiotic relationship among the women and between life and death as well. These women who "will not live to settle for less" lose their lives in the attempt to reach new possibilities for living. Here Rich asserts the belief (echoed throughout these poems) that what women seek, this new ground, is a space where love and language find meanings that transgress the rules of society and supercede the tradition of a male-dominated discourse. Like Marie Curie in "Power," achievement depends upon the sacrifice of one's life. In the face of such a sacrifice, Rich keeps asking, can we achieve this requisite freedom and survive?

If the climate in which women live proves stultifying, if our language has become too tainted to trust, can we find a world more congenial to an imagination that seeks a reawakening of the powers of language and a field for its own intelligence? What determines the success or failure of this enterprise for Rich is whether she can stake out a territory freed from traditional identities and associations; she cannot forget the history of poetry because it is not hers. As outsider, Rich seeks a way to reappropriate language, to find a means of forcing language to free itself from its patriarchal origins; yet Rich embarks on this search not in innocence, but with the knowledge that such a pursuit will necessarily require her to banish, repress, or "consign to oblivion" the impossibility of establishing an alternative language capable of reaching beyond male experience into exclusive relationships between women. Although love between women becomes a way of discovering fresh ground, of defining a world that will and can only be described by women, the play of desire and the formal character of language cannot, of course, simply be destroyed. Nevertheless, asserting the priority of experience, Rich turns to address the woman who seeks to map a territory for such a language and faces the problem of conceiving a poetics based on transgression, a violation of societal expectation. The desire to make things whole, to love "for once with all [her] intelligence," [1] becomes a move to cast out the relation of male self and female/male other, to reassert mother-daughter intimacy and thus validate the emotional self-sufficiency of women. Placing woman-woman relationships at the center of poetic attention may establish the experiential basis for a figurative discourse no longer dependent upon the traditional patterns of heterosexual romance.

Rich's poetics of transgression becomes a source of "truth" in her twenty-one love poems. In the center of the book she enacts the poetic theories she had asserted in the volume's beginning and the assertions she will return to at its close. Here Rich attempts to make a poetry that refuses to succumb to the lies she must utter when living within the confines of a heterosexist culture. These poems demonstrate the difficulties of fusing a poetics out of politics, for they raise a question fundamental to Rich's project: If women have been stifled by a society they reject, can a rejection of that society's mores in and of itself free the poet, and thus restore to her the power of an "original" language? On this subject, Rich remarks, "Heterosexuality as an institution has also drowned in silence the erotic feelings between women. I myself lived half a lifetime in the lie of that denial. That silence makes us all, to some degree, into liars." [2] To express, openly and without hesitation, her feelings as they develop in a lesbian relationship becomes a way of escaping the "silence and lies" that here-

---

1. Adrienne Rich, "Splittings," in *The Dream of a Common Language: Poems 1974–1977* (New York: W. W. Norton & Co., 1978), p. 11 [77].
2. Adrienne Rich, "Women and Honor: Some Notes on Lying," in *On Lies, Secrets, and Silence: Selected Prose 1966–1978* (New York: W. W. Norton & Co., Inc., 1979), p. 190 [200].

tofore governed "women's love for women." Out of this assertion of truthfulness, Rich discovers, on her own terms, new possibilities for "truth": "When a woman tells the truth she is creating the possibility for truth around her."[3] The relation of a lesbian ontology to poetic praxis is not, however, so direct as Rich would have us believe. Merely to eliminate an overt stigma, to reject the veil of obfuscation, will not of itself produce effective poetry, no matter how liberating a gesture for the poet's psyche. What this lesbian relationship, as a ground of experience, does offer the woman poet is the possibility of escaping the anxieties of male-dominated poetic influence. Ideally, Rich can thus draw on both female and male precursors while maintaining the authority that comes from a description of life that taps the more generally recognized emotions associated with eros, while simultaneously centering the poetry in a relationship that excludes male consciousness—hence, the male poet.[4] Helpful as sexual truth-telling may be, however, it does not resolve the problem these poems so starkly articulate: the difficulty of reinventing names for experience, of placing the female self at the center of the mimetic process.

In her essay, "When We Dead Awaken: Writing as Re-Vision," Rich discusses the relationship between woman's survival in this world and man's authority as the one who names what we experience:

> And this drive to self-knowledge, for women, is more than a search for identity: it is part of our refusal of the self-destructiveness of male-dominated society. A radical critique of literature, feminist in its impulse, would take the work first of all as a clue to how we live, how we have been living, how we have been led to imagine ourselves, how our language has trapped as well as liberated us, how the very act of naming has been till now a male prerogative, and how we can begin to see and name—and therefore live—afresh.[5]

In *The Dream of a Common Language*, the politics of experience becomes a question of style, for the poems either assert in a strong rhetorical voice or enact in a more muted conversational manner the distinction between gender-based differences in language. As Rich herself states, "Poetry is, among other things, a criticism of language."[6] More specifically in "Twenty-One Love Poems," Rich proceeds to make a myth out of the dailiness of her experience, because, as she asserts, "No one has imagined us." The female poet can, as Adam in the Garden, name rather

3. "Women and Honor," p. 191 [200].
4. Consider, for example, the echoes of Robert Lowell's *Notebook: 1967–68* in Rich's *Twenty-One Love Poems*. I would suggest that here Rich draws freely upon Lowell's tone, his form, and the recounting of the dailiness of his life because she claims for herself an alternative centrality in the poetic tradition.
5. See Rich's "When We Dead Awaken: Writing as Re-Vision," in *On Lies, Secrets, and Silence*, p. 35 [167].
6. Rich, "Power and Danger: Words of a Common Woman (1977)," in *On Lies, Secrets, and Silence*, p. 248.

than rename the world around her. This transference allows the woman to be both subject and object of consciousness, the agent of desire and its aim. The poem sequence's language, with its attempts to bear witness to the individual, private quality of an intimate relationship, moves between tones of understatement and forthright assertion of the difficulty of sustaining such a poetry in the face of a tradition of silence, in the face of "centuries of books unwritten piled behind these shelves"(V). These poems seek to combine a self-consciousness associated with establishing an alternative poetic ground based on a lesbian relationship, a world without men, and an attempt to convert a specific intimacy into a paradigm that maps the possibilities of such a relationship for a radically alternative poetics. Rich confronts the inherent problem of combining these aims as she questions the mythopoetic enterprise itself—the conversion of private experience into an alternative program: "What kind of beast would turn its life into words? / What atonement is this all about?" (VII). But Rich also sees this attempt as a kind of evasion of the even more disruptive goal of centering the female self and making that self the origin for naming all that stands outside it:

> And how have I used rivers, how have I used wars
> to escape writing the worst thing of all—
> not the crimes of others, not even our own death,
> but the failure to want our freedom passionately enough
> so that blighted elms, sick rivers, massacres would seem
> mere emblems of that desecration of ourselves?
>
> (VII)

The question of renaming the world is crucial because Rich understands the necessity of escaping the boundaries of convention to make a new world "by women outside the law" (XIII). Moreover, these poems mirror the conviction that only by choosing one's own life freely and converting one's choice into language can a woman poet begin to redefine poetry by appropriating the power of naming. The love poems close with Rich's assertion of the autonomy she seeks and the corollary mythos she would create:

> I choose to be a figure in that light,
> half-blotted by darkness, something moving
> across that space, the color of stone
> greeting the moon, yet more than stone:
> a woman. I choose to walk here. And to draw this circle.
>
> (XXI)

Echoing Aurora Leigh's decision, "I choose to walk at all risks," Rich shares her choice; the tradition reaffirmed continues.[7]

7. See Elizabeth Barrett Browning, *Aurora Leigh*, *The Poetical Works of Elizabeth Barrett Browning* (Boston: Houghton Mifflin Co., 1974), Book II, 1.106.

Yet such exclusionary tactics as Rich employs in the twenty-one love poems do not necessarily release the poet from her own linguistic anxieties; the word can never free itself of its accrued meanings as emotion here strives to do. If the woman poet discards traditional images, where will she discover her First Idea? Power inheres in the word; it cannot rid itself of centuries of connotation. Knowing this, Rich turns away from the outspoken word, the power of voice, to advocate a language that borders on silence. Thus the gesture of isolation, the exclusionary act itself, may, Rich speculates, provide an untainted source of female power. Consequently, the poems in this volume in various ways address the need to minimize language, to divest the word of its accretions of power by replacing it with actions identified as preserving and sustaining a woman's integrity. Rich most powerfully resolves the difficulties of her apparently contradictory poetic aspirations in "Paula Becker to Clara Westhoff" and "A Woman Dead in Her Forties," for both poems achieve the balance between intimacy and assertion toward which Rich strives throughout this volume. In both poems, the speaker's words are shadowed by death; in the earlier poem, Becker writes to Westhoff, and her "letter" acquires for us a sorrowful resonance as her mingled hopes for her work combine with her sense of bewildered regret as she unwittingly prophecies her death in childbirth. As in the twenty-one love poems, we are readers who overhear—only now the imaginative reconstruction of the letter Becker writes creates a further distance. Through this double distancing and tone of intimacy, Rich is able simultaneously to use her words in a conversational, muted way and to give her language dramatic force, for the letter itself is not a private document, but becomes through our reading a public performance. This same sense of violated yet shared intimacy controls "A Woman Dead in Her Forties," only here the survivor speaks of all she could never say while her friend was still alive. Again death endows her words with renewed pathos, and the difficulty of speech, the price of honoring the taboo of silence, is measured by the irrevocable silence of death itself. Once more, we overhear words meant for another, and this act of overhearing enables the poem to mediate successfully between a conversational language (the intimate voice) and the power to transform the language into performance, into the language of poetry.

Yet such poems, although they do balance, can only provisionally resolve the underlying linguistic questions to which Rich returns throughout her work. If the poet cannot even trust the words she writes, her voice must be relegated to silence, but if silence will not suffice, the problem remains: how to control distrust of the very language the woman poet must invoke. The claims to be made for silence, its capacity for interrupting the repetition-compulsion of naming, the danger either of echoing or antithetically mimicking the patriarchal voice, achieve an eloquent expression of her own:

Silence can be a plan
rigorously executed

the blueprint to a life

It is a presence
it has a history   a form

Do not confuse it
with any kind of absence[8]

But the power of silence casts its own shadow, for the refusal to speak
may not be a simple desire to escape the strictures of conventional dis-
course but may signify, in the absence of any interpretative gesture, the
negative act of willful withholding. The tension between these possibil-
ities cannot be resolved within silence but must seek its resolution in the
margins of discourse; by margins, I mean the outermost edges where
Rich can best mediate between the desire for speech and her need to
respect the communicative force of silence. The margins of discourse
become for Rich the thoughts that precede or follow conversations,
momentary impressions, the internalized voice to which she returns
throughout the volume.

   In "Cartographies of Silence," a mapping of the possibilities and dan-
gers of the word, the poet expresses her longing for a language that would
itself be a "pure" imaging forth; she desires an impossible linguistic form
that would transcend discourse through its own originating presence:

The silence that strips bare:
In Dreyer's *Passion of Joan*

Falconetti's face, hair shorn, a great geography
mutely surveyed by the camera

If there were a poetry where this could happen
not as blank spaces or as words

stretched like a skin over meanings
but as silence falls at the end

of a night through which two people
have talked till dawn.[9]

In this linguistic utopia, poetry would win freedom from voicing either
by the signifying power of physical presence (the camera's moving in
silently to survey Falconetti's face) or by the mutual plenum of meaning

8. "Cartographies of Silence," *The Dream of a Common Language*, p. 17.
9. "Cartographies of Silence," p. 18.

created by a night of intimate conversation. In both instances, a temporary resolution is achieved. The ultimate irresolution of the character of silence, however, does not allow Rich to evade the more precise demands of speech. In her earlier poems—one thinks particularly of "Shooting Script"—Rich attempted to apply cinematic techniques (splicing, close-ups, fade-outs) to writing, but in her most recent work, she insists upon the distinctions between the two media.[1] Despite her occasional envy of "the pure annunciations to the eye," what Rich keeps choosing "are these words, these whispers, conversations / from which time after time the truth breaks moist and green." These words, at the close of "Cartographies of Silence," complete the equation between the act of renaming the world and the power of speech. Like those celebrants of the Eleusinian rites, the woman poet celebrates her choice: "these words, these whispers, conversations" that will bring, as did the goddess worshipped by the hierophants, a return of spring to the world.[2] The woman poet through her very presence becomes, as in the myth of Demeter and Kore, the regenerative life force. Although Rich is drawn to silence, her poems refuse to relinquish the life-giving possibilities of an eloquence based upon the vocative powers of the word, the truth-telling capacities of the woman poet who defies convention to redefine the very nature of performative language.

The central paradox of this volume resides in the poems' assertion of this move toward a new mode of writing, toward a gentle poetics antithetical to the aggressions of the patriarchal tradition of Western poetry, while at the same time claiming the bold, heroic nature of this enterprise. Consequently, Rich shifts from the intimate voice of inner conversation to the rhetorical formulations of the need for an alternative form of power. Although the reader may initially be puzzled by this disjunction as she moves from poem to poem, the two modes are interdependent, for the apparently heterogeneous voices cohere around a common purpose—to strive toward overcoming the delimiting properties of language itself. The "radical change in sensibility" Rich at once explores and articulates depends in part upon the appropriation of Whitmanian expansiveness for women; she is here to experience, as *only a woman can*, "the rainbow laboring to extend herself / where neither men nor cattle understand."[3] She envisions woman as explorer—a miner whose headlamp, as we by now might expect, casts a ray: "a weight like death." Despite the lethal dangers revealed by the woman poet's light, she alone can enter sacred ground. We hear Rich invoking the Whitman of "The Sleepers," with all his confidence in the prepotent self, as she describes a woman's solitary voyage:

1. See Rich, "Shooting Script," sections, 1, 8, 13, and 14 [45–47].
2. "Cartographies of Silence," p. 20.
3. "Natural Resources," p. 60. The following two quotations are also from this poem.

> The cage drops into the dark,
> the routine of life goes on:
>
> a woman turns a doorknob, but so slowly
> so quietly, that no one wakes
>
> and it is she alone who gazes
> into the dark of bedrooms, ascertains
>
> how they sleep, who needs her touch
> what window blows the ice of February
>
> into the room and who must be protected:
> It is only she who sees; who was trained to see

She wanders all night in her vision, and her freedom draws upon the power Whitman had claimed for himself. Note how close Whitman comes to this assertion of universal consciousness as he appropriates the metaphor of birth to inform his return to the world of night, dreams, and death:

> I will duly pass the day O my mother and duly return to you;
> Not you will yield forth the dawn again more surely
>   than you will yield forth me again,
> Not the womb yields the babe in its time more surely than
>   I shall be yielded from you in my time.[4]

This is the voice of the divinating American poet—Emerson, the father; Whitman, the son—members of the descendental tradition of a powerful patriarchy that claims for itself the possibility of an awful knowledge, a universal transparency that enables men to see and know the dreams of their mothers and daughters. Women confront such a company, each of whom asserts that he is "the man who would dare to know us." In response, Rich creates experiences that exclude men; she envisions a world of women, a kind of love in which men play no part.

From this renewed ground of being, what kind of poetry? In lieu of aggressive consciousness, the powerful men of imagination, what possibility? Or to ask these questions in another way, can language survive if we divest it of its appropriative power over the world of things? This is the heart of the problem, and like other originating tensions, its power lies in its capacity to resist solutions. In the final passages of "Natural

4. Although in her discussion of literary influences ("When We Dead Awaken: Writing as Re-Vision," p. 39 [171].) Rich does not mention Whitman, he clearly has had an impact on her work. Rich's "The Corpse-Plant" (*Necessities of Life* [W. W. Norton & Co., 1966]) quotes Whitman in its headnote: "How can an obedient man, or a sick man, dare to write poems?" Both the tenor and scope of her recent work remind one of the Whitmanian assertion of an expansive intimacy. The passage cited here is the closing verse paragraph of the 1855 version of "The Sleepers."

Resources," the poem that earlier made Whitmanian claims for the female imagination, Rich turns to gentleness and a conserving stoicism as ways of combating aggression without diminishing the capacity of verbalization. "These scraps, turned into patchwork, . . . a universe of humble things"—what options do these offer? [5] Women must, Rich asserts, strive against the assaults of both life and language; she must seek to save; but the burden is in the labor, the bringing forth. Returning to the rainbow that *labors* to extend itself, the natural work only a woman can understand, Rich closes this poem with her counterclaim against the male tradition:

> The women who first knew themselves
> miners, are dead. The rainbow flies
>
> like a flying buttress from the walls
> of cloud, the silver-and-green vein
>
> awaits the battering of the pick
> the dark lode weeps for light
>
> My heart is moved by all I cannot save:
> so much has been destroyed
>
> I have to cast my lot with those
> who age after age, perversely,
>
> with no extraordinary power,
> reconstitute the world.

But can such stoic gentleness, or biological capacity, create an individuating language? Or is the very act of finding words and sending them out of oneself, an activity that must imply violation, a gesture of trespass against the world? Here Rich faces her most severe challenge: at once to speak of the place without violating its presence and to find a common language that repudiates the mode of aggression in favor of a discourse of conservancy:

> if I could know
> in what language to address
> the spirits that claim a place
> beneath these low and simple ceilings,
> tenants that neither speak nor stir
> Yet dwell in mute insistence

5. "Natural Resources," p. 66.

The poet searches for a spider thread that will lead her back to the origins of discovery, the answers that will inform her historical moment.[6] Seeking a "directive" that will lead her home, Rich turns to housewifely duties—"brushing the thread of the spider aside," a thread she earlier hoped might lead her to the source of lucid understanding, a thread that now she must sever rather than spin in order, paradoxically, to reform the thread of poetic continuity. Merely to preserve appearances is not to save them.

Yet if the gentle occupations of the housewife of language will not suffice, what alternatives remain for the woman poet? Rich explicitly rejects the American Romantics' belief in the poem as performative act:

> And we're not performers, like Liszt, competing
> against the world for speed and brilliance
> (the 79-year-old pianist said, when I asked her)
> *What makes a virtuoso?—Competitiveness.*)
> The longer I live the more I mistrust
> theatricality, the false glamour cast
> by performance, the more I know its poverty beside
> the truths we are salvaging from
> the splitting-open of our lives.[7]

To deny a language of competition, to reject performance—"cut the wires, / find ourselves in free-fall"—is to incur a risk akin to that of living in a world where conventional self-other relations are redefined, where the solace of precedent ceases to exist, where the tradition casts the world into a void:

> No one who survives to speak
> new language, has avoided this:
> the cutting-away of an old force that held her
> rooted to an old ground[8]

What that new poetry will depend upon are the origins of the poet's vision, and in the final lines of this volume's final poem, "Transcendental Etude," Rich shows us her vision through an extended simile:

> Vision begins to happen in such a life
> as if a woman quietly walked away
> from the argument and jargon in a room

6. Robert Frost's "Directive," with its language of domesticity and spiritual search for origins, may be the poem Rich is addressing, if only indirectly, in "Toward the Solstice." To assess just how far Rich has come from her first volume of poems, one need only compare her self-conscious echoing of Frost, Auden, and other male poets in the earlier work and her dialectical appropriation of the voices of past poets, both male and female, in her most recent work. (For analyses of this progress in Rich's poetry, the development of a clearly delineated feminist stance, see Albert Gelpi's essay "Adrienne Rich: The Poetics of Change" [282–99] and Wendy Martin, "From Patriarchy to the Female Principle: A Chronological Reading of Adrienne Rich's Poems," in *Adrienne Rich's Poetry*, pp. 130–48, 175–89.

7. "Transcendental Etude," p. 74 [88].

8. "Transcendental Etude," p. 75 [89].

and sitting down in the kitchen, began turning in her lap
bits of yarn, calico and velvet scraps,
laying them out absently on the scrubbed boards
in the lamplight, with small rainbow-colored shells
sent in cotton-wool from somewhere far away,
and skeins of milkweed from the nearest meadow—
original domestic silk, the finest findings—[9]

This would be a poetry of what is close, precious through personal association, and drawn from a domestic landscape.[1] Such a poetry would pull "the tenets of a life together / with no mere will to mastery, / only care for the many-lived unending / forms in which she finds herself." The woman, in a return to a kind of "negative capability" that results in imagistic poetry, would find herself

becoming now the sherd of broken glass
slicing light in a corner, dangerous
to flesh, now the plentiful, soft leaf
that wrapped round the throbbing finger, soothes the wound;
and now the stone foundation, rockshelf further
forming underneath everything that grows.[2]

It is she who protects by becoming, who re-creates by combining into the form of art the foundations of life, a life not of argument or jargon (a life of intellectual displacement), but a life so close to its sources, so open to experience, that it provides the foundations for a new home and a new world. The woman becomes this foundation as she creates her language out of what she knows, the acceptance of the common, the life-sustaining forces that allow her to grow and to write.

II

It is important to me to know that, through most of her life, Bishop was critically and consciously trying to explore marginality, power and powerlessness, often in poetry of great beauty and sensuous power. That not all these poems are fully realized or satisfying simply means that the living who care that art should embody these questions have still more work to do.

—Adrienne Rich, "The Eye of the Outsider:
The Poetry of Elizabeth Bishop"

9. "Transcendental Etude," p. 76 [90].
1. For a discussion of Rich's poetry in relation to Emerson, see Gertrude Reif Hughes, "Imagining the Existence of Something Uncreated: Elements of Emerson in Adrienne Rich's *The Dream of a Common Language*," in *Reading Adrienne Rich*, pp. 140–62. Hughes notes, "From beginning to end, *The Dream of a Common Language* recalls Emersonian visions and rhapsodies, because it affirms energies that are potentially limitless (or at least are still to be imagined). At the same time, these poems confirm the misnaming, miscues, and misunderstanding that beset women's energies, impeding women's access to them. Having begun the volume with three poems in which she rechannels those Emersonian ideas of power that are especially congenial to her, Rich ends it with a poem she calls 'Transcendental Etude,' as though to invite comparison with the Emersonian tradition," p. 155.
2. "Transcendental Etude," p. 77 [91].

To examine Rich's comments on Elizabeth Bishop is not only to learn what Rich values in her formidable predecessor but also to discover Rich's aspirations for her own work. If *The Dream of a Common Language* offers an alternative poetics based upon gender, Rich's most recent poems return with "still more work to do," testing and expanding the possibilities of a gender-based poetics as they reach deep into the pain of the body and far into the historical and social events that shape contemporary life. The audacity of Rich's 1986 book commences with its title, for in naming this collection *Your Native Land, Your Life*, Rich asserts an authority over the reader's experience as she invents a patriotism that locates its origins in Whitman's audacious claims for the poet as not merely representative, but also himself the embodiment of America in all its diversity and difference. Despite this wildly ambitious, thoroughly native assertion, however, Rich's more recent work preserves her earlier conversational, explicitly "nonperformative" diction; only now Rich is willing to confront the long-suppressed memories of husband and father, the men who also shaped her life. In this resurgence of openness, Rich returns to heterosexual as well as homoerotic experience, delving into her fund of recollection to address a "you" neither exclusively female-identified nor overtly adversarial. The dream of a common language has been extended to include the reimagining of a past that recognizes rather than rejects the sources of personal as well as cultural history; Rich incorporates the most threatening aspects of her past without subordinating her feminist sense of difference. What Rich asks of us is that we reexamine the relationship between ethics and poetics, between the conduct of our lives and the forms of its expression. That the relationship between the conduct of life and the praxis of art has not gone unexamined by American poets is a fact clarified by our poetic history. Yet with its incantatory power and its huge Whitmanian claims, *Your Native Land, Your Life* pursues this awareness from a position of marginalization that nevertheless asserts its authority to representation. Moreover, Rich's gender-inflected subjectivity is balanced by her deployment of the word as cultural sign and as expression of a distinctly decentered imagination. Thus, Rich works toward a feminist discourse that is at once inclusive and humane, that in exploring the rhetorical possibilities of its own gender-inflected identity registers the presence of others while acknowledging the figural powers of the natural world: the enunciation of a woman-centered Counter-Sublime.

Focusing on the experiential aspects of women's lives, these poems, while overtly asserting no special claim to rhetorical power, nevertheless betray mastery of a distinctive style of reading as well as writing. Surely, in the creation of the sustained illusion of conversation and the never obtrusive yet deftly figurative use of the natural, Rich displays the achievement of her craft. Technical skill does its work through pacing, line breaks, and subtle, often elusive rhymes. Interestingly, for one who explicitly disavows Whitman's overt will to power, Rich's language, with its imperative force and didactic assurance, may at times resemble his own. In "You who think I find words for everything" ("Contradictions: Tracking Poems," 29, p. 111 [130].) Rich opens with the readerly "you's" suppositions concerning the speaker and responds by challenging herself to break free from the words she herself writes. In a Whitmanian gesture that echoes the assertion, "he most honors my style who learns under it to destroy the teacher" ("Song of Myself," section 47, l.1236), Rich advocates a commensurate self-reliance that depends for its authority not on the body's individuating strength, but upon its shared, inherent vulnerability. The reality of pain becomes not an isolating reality but a force for relation beyond the suffering self.[3] Rich accomplishes what Whitman as nurse and wound-dresser had achieved before her—a deeply empathic sense of the other arising from that apparently least communicative of sources, the body in pain. What serves to isolate each of us, the inherently incommunicable experience of pain, Rich renders with a specificity that not only strives to articulate individuated suffering but also makes of that pain a relational phenomenon. The danger (one that Rich herself recognizes) is the possibility that personal and social suffering may become confused. Always alert to this danger, Rich writes of bodily pain as a way of working against the self's desire to close itself off, its yearning for definitive boundaries, for "clear edges." Instead, pain may offer a way of merging but not blurring identities, of restoring the connection between individual and social experience. As a result, the reality of pain becomes not an isolating condition but a force for feeling beyond the self.

* * *

The question for the empathic imagination is how to sustain compassion for experience beyond one's own without relinquishing the self's boundaries or an awareness of the *difference* between physical pain and political oppression. Rich knows that resemblance does not equal identity, for she confronts the risks involved in any simple equation of private suffering and social injustice. Although Rich's commitment to issues of class, race, and gender is not a new phenomenon, what she now explicitly engages is the univocal position of the exile. Recognizing the authority that exists in the position of marginalization, she draws upon this power to speak for and to other victims of oppression. Rich investigates and reimagines (as she had in her earlier work) historical women and delineates the relationship between their lives and her own in poems of praise and sympathy. Yet in terms of Rich's own poetic evolution, the

3. This intersection of the physical and political had long interested Rich. See, for example, "The Blue Ghazals," 4 May 1969: *"The moment when a feeling enters the body / is political. This touch is political." The Will to Change: Poems 1968–1970* (New York: W. W. Norton & Co., 1971), p. 24.

most revealing poems in "Sources" may be those that explore her rela-
tionships with her father and her dead husband. In choosing now to
converse with them through her poetry, Rich clarifies and extends her
quest for a woman's poetic authority. In *The Dream of a Common Lan-
guage*, Rich described a newly imagined commonality defined by gender
and based upon a rejection of men as both readers and lovers. The poems
in "Sources" do not so much relinquish as extend that search for a dis-
tinctive, personally valid aesthetic and moral vision. In *Your Native Land,
Your Life*, however, Rich explores the possibilities of an individuating
poetics while at the same time revealing an openness toward prior expe-
rience. This revisionary work of introspection yields a freedom from the
need for others to serve as sources of rejection. Rich lets go of a poetics
based upon selectivity or the creation of difference as the source of vic-
timization to fashion a "new" language that acknowledges difference as
a necessary and enabling fact that affords generous authority.

"Sources" investigates the question of strength, both moral and poetic,
and how Rich might discover such strength within her experience. It
might, therefore, be read as the "career of the woman poet" in its careful
delineation of the eventfulness of a woman's life and its articulation of
how these events, both literary and personal, inform a mature, aesthetic
vision that supercedes Rich's former, exclusionary stance. What emerges
from Rich's reclamation of her Jewish and heterosexual origins is a stronger
and more deeply empowered poetics based not on defense but upon
what Emerson, in an evocative phrase, described as the "flames and
generosities of the heart"[4]

* * *

Read as a whole, the poems of *Your Native Land, Your Life* are about
what is recoverable, what can be salvaged for an imagination that takes
cognizance of the sociohistorical realities of injustice, brutality, and ter-
ror. How does one accommodate human suffering without suppressing
the desire to praise the ahistorical natural world, the world of the king-
fisher, the lupines, the Pacific shore? How can one mediate between the
imagination's aversion to what is cruel, to what is painful? How does
one meet, in Elaine Scarry's words, "the rhetorical challenge of finding
a language that will at once communicate the torture of an other human
being's unknown suffering to someone who would rather avoid it but
who is needed to help alleviate the very thing she would prefer to for-
get?" (Elaine Scarry, *The Body in Pain*).

What can be saved for poetry when the words themselves, once writ-
ten, no longer remain the same, but are overnight transformed by the
social conditions in which we live?

4. Ralph Waldo Emerson, "Circles," *Selections from Ralph Waldo Emerson*, ed. Stephen E.
Whicher (Boston: Houghton Mifflin, 1960), p. 178.

Envisioning a utopia of fulfilled needs, "Poetry: III" describes an ordered existence freed from the obligations, enslavement, and guilt of life as we know it. Would such a utopia, the falling away of resistance and illusion, release the act of writing from the burden of guilt?

> would we give ourselves
> more calmly over   feel less criminal joy
> when the thing comes   as it does come
> clarifying grammar
> and the fixed and mutable stars—?

To be "fixed" and "mutable" is simultaneously to be immune to the workings of the poetic imagination and susceptible to poetic transformation. Unable to erase the cruelty of the world in a blaze of language, Rich continuously returns to the difficulties of writing poetry in late-twentieth-century America in the face of personal loss and extreme violence. "Blue Rock" bears the fullest exploration of this conflict, as a piece of lapis lazuli "shoots its stain / blue into the wineglass on the table."

> This is a chunk of your world, a piece of its heart:
> split from the rest, does it suffer?

This is the situation of poetry at the present time:

> At the end of the twentieth century
> cardiac graphs of torture reply to poetry
>
> line by line: in North America
> the strokes of the stylus continue
>
> the figures of terror are reinvented
> all night, after I turn the lamp off, blotting
>
> wineglass, rock and roses, leaving pages
> like this scrawled with mistakes and love,
>
> falling asleep; but the stylus does not sleep,
> cruelly the drum revolves, cruelty writes its name.

According to Rich, this has not always been the situation of the poet or her language but represents a distinct response to the horror of contemporary life. Even in terms of her own career, Rich can chart a historical change in consciousness:

> Once when I wrote poems they did not change
> left overnight on the page
>
> they stayed as they were and daylight broke
> on the lines, as on the clotheslines in the yard

heavy with clothes forgotten or left out
for a better sun next day

but now I know what happens while I sleep
and when I wake the poem has changed:

the facts have dilated it, or cancelled it;
and in every morning's light, your rock is there.

If external circumstances can alter a poem's words, how much greater a
loss whose origins reside in the mind's own failing powers?

> Someone said to me: *It's just that we don't*
> *know how to cope with the loss of memory.*
> *When your own grandfather doesn't know you*
> *when your mother thinks you're somebody else*
> *it's a terrible thing.*
> ("Contradictions: Tracking Poems," 24, p. 106)

What happens when the insignia of our individualities are effaced, when
each of us and her words are no longer remembered? The next poem in
the sequence extends this personal loss to the historical memory of the
holocaust: the anonymity of the dead, the realization that this horror has
for millions of us already occurred.

The final poem of the volume, with its conversational quietness,
description of physical pain, and yearning for closure, teaches what can
be learned from "the edges that blur," the coincidence of bodily and
social afflictions.

> You who think I find words for everything
> this is enough for now
> cut it short   cut loose from my words
>
> You for whom I write this
> in the night hours when the wrecked cartilage
> sifts round the mystical jointure of the bones
> when the insect of detritus crawls
> from shoulder to elbow to wristbone
> remember: the body's pain and the pain on the streets
> are not the same   but you can learn
> from the edges that blur   O you who love clear edges
> more than anything   watch the edges that blur
> ("Contradictions: Tracking Poems," 29, p. 111) [130]

Only by acknowledging the blurring of edges can poetry continue to
make connections between the personal and the public, between self
and world. With her Whitmanian, vocative "you," Rich sends the reader
forward. Cut free from her words and her pain, we are admonished to

learn through observation, through the synthesizing powers of the imagination. Not by confusing personal and historical pain, but by learning to experience the contiguities of private and public experience can we discover the courage to make choices: the will to change.

Rich writes with the ardor of someone constructing a world from memory rather than repression, who chooses to celebrate the capacities of an imagination informed by the experiences of gender, race, and class. This regenerative voice serves to encourage contemporary women poets to write without sacrificing either their marginality or their authority. Like Dickinson, Rich seeks to "have it out at last on her own premises," but those premises have extended beyond Dickinson's necessarily restrictive, nineteenth-century terrain.[5] Thus Dickinson's consciousness of competition falls away before Rich's hope of mutuality, as Rich's "plaine style" emerges from the complexities of Dickinson's encoded poetics.[6] For surely, Rich participates in the ongoing project of twentieth-century women writers who have begun to delineate a feminist poetics that flourishes on the margins imposed by the male-identified American Sublime.

5. In *An American Triptych: Anne Bradstreet, Emily Dickinson, Adrienne Rich,* Wendy Martin contextualizes Rich's poetry within a tradition of women poets. She writes, "Finally, Rich has written poetry that suggests alternatives to the city on a hill, the virgin land, and the machine in the garden, metaphors that have been used by writers and literary historians to describe the American experience. As a writer, as an activist, Rich had tried to bring a nurturing ethos to the larger society . . . Adrienne Rich has tried to envision a society in which all women can be at home." *An American Triptych: Anne Bradstreet, Emily Dickinson, Adrienne Rich* (Chapel Hill: The University of North Carolina Press, 1984), p. 234.
6. Helen Vendler's comment on Rich's style acquires renewed importance given the frequent critical objections to the sparse use of figuration in her work. Although writing specifically of *The Will to Change* (1971), Vendler's characterization applies with equal force to Rich's latest work. Vendler writes:

> I pause only to say that Rich's "music," so praised by her earlier reviewers and so ignored by most of her later ones, seems to me to reach its height of accomplishment in lines like these, as "hulls," "dull," "crust," "sunk," and "drudge" play one note while "margin" and "barges" play another, both soon to be reinforced by "gulls" and "rubbish" for the first, and "dark" and "harsh" for the second. The unobtrusiveness of these choices, choices perceived as such only when we ask why the lines adhere so to each other, is worth all the prettiness sacrificed in favor of their reticence.

Helen Vendler, "Ghostlier Demarcations, Keener Sounds," in *Parnassus* 2, no. 1 (Fall 1973); repr. *Modern Critical Views: Contemporary Poets,* ed. Harold Bloom (New York: Chelsea House Publishers, 1986). That reticence has come to include an increased use of the conversational and the illusion of transcribing speech. The music, however, continues, in its more reticent forms, unstilled.

Adrienne Rich: A Chronology

1929　Born in Baltimore, Maryland, May 16. Began writing poetry as a child with the encouragement and under the supervision of her father, Arnold Rich, from whose "very Victorian, pre-Raphaelite" library, Rich later recalled, she read Tennyson, Keats, Arnold, Blake, Rossetti, Swinburne, Carlyle, and Pater.

1951　A.B., Radcliffe College. *A Change of World*, chosen by W. H. Auden for the Yale Younger Poets Award.

1952–53　Guggenheim Fellowship; travel in Europe and England. Onset of rheumatoid arthritis.

1953　Marriage to Alfred H. Conrad, an economist teaching at Harvard. Residence in Cambridge, Massachusetts, 1953–66.

1955　Birth of David Conrad. *The Diamond Cutters and Other Poems*. Ridgely Torrence Memorial Award of the Poetry Society of America.

1957　Birth of Paul Conrad.

1959　Birth of Jacob Conrad.

1960　National Institute of Arts and Letters Award for poetry.

1961–62　Guggenheim Fellowship; residence with family in the Netherlands.

1962　Bollingen Foundation grant for translation of Dutch poetry.

1962–63　Amy Lowell Travelling Fellowship.

1963　*Snapshots of a Daughter-in-Law: Poems 1954–1962*. Bess Hokin Prize of *Poetry* magazine.

1966　*Necessities of Life: Poems 1962–1965*. Move with family to New York City. Increasingly active politically in protests against the Vietnam War.

1967　*Selected Poems* published in Britain. Honorary doctorate, Wheaton College. Orthopoedic surgery for arthritis.

1967–69　Lecturer, Swarthmore College. Adjunct Professor, Writing Division, Columbia University School of the Arts.

1968　Begins teaching in SEEK program at City College of New York, and continues 1968–72 and 1974–75. Eunice Tietjens Memorial Prize, *Poetry* magazine. Death of Arnold Rich.

1969   *Leaflets: Poems 1965–1968.*

1970   Death of Alfred Conrad.

1971   *The Will to Change: Poems 1968–1970.* Shelley Memorial Award, Poetry Society of America. Increasingly identifies with the women's liberation movement.

1972–73   Hurst Visiting Professor of Creative Writing, Brandeis University.

1973   *Diving into the Wreck: Poems 1971–1972.*

1974   National Book Award, shared with Allen Ginsberg.

1975   *Adrienne Rich's Poetry,* edited by Barbara Charlesworth Gelpi and Albert Gelpi (Norton Critical Edition). *Poems Selected and New, 1950–1974.* Lucy Martin Donnelley Fellow, Bryn Mawr College.

1976   *Of Woman Born: Motherhood as Experience and Institution. Twenty-One Love Poems.* Begins life with Michelle Cliff.

1976–79   Professor of English, Douglass College, Rutgers University.

1978   *The Dream of a Common Language: Poems 1974–1977.*

1979   *On Lies, Secrets, and Silence: Selected Prose 1966–1978.* Honorary doctorate, Smith College. Move to Montague, Massachusetts.

1980   Orthopoedic surgery for arthritis.

1981   *A Wild Patience Has Taken Me This Far: Poems 1978–1981.* Fund for Human Dignity Award, National Gay Task Force.

1981–83   Co-edits *Sinister Wisdom,* a lesbian/feminist journal.

1981–87   A. D. White Professor-at-Large, Cornell University.

1982   Orthopoedic surgery for arthritis.

1983   *Sources.*

1983
& 1984   Visiting Professor, Scripps College.

1984   *The Fact of a Doorframe: Poems Selected and New 1950–1984.* Move to Santa Cruz, California.

1984–86   Distinguished Visiting Professor, San Jose State University.

1986   *Your Native Land, Your Life: Poems. Blood, Bread, and Poetry: Selected Prose 1979–1985. Of Woman Born,* 10th Anniversary Edition. Ruth Lilly Poetry Prize.

1986–93   Professor of English, Stanford University.

1987   Honorary doctorate, College of Wooster, Ohio. Honorary doctorate, Brandeis University. Brandeis Creative Arts Medal in Poetry.

1989   *Time's Power: Poems 1985–1988.* Marjorie Kovler Fellow, University of Chicago. National Poetry Association Award for Distinguished Service to the Art of Poetry. Elmer Holmes Bobst Award in Arts and Letters, New York University.

1990 Honorary doctorate, City College of New York. Honorary doctorate, Harvard University. Bay Area Book Reviewers Award in Poetry.

1990– Member, Department of Literature, American Academy and Institute of Arts and Letters. Member, founding editorial group, *Bridges: A Journal for Jewish Feminists and Our Friends*.

1991 *An Atlas of the Difficult World: Poems 1988–1991*. The Common Wealth Award in Literature.

1991– Member, American Academy of Arts and Sciences.

1992 Honorary doctorate, Swarthmore College. Robert Frost Silver Medal of the Poetry Society of America. William Whitehead Award of the Publishing Triangle for lifetime achievement in letters. *An Atlas of the Difficult World* receives the *Los Angeles Times* Book Award in Poetry and the Lenore Marshall/*Nation* Award. Julia Arden Conrad, grandchild, born. Charles Reddington Conrad, grandchild, born.

1992 Spinal surgery.

1993 *Collected Early Poems, 1950–1970. What Is Found There: Notebooks on Poetry and Politics. An Atlas of the Difficult World* awarded the Poet's Prize.

Selected Bibliography

This bibliography does not list books and essays excerpted for this volume.

POETRY

A Change of World. New Haven: Yale University Press, 1951.
The Diamond Cutters and Other Poems. New York: Harper & Brothers, 1955.
Snapshots of a Daughter-in-Law: Poems 1954–1962. New York: Harper & Row, 1963; New York: W. W. Norton, 1967; London: Chatto & Windus, 1970.
Necessities of Life: Poems 1962–1965. New York: W. W. Norton, 1966.
Selected Poems. London: Chatto & Windus, 1967.
Leaflets: Poems 1965–1968. New York: W. W. Norton, 1969; London; Chatto & Windus, 1972.
The Will to Change: Poems 1968–1970. New York: W. W. Norton, 1971; London: Chatto & Windus, 1973.
Diving into the Wreck: Poems 1971–1972. New York: W. W. Norton, 1973.
Poems: Selected and New, 1950–1974. New York: W. W. Norton, 1975.
Adrienne Rich's Poetry, ed. Barbara Charlesworth Gelpi and Albert Gelpi. New York: W. W. Norton, 1975. (Revised and enlarged as *Adrienne Rich's Poetry and Prose*, 1993).
Twenty-One Love Poems. Emeryville, CA: Effie's Press, 1976.
The Dream of a Common Language: Poems 1974–1977. New York: W. W. Norton, 1978.
A Wild Patience Has Taken Me This Far: Poems 1978–1981. New York: W. W. Norton, 1981.
Sources. Woodside, CA: Heyeck Press, 1983.
The Fact of a Doorframe: Poems Selected and New 1950–1984. New York: W. W. Norton, 1984.
Your Native Land, Your Life: Poems. New York: W. W. Norton, 1986.
Time's Power: Poems 1985–1988. New York: W. W. Norton, 1989.
An Atlas of the Difficult World: Poems 1988–1991. New York: W. W. Norton, 1991.
Collected Early Poems 1950–1970. New York: W. W. Norton, 1993.

PROSE

Of Woman Born: Motherhood as Experience and Institution. New York: W. W. Norton, 1976; Tenth Anniversary Edition, with new foreword, 1986.
On Lies, Secrets, and Silence: Selected Prose 1966–1978. New York: W. W. Norton, 1979.
Blood, Bread, and Poetry: Selected Prose 1979–1985. New York: W. W. Norton, 1986.
What Is Found There: Notebooks on Poetry and Politics. New York: W. W. Norton, 1993.

UNCOLLECTED ESSAYS AND REVIEWS

"Review of *The Lordly Hudson* by Paul Goodman." *The New York Review of Books* (1st issue, undated, 1963): 27.
"Mr. Bones, He Lives: Review of *77 Dream Songs* by John Berryman." *The Nation* 198.22 (25 May 1964): 538, 540.
"Beyond the Heirlooms of Tradition: Review of *Found Objects* by Louis Zukofsky." *Poetry* 105.2 (Nov. 1964): 128–29.
"On Karl Shapiro's *The Bourgeois Poet*." In *The Contemporary Poet as Artist and Critic*. Ed. Anthony Ostroff. Boston: Little, Brown, 1964. 192–94.
"Reflections on Lawrence: Review of *The Complete Poems of D. H. Lawrence*." *Poetry* 106.3 (June 1965): 218–25.

"For Randall Jarrell." In *Randall Jarrell, 1914–1965*. Ed. Robert Lowell, Peter Taylor, and Robert Penn Warren. New York: Farrar, Straus, & Giroux, 1967. 182–83.

"Living with Henry: Review of *His Toy, His Dream, His Rest* by John Berryman." *The Harvard Advocate* 103.1 (John Berryman Issue, Spring 1969): 10–11.

"Poetry, Personality, and Wholeness: A Response to Galway Kinnell." *Field: Contemporary Poetry and Poetics* 7 (Fall 1972): 11–18.

"Review of *Women and Madness* by Phyllis Chesler." *New York Times Book Review* 31 Dec. 1972: 1, 20–21.

"Voices in the Wilderness: Review of *Monster* by Robin Morgan." *Washington Post Book World* 31 Dec. 1972: 3.

"Caryatid; A Column." *American Poetry Review* 2.5 (Sept.–Oct. 1973).

"The Sisterhood of Man: Review of *Beyond God the Father: Toward a Philosophy of Women's Liberation* by Mary Daly." *Washington Post Book World* 1 Nov. 1973: 2–3.

"Feminism and Fascism: An Exchange." By Adrienne Rich and Susan Sontag. *New York Review of Books* 22.4 (20 March 1975): 31–32.

"Women's Studies—Renaissance or Revolution." *Women's Studies* 3 (1976): 121–26.

"Review of *Women and Nature* by Susan Griffin." *New Women's Times Feminist Review* (Nov. 1978): 5.

"Review of *Gyn/Ecology: The Metaethics of Radical Feminism* by Mary Daly." *New York Times Book Review* 14 Feb. 1979: 10.

"What Does Separatism Mean?" *Sinister Wisdom* 18 (Fall 1981): 83–91.

INTERVIEWS

"Talking with Adrienne Rich." By David Kalstone. *Saturday Review; The Arts* 4.17 (22 April 1972): 29–46.

"Adrienne Rich and Robin Morgan Talk About Poetry and Women's Culture." In *The New Women's Survival Sourcebook*. Ed. Susan Rennie and Kirsten Grimstad. New York: Knopf, 1975. 106–11.

"Three Conversations with Adrienne Rich." By Barbara Charlesworth Gelpi and Albert Gelpi. In *Adrienne Rich's Poetry*. Ed. Barbara Charlesworth Gelpi and Albert Gelpi. New York: Norton, 1975. 105–22.

"An Interview with Audre Lorde." By Adrienne Rich. *Signs: Journal of Women in Culture and Society* 6 (Summer 1981): 713–36.

RECORDINGS

"Adrienne Rich Reading at Stanford." Stanford Program for Recordings in Sound, 1973. Introduction by Barbara Charlesworth Gelpi. Jacket notes by Albert Gelpi.

"Planetarium: A Retrospective 1950–1980." Washington, D.C.: Watershed Tapes, 1986.

"Tracking the Contradictions: Poems 1981–1985." Washington, D.C.: Watershed Tapes, 1986.

A SELECTION OF BOOKS ABOUT ADRIENNE RICH

Cooper, Jane Roberta, ed. *Reading Adrienne Rich; Reviews and ReVisions, 1951–1981*. Ann Arbor: U of Michigan P, 1984.

Diaz-Diocaretz, Myriam. *Translating Adrienne Rich: Questions of Feminist Strategy in Adrienne Rich*. Amsterdam & Philadelphia: John Benjamins, 1985.

Gelpi, Barbara Charlesworth, and Albert Gelpi, eds. *Adrienne Rich's Poetry: A Norton Critical Edition*. New York: W. W. Norton, 1975. [This earlier edition contains essays not included in this revised and enlarged edition and not published elsewhere.]

Keyes, Claire. *The Aesthetics of Power: The Poetry of Adrienne Rich*. Athens: U of Georgia P, 1986.

Lemardeley-Cunci, Marie-Christine. *Adrienne Rich: Cartographies du Silence*. Lyon: Presses Universitaires de Lyon, 1990.

A SELECTION OF BOOKS WITH CHAPTERS ON ADRIENNE RICH

Bennett, Paula. *My Life a Loaded Gun: Feminist Creativity and Feminist Poetics*. Boston: Beacon, 1986.

Blau DuPlessis, Rachel. *Writing Beyond the Ending*. Bloomington: Indiana UP, 1985.

Howard, Richard. *Alone with America: Essays on the Art of Poetry in the United States Since 1950*. New York: Atheneum, 1969; enl. ed., 1980.

Juhasz, Suzanne. *Naked and Fiery Forms: Modern American Poetry by Women, a New Tradition*. New York, Harper, 1976.

Kalaidjian, David. *Languages of Liberation: The Social Text on Contemporary American Poetry*. New York: Columbia UP, 1989.

Kalstone, David. *Five Temperaments: Elizabeth Bishop, Robert Lowell, James Merrill, Adrienne Rich, John Ashbery*. New York: Oxford UP, 1977.

Martin, Wendy. *An American Triptych: Anne Bradstreet, Emily Dickinson, Adrienne Rich*. Chapel Hill: U of North Carolina P, 1984.

Nelson, Cary. *Our Last First Poets*. Urbana: U of Illinois P, 1981.

Ostriker, Alicia. *Writing Like a Woman*. Ann Arbor: U of Michigan P, 1986.

Vendler, Helen. *Part of Nature, Part of Us: Modern American Poets*. Cambridge, MA: Harvard UP, 1980. [Part of the Rich chapter is included in this volume; the part not included is a review of *Of Woman Born*.]

Index